MW00795707

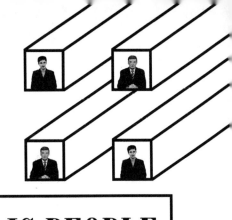

NEWS IS PEOPLE

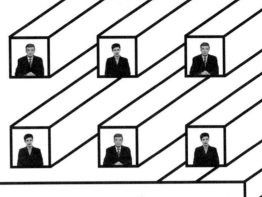

NEWS IS PEOPLE

The

Rise

of

Local

TV

News

and   CRAIG M. ALLEN

the

Fall of News from New York

Iowa State University Press / Ames

Craig Allen is the head of broadcast journalism at the Walter Cronkite School of Journalism and Telecommunication at Arizona State University. In his nearly 20 years in the professional mass media, he served as a local TV news director, anchor and producer. He has reported for newspapers and contributed to television documentaries in the United States and Great Britain. His other books are *The Global Media Revolution* and *Eisenhower and the Mass Media.*

© 2001 Iowa State University Press
All rights reserved

Iowa State University Press
2121 South State Avenue, Ames, Iowa 50014

Orders: 1-800-862-6657
Office: 1-515-292-0140
Fax: 1-515-292-3348
Web site: www.isupress.com

Authorization to photocopy items for internal or personal use, or the internal or personal use of specific clients, is granted by Iowa State University Press, provided that the base fee of $.10 per copy is paid directly to the Copyright Clearance Center, 222 Rosewood Drive, Danvers, MA 01923. For those organizations that have been granted a photocopy license by CCC, a separate system of payments has been arranged. The fee code for users of the Transactional Reporting Service is 0-8138-1207-0/2001 $.10.

♾ Printed on acid-free paper in the United States of America

First edition, 2001

Library of Congress Cataloging-in-Publication Data

Allen, Craig
    News is people: the rise of local TV news and the fall of news from New York / Craig Allen.
        p. cm.
    Includes bibliographical references and index.
    ISBN 0-8138-1207-0
    1. Television broadcasting of news—United States. I. Title.

PN4888.T4 A39 2001
070.1´95—dc21   00-053896

The last digit is the print number: 9 8 7 6 5 4 3 2 1

CONTENTS

ACKNOWLEDGMENTS

Even though seven years were needed in piecing together the far-flung history of local TV news, the book's most daunting moment is acknowledging the more than 200 people who in some way assisted the project. Most were past and present station managers, news directors, newsworkers and consultants who yielded their time, insights and direction during interview sessions. A complete list of those who contributed as sources appears in the Bibliography. While gratitude goes to all those who participated, several individuals played special roles not only in providing needed elements but also in encouraging the project to continue against what sometimes seemed impossible odds.

The book could not have been written without the cooperation of the news consultants Frank N. Magid Associates, Audience Research & Development (AR&D) and McHugh & Hoffman. Three additional consulting firms, Primo Newservice, Broadcast Image and Reymer & Associates, also gave vital support. The opportunity to draw from the consultants' private materials, although with the stipulations indicated in the Introduction, made possible the book's central theme of the need for class consciousness in news. In lieu of any central archive on local broadcasting, the consultants' materials provided individual TV histories of scores of U.S. cities. John Bowen of McHugh & Hoffman, Frank N. Magid, and Bill Taylor and Ed Bewley of AR&D personally helped the project come to fruition. Beyond acknowledgment, each needs to be credited for finally opening some of their secretive affairs to the public. Others from these firms who deserve special thanks are Jim Willi, Laurie Mullens, Sandra Connell and Elizabeth Anderson of AR&D; Joe George, Brent Magid, Charles Munro and Ned Warwick of Magid; Anne Bowen and Jacques De Suze of McHugh & Hoffman; and Larry Rickel and Tom Dolan of Broadcast Image.

No less indispensable were several people who gave inordinate amounts of time during interviews, supplied videotapes and materials and, in turn, helped facilitate additional contacts. Al Primo did double duty, both as the head of his consulting firm and as an authority on the innovation he helped pioneer, "Eyewitness News." Joel Daly, Bill Beutel, Al Ittleson, Ray Beindorf, Robert Nelson, Jerry Dunphy, Tom Battista, Lorraine Hillman, Max Utsler, Phil Nye, Melba Tolliver, Mel Kampmann, Bob Weaver, Jack Capell, Patrick Emory, Bill Applegate, Mike Davis, Larry Kane, Ray Miller, Lou Prato and Ed Godfrey always were "there" for the author—as often as not to clarify what must have seemed to them a minor detail on something that had happened 20 or 30 years in the past. Never once did they complain.

Nor did Roger Grimsby, Al Schottelkotte and Ron Tindiglia complain, even as they were interviewed over many months when they were in failing health. Discussions with these three individuals traced their substantial careers in local TV news, although as their stories neared completion, they had wanted to convey a message that became a theme of this book. It was that there is more to life than worrying about TV. When, sadly, each passed away, there was some comfort in knowing that part of them would live on.

What proved the greatest challenge was acquiring films and videotapes of local news broadcasts. While reading about these broadcasts did help, there was no substitute for actually seeing them. Several people were instrumental in making this possible, including John McGinty of the Marist College Film Archive; Andrea Kalas of the UCLA Film and Television Archive; Thomas Bohn of Ithaca College's Roy H. Park School of Communication Archive; Jean Suber and Steve Ferger of PROMAX; Steve Eisman and Paul Gluck of KYW; Jeanne McHale-Waite and Dan Sitarski of WCAU; Sandy Krawitz and Joan Dry of Bill Kurtis Productions; Jan Mode of WCPO; Lorie Reingold of KTRK; Harry Sweet of KCRA; Mike Rausch of KGW; and Jaka Bartolj of Slovenia's Pop TV.

Some of the most important papers and documents relating to local TV news are contained in the Radio-Television News Directors Association (RTNDA) Archive at the University of Iowa. Thank yous and compliments go to Robert McCown and his staff at Iowa for expediting access to 50 years of RTNDA materials. The same tidings are accorded Mary Ellen Brooks at the Hargrett Library at the University of Georgia, where the Arbitron Archive is located. Time spent in Athens combing through what seemed like endless Arbitron ratings books proved essential in documenting three of the most vital local TV news elements: Who was No. 1, when, and for how long.

Most of the funding for the project consisted of media research grants obtained through Arizona State University. Not enough gratitude can be given to Anne Schneider, dean of ASU's College of Public Programs, and Doug Anderson, director of ASU's Walter Cronkite School of Journalism and Telecommunication, who expedited financial support and took a personal interest in the subject.

No part of the project was more enjoyable than working with Judi Brown and the staff at the Iowa State University Press.

Others whose contributions are greatly acknowledged include Anne Bolen, Steve Trella, Charlie Van Dyke, Dan Forman, Nika Beamon, and Nick Lawler.

In addition to those who directly participated, several individuals got behind the book, sharpened its ideas and lent moral support. Heading this list is Professor Don Godfrey, the author's close colleague at the Walter Cronkite School. Dave Walker, the television critic of the *New Orleans Times Picayune,* was a consistent source of insight and encouragement. Others who assisted included Phil Alvidrez, news vice president of KTVK; Ron Bergamo, president of KSAZ; Pep Cooney, president of KPNX; and Brad Nilsen, president of KNXV.

Finally, thanks is given to the author's family, including Dorothy and Austin Allen, for the patience they demonstrated in the seven years it took to write the book.

From obscure beginnings a little over 50 years ago, local TV news has risen to become the largest component of the U.S. news media and a source of information to an estimated 150 million Americans. Each day almost as many people watch one of the nation's local newscasts as watch the Super Bowl. At a time when confidence in the news media is in decline, local TV news has nearly 70 percent public approval. For these reasons and more, local TV news has stirred curiosity in a wide range of individuals—from media experts who look askance at the "Six O'Clock News" to everyday Americans who have made it a daily part of their lives. Until now, a book-length account of local TV news has never been produced.

News Is People operates on several levels. Of interest to many readers will be the showcase of local news, the local newscast, which is followed from its origin as a 15-minute scheduling plug to its more recent status as the main attraction of local TV. Others may appreciate the book's behind-the-scenes thread, of news directors and newsworkers fighting for viewers and ratings points while simultaneously advancing almost every TV news "first." Also included is another facet, the criticism of local TV news, as vigorous as any the news media have ever seen.

However, the largest part of *News Is People* is devoted to a single theme, one universal in today's mainstream news media. It is a tug-of-war between the best-and-brightest individuals who deliver news and the average Americans who receive it. Journalism literature has not isolated this conflict, nor has it established that rather than being "gatekeepers," today's news defers to a bulwark of focus groups, surveys, ratings and Q scores. These guarantee that the average American, not the journalist, will win. Local TV news is essential to understanding the modern news process because it was the first component of the news media to absorb the systems approach. The result has been "people's news"—a formula of warm-and-friendly personalities, "action" visuals, brief soundbites, simple stories, and "news you can use." As traced in *News Is People,* this was no insignificant event. Today the "peopleization" of journalism is plainly seen in every mainstream information source from CBS News and *Time* magazine to ESPN and *USA Today.*

Crucial to the story of local TV news was the opening of the field to specialists called news consultants. As will be seen, it was through giant consulting firms such as Magid and McHugh & Hoffman that the "voice of the people" first entered newsrooms and tremendous change ensued. In standard works on the process of local TV news, including Edwin Diamond's 1975 *The Tin Kazoo,* Ron Powers' 1978 *The Newscasters,* and Jerry Jacobs' 1990 *Changing Channels,* news consultants are prominently discussed. These works illustrate how a fiercely competitive environment in local TV news inspired the hiring of consultants. They associate consultants with a drive for ratings and profits, and they document the consultants' remarkable spread. Such accounts, though, have been negative in tone and capture the research-consulting process the way journalists would prefer it be viewed: as an aberration rather than a force. Witnessing people's news on TV stations all over the country, for example, Powers urged Congress to "clean up the mess."

It does seem a "mess" to many. Consultants have been easy targets for those convinced that local TV news "dumbs down" the public and panders to a "lowest common denominator."

Still, the primary source has never been exposed in these discussions: the volume of audience research reports and accompanying materials in which the people, not journalists and critics, weighed in. While many authors have stressed the significance of the consultants' research and some have given their opinions as to what they thought it probably contained, it is unclear whether anyone who has previously written about the research actually has seen it. Applied research is proprietary and generally not available to the public. Thus, Job No. 1 was arranging access to at least some of these research studies.

The project took wing in 1994 when the three leading consulting firms, Magid, McHugh & Hoffman and AR&D, were persuaded to participate in a historical study. Vaults were opened, and out came a bounty of these companies' secret consulting reports. They were offered with the stipulation that proprietary sensitivities be observed and that they be used strictly for historical purposes. Throughout the book these stipulations are observed. Some of the most consequential reports, including the ones that launched the concepts called "Eyewitness" and "Action" news, are now on file at Arizona State University.

It was soon apparent why the release of this information did not threaten the consultants. First, it was old. The material consisted of audience research reports from 1957 through 1995. But above all, in these focus groups and surveys, average people had done little more than speak their minds about TV news. Millions of people have participated in these studies. In some cases they ranked content and personalities and produced the infamous "Q scores," while on most occasions they merely explained such things as why they preferred pictures over words, weather reports over political news, and female as well as male newscasters.

The richest of these data were those at the very beginning, when mass audience preferences for television news were first exposed and the news took its modern form. When asked about television news, respondents were of one mind on basic things. They insisted they were not news "junkies" and had more to do than ponder the details of current events. They told consultants they would most likely watch if given relevant stories that did not waste their time, anchors who were like the "friend next door," and as much style and technical razzle-dazzle as newsrooms could allow. They wanted news in simple conversational language. Rather than granite newscasters who spoke from Mt. Olympus, they wanted anchors who could smile. As time went on and the format for people's news became routinized, the consultants, still seeking competitive advantages, broadened their research into a range of market-specific issues. Nevertheless, the public's basic expectations for TV news were consistent year after year.

Not only was it obvious that the many alleged failings of local TV news—from happy talk and pictures to flamboyant coverage and the "news you can use"—had not been dreamed up by news consultants, but that consultants only had been a conduit for elements that everyday people had defined. The larger revelation was the sensitivity of local TV news to what the idea of "mass" media really means. When the first news consultants told TV journalists they were not "average Americans," and then explained that steamfitters, truck drivers, and office workers did fit this tag, they knew whereof they spoke.

While local TV news draws energy as a field devoid of great people and big events, one exception comes forth. He is Lloyd Warner, the person who spearheaded the first news consulting firm, McHugh & Hoffman. While his name has been insignificant in the field of mass communication, Warner was a seminal figure in American scholarship and one of the founders of the field of sociology. During the Great Depression, Warner, a Harvard and then University of Chicago professor, soared to worldwide academic acclaim for establishing the American system of social class.

Through painstaking anthropological studies that stretched over several years, Warner documented a small college-educated upper and upper-middle class of around 20 percent of the total U.S. population. Then he isolated what he termed the "middle majority," the 70 percent of lower-middle and upper-lower class Americans with high school educations or less, whose similar incomes, occupations and lifestyles limit their upward mobility. The fulcrum of local TV news was the division between these two groups. In research, preferences of the middle majority were dissimilar and sometimes diametrically opposed to those of the upper-middle class. The upper-middle class, its calling card a college degree, included almost everyone drawn to careers in the news media. They were and remain a small minority. Under Warner's tutelage, McHugh & Hoffman began the process of taking TV news out of the hands of newsroom bourgeois and passing it to the masses. Although Warner never set foot in a newsroom, his fingerprints are all over the local TV news seen by scores of millions today.

Thus, *News Is People* is more than merely an account of the "Six O'Clock News." By looking at TV news not from a media but from a sociological perspective, one sees new ideas and possibilities. If local TV news is flawed, the problem may be that it fails not the American public at large but only the upper-middle class, a small yet vocal group. That two-thirds of Americans not only use local TV news but say they approve of it is evidence the field actually succeeds. As for "dumbing down," Warner and his colleagues saw this as upper-middle class grief. They knew that IQs vary among individuals, with those in the upper-middle class at around "125" and those in the middle class at "100" and thus had rendered "dumbing down" a relative concern. Warner never taught a media course. Yet he did teach those in sociology that a person's status, IQ and all, was an accident of birth. People, he said, must be accepted for who they are. Accordingly, Warner enlightened many that use of the term "lowest common denominator" is analogous to a racial slur. Finally, Warner insisted that if a person articulates his or her own interests and needs, whether they be pictures, weather reports, or smiling news anchors, it was not right for the upper-middle class to say "You're wrong."

The main lesson of local TV news is that understanding the mass media begins with understanding the masses. It can be an elusive lesson on a college campus or in a newsroom, where upper-middle class meets upper-middle class. Yet those whose instinct may be to say the Great Depression is over, "Joe Six Pack" a thing of the past, might judge these facts: According to census data published in 2000, 55 percent of Americans had high school educations or less and only 23 percent had college degrees. Forty-four percent were in the two lowest of seven income brackets, while more than 60 percent belonged to single-parent families. The same number of families were headed by blue collar workers or the white collar working class. While 30 percent had risen to salaried occupations, the rest continued to work by the clock. With the mass media in a state of unprecedented upheaval, these remain powerful considerations. As much as the media may change, experience suggests the mass will remain the same.

Yet local news, to be sure, is more than just this. Nowhere in the news media is there a story more colorful. Only in local TV news does a bow-tie help save an entire television network. Only here do Newton Minow, Ted Baxter, Marshall McLuhan, and Patty Hearst have fundamental meaning alongside tens of thousands of mostly young newsroom lights who were "on your side" and "moved closer to your world." It is an urban study that takes in almost everyone's hometown. It is a generational study in which TV generation baby-boomers engage their war-hardened pre-TV elders in a philosophical armageddon over what TV news should be. In the end it brings a 21st Century spin to what McLuhan with his metaphor of the "global village" may have had in mind.

As much as by any other element, *News Is People* was inspired by a restlessness with a TV news literature dominated by accounts and memoirs of the three original networks. Calls for an alternative history of television news reached a crescendo as the book came together in the 1990s, this as the ABC, CBS and NBC nightly newscasts plummeted in the ratings and questions multiplied as to whether the volume of network-dominated literature had power to explain TV news in its current state. Countered here is a perception left from this literature that local TV news was "little network news" and that the networks established a model for broadcast journalism that smaller local newsrooms obediently followed. In reality, every significant development in local news was a revolt against network news. That local news prevailed in these revolts helps explain the shrinkage of network news today.

The story quite naturally is keyed to TV institutions. Pioneers such as Storer, Westinghouse, Belo and King—buried under mounds of network history—at last see daylight. But new and important light shines on the New York networks themselves, a vortex of events in local TV news. ABC, CBS, and NBC were not just networks but owners of the nation's largest local television stations. Enormous profit from these powerhouse local stations was crucial to keeping the networks alive. A dominant theme, network-local antagonism, had roots in network-owned local newsrooms, where scorned yet profitable people's newscasts were indirectly footing the bill for critically acclaimed but money-losing network news divisions.

At the local level, NBC played a middle-of-the-road role. Initially knocked off balance in competition with the people's newscast, the NBC local stations reeled under an executive who denigrated the cause of women and then sat back as NBC's flagship outlet in New York scored a zero rating. Sometime after this, NBC separated its network and local news departments, attracted new leadership, and went on to become one of the field's most progressive entities.

If the story has a hero, it is ABC, the broadcast institution that least interests the experts. ABC was television's greatest underdog. Its current strength as part of the Disney empire stems from its tradition of not fighting the people. This started with one of the most inexplicable events in the annals of American television, when the gnat called ABC invented a concept called "Eyewitness News" and then scored not measured but Carthaginian ratings victories over NBC and CBS. The ABC stations were among the first to hire news consultants, the first to implement research, and the first to advance women and minorities, and they elevated a TV news paradigm in the face of the most malignant elite criticism in the history of American journalism. Yet all along it was plain that what experts were calling the "Almost Broadcasting Company" was a King Kong in the making.

Finally comes CBS, a "tiffany" network that couldn't find its backside with both hands. The local CBS station is credited with the first long-form news as well as with technical feats that led to VCRs and home video. Yet TV news had no greater turning points than when CBS fired local "Walter Cronkites" in Chicago, Philadelphia, and Los Angeles. Then, battered by ABC, the local CBS went on to fire news directors, reporters, producers, and more anchors, en route to its 1970s reputation as the lord high executioner of TV news. One of many attempts to rebound was a promotional cavalcade in which CBS had a local news anchor dress in a costume that made him look like a cross between Porky Pig and the Werewolf of London. While this was happening, the national media began a search-and-destroy campaign against "Eyewitness News," with the confused CBS leading the charge. Cronkite publicly denounced the nation's local station managers and news directors as "suckers for a fad—editing by consultancy" at the very moment CBS itself, at the local level, had made a massive commitment to news consulting. Nothing has more dominated the literature on television news than the continuing efforts by authors to cheer a "CBS tradition." This "tradition" as revealed here will amuse the reader as nothing else.

The book is a history, and while the main theme of people's news has stood the test of time, many circumstances have changed. Tensions between network and local news have eased as the former realizes its dependence on the latter. The Fox network, built from owned local TV stations that don't have to carry a newscast from New York, exemplifies the 50-year trend. In addition, specific TV stations characterized here as winners and losers may not be those today, and the parts of the book recounting criticisms do not necessarily reflect the current views of the same critics. Given local TV's far-flung structure, it was impossible to account for some conflicting claims of what was first. It should also be noted again that a promise by the author was made, and kept, that personal and professional sensitivities be upheld in using the confidential consulting materials.

Finally, in establishing the decline of the New York networks, the objective was not to diminish their landmark contributions to broadcast journalism. Indeed, one of the highlights of the project was the opportunity to involve Cronkite and his CBS staff in the research. Cronkite would argue that CBS, too, had a people's news tradition, which in his personal case—as the reader will see through actual research on Cronkite—was true. More persuasively, Cronkite was committed to accuracy, immediacy, enterprise, and hard work, elements of journalism that should bind national and local news. Although he is wrong, it is impossible not to be impressed with Cronkite's steadfastness in pleading that television's local level infected the information process. Just listening to Cronkite say the words "Eyewitness News" was an unforgettable experience.

Still, the times have changed. For better or worse, local TV news is in step with them. It is a field that can serve everyone, its detractors and proponents alike, by giving the story of TV news a fresh start.

NEWS IS PEOPLE

1

Famous for Fifteen Minutes (1947–1959)

World War II was over, and the troops had returned. To GI Janes and Joes who had gone forth from the nation's largest city, homecoming had meant Coney Island, the Bronx Zoo, Brooklyn Dodgers baseball games and the *New York Daily News.* "All news is local," Joseph Medill Patterson had proclaimed in founding the *Daily News* in 1919. Indeed, nothing in New York better said "New York" to the millions of average people who lived there.

They printed it vertically like a magazine in what printers called a tabloid design. The *Daily News* was the source of this term "tabloid," although not because of its shape but because of what was on the cover and carried inside. There were pictures everywhere, lots of big headlines, and stories about cops and killers, dogs and debutantes and where to go to buy shoes. The city's elite snickered at this newspaper, but with the war over and local happenings being the big news, at least to those Janes and Joes, the aging Patterson was not perturbed. With a daily circulation of three million, five million on weekends, the *Daily News* was the most widely read newspaper in U.S. history. On East Forty-second Street, chiseled in black marble over the main entrance to the *Daily News,* were the words "He made so many of them," the rejoinder to Abraham Lincoln's famous remark "God must have loved the common people . . . ." Fittingly, it was inside that building that local TV news began.

To succeed with the masses, the *Daily News* had had to keep up with the masses, so it was far ahead of most in spotting the fast approach of television, the new people's medium. In the span of just a few weeks in 1946, it had applied for and received from the FCC a TV license for New York, a big moment for the newspaper. The celebrating ended just as quickly. With nearby cities as large as Baltimore and Boston with no TV stations, New York already had three, and a fourth was on the way. Ominously for the *Daily News,* each was owned by a network, and each was a flagship of chains of outlets that soon would stretch from coast to coast. On Channels 2 and 4 were CBS-owned WCBW (later WCBS) and NBC-owned WNBT (later WNBC), while on Channel 5 was WABD (later WNYW), owned by the Dumont network. Beginning test patterns on Channel 7 was ABC's WJZ (later WABC). Off by itself on Channel 11, the *Daily News* signal, was New York's first independent station. Lacking a national advertising base, Channel 11 had no hope of enlisting marque attractions such as Channel 4's Milton Berle and Phil Silvers or Channel 2's Ed Sullivan, hit entertainers eventually known nationwide.[1]

What Channel 11 could do, though, was offer a local news service. Local news was the specialty of the *Daily News.* Scrambling to get anything on the air by the spring of 1948, there were indications a televised local news show might carve a definitive competitive niche.

Although Channels 2, 4 and 5 had been carrying 15-minute newscasts, they were filled with national and worldwide news. Moreover, the nightly news on Channel 4 had just taken on a national sponsor, Camel cigarettes, and a nationally known newscaster, John Cameron Swayze. Smiles appeared at Channel 11 when Channel 4's local newscast, the "Camel News Caravan," was beamed down the NBC line as the first network news. That was in February 1948. Others seemed sure to follow, so no one at Channel 11 was surprised when CBS transferred a photogenic network radio correspondent named Douglas Edwards to Channel 2, where the first CBS evening news would originate a few months later. "The networks did not add a local newscast," recalled Leavitt Pope, one of the first *Daily News* executives moved to Channel 11, and "this was crucial in deciding what we were going to do. . . . Our plan was for a people's newscast," one that would target the masses and counter the "big journalism" ventures on the network stations.[2]

A people's newscast was auspicious for an important additional reason. Since the 1920s, when it had conducted streetcorner interviews to document the people's preferences, the *Daily News* had relied on research in news decision-making. Patterson, in fact, had demanded research as a way to suppress the managers' "country club" instincts.[3] "We knew," Pope would explain, "that not many of us were like the people we served. There were differences we had to know." The research would advance into regular readership surveys. Despite seat-of-the-pants survey techniques, and scoffs from professional researchers, the *Daily News* nevertheless had ferreted a forward-looking parameter: a breakdown of news preferences by social class. In 1948, the newspaper had gone so far as to advertise one of these studies, which showed to no one's amazement its overwhelming acceptance in New York's "Middle Class," exactly 60.1 percent of the population.[4] While it was not known how the *Daily News* had arrived at this figure, it was nearly identical to an authoritative measure soon to shape all of local TV news. New York's middle majority was not just loyal to the *Daily News;* in 1948 they were buying TV sets at fever pitch.

Thus, with the stakes very high, Channel 11 pulled out the stops. Its 1948 news budget of a half-million dollars exceeded amounts then being spent to get entire TV stations on the air.[5] F. M. Flynn and Allen Martin, Channel 11's general manager and news director, followed Pope, the vice president for programming, to the television operation. Twenty-six additional people joined the news staff. John Tillman became the first local news anchor; Joe Bolton, the first weathercaster; and Guy Lebow, the first sportscaster. The chief photographer appropriately was named Ed Clarity.[6] In the meantime, the *Daily News* had purchased for Channel 11 a half-dozen portable film cameras, as many news cars, a high-speed film processor, and two huge remote trucks with live capability. Channel 11 even had an airplane for aerial coverage.[7]

The plan was pinned to two polished local nightly newscasts, one initially of 10 minutes at 7:30, the other initially of 15 minutes at 11, following prime time shows. Local TV's "Eleven O'Clock News" had begun as a special piece of Channel 11 strategy. At that hour, all stations but Channel 2 had signed off. The research had indicated that if viewers could be persuaded to stay up for an 11 p.m. newscast, their dials already would be set on Channel 11 when the next day's programming began.[8] Not only this, the 11 o'clock hour and the station's position on the TV dial worked wonderfully in news promotion. An advertising campaign touting "Lucky 'Levin" was seen all over New York.[9]

Promotion also rested on naming the new TV station. In picking the call letters, Channel 11 wanted a handle, not a stuffy corporate abbreviation. It also wanted to drive home its companionship with the immensely popular *Daily News*. Because the *Daily News* bannered itself as New York's picture newspaper, the call letters "WPIX" were selected. "[P]ronounce it Pix," the *Daily News* urged.[10] Spinning from the call letters was the newscast title, "Telepix Newsreel." "Now that the radio wave can be made to carry pictures as well as sound," read a gigantic promotional ad, "WPIX brings to Television the experience of The News." The station promised to "find, get and deliver stories [and] to be always a reliable medium of information, education, and understanding."[11] A final preparation was announcing the station's motto: "First On Scene, First On Screen."[12]

Local TV news began with a flourish. "Telepix Newsreel" debuted on June 16, 1948, the station's second day. The big event in New York at that moment, and the lead story, was Channel 11's own sign on.[13] The next day, when word came that a DC-6 airliner bound for LaGuardia Airport with two dozen New Yorkers on board had crashed in Pennsylvania, a WPIX newsreel crew boarded the newsplane and winged to the scene. That evening, while the network stations carried week-old material from Jerusalem and Berlin, the 7:30 p.m. edition of "Telepix Newsreel" was dominated by updates on the crash. Between programs, a WPIX announcer kept telling viewers "film at 11," a phrase that stuck. In what the national trade newspaper *Variety* termed a "news gathering feat," the New York audience saw a complete visual report of the tragedy less than 10 hours after it had occurred.[14] "Television Row was talking yesterday about the dramatic news beat of WPIX," Ben Gross of the *Daily News* wrote. "Put this down as the first of WPIX exclusives. There will be many more to come."[15]

Gross's prediction was accurate: By the end of 1948, features that would still define local TV news 50 years later had already been demonstrated. WPIX became the first local station to originate an entire newscast from a remote location, this at the Republican convention in Philadelphia. The local angle was New York Governor Thomas Dewey's presidential nomination. WPIX then introduced a technique called the "mini-documentary" in a week-long series of reports previewing the startup of Idlewild Airport. The first reporter "live shots" were seen when WPIX covered the opening of the airport that August. Later, when two Navy ships bound for New York collided 1,200 miles off shore, out of range of the four-seat newsplane, WPIX scooped the local and national media by reaching the scene in chartered 50-seat DC-4.[16]

In a turn of events even more portentous, WPIX became the first TV news organization to discover the medium's true challenge: not the occasional big events but the days, weeks, and sometimes months when nothing big occurred. As "Telepix Newsreel" fell into a routine, viewers usually witnessed events carried on a typical day in the *Daily*

News. The "little news" agenda was dominated by fires, crimes, and outbreaks of isolated violence, so much that there was barely a day when police, firefighters, and mayhem did not appear. Even more frequent were political events, council meetings, public proclamations, groundbreakings, and the arrivals of celebrities.

In an attempt to liven this daily array of "blotter" news, WPIX humanized its reporting. The news personalities sometimes broke from the script and chit-chatted, this informality visible when WPIX heralded a TV version of a popular *Daily News* column known as the "Inquiring Fotographer." It was the advent of TV's "man-on-the-street" interview. From this followed consumer stories: advice on buying new cars and tips for beating the crush of holiday mail. Feature stories, which on one WPIX newscast had included updates on a baby platypus at the Bronx Zoo and reports on children in a Bronx neighborhood leaving for summer camp, often were the most popular news items of all.[17] "People hear too much talk [and] too many high-sounding words," WPIX news manager Carl Warren remarked. "If we've learned one thing, it [is] that the television audience wants less talk and more of the on-scene feel. . . ."[18]

Convinced they were on to something, Warren, Pope, and the others were heartened by the first Nielsen ratings in 1948, which not only showed "Telepix Newsreel" as one of WPIX's most-watched programs. With a 15 percent share of the audience, it had almost as many viewers as the nationally sponsored network newscasts on Channels 2 and 4.

Yet in the city where the big networks were born, and opinions on the media were formed, network news already was king. Despite a surprisingly large audience, "Telepix Newsreel," like the *Daily News* itself, was passed off as a carnival act. It was something new for New York's many media critics to harpoon. Only a month after the debut, a July 1948 *Variety* article summed up the reaction by first questioning whether WPIX's newscast, containing news that either could be filmed or covered live, even constituted journalism. Then hailing the networks' strides in digesting national and global events, *Variety* went on to condemn the local approach on Channel 11—"stunts, entertainment, and people on the street"as a "tabloid technique" by comparison.[19]

While WPIX pressed on in New York, more trial and error had been unfolding in Chicago and Los Angeles. In the nation's second- and third-largest cities, the impetus for local news had been the same as in New York: a struggle by independent stations against the iron grip of the networks. In Chicago, WBKB, then an independent outlet, had initiated a local newscast in 1947. A year later, the first local news competition appeared when a more ambitious effort, the 15-minute "Chicagoland Newsreel," was started by rival WGN just days before WGN lost the CBS affiliation to WBKB.[20]

More spirited was the activity in Los Angeles. KTLA, the first TV outlet on the West Coast, was a "sister station" to Chicago's WBKB; this meant they were owned by the same company, in their case, the mammoth Paramount Pictures corporation. Planning to use television for its motion picture distribution, Paramount was forced to abandon this idea following its breakup by the Justice Department in 1948. By then, long past the point at which it could jockey for a network affiliation, KTLA was resigned to a future as an independent, as was an outlet called KTTV, owned by the *Los Angeles Times*. KTTV had just had its affiliation stripped when CBS purchased the station that became KNXT, later KCBS. KTLA and KTTV responded immediately with local newscasts. Their competition in the late 1940s marked the first TV "news war."

The battle between KTLA and KTTV initially shaped up over live coverage of breaking events. A landmark in television news, and one which exquisitely depicted the power of people's news, occurred on April 8, 1949, when a three-year-old girl named Kathy Fiscus stumbled into a 110-foot abandoned well in the Los Angeles suburb of San Marino. While the network stations continued with their entertainment programs, the two Los Angeles independents dispatched several tons of mobile equipment, including large banks of flood lights, and provided around-the-clock live coverage of an eventually unsuccessful rescue attempt.[21] With newscaster Stan Chambers giving descriptions, KTLA remained on the air for 25 hours. KTTV, though, was able to tout its slightly longer coverage of 27 hours.[22] In a study of this event, Dartmouth's Mark Williams noted that "in many ways television was making news by covering news. The overwhelming public interest and concern for Kathy's rescue, which by many accounts virtually brought the city to a standstill, merged in a silent way with . . . television, still new to most as an apparatus, and especially new as a primary source of 'live' news coverage."[23]

While the two stations would tangle in many similar contests, including their continuous coverage of a child kidnapping in 1951, KTLA's technical prowess proved no match for KTTV. It was masterminded by a producer-engineer named Klaus Landsberg, who had escaped Nazi Germany and, while working for the Dumont company, had invented the system that made live news possible. In 1952, Landsberg arranged another local news watershed, KTLA's live coverage of an atomic bomb explosion 300 miles away in Nevada.[24] As Sherrie Mazingo of the University of Southern California would write, "The preliminaries to this telecast as well as the telecast itself were as anxiety-ridden and suspenseful as any movie scene from Hollywood."[25] Landsberg died three years later, his large yet scarcely acknowledged legacy to television news the first use of portable video cameras, the first truly mobile live transmitters, and in 1958 the first live TV news helicopter. All of these had come at KTLA.[26]

Nevertheless, because of something still newer, KTTV would wind up the champion of Los Angeles TV news throughout the 1950s. KTTV's innovation was the first six-figure TV news star.

Not long after the Fiscus spectacle, the family that owned the *Los Angeles Times* and KTTV amassed salaries and benefits totalling more than $150,000 to hire as KTTV's newscaster a nationally known radio commentator named George Putnam. At the time, Swayze and Edwards, the network anchors on NBC and CBS, were earning one-tenth as much. Putnam had been the understudy to NBC's Walter Winchell, by far the era's best-known radio news figure, Edward Murrow's later reputation as the father of radio news notwithstanding. Unlike the shrill and chattering Winchell, Putnam had what Winchell had called "golden pipes." Winchell had been so impressed by Putnam's remarkably rich, resonant, and ear-catching delivery that he blazoned Putnam's voice as "the greatest in American radio."

On television, Putnam kept this commanding presence. Even so, he came through as a passionate and gut-level newscaster, particularly when he shared what most recognized as conservative political views. He was the first TV news sensation. Each night, Putnam stood beside an American flag, signed off with his signature line "Here's to a better, stronger America," and then winked at the camera.[27] In Los Angeles he was as much a household name as Humphrey Bogart, Grace Kelly or any of the other international celebrities who lived there.

Putnam offered a distant glimpse of a star system destined to proliferate in and then dominate local TV news. In a 1953 survey, KTTV news manager Bob Allison disclosed that Putnam was earning almost as much money as that defraying all the station's other news expenses, including the salaries of 10 other people.[28] This talent fee, though, was more than offset by KTTV's 35 percent share of the audience. Flush with ad revenues from this "35," a stratospheric rating, KTTV could have paid Putnam's salary several times over. Indeed, every time Putnam renegotiated his contract, more money came his way. By

1960, Putnam was earning $350,000, an amount that in real terms would have equaled well over a million dollars in 1983, the year the first seven-figure local news salary, commanded by New York's Ernie Anastos, actually was paid.[29] "Was I bashful about the money? Not for a second," Putnam would relate. "Channel 11 [KTTV] had accountants, and they were not about to give me a penny more than I was worth." Putnam also was oblivious to criticisms of his wink-at-the-camera delivery. "All of the so-called experts felt my style was not in keeping with 'good journalism.' I said, 'Who cares about them?' Whenever the red light went on," Putnam stated, "I tried to be myself . . . [and] the people responded. If you can reach the people, that's all that matters."[30]

Personalities like Putnam and spectacular coverage like KTLA's cut grooves that would extend far into the future. Yet almost immediately these path-breaking independent stations were overshadowed. Television had just entered its "Golden Age," the leading event the FCC's lifting of a four-year "freeze" on station licensing in 1952, which brought 555 new local TV stations to the air. In a defining moment in U.S. TV, all of them would affiliate with one of the New York networks, ABC, CBS or NBC. From this point onward, three big networks and hundreds of otherwise autonomous local stations would be locked in a relationship never as harmonious as many made it out to be. On paper, the local stations actually mastered the arrangement. They controlled all the transmitters, but as long as New York had a monopoly on the nation's popular programs, the networks were in charge.

Indeed, from the beginning of the network-affiliate system, the affiliates relied on the networks for entertainment fare. Hit shows such as "I Love Lucy" were turning millions of dollars in profits, and local stations had hastened to get these offerings on the air. Even though the freeze had ended and the FCC had ordained more local fare, the rush to affiliate began a dark period in the development of local TV. Interestingly, local origination had been more robust during the freeze than immediately after it, this because network lines leading from New York had yet to extend from coast to coast. Pre-freeze stations in the Midwest and Far West had to produce their own shows. Yet after the freeze, only a handful of stations spearheaded local programming. Fewer still emerged as leaders in local TV news.[31]

This short list of early news-active stations was not unimportant, though. It had included an extremely significant contingent of local TV properties: those actually owned by the big networks. In the policy statement ending the freeze, the FCC had limited to five the number of stations a company could own. Even the networks could hold no more than five local licenses. Although this was a small number and would not appreciably increase until the FCC lifted ownership rules in the 1980s, power concentrated in these five-station groups. Each network had used its muscle to arrange its five stations in the very largest cities. Crucial to the networks' bottom lines, these network owned-and-operated stations, known as "O and Os," were carefully followed throughout the TV industry. Notable among them was WNBC in New York, which reinstituted local news in 1954; for the next 15 years, WNBC was the pillar of local TV news. It commanded more viewers than any station in the country. Almost as much of a local news powerhouse was Washington's WTOP, half-owned by CBS. It was there that future CBS anchor Walter Cronkite was first seen in TV news. Also resource-laden, two other CBS-owned stations, WBBM in Chicago and WCAU in Philadelphia, were dominant in their markets.

These network-owned local newscasts were informative but by most accounts not very interesting to watch. Operated by the network news divisions, they were facsimiles of network newscasts. They kept visual effects to a minimum, avoided video technology and seemingly aspired to be "televised newspapers." One man read out loud all the news. This approach, known to insiders as the "man-on-camera" format, was the most efficient means for compressing the day's news into a 15-minute time span, the limit of all network and local newscasts.

Against this man-on-camera idea, though, a new thread in local TV news began to twist. According to a local news newcomer in Minnesota, Bill Tucker, "The thing that caused many in local news to question network news was a sense [the networks] lacked creativity, that they had a single idea when here you had this new medium with all sorts of new possibilities." The problem in 1953, as Tucker saw it, was pinpointing the cities where more had been done. "Back then," he explained, "there were no consultants, nobody who could tell you what was happening in different cities. The networks were all you knew."[32]

So Tucker, intrigued by the possibility that there were varying techniques in TV news—and by his notion that one city's local TV news could be modeled on the local news somewhere else, that ideas could be transplanted into others—took on the task himself. He defined a function news consultants later would assume. It started when Tucker, halfway through a master's degree program at the University of Minnesota, proposed as a school project the first national study of local news. Even though he had just been hired as a news writer at Minneapolis-St. Paul station KSTP, he won the support of station owner and broadcast pioneer Stanley Hubbard, Sr., a person who like

Tucker had been restless with the network concept and interested in everything Tucker might find out. Hubbard and his sons, the heirs to KSTP, eventually would become famous for bucking the establishment. They were synonymous with the contempt leading local broadcasters often directed at New York. Though KSTP had been NBC's first local affiliate, in 1977 the Hubbards would stun the TV industry by dumping the "peacock" network and switching to the then-weak ABC. In 1984, the Hubbards struck again by instituting a satellite news cooperative called CONUS. With CONUS local newsrooms could obtain distant news feeds without contact with their networks. Tucker had started the Hubbards thinking in maverick terms. As their "Marco Polo," Tucker traveled around the country and brought back glowing reports of how local TV news in at least some cities had progressed.

An example was the first city Tucker contacted, New York, where he studied WPIX. In filling out a preliminary questionnaire, news director Walter Engels detailed the ways the WPIX newscast had departed from the networks' man-on-camera format. WPIX had emphasized its "friendly" news team and had established a format that stressed interviews with people on the street.[33]

Expecting WPIX to be the most progressive in local news, Tucker subsequently found that Baltimore's WMAR, a CBS affiliate, actually had a more sophisticated news. This station claimed 23 pieces of equipment, including two sound-on-film "Auricon" cameras and six silent "Filmo" cameras.[34]

Yet even WMAR was outdone by NBC affiliate WBAP in Fort Worth-Dallas, which reported no fewer than 17 film cameras, more than the NBC and CBS networks put together.[35] This wild enumeration of field cameras piqued the curiosity of Tucker, who quickly pencilled "Fort Worth" on his travel itinerary. When he arrived at WBAP, Tucker found that all this hardware was, in fact, being used. He was awe-struck to discover that WBAP's "Texas Newsreel" literally was just that: 15 minutes of continuous filmed reports dressed as newsreels—with *no newscaster.*

WBAP's 1950s newscasts under news director Jim Byron were the antithesis of the Swayze-Edwards newscasts on the networks. Byron's no-newscaster newscast continued until 1963, when expansion to a half-hour did finally necessitate a presenter. Until then, Byron fulfilled the hope of many later news directors who would yearn for a newscast without "star" anchors. CBS's Walter Cronkite, by then a correspondent and special events anchor, said he had shared this yearning. "We discussed at CBS many times . . . the possibility of getting rid of the anchor person," Cronkite stated in a 1989 interview.

"But . . . every time we studied other ways to do the evening news broadcast, we came up with the fact that [a newscast with personalities] was best."[36] Even so, all through this period, Fort Worth's NBC affiliate demonstrated that a newscast without anchors could be done.

Of all the questionnaires, none was more eye-opening than the one from CBS affiliate KFMB in San Diego. This was because its news director was one of the "big" and "great" figures from network news. He was Paul White, the first director of CBS News and a Peabody Award winner, who had moved to San Diego because of an arthritic condition. Tucker would find White an individual much affected by his experience in local TV news. Struck by television's potential for reaching everyday people, White's thinking had moved far afield from that recalled by his former colleagues in New York.

White had told Tucker "there's nothing wrong with trying to make [TV news] as interesting (or 'entertaining') as you can." For example, "in the local reel one night, I wrote for the announcer: 'Did you ever see a baby giraffe try to get on his feet for the first time? Well, take a look at what happened today at the Zoo.'" Another example had come when White stationed a KFMB photographer outside a flower shop before Mothers' Day, "in the hope that a grubby little boy would come along, look in the window and come out with posies. It did happen, it was unrehearsed and it made as charming a bit as we've ever filmed." Another concept was the "twister" shot, filmed items ending with the unexpected. "A good example might be a heat wave story," White explained. "We did the usual beach scenes . . . and then ended up with a cute three-year-old girl in a head shot carrying a parasol pirouetting before the camera. Then, as she turned and walked away, it became apparent that she didn't have on a stitch and we shot her . . . for a two-or-three second finale."

White had been so enthralled by the potentials of little journalism that his single-spaced, typewritten comments spilled over onto two additional pages of the questionnaire he returned to Tucker.[37] When it came time for the field's major trade organization, the Radio-Television News Directors Association, to pick a namesake for its most prestigious award, it would honor the man who'd been impressed with the baby giraffe and the grubby little boy.

Tucker felt the 1950s' most progressive newscast, and the one later emulated by Hubbard, was that seen by Miami viewers on CBS affiliate WTVJ. With a "65" share, WTVJ had the highest ratings of any local newscast in the country, and Tucker could see why. In Tucker's words it was "distinctly non-network" and had a "home" station touch. Tucker's report noted a "living room setting" highlighted by a broad "window with [a] downtown picture of Miami illuminated from [the] rear." This "skyline" innovation eventually would be seen on local TV newscasts in every city. Yet according to WTVJ news director Ralph Renick, content had made the difference in the ratings. Unlike White, Renick stressed crime news. In fact, by Renick's own account, his newscast might have been titled "Miami Vice." "[Our] concentration [is] on 'Spot News,'" he emphasized, "we gear our operation to having an MP cameraman at the scene when news is happening—this takes radio-equipped wagons [and] co-operation with police and fire agencies." Good breaking news, he insisted, "can be done."[38] With this type of news philosophy, Renick would ascend as another TV news great. He was the only local TV news figure ever to win that Paul White Award.

Tucker had gone on to isolate about four dozen other progressive local stations. Yet hundreds of others were doing as little in news as they could. In one respect all local news had been bolstered by the licensing boom, for under FCC rules each station had to devote one hour out of 10 to programs relating to news and public affairs. Every city graced with a new TV station also had a new source of local news.

However, to owners, and patently to an FCC that had to force-feed news, it was inconceivable that newscasts could compete with entertainment programs. Back in 1948, for example, the "15" share delivered by WPIX had been considered a feat. Still, that "15" had paled next to Milton Berle's "86." The rest of the Golden Age brought one clue after another to the difficulties TV news would face. Savaged in the ratings, Murrow's acclaimed "See It Now" documentary series on the networks had just been canceled. Likewise, for not meeting ratings expectations, the CBS and NBC network newscasts had been pulled out of prime time and pushed into earlier time periods with fewer viewers. Because of the ratings predicament, NBC's Swayze, the first network news anchor, was fired in 1956 and replaced by Chet Huntley and David Brinkley.

The troubles were illustrated in many other ways, none better than in model blueprints by architectural firms building the first TV stations. One drawing by Kramer, Winner, Kramer of New York showed a local newsroom no larger than an adjacent restroom.[39] Consistent with this blueprint was a prototype personnel chart circulated to local stations by CBS. It listed 51 station personnel—and one "local news man."[40] That this "one man" was doing little more than trimming dispatches from wire services and reciting them on the air, a practice known as "rip-and-read," was documented by the RTNDA, which had just shown in a survey that only 17 percent of network affiliates had people who wrote their own news stories.[41]

All this had exposed a problem in TV news that was not easily managed and that would never really go away. The public was indifferent to news. As Tucker commented, "Janes and Joes were not news junkies. Not a little but a lot was needed to get them to tune in."[42] Mindful of this, hundreds of TV stations carried local news only to satisfy the FCC. All over the country, home screens bore a lone newscaster sitting behind a desk or standing at a podium and reading news dispatches out loud into a camera, one dispatch after another, the simplest way news could be telecast. Indirectly, the big networks influenced this inaction. They had legitimized the man-on-camera format, which local stations could emulate for almost no money. Beyond this, the networks had virtually dictated the newscast's 15-minute time frame. Because at the dinner hour the networks carried 15-minute newscasts, local stations had to have a similar 15-minute report. A local newscast longer than 15 minutes would consume part of the next half hour and throw schedules out of whack. At 11 p.m. NBC affiliates additionally were blocked because the "Tonight Show" with Jack Paar began at 11:15.

Moreover, cleaving to yet another network norm, the news-only newscast, the first local newscasts did not contain weather and sports. Challenged each night merely to fill 15 minutes, many stations did carry forecasts and scores. Yet only at independent stations were weather and sports integrated into a single newscast. In the beginning, weather and sports were separate programs, each with their own theme music and credits and always their own sponsors. Across the country, the viewers' 15 minutes of local news frequently consisted of five minutes of news, followed by five-minute weather and sports telecasts.

The networks, though, had not decided everything. Indeed, two local concepts had risen as the hallmarks of TV news in the so-called Golden Age.

The first was a grabbag of ideas aimed at getting people to watch those weather programs. In most cities, 1950s weather reports were known less for their forecasts and more for the gimmicks local stations had devised. At WSM in Nashville, for example, poet weathercaster Bill Williams delivered his forecasts in verse. "Rain today and tonight. Tomorrow still more rain in sight," he would report.[43] New York's WNBC also had poetry, only that station's weather program featured two local celebrities, an actual weathercaster dressed like an artist, in a smock, named Tex Antoine, and Antoine's artistic creation, a puppet named Uncle Wethbee.[44] At WITI in Milwaukee another weatherpuppet actually delivered the forecast. Albert the Alleycat was so popular that it later was rated as a top Milwaukee news personality.

Back in New York, yet another concept had been unveiled in the attempts of WCBS and WABC to compete against WNBC's Antoine and Uncle Wethbee. Both stations hired females. Carol Reed started at WCBS, followed by Janet Tyler at WABC. After Tyler departed, WABC divided the assignment between a former Miss Chicago named Penny Wright and a former Miss Florida named Jan Crockett, who played a ukelele. Station manager Joseph Stamler revealed WABC's strategy: "We feel that women—or ladies—have greater acceptance than men, because, well, with the contribution of an attractive-looking personality the men prefer to look at and the women are attracted to because of the fashions they wear, we've really got a two-fold program."[45] By the mid-1950s female actresses, models and beauty pageant winners were working weather maps at local stations all over the country, including Washington's WTTG, which hired singer-dancer Cindy Dahl, and Miami's WITV, where Maxine Barrat appeared each night in a bathing suit.[46]

More conspicuous than even this development was local TV's other Golden Age innovation, the routine use of main newscasters in advertising. NBC News undoubtedly helped legitimize this practice by heavily identifying Swayze with Camel cigarettes. Yet long after the "Camel News Caravan" disappeared in 1956, the newscaster-as-merchandiser flourished at the local level. Thirty-second commercials had not yet been invented. Sponsors purchased entire programs on a sustaining basis and, no differently than the stars of entertainment programs, newscasters had to perform their commercials.

Viewers in Providence grew accustomed to seeing WJAR's Russ VanArsdale finish his newscast by hoisting a glass of Knickerbocker Beer.[47] In Philadelphia, WCAU newscaster John Facenda did the same for Eslinger Beer, while WCAU sportscaster Jack Whitaker gained acclaim for pouring a local brand of wine into a glass that rested on a white mink stole.[48] Others sat on sofas and chairs for local furniture stores and delivered monologues lauding local utility companies.[49] At WTVJ, Renick's benefactor was the local Frigidaire distributor. The most memorable of Renick's hundreds of appliance commercials occurred when a WTVJ employee placed some used diapers in a refrigerator a surprised Renick opened while on the air.[50] The sustaining news sponsor of Cleveland's WEWS was a munitions contractor called the Cleveland Tank Plant, so toy tanks were placed on the news set.[51]

Because of this practice, a dilemma that became common in local news had occurred at another Cleveland station. At WJW sportscaster John Fitzgerald feared for his credibility when after years of touting the Carling Brewing Company the station found a new sponsor—another brewery. "You can't just go on one night and say you like one brand of beer, and then go on the next night and say you like someone else," Fitzgerald complained.[52] Fitzgerald survived but wished he had had the problem of WBBM newscaster Fahey Flynn, who was so popular in Chicago that his many sustaining sponsors had to be juggled. Flynn was the spokesperson for Standard Oil, Illinois Bell, the Santa Fe Railroad, and Illinois Blue Cross.

Not all of these sponsorships were arranged locally. Years before news consultants appeared, far-flung local newscasts had been networked by huge corporations, most notably the Standard Oil Company of New Jersey, later known as Exxon, which sustained newscasts called "Esso Reporter" at 100 local stations in the East and Midwest. These Esso newscasts featured the Standard Oil theme music, company logos on the jackets of the newscasters, and a special "Esso Reporter" studio sign devised by the company's ad agency. Cronkite had been an "Esso Reporter" on Washington's WTOP. Esso's success inspired two of its biggest competitors. Standard Oil of Ohio's "Sohio Reporter" became an institution in the upper Midwest.

Then came Atlantic Richfield, later known as ARCO, which sustained weather programs at 40 local stations, mostly in the East. Newly christened "Atlantic Weathermen" delivered forecasts dressed as service station attendants. It was not until 1964 that the last of these "Atlantic Weathermen," Miami's John Lascelles, faded away.[53] While the service station garb seemingly made the work demeaning, TV forecasters jumped at the chance to be an "Atlantic Weatherman." They earned top dollar and looked forward to expense-paid trips to the Bahamas for conclaves on weathercasting and gasoline products.[54]

Of all these national sponsorships, the most ubiquitous was that of the Continental Baking Company. For a short time, viewers in about two dozen cities saw a newscast called the "Hostess Cinnamon Dainty Report."[55]

Videotape was a four-year-old toy when the 1950s ended and not available for archiving newscasts. Only a handful of local stations filmed their newscasts with kinescope reproduction, and fewer still preserved them. One of probably a half-dozen local stations that did save their first newscasts was KGW, the NBC affiliate in Portland, Oregon. A 1959 edition of KGW's 11 o'clock news called "Nightbeat" was a glimpse of what viewers encountered when they tuned to 1950s local news.

This program, all in black and white, opened with a 30-second opening film montage of native Americans in costume at a nearby Indian reservation. In fuzzy white letters the word "Nightbeat" was superimposed over the film, while music resembling "Pomp and Circumstance" was heard. Next, viewers saw newscaster Ivan Smith standing at a podium. The news consisted of this dashing, resonant, and serious-looking Smith reading out loud a succession of dispatches, with an occasional film. After seven minutes, he concluded. Commercials followed and then a sports program began. Viewers saw sportscaster Doug La Mear read sports stories much as Smith had read the news, although sitting at a desk somewhere else in the studio. After La Mear handled commercials for a local tire company, viewers saw between a national-regional map and a giant logo for a household finance company weathercaster Jack Capell, and, then, Capell's weather program. Prominent on the national map was a picture of a covered wagon, which Capell was using to track the progress of a wagon train expedition to Oregon, then marking its centennial. "Nightbeat" ended with the same film and music seen at the beginning, only this time superimposed with credits listing all the news services KGW had used. After the music rose to a swell, an announcer chimed in and urged the audience to stay tuned for Jack Paar.[56]

Thirty-six years later in 1995, the first employees of KGW gathered for a reunion. Such events were to become a ritual in the 1990s as the startup stations of the 1940s and 1950s marked 40- and 50-year anniversaries. The same year KGW held its affair, veterans of Philadelphia's KYW renewed acquaintances. Another station of consequence, New York's WABC, also staged a reunion.

While nostalgia was the order, these events were rife with riveting reflections on the evolution of television news. For example, at the KGW reunion, the 1959 "Nightbeat" triumvirate of Smith, La Mear, and Capell were the celebrants. Yet another person who was not invited to the gathering was acknowledged again and again. He was Frank N. Magid. Following its dominance in Portland through the 1950s and 1960s, KGW's fortunes would slip in the 1970s, at a time when a No. 1 rating stopped being a public vote of confidence and became instead a managerial expectation, or so it had seemed. Magid, a news consultant from "somewhere in Iowa," was brought in and according to Capell, "everything changed."[57] There were ratings pressures, new personnel and constraints on the way the veterans had done their jobs. Thinking about this gave the past a glow. As primitive as their early efforts were, and notwithstanding weathergirls and sustaining sponsorships, pioneers in reunion had not just fond assessments of the 1950s. To many these had been the best years local TV news had ever seen.

Among them was Richard Ross, KGW's eventual news director, who through most of the 1950s anchored news on KGW's sister station, KING in Seattle. If anything had energized Ross and told him television was "the place to be," it had been the public's unabashed reaction to the new medium, seemingly a miracle. "You wouldn't have believed it," Ross related. "People would not just come up to me and shake hands. I could walk down any street in Seattle, and they'd holler at me from a block away." Ross remembered not just an adulation and appreciation for local TV newscasters. "I'd get mail," he said, "from people who told their children not to undress in front of the TV set because they thought I could see them. It was amazing. Being in television in that era was the most unforgettable experience of my life."

This sensation was not confined to Ross. To have a job in local TV news was to Oklahoma City newscaster Ernie Schultz "a dream come true." When Schultz was told "You're hired," he "couldn't believe it was happening," and he felt "everyone who worked in TV news felt that way."

Indeed, Boston newscaster Jack Chase couldn't wait to leave for work each day. "To me," said Chase, "it was always fun and exciting, and I enjoyed every minute of it." One of the most overwhelmed was another Boston newscaster, Jim Jensen. "I thought if I made a hundred-and-a-half a week . . . I'd have a great life," Jensen would exclaim. "Life was terrific. I thought if I'd ever made a nickel more than that, I'd be happy for the rest of my life."

Yet as Dallas newscaster Eddie Barker pointed out, "We were not stars—that was the thing about the 1950s. . . . We were journalists who happened to be on television. . . . Management left us alone to do our jobs." Cincinnati newscaster Al Schottelkotte recalled the same. "I had ideas on what was effective and a free reign in implementing them. Management backed what I'd do every single time."

Surrounding all this enthusiasm was a feeling that the best was yet to come. "News departments were just beginning to expand," noted Cleveland newscaster Bill Beutel, "and everyone was talking about technology, electronic cameras, satellites, you name it. You couldn't help but think TV news was just going to get better and better."

Indelible to New Orleans newscaster John Corporon had been a conversation he had had in the mid-1950s, "when someone told me there's something new coming on called 'videotape' that does for video what audiotape does for the voice. I said, 'This can't be.' . . . The reason it was especially a lot of fun was that no one had been down that road before."

Beutel and Corporon would both wind up in New York: Corporon, a later news director of television's first local news operation, the one at WPIX; Beutel, for 16 years to sit on a news set alongside Roger Grimsby, the two of them playing a formative role in local TV news analogous to Walter Cronkite's in network news. Grimsby, a Milwaukee and St. Louis newscaster in the 1950s, had a more cutting perspective on the local news of that decade, as well as many other things. "Yes, being a news director meant something then," Grimsby observed, "but you could do what you wanted because the public didn't care about local news. They wanted entertainment. . . . I don't think we were as big as a lot of us liked to remember. In fact, we were a lot like the people [artist Andy] Warhol talked about: famous for 15 minutes."[58]

The last thing Grimsby and most others expected as the 1950s ended became a reality practically the moment the 1960s began. It was the first glimmer that fame in local TV news might be tremendous, that it might outstrip Warhol's span of time.

2

Big News,
New Rules
(1960–1962)

The first watershed in TV newscasting occurred the night of October 2, 1961, when a Los Angeles station called KNXT crashed the 15-minute time barrier and offered viewers a continuous hour of news. What KNXT had named "The Big News" had a big legacy. Its personification and a fixture in Los Angeles TV news for the next 35 years, a stentorian-voiced local anchor named Jerry Dunphy, was so much of a paragon in the entertainment capital that he became the real-life model for the Ted Baxter character on the hit "Mary Tyler Moore Show" comedy series. Anyone in America who could identify Baxter also could identify Dunphy.

However, the plot behind the real "Big News" was vastly more compelling that anything fiction writers could devise. Hardly a comedy, Dunphy's hour-long newscast altered the thinking on TV news. Opening the confines of the newscast while never losing sight of what would be popular, KNXT finally demonstrated that news and entertainment could co-exist. For the first time in television, a TV newscast would turn a significant profit. Long-form news was a local creation. Two more years would elapse before the New York networks unveiled their version; half-hour newscasts started in September 1963 on NBC and CBS. By the standards of local TV news, these network half-hours were already a blip.

The story of "The Big News" in far-off and forgotten Los Angeles would drip with implications, including more people's news techniques and local TV's first serious reaction to New York's indifference. Yet at the exact moment "The Big News" was being conceived, a different event in Washington, D.C., had pointed the field even further ahead. The Federal Communications Commission had just saddled KNXT and all other local stations with a new policy called community ascertainment. Ascertainment was the legal term for audience research, a new, strange, and expensive practice. Maddened by weathergirls, sustaining sponsorships and almost everything else on TV, the FCC's solution was giving the public a voice. In Washington, lawyers, leaders and FCC commissioners naturally assumed that once the public could speak, it would holler "Get this trash off the air." This policy decision not only was important to local broadcasters; it was unveiled in the 1961 speech that saw FCC chair Newton Minow reduce television to a "vast wasteland."

Media experts were so spellbound by the "wasteland" phrase that they lost track of what Minow's speech had been about. Its subject was community ascertainment. By forcing broadcasters to seek public input, the FCC empowered the masses. When the research began, people "out there" would give the experts a surprise. They liked TV just as it was. If television was a wasteland, it was not a wasteland to them.

In addition, the FCC's research requirement was about to give birth to news consultants, who, in turn, under an official government mandate, would soon bear the people's demand for people's news. Ironically, what experts eventually would assail as more "wasteland," news consulting, had been put in motion by Minow's speech.

In 1961, the year John Kennedy became president, Alan Shepard rode into space and the Berlin Wall went up, another event had great significance in shaping the outlook and destiny of the nation. It was the migration of Americans to Southern California. Each day in the 1960s, 1,000 new people headed west and settled in the Los Angeles Basin, a population shift that left California with the world's seventh-largest economy and more votes in the Electoral College than the combination of 15 other states. In impact not even the Gold Rush a century earlier came close. Yet Americans living in the 1960s never would have known by watching the "CBS Evening News." The networks had invested in overseas bureaus and had arrayed their main correspondents in New York and Washington, D.C. When California made the network news, the occasion usually was an offbeat feature about counter-culture artisans or chimps at the San Diego Zoo.

Reminded of this again and again was a California immigrant named Robert Wood, the general manager of KNXT, a TV station owned by CBS. Officially, Wood was part of the CBS hierarchy, but in distant Los Angeles, he and his assistants felt at the end of the earth. Almost nothing about Los Angeles ever appeared on the network news. "We felt second class in the attitude they had that we were kooks and nuts out in a place where news didn't happen," related Robert Nelson, one of Wood's lieutenants. "Bob [Wood] saw an opportunity because the networks didn't care . . . [and] because Los Angeles had a need."[1]

All along, Wood had sensed that the indifference of New York might work to his advantage. His vision, a full hour of local news at 6 p.m., was not even open for discussion at KNXT's more-prized sister stations, WCBS in New York, WBBM in Chicago and WCAU in Philadelphia, for this would upstage the network news broadcasts. "But out here on the Coast," recalled Ray Beindorf, KNXT's sales manager and second-in-command, "we weren't given much credit, so anything we did in news didn't matter to them. As long as it made money, New York didn't care."[2]

Symbolically, Wood's first supporters were not in New York and, indeed, were part of rival NBC. In late 1960, Wood traveled north to Sacramento upon learning that two brothers named Robert and Jon Kelly, the owners of NBC affiliate KCRA, were about to unveil a 45-minute evening newscast. This broadcast, which would debut in Sacramento on February 20, 1961, as "Channel 3 Reports," was TV's first long-form newscast, although not the trend-setter "The Big News" would become.[3] Wood was awe-struck that a station in the thirty-fourth market could pull off this feat, and he noticed in Sacramento how much "Channel 3 Reports" dwarfed NBC's network news. Although "Bob went on to great success at the network level," eventually as CBS president, "he was one of us," Robert Kelly recalled. He encouraged local stations "to be captain of [their] own ship, not the dinghy trailing along behind." Realizing he could be reprimanded for fraternizing with NBC, Wood nevertheless visited the Kellys and KCRA several more times. During one trip to Sacramento in early 1961, he had told CBS headquarters in New York that he was taking a "vacation."[4]

Back in Los Angeles, many factors had pointed to the viability of an hour-long newscast. Discussions repeatedly revolved around the recent move of the Brooklyn Dodgers to Los Angeles and how the Dodgers and the forthcoming opening of Dodger Stadium were captivating Southern Californians. In addition to the Dodgers, Los Angeles was bursting with other types of local news. Freeways were snaking miles and miles into distant suburbs; houses could not be built fast enough, and every resident was affected by an air pollution problem of unprecedented magnitude.

Yet KNXT had no intention of limiting "The Big News" to local news. To the contrary, it was the first strike against the convention that only the networks could report national and international material. Key to "The Big News" was the three-hour time difference between New York and Los Angeles. In sales brochures, KNXT actually would banner the fact that its own network news, recorded for later playback, was out of date.[5] It also would emphasize that all CBS News material could be edited right there in Los Angeles for a more timely and localized perspective. No factor was more vital in the planning than the public's demonstrated appetite for local coverage. This was the city that had ground to a standstill during the Kathy Fiscus episode in 1949, and the late Klaus Landsberg had left a legacy of live coverage spectaculars.

Ultimately, "The Big News" hinged on a single question, whether to add news in KNXT's 6 p.m. time period or continue with a Monday-through-Saturday strip of assorted syndicated programs produced by a company called ZIV that included "Sea Hunt," "Lockup," and "Dangerous Robin."[6] While this "Six Pack" had marginal audiences of 10 to 15 percent, it cost little and thus made money. Because news expansion would cost hundreds of thousands of dollars, big numbers would be needed for the same. To Wood "it was all a matter of dollars and cents," related Beindorf. "He was battling the perception that news was a great loser. Bob was committed to making it work, but from where he stood he was out on a limb."[7] Wood was convinced local news, not network programs, determined a viewer's impression of a TV station. It followed that KNXT could gain an advantage with a powerful local newscast. However, Wood's tribulation was the certainty that CBS corporate management would demand instant results. If KNXT bought new equipment and hired a new news staff and then had to put "Sea Hunt" back on the air, the sell-off of the equipment and the layoff of the news staff would leave Wood out on the street with them.

Imperative to Wood had been Beindorf's okay. Beindorf and his sales staff would have to find sponsors.

Still, the heavyweight in the deliberations was Sam Zelman, a longtime newspaper reporter who had joined CBS News in New York. Zelman was the only person at CBS News Wood could sway. "Bob Wood approached me in New York and said 'How would you like an hour for news?' I said, 'That would be great.'" Zelman felt that pioneering a long-form news program in Los Angeles or Atlanta, where he ended up, was more meaningful than continuing to fill a blip newscast in New York. Eighteen years later Zelman would be hired by Ted Turner as second-in-command to Reese Schoenfeld at Turner's Cable News Network, the first 24-hour TV news service. After Zelman arrived in Los Angeles and became KNXT news director in April 1961, Wood announced that KNXT not only would push ahead with "The Big News" but would time the startup with the new TV season that fall. The onus then passed to Zelman. "Some of us, including me perhaps, had flashes of there not being an audience, that an hour would be too much," Zelman recounted. "[We] wondered where all the news would come from."8

The audience did tune in, and enough news was found. Yet long before the first program, it became apparent that "The Big News" was not destined to be the hour-long "newspaper of the air" that Zelman had foreseen. Just 16 months after the premier, in February 1963, Zelman would resign. What had troubled Zelman, a newspaper man, were the rudiments of people's news. He did not appreciate the incessant sales and promotional activities that accompanied "The Big News." Yet worse was sentiment that each "Big News" had to be an event—not a record of information but a "show." A thorn was newscaster Jerry Dunphy, who, whether Zelman liked it or not, was going to be the star of this show.

Unlike Ted Baxter, Dunphy did have credentials as a newsperson. Still, he had risen as a talent and was hired by KNXT to topple the popular George Putnam, the star anchor on KTTV. At age 37, Dunphy was young for this role. Starting in Peoria, Dunphy's rich voice and dashing appearance—tinges of silver hair complementing an otherwise youthful look—had caught the attention of many. He was named main newscaster at WXIX in Milwaukee in 1955 and by 1958 had joined Chicago's WBBM as a backup to a dominating local anchor known for his bow-ties named Fahey Flynn. In 1960, Dunphy had wrestled with two offers. He could go to New York and become the new host of NBC's "Today Show" or to Los Angeles to anchor at KNXT. Dunphy opted for local TV because it paid more: $65,000 in his first year. This was an amount that in 1961 equaled the cost of the most expensive Rolls Royce, a vehicle Dunphy later would own. To compete with KTTV's Putnam and his $350,000 salary, KNXT had to open its purse. Still Dunphy's paycheck bothered Zelman, the head of the news department, who was paid one-third as much.

The showy nature of "The Big News" would reveal itself in other ways. Zelman had taken a forward step by designating a second tier of newscasters and assigning them specializations like the "beats" of newspapers reporters. This group was to blossom into one of the most imposing reporting teams in the history of local television; and the first of these personalities had, like Dunphy, been screened in a talent search. In 1961, television was still many years away from permitting anyone but handsome and charismatic anchors to report events on camera.

One of these individuals, who had been making news rather than covering it, would compensate for his lack of journalistic experience by defining a key provision in people's news. He was Ralph Story, nationally known as the former host of CBS's ill-fated "$64,000 Challenge," a program found to be rigged during the quiz show scandals two years before. Making a comeback in local TV news, his assignment for KNXT was a feature called "The Human Predicament." Realizing Story would be laughed off if given the police beat or city hall, KNXT told him not to worry about the "blotter" and instead to make news out of everyday events directly affecting average people: senior citizens returning to school, commuting problems on freeways, and the fuss over keeping up with fashion trends.[9] "The Human Predicament" became the single most popular feature on "The Big News." Although its concept of looking at news from a people's perspective eventually would sweep into every local newsroom, Story's segment was radical at the time.

Plans finally gelled in a warmup broadcast on August 1, 1961, not as a real newscast but as a special closed-circuit presentation for prospective advertisers. "During the next few minutes I'm going to tell you about one of the most exciting news program developments to hit the Los Angeles television scene in many years. Starting on October 2nd, KNXT will present a full hour of news . . . ," Dunphy began. Why did Los Angeles need this news? "First, the public's thirst for news has never been greater. The true story of the world today with a gun at its head vitally concerns every viewer." Second, because of "jet transports and high-speed film processing . . . television can do this more effectively now than ever before."

As the production continued, Dunphy walked to a chart that outlined the format Zelman had finalized. Sportscaster Gil Stratton and weathercaster Bill Keene appeared within the single KNXT newscast, not in separate programs as in the past. Story's "Human Predicament" was also extolled. Then, listed as nothing more than another team member was Douglas Edwards, his 15-minute network newscast from New York just a followup segment. "Already, the publicity is starting to roll. Soon, all of Southern California will know of 'The Big

News'—and they'll be waiting for it—the first daily full hour news program," Dunphy concluded.[10]

The first actual edition of "The Big News" on October 2 began with more fanfare—newspaper ads, billboards, and previews all day on sister radio station KNX.[11] That October, and every night for the next 13 years, Los Angeles viewers saw a 30-second animated intro-duction that showed in the backdrop of outer space the planet Earth. As the Earth enlarged and the perspective homed in on Los Angeles, an announcer said, "From man's new frontier, the limitless reaches of space. From the world we live in. From the United States of America. From Los Angeles, comes the story of today—The Big News!" Ac-companying the opening were telemetry signals presumably from orbiting satellites. Succeeding programs would follow the format Zelman had developed. With his signature line "From the desert to the sea," Dunphy coordinated the hour-long juggernaut and thus was the first person who could truly be called a newscast "anchor." The broadcast never really escaped a thick network look. Most filmed re-ports were elongated interviews, then a staple of network film coverage. Noticeably, Dunphy rarely smiled.

Yet prospects for "The Big News" increasingly brightened. Prof-its were plowed back into the broadcast so that by the mid 1960s "The Big News" was far and away the nation's premier local news-cast. KNXT's original 10-person news department swelled to 35 people by the end of 1962, to 59 by 1966. One month after the debut in 1961, KNXT interrupted regular programming for continuous cov-erage of a tremendous fire in the posh Bel Aire district. It was the first time a network-owned local station had originated a live cover-age spectacle. In June 1962, Dunphy and a KNXT crew traveled to Europe for reports on U.S. military commitments there, another local news first. A year later, KNXT became the first station to open a bu-reaus in other cities, including one in Washington, D.C. In 1966, Dunphy became the first local newscaster to report on the fighting in Vietnam.[12] By then KNXT had assembled an all-star cast of reporters including Bill Stout, Joseph Benti, Clete Roberts, Saul Halpert, Paul Udell, and Rick Davis.

The bottom line was the bottom line. In the November 1962 rat-ings, 13 months after the first telecast, "The Big News" registered a 28 percent share of the audience throughout the hour-long time period. Competing against six other Los Angeles stations, KNXT's "28" was a very large number and more than proved the prospects of long-form news. It placed KNXT first in the ratings and enabled Beindorf to more than double the cost of a 60-second ad, from $1,300 to $2,800.[13] Because there were 18 minutes of advertising each night and 260 weekday "Big Newses" each year, KNXT was grossing three-quarters of a million dollars, far more than Dunphy's salary and all other expenses. Instantly, "The Big News" had become television's first news profit center.

More important to the future, though, was a schism between Los Angeles and New York that hardly narrowed and, in fact, had widened because of the success of "The Big News." Although CBS did open a bureau in Los Angeles and its coverage did increase, viewers there and around the country usually saw offbeat and freakish California subjects that had nothing to do with the way tens of millions on the West Coast were coping with life. To them "we were a feature factory," Beindorf would note. "You could not convince the New York group that our news meant anything."[14] Indelible to Nelson was the day in 1962 when he was told by a CBS executive, "The people of New York won't watch an hour newscast; that's something just for you 'Coasties' to do."[15] Another event that had angered those in Los Angeles was Walter Cronkite's refusal to do promotional messages for KNXT's local news, a courtesy he had extended to other CBS stations.[16]

The Coasties had tried to tell New York to pay attention, that the future of the network's own news was at stake. Later when network news began to decline, CBS News would attempt to right itself by proposing its own hour-long newscast. For an hour-long network newscast to appear, however, local stations had had to give their okay. It was apparent as early as 1965, because of "The Big News," that long-form network news was D.O.A. That year CBS president John Schneider first floated the idea before CBS local stations. Immediately, KNXT's Bob Wood said no. "We do not . . . favor, nor could we be expected to endorse, any effort on the part of CTN [CBS television network] to lengthen its own Monday through Friday news service. Such action would cause us to shorten our deeply entrenched local news or move it to an earlier time period. Neither, in our judgment, would be advantageous to KNXT."[17] The network blip would remain a blip for as long as TV endured.

New local newscasts of at least 45 minutes soon commenced on WTOP in Washington, KSD in St. Louis, and WLWT in Cincinnati. Each local news expansion would prove another nail in the coffin of extended network news.[18] Eventually, KNXT and most big-city local stations would carry as much as four hours of local news at the dinner hour.

Even so, long-form newscasts were a rarity in the early 1960s. In most places local news traditions of the 1950s had continued.

Fifteen-minute newscasts were still the norm. So was the practice of turning local TV stations into relay devices for network entertainment shows. Safe under the shield of their networks, stepping away was unthinkable to most local station owners.

The Federal Communications Commission thought otherwise. In Washington, far removed from the swirl of activity in Los Angeles, the FCC was sharpening its regulatory knife but unsure how to direct this dagger. Although under the 1934 Communications Act the commission lacked power to censor programs, sentiment was running high that something had to be done.

A fitting example of TV's alleged failure to satisfy the public interest was a loophole local broadcasters had found for skirting the FCC's news-and-public affairs requirement. Even though 10 percent of airtime had to be devoted to these topics, practically every TV station fulfilled the quota with low-effort interview shows in viewing "ghettos" when few watched. The compulsion of local stations to clear hour upon hour of seemingly insipid network entertainment programming, and profit as a result, questioned whether "local" television even existed. A study just conducted by Gary Steiner and published in *The People Look at Television* had found that only three percent of viewers knew their local TV stations as "local TV stations." Ninety-seven percent thought the networks owned all the channels.[19]

From its earliest days, the FCC had sought localism as a check against the network system.[20] Its chain broadcasting report in 1941, showing how NBC dominated hundreds of local radio affiliates, led to the 1943 breakup of the NBC Red and Blue radio networks, the latter to become ABC. The commission's 1946 *Blue Book* had been the hoped-for final word. It had affirmed that "local self-expression still remains an essential function of a station's operation . . . . [S]uch programs should not be crowded out of the best listening hours."[21] The *Blue Book*, though, was honored in the breech, with the FCC so consumed with matters relating to television, including its "freeze" on station licensing between 1948 and 1952, that enforcement was impossible.

Yet distress that had started in radio not only transferred to the new medium but grew more intense. The FCC circulated its first rules about payola when the quiz show scandals in 1959 offered a glaring example of how network programs merely switched on by hundreds of affiliates had created a pathetic public spectacle.[22] Then for the second time, the FCC brought anti-trust action against NBC, which had grabbed a Westinghouse-owned local TV station in Philadelphia, an event that later would loom large in the evolution of local TV news.[23] Prominent in every allegation had been annual FCC filings showing that recently licensed TV stations had turned profits long before their owners said they would. Broadcasters had been given latitude until the early 1960s because of the plea that most would lose money. Yet three-fourths of local stations were profitable by 1958.[24]

In July 1960, Frederick Ford had served on the commission for only two years and had been its chair for only a few months. Yet in this short span of time, Ford had rejuvenated one of the FCC's abiding debates: defining the term "public interest, convenience, and necessity," the rationale behind its licensing procedures. To renew a license, all one had to do was fill out a four-page questionnaire. If a broadcaster could document merely that the transmitter had been turned on, a case could be made that the public interest had been served. Yet characterizing television as a compendium of game shows, soap operas, and slapstick comedies, Ford fumed because his FCC had no way to disagree. Summoned to Capitol Hill, Ford complained at a Senate hearing that under the Communications Act the commission lacked authority to set program standards. "I don't see how we could possibly go out and say this program is good and that program is bad," Ford testified. "That would be a direct violation of the law."[25]

Still, it was hard to imagine that viewers in the inner cities of the East were best served by the same programs as viewers on the farms of the Midwest. If this could be proved during license renewals, Ford knew, the network-affiliate noose could be loosened. Accordingly, the main order of business at the FCC in 1960 was a new statement on programming policy, its cornerstone a new and legally sound idea for better ensuring the public's interests and needs. The FCC decided that if it could not determine interests and needs, then neither could the broadcasters. The public would have the final say. On July 29, 1960, after a 6-1 vote, the FCC approved a new policy, which read: "In the fulfillment of his obligation the broadcaster should consider the tastes, needs and desires of the public he is licensed to serve in developing his programming and should exercise conscientious efforts not only to ascertain them but also to carry them out as well as he reasonably can." News was among 14 program types explicitly under the jurisdiction of this new FCC rule.[26]

Few ears immediately perked, though, the policy having been rendered in the middle of an election campaign. Ford was an appointee of outgoing President Dwight Eisenhower, and he had signed the new policy as a lame duck FCC chair. Political protocol required that Ford defer rulemaking until after the election just three months away. John Kennedy won the election that November but did not appoint Ford's successor until just days before the inaugural in January 1961. Thus, for six months, the FCC's policy statement was in limbo. When Kennedy took office, 500 radio and television license renewals were on hold.[27]

Kennedy's choice at the FCC was Chicago lawyer and Democratic party political insider Newton Minow, barely 35 years old, whose interest in broadcast regulation stemmed from difficulties he had had in arranging "equal time" for presidential candidate Adlai Stevenson in 1956. Anxious to learn where Minow stood on pending issues, broadcasters invited the new FCC chair to speak at their major industrial conclave, the annual convention of the National Association of Broadcasters that spring in Washington. Minow accepted the broadcasters' invitation, and when the convention convened on May 9, he satisfied their curiosities with a vengeance.

Minow's speech before the NAB was made famous by his assertion that the nation's airwaves amounted to a "vast wasteland." This phrase, however, was not the only passage that had resounded in the hall that day. The thrust of Minow's speech had been the announcement of the first full-scale FCC licensing crackdown. Minow expanded on the same matters as had Ford, that "[t]oo many local stations operate with one hand on the network switch and the other on a projector loaded with old movies." Minow said this would change. "I say to you now," he proclaimed, "renewal will not be pro forma in the future. There is nothing permanent or sacred about a broadcast license." Minow concluded by informing broadcasters that new instructions on license renewals were on the way.[28]

Those who had heard the "wasteland" oration already knew what these instructions were going to be: Ford's new policy. Unfolded in a series of steps, Minow's procedure ushered in what his staff called community ascertainment. Under the plan, broadcasters were to venture into their communities and consult civic leaders as well as a cross-section of the general public. The objective was a "prudent, positive and continuing effort to discover and fulfill the tastes, needs and desires of a [licensee's] community for public service."[29] After the fact-finding, broadcasters were to respond to what they had learned and at the three-year intervals, when their licenses were due for renewal, make available to the FCC all the results. Station managers "must prove they have diligently studied their markets to find out what people ought to get from radio and TV."[30]

Broadcasters were caught off-guard by Minow's resolve. Accustomed to renewing licenses with those four-page forms, they dreaded reams of paperwork. Fifteen broadcasters immediately wrote personal letters to the FCC in protest.[31] It was mid-1961, and the policy statement had stood in abeyance now for almost a year, officially as an "interim report" with no rulemaking. There had seemed a strong possibility community ascertainment would die in bureaucratic red tape or be reconsidered. FCC commissioner Rosel Hyde had written a perceptive dissent, arguing that the unbridled popularity of television was the best evidence that public interests and needs were, in fact, served. Broadcasters could probe the public in a million ways, Hyde insisted, but the result would be the same. Finally, in 1962, federal judge David Bazelon in ruling against the owner of Suburban Broadcasting upheld the FCC's authority to join ascertainment to license renewals.[32] Community ascertainment was a fact of life for everyone who owned and operated a local television station.

Losing a license was the TV death penalty. Without licenses broadcasters had to go out of business. Thus, they viewed community ascertainment as a policy from hell. It was as if car owners had just been told they needed a college dissertation to renew a driver's license. The ascertainment documents were not to be submitted to the FCC but, instead, to be kept at the station in files that could be inspected by anybody who walked in. This made ascertainment especially frightening because groups seeking to challenge a license would have inside information. Meanwhile, the FCC, much like the IRS, planned to conduct audits. At its discretion, it would select certain stations for on-site inspections without announcing them in advance.

The broadcasters' disdain came to rest on the methods that underlie the policy. They seemed as nebulous as they were exhaustive. Nervous station owners who had started working on ascertainments in 1961, on the basis only of the interim report, had been thoroughly confused. As he'd promised, Minow did follow through with operational guidelines. Policies requiring broadcasters to interview civic leaders were clarified. However, understanding still broke down over the sketchy procedures mandating direct input from the audience. When the official FCC Rules and Regulations were revised in 1961, broadcasters read, "Each licensee or permittee of a commercially operated TV station shall place in the station's public inspection file documentation relating to its efforts to consult with a roughly random sample of members of the general public . . . ." According to the new rules, this documentation had to be a "survey," and it had to stratify the population by "age, ethnic, and geographic" criteria. Finally, the "number of people surveyed" was to be a key factor in the commission's determination of compliance.[33]

The FCC had not used the term "audience research." Yet, without a doubt, audience research was what the FCC wanted. Just glancing at the new rules, station owners easily could see that terms such as "survey," "random sample," and "stratification" related to some sort of research procedure. It was from there that questions had multiplied. Most local stations already paid heavily for formal research in reports sold to them by the ratings services. Could ratings surveys, which lacked detail, be used in community ascertainment? Most stations routinely gathered informal input, such as when people called in to comment on a show. Could these fulfill the commission's demands?

By 1961, many broadcasters knew at least one thing about professional research, that it could cost a king's ransom. Despite periodic claims by professional researchers that their data could improve ratings and profitability, broadcasters balked. Chained to their networks, they had no need for such extravagance. Still, if professional research could serve two purposes—ratings and renewals—it might be cost-effective. What the FCC expected in a community ascertainment survey was something likely to be discovered by stations in the Southeast and industrial Midwest, which were up for the next round of license renewals. With Minow's speech at the NAB convention ringing in their ears, the owners of the largest TV properties in these regions—those with the most to lose should their licenses be revoked—were in a mood to take no chances.

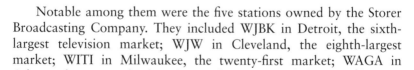

Notable among them were the five stations owned by the Storer Broadcasting Company. They included WJBK in Detroit, the sixth-largest television market; WJW in Cleveland, the eighth-largest market; WITI in Milwaukee, the twenty-first market; WAGA in Atlanta, the twenty-third market; and WSPD in Toledo, in market No. 50. These Storer television stations had licenses due to expire in 1963.

If KNXT had "The Big News," stations in the Storer group exemplified the little news. They were classic examples of network affiliates that confined news to 15 minutes, kept investments to a minimum and skimmed a news audience from adjoining entertainment programs. WJBK had a three-person news department. WJW had four.

Milwaukee's WITI and Atlanta's WAGA were the largest stations in the country without network newscasts. They refused to clear them. The "CBS Evening News" would not be seen in Atlanta until 1966. "At WAGA," general manager Ken Bagwell explained, "we carried reruns of 'Amos and Andy' until the sprocket holes wore out."[34]

The moment Minow announced his license crackdown, the Storer group accepted audits as a fait accompli. It began plotting a strategy in late 1961, two years before what seemed a certain day of reckoning. A shortage of local news, while enough trouble for most local stations, was a relatively minor worry at Storer, a company operating under a cloud.

Although Storer was not sanctioned, its management had just been implicated in the biggest influence-peddling scandal in FCC history. For several days in March 1960, the nation's capital had buzzed over rumors that Storer had given free rides on a company airplane and a vacation on a company yacht to then-FCC chair John Doerfer. Acting quickly to head off a certain Congressional investigation, Eisenhower fired Doerfer. Ironically for Storer, it had been Doerfer's dismissal that had allowed Frederick Ford to take the reigns at the commission and then propose community ascertainment.[35]

Potentially of greater interest to the FCC were the maneuvers that had enabled Storer to purchase the profit-laden Milwaukee station back in 1958. It had done this from proceeds gained from its sale of KPTV in Portland, Oregon, the nation's first UHF station and a spearhead of the FCC's then-sputtering vision for expanded UHF broadcasting. Storer had supported KPTV for only four years. Immediately after Storer sold it, KPTV merged with a VHF station in Portland, and the first UHF channel went dark. This had been a major FCC setback. Storer was immersed in allegations it was trafficking in local stations.[36]

It didn't help that Storer was one of broadcasting's big fish. In 1961, Storer was the nation's sixth-largest broadcast company and exceeded in size only by the three networks, ABC, CBS, and NBC; Westinghouse; and a group then called Metropolitan Broadcasting, later Metromedia. Founded in Toledo in 1927 by George B. Storer, Sr., the company had started as a small yet active and profitable radio group. In the 1930s, it had attempted a radio network to compete with CBS and NBC. While this venture failed, Storer moved fast when television arrived in the 1940s and obtained three of the coveted 108 TV licenses granted by the FCC before its freeze in 1948. These stations were WJBK, WAGA, and WSPD; WJW, purchased in 1954, also was a pre-freeze station. The Detroit, Cleveland, and Atlanta stations were affiliates of the dominant CBS network. Mainly because it owned CBS affiliates in two of the 10 largest markets, Storer was flush with income. Its annual revenues in 1961 of $37 million were the largest of any non-network broadcast group. Not only this, but on the eve of its license renewals Storer posted first-quarter 1962 revenues double those of a year before, remarkable because CBS entertainment programs had just taken a dip in the ratings.[37]

Money continued to accumulate, and because of the FCC, Storer would have a hard time spending it. It had long ago reached the five-station maximum. Through the mid-1960s, Storer again and again would test this limit so it could buy more TV stations.[38] Storer's hopes would be realized many years later when the FCC did relax the rules. In the 1990s these Storer stations would form the core of a company owned by Rupert Murdoch called New World Broadcasting, TV's first super-group and part of Murdoch's Fox TV conglomerate.

In the 1960s, Storer did claim additional UHF licenses in Boston and San Diego, but because the FCC stood firm and said "no more," Storer's wealth started to go elsewhere. One of the major developments on Wall Street in 1965 was Storer's purchase of Northeast Airlines from billionaire Howard Hughes.[39] Storer then assumed a controlling interest in the Boston Gardens sports arena. Not long after this, Storer would acquire its first local cable television franchises, eventually to become the nation's third-largest multi-system operator.[40] This buying spree was made possible by the profits generated from its original TV stations. Thus, much had been riding on Storer's first post-Minow license renewals.

As in all big groups, major decisions at Storer were not left to local station managers but made at the corporate level. By late 1961, the topic of community ascertainment had reached Storer's highest corporate tier, in discussions between company chair George Storer, Jr., general counsel Warren Zwicky, and TV vice president Bill Michaels. These men communicated at a distance. Storer worked at corporate headquarters in Miami; Zwicky, usually in Washington. Michaels ran the television division from an office in the Detroit suburb of Birmingham, close to WJBK, Storer's largest station.

Storer's plan was simple: it would not fight the FCC but cooperate to the nth degree. "If Minow says 'jump,'" Zwicky said, "we are going to answer, 'How high?'"[41] Storer asked Michaels to find out how much detail would be needed in the public survey. Michaels estimated that "[i]n each of the five markets we want questions devised in such as fashion that the stations ascertain a minimum of five general subjects." This would exceed the requirements of the FCC, which had indicated that only two subjects, "needs and interests," be assessed.[42] Zwicky, the lawyer, agreed, insisting the process had to be "serious, complete, and credible."[43]

These executives had been undaunted by Phase One, the interviews with civic leaders, because the station managers would personally conduct them. Michaels knew the managers would protest, but he accepted no arguments. The FCC had stated only that "50 per cent of all interviews must be conducted by management level employees."[44] Having all interviews so conducted would show the FCC "superior compliance."[45] Whether this could be shown in the second phase, the public survey, was a question not so expeditiously resolved.

Indeed, not long after the initial exchanges between Storer, Michaels and Zwicky, the public survey had become an albatross. Earl Kahn, the researcher assigned to McHugh & Hoffman who ultimately supervised the surveys, recalled "numerous questions" he had directed at Zwicky and others, only to receive educated guesses. Because of such quandaries, the FCC soon would provide more precise direction.

Yet as of 1962, the FCC had not specified whether the survey interviews had to be face-to-face or if telephone contacts could be used. Worse yet, the FCC had only broadly hinted at the total number of people needed. As a rule, many assumed 100 interviews was about right. However, language mandating "demographic stratifications," which meant the total group had to be divided and divided again, strongly suggested samples of 200, 300, or larger. There were loose guidelines over whether survey items could solicit yes-no or multiple choice responses or instead needed open-ended commentary. That the FCC had referred to "conscientiously consulting the public" slanted toward the latter and added to the anguish. Open-ended interviews were the most time-consuming. Most troubling was one provision the FCC had specified, that the survey must be original and defrayed by the applicant. This meant a TV station could not send someone to the library to look up second-hand digests of public opinion polls. According to Kahn, "The Storer people had an image of their employees dropping what they were doing and taking to the streets to work on a research project."[46] As disruptive and crude as an employee-conducted survey promised to be, many station owners did opt for this to get past their first ascertainments.

The five Storer stations were not to be among them. By late 1961, the Storer executives had decided to hire a professional research organization. All along it had seemed that a professional survey was what the FCC really favored. Within a few years the FCC would make this official. Because they usually were more rigorous, surveys conducted by professional research firms would be upheld in FCC policy-making. Nevertheless, Storer's decision had not been easy because of what seemed inordinate costs. The fee for just one professional survey, with enough interviews to satisfy demographic stratifications, was around $5,000. For the same amount, a TV station could replace a new studio camera, pay a month of utility bills, or defray numerous other costs. The Storer executives had to multiply the $5,000 figure by five to account for all the TV stations in the group. Yet given the tens of millions of dollars at risk in a license revocation, a $25,000 expense was a pittance. Also comforting was knowing that a professional survey would wow an FCC auditor.

All that was left was selecting the research firm. Those known to Michaels were market research operations with little broadcast experience. They included two local Detroit firms, Market Opinion Research and Milton Brand and Company. Additional possibilities were Opinion Research of Princeton, New Jersey; the Merwyn Field group of Los Angeles and Burke Marketing Research of Cincinnati.[47] Michaels also knew of another candidate, Frank N. Magid Associates located in Cedar Rapids, Iowa.

However, Michaels saw a drawback in hiring any of these companies. While they all had impressive credentials in field research, each was strictly a research supplier with a forte in gathering data. Because ascertainment reports had to have narrative statements, Michaels was hoping for a company that could help with the analysis and the writing. If Storer was going to spend $25,000, Michaels reasoned, then let the contractor do as much of the work as possible.[48] In early 1962, with resources to go anywhere in the country, Michaels' search ended almost around the block from his suburban Detroit office.

That March, Michaels was paid a visit by two individuals who had just resigned from top positions at the Detroit-based Campbell-Ewald advertising agency. Philip L. McHugh had been the vice president of the agency's television division, and Peter S. Hoffman had been that division's second-in-command. Their mysterious departure from Campbell-Ewald had just made headlines in trade publications from coast to coast. Campbell-Ewald was no ordinary ad agency but rather on the strength of a single local client was one of the world's five largest. That client was General Motors, the world's largest corporation and second-largest advertiser. General Motors was spending millions not merely to advertise on national television. Well into the 1960s, sponsors such as GM controlled entire television programs and hired agencies like Campbell-Ewald to produce and direct them. The two men greeting Michaels had been among the most influential in TV. The hottest show then on the networks, NBC's "Bonanza," had been the brain-child of these two executives.

In the meeting, an interested Michaels finally found out what had happened. Campbell-Ewald's owners had scolded McHugh for spending lavishly on audience research and then had reacted passively, McHugh violently, when on the basis of this research McHugh had said that entertainer Dinah Shore needed to be taken off the air.[49] While this was the kind of inside intrigue most broadcasters lived for, McHugh and Hoffman were not in Michaels' office to recite war stories.

They wanted his business. In a small office in Birmingham not far from Storer's television headquarters, the former Campbell-Ewald executives had established what they were calling a "consulting" firm. As the first broadcast consultant, the firm McHugh & Hoffman would operate just like consultancies in big business: it would conduct public research studies, analyze findings and prepare narrated written recommendations.[50] A decisive advantage of McHugh & Hoffman was its exclusive contract with the world's largest applied research firm, Chicago-based Social Research, Inc. Headed by two well-known academic researchers, W. Lloyd Warner and Burleigh B. Gardner, SRI had become a behind-the-scenes fixture in the operations of numerous blue chip corporations.

McHugh and Hoffman had walked out at Campbell-Ewald somehow assured that, backed by SRI, they would land a contract with CBS, where McHugh had worked under Frank Stanton in the 1930s and 1940s, or with the media department at the Chrysler Corporation, where Hoffman had connections. To the partners' dismay, these opportunities were not materializing. Initially, they thought of Storer as a step down, only later to realize Storer's corporate muscle. While McHugh pitched Michaels on the idea that research could help the Storer stations in the ratings, and Michaels fully intended to get around to this in due course, the Storer vice president was interested for one reason: as so-called "consultants," McHugh and Hoffman were the perfect people to sic on community ascertainment.[51] McHugh was up to the task, later confirming to Michaels that "[our] yearly market studies are of particular value to Storer management as effectively meeting the Federal Communications Commission's requirements."[52]

With time of the essence, Michaels went ahead and signed a contract with McHugh & Hoffman. Corporate chair George Storer, Jr., contacted by telephone in Miami, gave his approval. Because of other commitments, it was not until weeks later, on May 1, 1962, that Storer was able to travel north to Detroit to put his signature on the agreement, the first contract between a local broadcaster and an outside re-search-consultant. It happened in a small ceremony in Michaels' office, with McHugh, Hoffman, Storer and WJBK manager Larry Carino on hand. The main provision was professional research surveys in Detroit, Cleveland, Milwaukee, Atlanta and Toledo at a total cost of $42,500.[53] This was almost double the $25,000, $5,000 per survey, that George Storer had anticipated, and he had momentarily backed off. However, McHugh explained that the added money would defray an extra level of consulting services he and Hoffman would provide based on the research. At that point no one suspected that this $17,500 premium would lead McHugh & Hoffman into news.[54]

By the end of 1962, McHugh & Hoffman had signed several additional stations by making the same pitch for community ascertainment. Notable among them was KNXT in Los Angeles, the bastion of "The Big News." In the meantime, trained field researchers from SRI had filtered into the five Storer cities and on schedule had placed finished surveys in each station's public inspection files. Defying Minow's "wasteland," they showed overwhelming mass audience approval for programs on TV. No broadcaster had expected otherwise, not with 15 years of Nielsen ratings also sky high. Yet Storer's first ascertainments did have a major surprise. No one from the FCC examined any of the documents. One by one the stations received postcards from the commission with notifications their licenses had been renewed.

It had occurred all over the country. License renewals still ended with a rubber stamp. Rumors spread that Minow's crackdown had been a big and expensive bluff. While this wasn't true, the commission finally conceded that only one percent of renewal applications were ever audited.[55] Minow and his successors would plead for more government money to expand the inspections. Although the audits never did expand, broadcasters' anxieties recurred at three-year intervals— as did more confusion. Consequently, the commission circulated more and more materials to clear up questions.[56] A decade after the policy took effect, the FCC would publish a 16-page ascertainment "primer," a significant development for firms like McHugh & Hoffman because this primer had actually endorsed professional research in license renewals.[57] In 1976, just eight years before ascertainment came to fruition, the commission would publish another primer.[58]

Finally, in the 1980s, a conservative trend swept the FCC. One of it first steps in deregulating TV was the dumping of community ascertainment.[59]

Yet after Ford and Minow, a research genie was out of the bottle. When it came to television and news, not the experts but the people would have the last word.

3

Class Conflict

Research. For most it conjures images of test tubes, laboratories, and scientists in white suits. Television research was not this. The science of media research was written in person-to-person encounters, in which clipboards, tape recorders, two-way mirrors and computers were tools. Discoveries consisted not of new inventions and medical cures but models that could predict the way people watched TV. Since the 1940s the Nielsen ratings had churned out data on the numbers of people who watched. In the 1960s the intriguing question had become *why* they watched. The new firm McHugh & Hoffman had a need to know.

It was promised answers by some of the most esteemed figures in academic research, among them the very people who had pioneered the social sciences. The tiny consulting operation that had joined the giant Storer Broadcasting Company had as its official partners Phil McHugh and Peter Hoffman. Yet the early identity of news consulting had been drawn around McHugh & Hoffman's two unofficial partners, William Lloyd Warner and Burleigh B. Gardner, world renowned sociologists and the directors of that corporate research colossus Social Research, Inc. McHugh & Hoffman was an extension of SRI and thus had been launched from the shoulders of giants.

Research of the sort SRI produced would be integral at every subsequent phase of television news. Its thread could be followed back in time past the origin of television to the era of Calvin Coolidge, Charles Lindbergh and Babe Ruth. It was during the 1920s that

Warner and Gardner, fresh from service in World War I, had met each other at the Harvard Business School. There they had been students of two famed Harvard professors, Elton Mayo and Fritz Roethlisberger, who in 1927 were abuzz over a study they had just published about workplace productivity.

Business schools such as the one at Harvard had been enclaves of executives, managers and corporate elite-to-be. Learning business had meant finance, boardroom protocol and cost-benefit procedures. As late as the 1920s rank-and-file workers had been regarded only as units of production and no different than machines. It was almost on a whim that the Harvard group decided to measure the effects from dimming the lights at Western Electric's Hawthorne, Illinois, assembly plant. Expecting productivity to drop off, the researchers were astonished when in the dark production actually increased. There was only one explanation: The workers knew they were being watched and wanted recognition.[1]

Rather than a bust, this famous Hawthorne Study would change the course of American scholarship. Its revelation, that the faceless masses were actually human beings with feelings and needs, heralded a new area of academic study. It would inspire a string of path-clearing worker studies by Gardner, including his 1945 *Human Relations in Industry*. For Warner, the Hawthorne Study would lead to much bigger things.

Departing for Australia in 1929, Warner had wanted to know more about aborigines sheltered from industrialization. Using a procedure called "qualitative" analysis, Warner had another "ah-ha" experience when he discovered that even the most primitive societies revolved around an elite-mass social order. Warner saw among the aborigines exactly what his teachers had witnessed at Hawthorne, a small elite class oblivious to a huge inferior class. The continuation of this research work in the United States set the stage for a seminal social scientific breakthrough.

In 1930, Warner and a team of graduate students began a study of those in Newburyport, Massachusetts, one of the nation's first communities. They remained for five years and interviewed every one of Newburyport's 17,000 residents. By this time, Warner had become a professor at the University of Chicago. From that campus in 1941, Warner published *The Social Life of the Modern Community*. It was the first volume in what scholars around the world would know as the "Yankee City" series.[2]

In it Warner became the first person to publish direct evidence of class stratification in the United States. While scholars had long acknowledged the idea of an American social class system, it was

Warner who actually demonstrated it. With exacting documentation, Warner countered one of America's most cherished notions, that it was a "land of opportunity," and he argued that only in the imagination of the nation's elite did equality exist. Warner became America's answer to Karl Marx, and like Marx, Warner had noted unequal economic opportunities. Yet Warner's achievement was in revealing that the American class system was elusive. In America it was possible to have "Beverly Hillbillies," people who had lucked into millions but rose no further than the lowest order.[3] "Great wealth did not guarantee the highest social position," Warner stated. By identifying individuals not just by their incomes but by additional factors— occupation, education, neighborhood, social interaction, church attendance and self-perception—an American class system was evident.

In diagrams the hierarchy took the shape of a diamond, actually a scatterplot of the data, which illustrated how the smallest classes were at the top and bottom, the largest classes in the middle. Because the hierarchy had existed since Newburyport's founding around the time of the Pilgrims, Warner postulated that America's class system was fixed and not likely to fundamentally change. The diamond was affirmed in followup studies in Natchez, Mississippi; Rockford and Quincy, Illinois; and Kansas City. By the end of World War II, Warner's social class diamond had become standard in social scientific literature. The diamond would be observed in what grew into hundreds of supporting works.[4]

About 3 percent of Americans belonged to an "upper" class. Below this was an "upper-middle" class of about 15 percent. The diamond then bulged noticeably to depict a "lower-middle" class, around 30 percent, and an "upper-lower" class, the largest grouping at 35 percent. The diamond then shrunk to reflect a "lower-lower" class, the remaining 13 percent.[5] "By social class is meant two or more orders of people who are . . . in socially superior and inferior positions. Members of a class tend to marry within their own order . . . [and] children are born into the same status as their parents." America, Warner said, "distributes rights and privileges, duties and obligations, unequally among its inferior and superior grades."[6]

For this, Warner rose as the preeminent social scientist of the mid-20th Century. His "Yankee City" series was praised by scholars from Princeton to the Sorbonne.[7] Backdropped by the ravages of the Great Depression, Warner's class theory spread not only to other sociologists but to political scientists, economists, progressive historians, and social critics. Important in numerous fields would be the concept of "socio-economic status" that Warner had defined.

Meanwhile, his critical appeal for "class consciousness" found many attentive ears.

Controversy abounded, too, as some labored with Warner's qualitative methodology, several with his generalizations.[8] Historian Stephen Thernstrom went back to Newburyport and in his 1965 "Yankee City Revisited" showed that Warner had distorted some of the history of that community. Yet even Thernstrom found merit in the centerpiece of Warner's works, the social class diamond and the inequality it illustrated.[9]

Warner's acclaim led to myth-making, though, namely that he was an active liberal social crusader. Few doubted that Warner was moved by the masses. He was impatient and disturbed by his peers in the upper-middle class, the nation's college professors and knowledge-shapers, who said they had read the "Yankee City" series and still expected all Americans to be like them: part of the upper-middle class. Yet Warner's roots were in the Harvard Business School. Warner had been a devout believer in capitalism and one of the first to articulate the view that a success in the marketplace was a success for society. With Gardner he started on a commercial trajectory, leading to their biggest project ever, the private research company called SRI.

The fist step came when Warner was appointed to a regents post at the University of Chicago, where he led that school's Committee on Human Relations and Industry (CHRI), set up by President Franklin Roosevelt to help plan postwar reconversion.[10] One of the first CHRI assignments was a research venture with sizable financial support from Sears. The world's largest retailer, while anticipating a boom in sales, had had a thicket of anxieties. From a study on refrigerators, Warner and Gardner garnered evidence soon to have far-reaching implications in the postwar consumer market and, then, in TV news.

Sears was troubled because of a shortage of employees in service departments. This meant customers might wait weeks when their appliances broke down. The research showed that, unlike upper status customers who were likely to complain and demand instant attention, two-thirds of customers in the two biggest classes, the lower-middle and upper-lower, were not worried. They liked Sears, often were on a first-name basis with sales clerks and knew their refrigerators would eventually get fixed. As Gardner later recalled, "The typical reaction was not a complaint against Sears, but rather an understanding of the difficulties." Sears executives couldn't believe what this research had shown. It was then that Warner told them why: the Sears executives never shopped at their own store.[11]

Reaction to the Sears study had been another illustration of upper-middle class isolation. Its larger outcome, however, was in indicating the viability of class-based research in the consumer marketplace. In the 1940s, target marketing, such as it was, was confined to gender, geography, age and race—demographic criteria. Demographics were simplistic and, in the development of many products such as lipstick and bicycles, could be intuitively assumed. Warner and Gardner proposed more powerful target marketing by augmenting demographics with class criteria.[12] For example, the research was indicating that the roughly 16 percent of lower-lower class members, whatever their gender, age, and race, lacked buying power. At the opposite extreme, the tiny number in the upper class had immense buying power, but they hardly ever made everyday buying decisions. The 15 percent in the upper-middle class met the buying-power and buying-decision criteria but were problematic because of their small numbers.

Only two of the six classes, the lower-middle and upper-lower, satisfied all criteria. Not only were their within-group characteristics extremely similar; together, the lower-middle and upper-lower classes formed a very homogeneous grouping, in effect a superclass comprising 65 percent of the population. Warner and Gardner christened this superclass the "middle majority."

Looking toward a postwar consumer boom, they were eager to get a jump on other market researchers hot on the same idea. Working out of their offices at the University of Chicago, Warner and Gardner started conducting class-based research for several companies; this went on for about six months until president Robert Hutchins told them to move off campus. Along Lakeshore Drive near Chicago's Gold Coast, they formed SRI. Not wanting to alienate his two academic all-stars, Hutchins permitted an arrangement that almost made SRI a University of Chicago branch campus. While Gardner resigned to be the full-time head of SRI, Warner officially remained at the university, a very fortuitous move. Warner would skim the creme de la creme from each University of Chicago graduating class and with salaries upwards of $50,000 place them at SRI.

A nucleus of 15 specialists and 200 assistants and part-time staff were employed by SRI when it joined with McHugh & Hoffman in 1962.[13] It was a highly select group. The 15 specialists had between them 40 advanced degrees. They had been required to take IQ tests. Their average IQ of 200 placed them in the ninety-ninth percentile.[14]

SRI's list of clients read like the Fortune 500. While Americans went about their daily activities, consumer products on which they came to depend—everything from Purina Dog Chow and Pet Milk to the Kenmore dishwasher and the Chevrolet Impala—had spun from input they had given SRI. Clients included General Motors, the Bank of America, United Airlines, General Foods, General Mills, General Electric, Pillsbury and Ralston Purina. Warner's first foray into the mass media was a soap opera study for NBC in 1948.[15] In another preview of things to come, Warner's class system was the inspiration when two of his University of Chicago associates, Donald Horton and Richard Wohl, published a 1956 study that established an effect they called "para-social interaction." It was a vicarious "bonding" effect between personalities and working class TV viewers. Years later this Horton-Wohl study would be applied by news consultants in the selection of TV news anchors.[16]

Gardner had tried to keep SRI to a low profile. Data generated in applied research comprised the trade secrets of corporations. Thus, the research process worked best when it operated in stealth. Even so, SRI was too large and partnered with too many big corporations to keep its cover for long. As would be the case when the news consultants were revealed, SRI's first public look was an unflattering exposé.

This had come in a 1957 book by Vance Packard called *The Hidden Persuaders*. It became a nationwide best-seller. Packard wrote, "The 'social scientists' who availed themselves of the new bonanza ranged . . . from 'buck happy' researchers to very serious, competent social scientists, including some of the most respected in the nation." Packard explained that the "fourth and fifth classes, the middle majority, fascinate merchandisers because they constitute, together, about 65 percent of the population [and] make up a great concentration of the nation's purchasing power." According to Packard, "Mrs. Middle Majority is simply delighted . . . ." But Packard was not. "The most serious offense many of the depth manipulators commit," he concluded, "is that they try to invade the privacy in our minds—privacy to be either rational or irrational—that I believe we must strive to protect."[17]

Yet Warner's company had a problem, and it had nothing to do with bad publicity. Despite SRI's big names, vast research capacity and 200 IQs, the TV revolution had been passing it by. The researchers realized that without an entre into the TV industry, they'd miss out on the era's most important social phenomenon. It was to resolve this dilemma that SRI's relationship with McHugh & Hoffman would take root. Phil McHugh and Peter Hoffman were two people Warner and Gardner had very much wanted to get to know.

As head of one of the largest ad agencies, McHugh had been a kingpin of television during the medium's Golden Age. His assistant at Campbell-Ewald, Hoffman, also had connections and clout. McHugh was the person who had brought Bob Hope to the TV airwaves and by the end of the 1950s had turned two obscure singers, Andy Williams and Pat Boone, into national celebrities. McHugh's other credits included "Route 66," "My Three Sons," the sensation called "Bonanza," and, fatefully, "The Dinah Shore Show." McHugh was valuable to SRI not only as a TV insider; McHugh actually savvied Mr. and Mrs. Middle Majority. McHugh would become obsessed with research, and he was convinced average people controlled TV.

The product of a broken home, McHugh had dropped out of Notre Dame University in 1938 in order to take a job in the then-small research department at CBS in New York. Making good when CBS auditioned him as a studio director, McHugh then teamed with Paul White in initiating the "CBS World News Roundup," famous for Edward Murrow's reports from war-torn London. After serving in the war himself, as a captain in the Navy, McHugh returned to CBS, only to leave in 1947 to expedite his move into television, then dominated by ad agencies. After four years at the Tracy-Locke agency in Dallas, McHugh in 1954 was named vice president of Campbell-Ewald in Detroit and put in charge of all programs sponsored by General Motors.[18]

It was at Campbell-Ewald that McHugh met Hoffman, who had earned a degree from Dartmouth after leading troops into combat during the Korean War. Rising as a lieutenant in the Army's elite Rangers corps, Hoffman recalled that "you get to know a lot about the average American when you've got an enemy shooting at you and it's up to you to see your buddy gets through."[19]

Although a familiar face in Hollywood and sometimes mentioned in the gossip columns, McHugh wasn't big on the glitter. He had a plain-spoken, combative personality that often created difficulties but nevertheless was effective in getting things done. His career had been shaped by his first job, in the CBS research department, where he had helped CBS president Frank Stanton and Columbia University professor Paul Lazarsfeld in the first studies of radio listeners. While only an assistant to Stanton and Lazarsfeld, McHugh was struck by the potential power of research and could see a day when the people's voice could make or break broadcasting's greatest stars. According to his daughter, McHugh had said as much to Bob Hope, and Hope would have reason to agree. Although one of the nation's premier celebrities, McHugh had seen research showing that Hope's NBC television show for GM was losing its appeal. Viewers had tired of seeing Hope week after week. A year later, Hope's Nielsen ratings tumbled, and McHugh took him off the air.[20]

McHugh's interest in research was cemented during his tenure at Campbell-Ewald. The agency's major client, General Motors, was thriving because of its own contract with SRI. The automobile breakthrough of the 1950s, the 1955 Chevrolet, known for its V-8 engine, had materialized after SRI had told GM of the public's interest in a high-powered car at a regular vehicle price. Through another Campbell-Ewald executive named John Bowen, who'd been involved in GM product development, McHugh met Warner for the first time. Further contact between McHugh and SRI finally led to the TV opening SRI had sought.

Partnered with Campbell-Ewald, SRI plied its research in the development of the agency's TV shows. Unknown to the public, those hit shows "Route 66," "My Three Sons," and "Bonanza," like the Chevrolet automobiles they advertised, were shaped during SRI research studies in the late 1950s.[21] Essentially, this research had shown that the novelty of television had worn off, that the middle majority no longer would watch just anything but wanted more novel fare.[22] The public got this in actor Fred MacMurray, who had been stereotyped by his "bad guy" roles in the movies. In "My Three Sons" he was seen as a kindly unmarried father who raised those three sons. The same concept, which had tested extremely well in SRI's research, inspired "Bonanza," a Western drama in which actor Lorne Greene, playing the role of Ben Cartright, raised three sons named Adam, Hoss, and Little Joe. "Bonanza" had formed around an additional SRI finding, that the middle majority wanted TV shows to look as sophisticated as motion pictures. "Bonanza" was the first television program shot on location, and because it was filmed in color, it was an impetus for the middle majority's purchase of color TVs.[23]

Although the public did embrace the new genre of filmed situation comedies and on-location drama, passage out of the Golden Age had not come easily for ad agencies like Campbell-Ewald, which still produced the programs. A television standard had been live sing-joke-and-dance variety shows. These programs not only were cheap but often were start-to-finish showcases for the products clients needed to sell. Every time an SRI study had pointed to the public's discomfort with these shows, and McHugh had delivered this news, top executives at Campbell-Ewald had resisted. Programs like "Bonanza" were enormously expensive, and out on the Ponderosa there were few opportunities for the actors to tout GM cars.

Events came to a head in that scrape over "The Dinah Shore Show." Shore had been virtually a corporate symbol of General Motors. Her jingle "See the U.S.A. in your Chevrolet" had resounded from coast to coast. Yet so many lower-middle and upper-lower research respondents had answered the "Why do you watch?" research question with "I don't know" that SRI had predicted Shore's demise. To no avail, McHugh had insisted that Shore's program be canceled and replaced by another venture like "Bonanza." At the time Shore still had high Nielsen ratings. However, the research showed that this would change the moment a competing sponsor developed a fresh alternative. The company Brylcreme finally did the trick by moving the popular drama "77 Sunset Strip" into the ABC time period opposite Shore's program on NBC. Her ratings collapsed.

By then, McHugh had bolted the agency. This had affected SRI, which had attained a major position in television through Campbell-Ewald. With McHugh gone, SRI's future in TV again was in question. Before the showdown over Dinah Shore, Warner had contacted McHugh and had encouraged him to go it alone, as an independent contractor who could help SRI secure another client in the big media. It was based on these discussions with Warner that the then-unemployed McHugh founded McHugh & Hoffman. This came on March 2, 1962, when McHugh opened a storefront office in Detroit and spent most of the day writing and distributing a press release announcing the new firm. For the first time, the release proclaimed, companies could obtain research and interpretation "from a completely unbiased point of view."[24]

The formation of McHugh & Hoffman was a closing event in the long career of Warner, who retired later in 1962. Although not officially as a director of SRI, Warner continued to advise McHugh & Hoffman until he died in 1970. The relationship that formed in March 1962 would be common among many future news consulting operations. One entity performed the research, while another entity did the consulting. SRI and McHugh & Hoffman meshed in these roles. In May 1962 McHugh & Hoffman signed that contract with Storer for the ascertainment studies. Realizing, though, that SRI wanted to remain in "big" television and not relegated to local TV, McHugh had promised that a national-level contract would ensue.

To McHugh's dismay, no takers were found. Trading on his friendship with Stanton, CBS did throw a bone, a contract with KNXT and the four other CBS TV stations, mainly for ascertainment. Yet at the network level, McHugh's overtures were denied. The networks were not licensed by the FCC and thus had no research obligation. Familiar with the networks' own internal research, the fiery McHugh would argue that it was superficial and that SRI's was better. This tactic did not win McHugh many friends.

At NBC, for example, Hugh Beville, the network's vice president for planning and research, had pegged McHugh and Hoffman as "middle men" who only added to the cost of SRI's already expensive research.[25] NBC research director Tom Coffin, meanwhile, was skeptical about the whole McHugh & Hoffman-SRI arrangement. "SRI's weakness is [that] it is long on conclusions and short on documentation," he told Beville.[26]

Mainly because of Beville's ongoing interest, McHugh & Hoffman did secure some spot consulting contracts for NBC, notably one arranged in October 1962 when Johnny Carson had debuted as host of "The Tonight Show." NBC executives had been unsure about the decision to hire Carson and had questioned whether a plain-looking Nebraskan like Carson could fill the shoes of the slick and New Yorkish Jack Paar. McHugh & Hoffman helped keep Carson on "The Tonight Show," where he would remain for 30 years. According to the research, many indeed had perceived Carson as an "amateur." However, the middle majority had warmed to Carson precisely because of the factor the NBC executives had feared: that he was from Middle America and, unlike Paar, "not a smooth-and-calculating professional."[27]

Even so, network opportunities would be rare. An impetus for the eventual people's news movement would be McHugh's personal contempt for what he felt was the arrogance of the network establishment. This feeling had gelled in 1962, when his firm had failed to win a permanent contract on network row.

Part of the problem had been a stigma about "qualitative research." Ahead was a day when millions of Americans would be chosen for focus groups, auditorium screenings and detailed surveys on the telephone. In 1962 these techniques had close to as much credibility as that year's New York Mets, a famous last-place baseball team. The television industry had been weaned on numbers, the Nielsen ratings. Yet when "why" questions were asked, numbers were not produced. Qualitative research was a gush of opinions, feelings and anecdotes, its value and high cost very unclear to broadcasters.

Nevertheless, qualitative research had a rich tradition in academia. Warner's University of Chicago had been at the very crossroads of this tradition. Qualitative inquiry had beckoned some of the world's top minds because it was a liberating procedure designed to wrest the study of human beings from the iron grip of "science." It was part of a ferment stirred by European philosophers who had urged "naturalistic" investigation. Attracted to qualitative research were scholars who detested the reduction of human experiences to numbers and who preferred a method that placed value on an individual's own expressions. In the United States qualitative inquiry had begun at scattered universities, most notably the University of Chicago. By the 1940s, when Warner published his first social class studies from there, the University of Chicago had become the center of the qualitative universe.[28] Every specialist at SRI had passed through the world-renowned "Chicago School" of qualitative analysis. Frank Magid, who had just formed a small applied research firm that eventually would compete with McHugh & Hoffman, was an expert in qualitative analysis and as a doctoral student at the University of Iowa had been trained in the "Chicago" technique.

Qualitative research actually had much in common with numerical research, including its most vital component: random sampling. Researchers never probed for class divisions. Warner had predicted that if a population was randomly sampled, the diamond distribution would automatically appear. And with 300 to 500 people in a random sample, the consultants could project their findings to thousands and even millions with 95 percent probability. Focus groups, which only had a dozen respondents, fell short of this and thus would remain peripheral to main research. The key data came in big qualitative surveys, in which researchers, like census-takers armed with special questionnaires, went into people's homes.

It was the questionnaire that made the qualitative method unique. Rather than scads of yes-no and multiple choice items, easily convertible into numbers, qualitative surveys had few questions and forced open-ended responses. Open-ended questions presupposed nothing; TV viewers could freely express their feelings.

The general technique was visible in the questionnaires McHugh & Hoffman and SRI had used in the 1962 studies for Storer. The one used in Cleveland had contained only 11 items. "Do you, personally, have any interests or needs that you would like television to give more attention to?" was the first question. After listing public affairs programs they could recall, respondents were asked to "describe some [programs] that you thought were especially good." Then, "Which that you have seen recently seemed a bit tedious or boring?" Finally, "Which local station seems particularly alert to the needs and problems of the community in which you live?"[29]

The data were voluminous and the analysis of it time-consuming. According to SRI's Earl Kahn, "as you read the verbatim responses you'd reach a point when you detected a pattern." Key words and some types of responses could be entered into computers, and this did expedite the process. Still, a single qualitative project often required weeks to complete.[30]

Years later the process would be handled extensively by computers. Advancements would enable digital transcription of voice interviews. With digitization, key patterns in volumes of open-ended data could be discerned almost instantly.

Even so, the consultants' research technique never would stray far from the original precepts of the famed Chicago School. And from it not one but two bowling balls, qualitative research and class-based interpretation, were about to roll through TV news. New to news would be the expression: "15 versus 65." "Fifteen" was the percentage of America's college-educated professional elite, Warner's upper-middle class; in it were those who aspired to be news reporters and who savored great people and big events. "Sixty-five" was the percentage of high school-educated "working class" Americans, the everyday people, who shared little with journalists and celebrated interests and needs all their own. Class conflict was inevitable. Yet no less apparent was which side would win.

Who were these people? One thing was clear: No one was talking about the poor, tired, huddled masses immortalized on the Statue of Liberty. Repeatedly, Warner would caution that because of America's bounding postwar prosperity, class divisions were obscured. Indeed, it was the unprecedented economic clout of the American working class that had made the middle majority so attractive to advertisers. Unlike the upper-middle class, with its business executives, managers, doctors, lawyers, accountants and college professors—and journalists—the middle majority took in shopkeepers, store clerks, file clerks, public school teachers, secretaries, administrative assistants, carpenters, mechanics, electricians, plumbers, toolmakers, crane operators, waiters and waitresses, railroad brakemen and switchmen, ministers, fruit packers, millwrights, molders and assembly line workers. Whether white collar office workers or blue collar factory workers, the middle majority was held to fixed hours determined by someone else. They lived for "quitting time" and the weekend. The chief symbol of their lives was the time clock.

There were countless other symbols, too: the frame house, the eight-passenger station wagon, the bowling alley, the football game. Yet in reaching understanding, more important were the parameters developed by the Warner group. To determine a person's social class,

SRI had developed an index of four leading criteria: income, education, occupation and census tract. Based on these four criteria, a demarcation line between the upper-middle class and the middle majority was readily seen.

The first parameter always would be income. In the 1962 Storer TV studies, SRI had found that from the bottom of the upper-lower class to the top of the lower-middle class, the entire middle majority, family incomes varied by only $6,000, from $4,000 to $10,000 per year. In contrast, incomes in the small upper-middle class ranged enormously, from $10,000 to $25,000.

The next component of the research was occupation. The middle majority was characterized by people whose jobs were regimented, most rank-and-file workers. The lower-middle class was comprised of hourly white collar and skilled blue collar workers. The upper-lower consisted of semi-skilled and unskilled workers who also had regimented occupations and worked by the hour. In contrast, the upper-middle class barely could be classified by occupation. Doctors had no occupational links to airplane pilots, who in turn had little in common with college professors. Members of the upper-middle class, while dedicated to their careers, were salaried and relatively free to work on their own time.[31]

Another component of the index was place-of-residence analysis, this determined by studies of census tract. Lower-middle and upper-lower individuals owned and as often as not rented smaller dwellings in more crowded neighborhoods and areas. In contrast, upper-middle class individuals generally owned newer and larger homes, often in prestige neighborhoods.

Finally came education. In both the lower-middle and upper-lower classes, formal education ranged from about 9 to 13 years; although some had trade school training, middle majority Americans had in common the fact they were high school-educated. As for post-high school education, SRI noted that 20 percent of those sampled had in fact enrolled in college but had not made it past their freshman years. More people had left college than had completed degrees. The upper-middle class had considerably more education than the middle majority. Virtually all members of the upper-middle class had baccalaureate degrees. Some had advanced degrees. A four-year college degree tended to be the calling card of the upper-middle class. Around 20 percent of Americans had degrees in 1962.

Alone, these factors had suggested conflicting perceptions of TV between the 15 and 65. As SRI's Lee Rainwater would write, "The clearest indication of social differences in attitudes toward [television] comes from the upper-middle group as it describes its increasing boredom [with TV]." At the other extreme, "upper-lower and lower-middle class families . . . value the TV set as a status symbol [and] are very dependent on it." Remarkably, more middle majority families than upper-middle class families were planning to buy the first color TVs, even though in 1962 these new sets were very expensive.

More had been learned when the researchers checked something very simple: where in the home the TV set could be found. Without exception, the lower-middle and upper-lower class installed their TV set in their living room. Those in the upper-middle class frequently placed theirs in a bedroom, a den, a children's playroom or a basement, indicating in addition to larger homes more fragmented families who did not rely on television as a center of activities. The middle majority definitely did; television was a reflection of family units more tightly knit.[32] Half of working class respondents lived within one linear mile of a parent, sibling, in-law, aunt, uncle, cousin, grandparent or grown child.[33] Family would remain a vital source of insight into the viewing behavior of average Americans.

Another was intelligence. The best-known means for determining this was the method developed in 1905 by French psychologist Alfred Binet who used comprehension, memory and reasoning tests to determine a mental age. Dividing mental age by a person's chronological age produced an "intelligence quotient," or IQ. A person of average intelligence, whose mental and chronological ages were equal, was said to have an IQ of "100." The plotting of IQs followed a normal distribution that took the form of a bell-shaped curve.

That the bell-shaped curve looked similar to a Warner social class diamond, cut down the middle and laid on one side, clued the researchers to a since-taken-for-granted fact: that IQ correlates with social class. According to SRI's Richard Coleman, an authority on intelligence testing, the average IQ of individuals in the upper-middle class was 122, the ninetieth percentile. In contrast, of the two groups in the middle majority, those in the lower-middle class had an average IQ of 108; in the upper-lower class, IQs averaged 93. The midpoint of 100 was the fiftieth percentile. Although the numerical difference between 122 and 100 did not seem large, the distance between the ninetieth and fiftieth percentiles was gaping.[34] "We at SRI were divided on whether IQ had a heavy genetic component [or could] vary by the environment," Coleman would relate. Yet at SRI, this hotly contested issue was left at that. Warner had emphasized that social class just like heredity were accidents of birth. So it didn't matter whether IQs were natured or nurtured. In either case, they were beyond a person's control.

It didn't require even a 50 IQ to understand the implications. "Intelligence was fundamentally important in television news," Coleman summed up, simply "because with it was how much a person could comprehend." Later, Coleman would scoff at those who accused the mass media of "dumbing down" the people. "Intelligent individuals learn to think twice about making that claim in public," he said, "because intelligence is relative." He recalled many instances when the research community was singled out for "dumbing down," largely by critics with mass media backgrounds. "We knew from probability [that our critics] had IQs of 120, maybe 130. Noting that he and his colleagues at SRI had IQs of 200, Coleman would comment: "To us, they were the ones doing the dumbing down."[35]

Local newsrooms soon would reverberate with the term "Joe Six Pack." Discovering him, in that Hawthorne plant and elsewhere, had been one of America's foremost scholarly achievements. "Joe Six Pack" was not likely to become a doctor or a lawyer anytime soon. According to Coleman, "Warner said it best: 'Different strokes for different folks. People of high status can't just stroke the masses into becoming better human beings.'"

Coleman went on to publish his own acclaimed work, the 1971 *Social Status in the City.* Undertaken during the same period he was conducting TV news studies for McHugh & Hoffman, Coleman's book was the first look at class stratification in large urban areas.

Highlighted in the book was a lift truck operator named Jim Meadows, who described his life. "Fall is my favorite time of year," Meadows related. "That's football season and all three of my boys have played on the team. . . . Every Friday night in the fall for five years now, Thelma and me have been wherever the team was. . . . Thursday night I stay home, and Thelma goes to a canasta club meeting with some of the girls. As you can see for yourself, we have a pretty good time. . . . Physically, I'm thicker in the middle than I used to be or ought to be—but I enjoy a good brew and a thick steak, so what the hell!"

Another person who had told about his life was a pipefitter named Eddie Morris. "Television has been a godsend," he proclaimed. "If you were to ask me what the greatest invention of all time was, I'd name that little box with the eye in it."[36]

In the Chicago School, people like Meadows and Morris were the experts of the "little box." Empowered through research, they were about to change the concept of TV news.

4

The Network Way (1963–1964)

Heading into the 1960s, network news had been worth its weight in gold to the experts and opinion leaders ordering discussions about American TV. Since 1941, when the first network news anchor, CBS's Richard Hubbell, had flickered onto a handful of TV screens, the network's man-on-camera concept had ruled. With Roper Polls suddenly showing television racing past newspapers as the nation's main source of news, experts were quick to pin this achievement on NBC, CBS, and ABC. Nevertheless, in one of the precipitous passages in TV history, Americans "out there" had found something wrong with news from New York.

For years no one had gotten underneath the Nielsen ratings and Roper Polls to find out how average people really felt about network news. This changed in 1962 with the arrival of McHugh & Hoffman and those first qualitative studies of television by the Warner group at SRI. More were on the way, and the results were a bolt from the blue. The folks didn't like Walter Cronkite, couldn't understand half of the news and found most of the rest too boring for words. But the biggest surprise was an expression of benign neglect. The people confirmed that network news was on. Yet the picture painted countless times by media experts, of millions of Americans sitting in rapt attention and engaging in a nightly news viewing ritual, was not even close to the real thing.

The networks themselves knew nothing of these discoveries. They had just told SRI and McHugh & Hoffman to get lost. Yet right from the start, research foretold of a big journalism destined to shrink—and of a new opportunity for those in command of the data, the people of local TV news.

From the beginning and for as long as research was performed, network news would have no problem attracting the 15 to 20 percent of viewers in the college-educated upper-middle class. Of this SRI was certain.

At that moment in 1962 when one team of SRI researchers had been plowing through the Storer ascertainments, another led by sociologists Ira Glick and Sidney Levy had just finished the first root-to-branch look at TV viewing behavior. Referred to as an "X-ray of the TV audience," a summary of this mammoth project, involving 13,000 personal interviews, made the front cover of *Broadcasting* magazine.[1] Glick and Levy published the completed version in *Living With Television,* a book that would revisit upper-middle class resentment with the general state of American TV. News was the only program elite viewers did not protest. They appreciated network news and its man-on-camera format because it was "no nonsense" and rich in words and substance. Further, the upper-middle class was drawn to the province of network news: national and world affairs. Only in passing did the upper-middle class audience even mention the viewing of local news.[2]

The soon-to-be-prominent Frank Magid firm knew the same. Although not yet active in news consulting, an upper class preference for national-world events, against diminished interest in local news, had been detected in some early Magid studies. Eventually, this feeling would resound in Magid's research.[3]

By 1963 everyone had expected similar approval from the middle majority, that superclass of lower-middle and upper-lower TV viewers four times larger than the upper-middle group.[4] After all, the television networks had been trumpeting for the last three years those Roper polls, in which nearly two-thirds of Americans named television as the most-used and most-believed source of news. In addition, network news Nielsen ratings were on an upswing. NBC's "Huntley-Brinkley Report" was a much talked-about program, and more was expected from CBS, which had just replaced Douglas Edwards with Walter Cronkite. ABC was very weak and not a factor. Yet alone, the NBC and CBS newscasts reached 30 percent of all U.S. homes, almost 70 percent of those tuned in at seven p.m., the hour when network news was seen. All of this suggested strong support among the masses.

The researchers were astounded by what was actually found. "[TV news] is absorbed while people are doing other things, such as shaving, eating breakfast, having dinner, etc.," Glick and Levy wrote.

"Most viewers have some awareness of news programs and may pick up something from the . . . evening shows. Still, the average viewer is able to talk at length about television without mentioning these programs."[5]

In fact, interviewers had had to work for any type of viewing reaction relating to network newscasts. It appeared that numerous middle majority viewers were watching network newscasts only because they preceded prime-time entertainment shows. Moreover, suspicions loomed that a high percentage of middle majority respondents who wrote in Nielsen ratings diaries they watched network news really didn't; they were worried by what others would think if they wrote "cartoons" instead. SRI had been alerted to this in its own research. Respondents had tried to impress interviewers by saying they viewed the news, even though many who answered "yes" drew a blank when asked to describe basic details.[6]

The plot thickened. Intrigued by this anomaly over news viewing in the 1962 Glick-Levy study, which SRI had paid for on its own, McHugh & Hoffman scraped together a budget to have the company conduct two more special surveys. The first was supervised by Lee Rainwater and circulated to McHugh & Hoffman's handful of clients in February 1963. The second was headed by Richard Coleman and distributed in March 1964. This time respondents were pressed. Those who said they watched network news had to "come clean" and give their true feelings.

Arriving first, Rainwater's findings were the most eye-opening. In response to probes about specific network news viewing experiences, one lower-middle male simply threw up his hands. "I had read the newspaper and had tuned to the radio and TV newscasters dealing with the facts and I never quite understood the issues involved," he admitted. In a similar query about a Huntley-Brinkley special report, a lower-middle female told the interviewer, "No point seemed to be made. It jumped from one subject to another. Didn't get the point across. At the end, I was asking myself, 'Why did they do that?'" When quizzed on distinctions between CBS and NBC news programs, another lower-middle class female just shrugged. "I don't think it makes much difference which one you watch. I don't think there is much choice between them. Truthfully, after awhile it is all boring," she said.

Of interest had been a question about news coverage of the 1962 election campaigns. Given the chance to speak freely, one lower-middle male didn't mince words. "Politics are a pain in the neck. They are something that everybody has made their minds up about. Why add to your miseries by making you listen?" he spouted. In a gentler tone, an upper-lower female hemmed and hawed and finally conceded that politics are "kinda' hard on me." On election night, she said, she and her "poor kids got restless and bored. . . . [T]hey got into arguments and couldn't find anything to do. I thought it was too bad they didn't leave plays on one channel at least. We can't expect kids that little to watch and understand [political coverage]."

Bewildered, Rainwater did learn one thing: why TV had just surpassed the newspapers. In their own words, average Americans said they were not keen on reading when there were other ways to get the news. "People find it easier to sit down and listen instead of sitting down and reading," an upper-lower male explained, his response identical to many. Another middle majority respondent volunteered, "I think by listening to a man who knows the score you can learn more about the subject than by just reading an account of the event in the paper. . . . Most newspaper[s] are too involved to understand easily."[7]

Coleman's study a year later confirmed what Rainwater's had shown. Following up on the matter of network television being the main source of information, Coleman showed that the networks were being watched. Yet stunningly, when given the opportunity to explain the information they did receive from the networks, average people had spoken of more than the evening news. Coleman's team had respondents react to the question, "What public affairs shows have you found interesting in the past few months?" This was done entirely by unaided recall. No list of programs was provided. The responses had included "The Tonight Show With Johnny Carson," an entertainment special on the Fisher quintuplets, and "The ABC Wide World of Sports."[8] Actual newscasts were not even mentioned by numerous respondents. "The conventional wisdom always taught you that professional journalists decide what is news," Glick would recall. Yet to average people "anything reality-based" could be that.[9]

By no means had network news been indicted. Much like those Sears refrigerator users 20 years before, middle majority TV viewers were kind. Overall perceptions of network news were positive, and most respondents noted that relative to local newscasts the networks had a more professional look. Seeing it as a personal obligation like going to church, or as a way to keep up in the next day's chit-chat with friends, even lower class respondents considered the viewing of news a good thing.

On the other hand, network news was flawed. Breakdowns in interest and understanding, coupled by sentiment that the New York networks were captivated by a distant and unknown world, kept the researchers coming back. Probing further, they would reach another unexpected conclusion, that perceptions of newscasts were not usually determined by news content. The anchors who delivered the news, a seemingly insignificant factor to professional journalists, had meant everything to the middle majority.

SRI was quite simply bowled over by the intensity of this finding. Middle majority respondents who said they watched network news but couldn't recall details often redeemed themselves with voluminous descriptions of the anchors, the sound of their voice, what they wore and even the cut of their hair. As an example, they had a definite perception of the man who had just taken the reins at CBS, Walter Cronkite; he was TV's greatest stick in the mud. In the 1963 study several had volunteered that Cronkite came off not as a news reporter but as a "history teacher."

So many respondents had reacted to Cronkite's superficial, stick-up-the-back delivery that Rainwater had questioned what CBS had hoped to accomplish by taking Douglas Edwards off and putting Cronkite on. It was obvious, too, that CBS had been getting the same input, for it would refuse to allow Cronkite to anchor the 1964 political conventions. Rumors were rampant that Cronkite would be fired. Even so, in this earliest of data, Rainwater had spotted a ray of light. Cronkite might survive, Rainwater wrote, through "his willingness [at times] to display some emotion and allow the public to see and think of him as a person." Instructive had been an otherwise reticent lower status respondent who had opened up with a gushing account of how Cronkite had abandoned his serious newscaster image and shared this respondent's own concerns in May 1962, when astronaut Scott Carpenter was believed to have perished on his Project Mercury space flight.[10]

Yet in 1963, it was not Cronkite's newscast but rather NBC's "Huntley-Brinkley Report" that the researchers had most wanted to explore. NBC had the highest ratings. Despite a positive view of NBC, widespread were "growing dissatisfactions." Again, there were cases of average viewers saying they regularly watched Huntley-Brinkley but not being able to offer concrete observations proving they had. While they fluidly reacted to personal images of Chet Huntley and David Brinkley and considered them "friends," they gave little indication they expected to gain anything personally meaningful from their newscast. Interest and comprehension difficulties were linked to two anchors "too patronizing and condescending."

In some situations, according to the research, comprehension had completely broken down. "Lower status people, especially, are prone to feel that occasionally Huntley or Brinkley flaunts his superior knowledge in the viewer's face." SRI concluded that the

"Huntley-Brinkley Report" had top ratings because "it was an ideal news program for people who are not vitally interested in the news." Coleman noted that "for the first time in our surveys this year we found a marked amount of criticism of Huntley and Brinkley." Meanwhile, "Cronkite's main appeal is to the [upper] middle class. He seems to conduct a show that is 'above the heads' of many blue collar people. He goes into details of foreign news and domestic affairs that make events somewhat too complicated for them to understand."[11]

What had middle majority viewers been seeing that would account for these perceptions? Vanderbilt University would begin the only public archive of network newscasts in late 1968. One of its first preserved programs was the January 2, 1969, edition of the "Huntley-Brinkley Report." Although this was not a 1963 broadcast, it was probably quite similar to the newscasts evaluated in the 1963 research. This NBC program contained 10 items in five segments separated by four groups of commercials. It began from Washington, where Brinkley introduced a two minute-forty second filmed report from John Chancellor, who summarized the day's events in Congress, including the renaming of John McCormack as Speaker of the House. Seven Senate and House members gave statements on Congressional affairs during the course of this opening story, which comprised the entire first segment.

As this broadcast continued, two minutes of commercials were shown. From New York Huntley then appeared. A thirty-second on-camera lead-in preceded a three minute-twenty second film from Paris about talks between French and Soviet foreign ministers on tensions in the Middle East. Huntley's lead-in and the film comprised the second segment.

After more commercials, Huntley made his second appearance and gave a two minute-forty second chronology of the day's meetings of President-elect Richard Nixon. Two subsequent reports covered the fighting in Vietnam and the Paris peace talks. The second-to-last segment returned to Washington, where Brinkley again introduced Chancellor, who gave a two minute-fifty second report on the procedure by which the Electoral College would officially name Nixon as president. The last segment contained a four minute-ten second report on the winter migration of Canadian geese.[12]

The same night, the "CBS Evening News" was similar. Four minutes were devoted Congress, three to Vietnam and the peace talks and almost two minutes each for the day's activities of Nixon and outgoing President Lyndon Johnson. The CBS newscast contained 10 stories and ended with a two minute-thirty second commentary by Eric Sevareid on the problem of filibusters in Congress.[13]

Newscasts like these were informative, but according to the research they were more informative to the upper-middle class than the mass of TV viewers. The tradition of network news would be exemplified on August 16, 1977, when the "CBS Evening News" would be headlined by the fifty-ninth day of discussions between White House officials and Congressional leaders on a new treaty for the Panama Canal. Another event that had occurred that day, the death of Elvis Presley, was second-segment fare.[14]

Most lower-middle and upper-lower class respondents had never been to Washington, let alone to Paris or Geneva. Were the nuances of French and Soviet foreign ministers worth three minutes of their time? Canadian geese four? "It was the first time we had gone in and really looked at the way the average person watched a TV newscast. . . . What the networks did and what the people were saying were like night and day," Hoffman recalled.[15]

To Hoffman and his partner McHugh, it was easy to see why findings such as these were important. The local stations that had just hired them as consultants had newscasts that looked just like the network's. Yet in network news, average people were not just getting the wrong things; in some cases, they weren't "getting it" at all. The consultants recognized that something would have to be done. Neither McHugh and Hoffman nor the research team at SRI had any experience in news. How to revise their clients' local newscasts had loomed as a question as these mixed reviews of the networks piled up through the end of 1963. Then out of a dark event came a thunderbolt. It was a new research report in early 1964.

Its subject was the Kennedy assassination the previous November, instantly hailed as network TV's "finest hour" because of four days of uninterrupted news coverage. A team of SRI researchers was in the field within two weeks of the fatal shots in Dallas on November 22. On short notice the study was small, with SRI able only to randomly sample and probe viewers in three cities. Although circulated privately, it would remain the only known examination of middle and lower class TV viewing during the assassination. The results would give the consultants the raw material for their first forays into TV news.

The assassination study was circulated in February 1964, with McHugh & Hoffman headlong into its first local news consulting assignments. Between 10 and 15 percent of lower-middle and upper-lower class viewers, the middle majority, felt television had devoted too much time to the tragedy. These respondents believed too many regularly scheduled entertainment programs had been pre-empted, particularly on the Sunday and Monday nights after the assassination when their interest had begun to wane. Indeed, according to William Manchester's account, 10 percent of local stations had cut from the networks and run commercials while President Kennedy lay in state.[16] But this was not unexpected. The small number with muted reactions served as a reminder that the average person did not have an instinctive interest in news, whatever the event.

Yet in bold terms, the thrust of the study had been an opposite perception. The vast majority of middle and lower status viewers "[had] been 'glued' to their television sets almost in hypnotic fashion." Most respondents had watched at least 12 hours of coverage, and some could recall the entire drama. "I was simply stunned while watching it," one respondent said, adding that "[m]y children knew something happened even if they were too young to fully understand." Another would relate, "I watched TV almost constantly. I think I watched everything that was on. . . . There was never a time when it wasn't interesting." Another lower class woman "thought they did a wonderful job of bringing some sort of order out of all that confusion. . . . I began to wonder if [Lyndon] Johnson would be able to carry on" but was relieved upon "seeing him, and the way he helped Mrs. Kennedy."

Importantly, middle majority reactions were not limited to the happenings in Dallas and Washington. Over and over, respondents had described the sensation of sharing the tragedy with the network news anchors. In meeting this expectation, many NBC viewers drew blanks over Huntley and Brinkley, who in a fashion described in the preceding research had appeared unmoved by what they were reporting. Most NBC viewers had avoided comment on Huntley and Brinkley and had responded to a backup anchor named Frank McGee, who to them had seemed warm, more comforting, and not above the events.

But Cronkite's research was off the boards. CBS viewers felt they'd been led through the tragedy by Cronkite, who again, as in the Project Mercury flights, had dropped the serious newscaster facade and come off like a member of the family. "He was straight but you could tell he was holding back tears. That's what we all felt," one person noted. This viewer had recalled the scene correctly. More than once Cronkite had choked up, including at the key moment when he'd told the nation Kennedy was dead.[17] "Walter Cronkite . . . made you feel as though you were actually on the scene," another volunteered. Emotional and out of character for a newsman, Cronkite "seemed at one and the same time to be humanly touched by the events, yet master of the situation," SRI emphasized. It was the same Cronkite trait SRI's research already had isolated, only now demonstrated before an attentive audience of millions during an event they'd remember for the rest of their lives.

SRI would conclude that visualization had steered almost every indelible impression. "Television made the experience infinitely more meaningful and emotionally rich than could radio," the report read. Yet middle majority viewers had not "taken it all in." Instead, their strongest reactions came when they could actually see events unfold, these "high points"—the shooting of Lee Harvey Oswald and the burial of Kennedy. "These are, of course, the most highly emotional and human moments, . . . those which are most nearly human and dramatic in emotional terms [and] have the widest impact." The overall effect was illustrating, in SRI's words, that "[i]ssues and intellectual concerns run a poor second" when news is carried on TV.[18]

The Kennedy assassination was an epiphany to those with access to this research and whose task was reconsidering the structure of the TV newscast. McHugh & Hoffman had just such a task. The abiding finding in the research was a metaphor that Hoffman would recount many times. That November, he said, "the people had seen a TV news that didn't look like TV news."[19] He had been referring to those nightly network newscasts that had droned on and on. Warm and caring newscasters made a difference to average people. So did content that hit home. They wanted to see events with their own eyes. Few were aware that JFK's last act was precipitating people's news.

Much more lay ahead for network news, a field that would come of age during the uncanny progression of history-making events that marked the rest of the 1960s. After the tragedy in Dallas, the networks again captivated the public with extended coverage of the assassinations of Martin Luther King and Robert Kennedy, the stormy 1968 Democratic convention and missions to the moon. Racial discord, urban unrest, student violence and the Vietnam War—all happening simultaneously—gave the people additional reasons to tune in. By 1969, the three networks' newscasts would be seen in 50 percent of all American homes and 85 percent of the homes tuned to TV at newstime, then a heralded display of TV news progress. Later, though, these 1969 numbers would have a different distinction—as the highest ratings network news ever would achieve.

Yet nothing that occurred on network row would have greater meaning to TV news than the rise of Walter Cronkite as the personification of the field. Not just network but local news would have a stake in the Cronkite phenomenon, as future events would show. Indeed, 15 years after retiring from CBS in 1981, Cronkite still was perceived as the best-known figure in TV news.[20] Most media experts had one explanation for Cronkite's stature: his factual and authoritative reporting, starting with that onslaught of news in the 1960s. Yet it was obvious this wasn't the real reason. Numerous other network news anchors had covered the same events with the same facts and the same levels of authority. They had included Chancellor, Sander Vanocur, Harry Reasoner and Howard Smith. All of them would be forgotten by most Americans almost the moment they left the air. Even Huntley would suffer this fate.

Cronkite stood out, the research had shown, because he was the first people's newscaster. Cronkite may not have known it at the time, but his career-shaping moment had been the Kennedy assassination in 1963, when in the shadows of Huntley and Brinkley he alone had dispensed with the nightly newscaster act and showed Americans who he really was. The data had indicated that Cronkite had undergone a metamorphosis. The more Cronkite loosened, the more intense his attraction became. Cronkite's image as a real person would be galvanized by his coverage of the space program. Viewers who saw the launch of the first Saturn Five rocket on November 9, 1967, didn't know what was louder, the rocket or Cronkite's screaming and yelling as it took off. "Look at that thing go!" Cronkite thundered, and there hadn't even been any astronauts on board.[21] Tears returned on July 20, 1969, the Apollo 11 moon landing. "Say something Wally. I'm speechless," Cronkite told astronaut Walter Schirra, his co-anchor.[22] Cronkite was the only newscaster who had the sense to behave this way, the way any real person would, while on TV. That had made the difference.

Less than two years after Dallas, three years after questioning his future at CBS, SRI's research would peg Cronkite as "humane," a term it had never before used in news. This image in a news context, coupled by Cronkite's ability to reach millions, was daunting. "The characteristic that distinguishes him from other network newscasters is his sincere delivery and his great appeal as a personality. Respondents say that Cronkite delivers the news with a sincerity which mirrors their own reaction to current events,"[23] SRI summed up. This feeling about Cronkite would never dissipate. "He's factual but yet not unfeeling. He's shown, on occasion, emotion over certain news stories," volunteered a lower-middle female in 1977 research. "And he has an aura around him that gives you confidence in him," another affirmed. According to an upper-lower male, "He has a nice way about him. You know, he's very easygoing and relaxed and speaks very well . . . He's a good man." That an upper class female in the same study had commented "I like just everything about him" was noteworthy.24 As SRI's Richard Coleman explained, "Cronkite was the only [newscaster] who could play both sides. He had the respect of the upper-middle class because of his seriousness, but he also had the admiration of the middle majority because he came across as a real person."25

Cronkite never had access to the qualitative research the consultants had performed on him. Indeed, Cronkite detested research as an impediment to good journalism. This might have averted the cloud that lay ahead, when the consummate people's newscaster would lead an ill-fated campaign against people's news.

With Cronkite as its symbol, the network way had seemed the only way. In reality, the moorings between network and local news were coming loose. Live coverage of history-making news, the foundation of Cronkite's acclaim and the forte of the networks, was not something local stations could accomplish. The only issue in local TV was regular nightly newscasts, a crucial area that had still shaped up as a void. If the Kennedy assassination had been a lesson in the potentials of TV news, no less revealing after its four riveting days was that which was learned on the fifth. As the networks resumed their regular schedules, Cronkite and the others fell back into their man-on-camera routines, with more chronologies of Congress, more European ministers and more geese. "They tell me things about the world scene [that] don't pertain to what I have to worry about. Like I worry about keeping my job and they focus on Lebanon's civil war. That is not part of my life," a lower-middle male would state. "I like it [network news] but I would like to see more stories that apply to our lives more. Like bottle-feeding babies and health stories," a lower-middle female similarly would complain. According to an upper-lower male, "When they get to carrying the same story for fourteen days in a row . . . it gets pretty boring."26

The network way was the wrong way for the consultants of local TV. Armed with insights from the best research money could buy, they finally were ready to act.

5

News for the Middle Majority (1963–1967)

The "people's newscast" was a news broadcast that mixed news, sports and weather; was headlined by a two-person usually male-female anchor team and had weather and sports anchors in dominant supporting roles. Exhaustive visualization was another defining feature, as were reporters who went to the scene and used pictures to communicate stories. Short interview clips called "soundbites" were in. The paradigm of words, known in TV as the "talking head," was out. Action, too, was a goal, as were eye-catching studio sets, mood-changing music and soft-sell promotion. Blotter news like meetings and news conferences was limited so that investigative exposés, medical reports, consumer affairs, personal money matters and lifestyle news could be seen. All the anchors and reporters conversed with one another in a way that made the viewer their friend. Put all together, the people's newscast was an electronic extension of a viewer's family; its binding symbol, the smile.

Soon virtually all television newscasts looked like this. Yet when the modern people's newscast began its ascent—in Detroit, Cleveland, Atlanta, Milwaukee and Toledo—nothing like it had ever been seen.

This turning point in TV news was accompanied by another, one that had occurred at the Broadmoor Hotel in Colorado Springs on September 8, 1962. That day had begun with McHugh & Hoffman stymied by those first curious findings on network news viewing and not sure what to do. When the day was over, news consulting was born.

Bearing SRI's research for Storer Broadcasting, and an announcement so surprising he feared being laughed off, Phil McHugh had traveled to Colorado for a Storer managers retreat. Until this meeting McHugh & Hoffman had no specialization, particularly in news, and had planned to perform general program advising and ascertainment research. Standing in front of an easel and pointing to a large colored rendition of Lloyd Warner's social class diamond, he started in on those troubles middle majority viewers were having with network news. McHugh then moved to something else he felt even more significant, a sinkhole underneath the very foundation of network TV: entertainment shows. While crucial in a station's immediate ratings count, network entertainment programs could not instill "brand loyalty" over the long haul. Average people were impulsive, McHugh said, and that was why even the most formidable network entertainment schedule was certain to lose favor in time. "[A]utomatically staying with one [network] is a clearly diminishing practice even in quite low status groups," the studies had affirmed.[1]

But local news, McHugh declared, was different. Not only was local news immune to cancellation; average viewers expected local stations to be permanent windows on their communities. In contrast, the networks were perceived as being hundreds of miles away. "Joe Six Pack" was scanning TV listings and choosing a night's viewing by giving first look to the station he favored for local news.[2] Local news, McHugh said, thus beat a path to the bottom line.

The Storer managers could not believe their ears. Entertainment was the gospel of TV; news, something to be handled like used diapers. "It is an expensive area to develop, because it takes qualified newsmen, cameramen, and directors behind the scenes," McHugh elaborated. Nevertheless, "it is an area where future investment must be made over the years if the goal of the Storer television stations is to be number one." When one of the managers asked for a figure and McHugh threw out $75,000, another told McHugh he was out of his mind. "We can only report what we have learned from these studies," he replied. "News is the major ingredient toward the Storer stations becoming number one in their markets."

The next question was directed at the man who had hired McHugh & Hoffman, Bill Michaels. Would not he, the company vice president, look askance at a station manager who might have to report losses because of gigantic news investments? Michaels told the managers not to worry—and more. "You must follow the McHugh &

Hoffman recommendations," he decreed.3 Finally hitched to TV news, the consultants had a green light to proceed.

Pie-eyed by research data, McHugh and Hoffman had heard enough from the SRI Ph.D.s. The consultants had made astounding claims about the ratings potential of local newscasts. Now they had to prove them. Without delay, the two men worked up a travel itinerary that shuttled them between WJBK in Detroit, WJW in Cleveland, WAGA in Atlanta, WITI in Milwaukee and WSPD in Toledo. These were the stations that had hired McHugh & Hoffman to avert license revocations in the wake of Newton Minow's 1961 crackdown. By 1963, even by McHugh's estimation, they were still a wasteland. Little more than network relays, their local airtime was consumed by syndicated fare from Hollywood—old movies, "Leave It To Beaver," "Sea Hunt," a teenage pop music program called "The Lloyd Thaxton Show" and the "Jack La Lanne" exercise show.

Every Storer newscast either was in last place or close to it. When asked about this, news staffers were blasé. Whatever the ratings, the newsmen thought they were doing a great job. Even less responsive were the managers, who acknowledged the low ratings but had had a ready excuse: powerhouse local newspapers that owned competing TV stations.

The research indeed had shown that local newspapers were giving TV stations a halo effect. In Detroit, Storer's largest market, WJBK's "Esso Reporter" barely registered because of the middle majority's intense esteem for the *Detroit News,* the owner of competitor WWJ. Detroit's newspaper station, WWJ, had a strapping 40 percent share. In Cleveland Storer's WJW and its "Sohio Reporter" were being walloped by the local news on WEWS, the TV station named after newspaper baron Edward W. Scripps and the arm of Scripps' *Cleveland Press.* In Atlanta, Storer's WAGA was so far behind WSB, owned by the *Atlanta Constitution,* as to defy rational hope. Storer's only glimmer was WITI in Milwaukee, although this was largely because of WITI's weather program and its popular weatherpuppet "Albert the Alleycat."4

The basic news consulting regimen fell into place. New employees with backgrounds in advertising or applied research were hired to help the partners service the accounts. Officially titled "account executives," most broadcasters would know such figures simply as "consultants." Travel dominated their lives. Inordinate activity took place in hotel rooms, where hour upon hour was spent monitoring the local newscasts of clients and competitors. Weekly station visits settled into monthly and then quarterly contacts, with major visits coinciding with annual surveys. It was a cyclical system of research-consulting, more research-more consulting. Because all of McHugh & Hoffman's research was performed by SRI, it had to be dovetailed with SRI's Fortune 500 accounts.

The process revolved around recommendations given by the consultants to their client TV stations. Extending from the research, these recommendations were listed 1-2-3 in reports. After they were turned over, usually in locked-door meetings, the consultants then did all they could to ensure this advice was followed. No client was obligated to follow any recommendation, and, typically, several were postponed or completely ignored. Yet the big ones usually were implemented. Non-compliance defeated the purpose of the high-priced consulting contracts they had signed.

These sets of recommendations came to be known as "action plans," although the first by McHugh & Hoffman barely were that. The first year saw a scattershot of ideas, some quick-fixes as suggested in the research, others the outcrop of the consultants' own experience and intuition. The earliest consulting reports were only 20 pages long and looked more like a college student's term paper than the 400-page volumes they would become. Even so, what these early reports lacked in detail was offset by some of the lasting people's news practices they inscribed.

For example, McHugh & Hoffman's first standing recommendation was expanding 15-minute newscasts to a half-hour and folding Storer's separate news, weather and sports programs into a single show, a move never before accomplished throughout a large group. WJBK's news program with Carl Cederberg absorbed a three-minute program called "Miss Fairweather" with Jeanne Dishong and the five-minute "Bill Flemming Sports." Identical mergers took place at WJBK's sister stations after Hoffman had advised: "[N]ews and weathercasters make an important package. . . . [The viewer thinks] he is getting more news."[5]

Yet at WJBK more had transpired. It was the first application of anchor-specific research data, with something insiders knew as "Q scores." The conclusion that "the gimmick of weathergirls has run it course" was evident in the dismal showing of "Miss Fairweather" when paired in the research against WWJ weathercaster Sonny Eliot. With a Q score of "63," Eliot was far and away the

No. 1 news personality in Detroit.[6] McHugh & Hoffman would help WJBK locate a new meteorologist named Jerry Hodak. The consultants' push for professional meteorologists looked ahead, but no more than these early clues as to the importance of weather in people's news.

Another step was adding editorials. Not wanting essays on the great events of the times, the consultants would advocate editorials as rote learning devices for the many lower-middle and upper-lower class viewers with comprehension difficulties. Middle majority viewers had ceaselessly complained of the networks' shortage of background information. Without it, news often made no sense. Not only were the networks writing stories by incorrectly assuming everyone knew the previous day's details; there was no way a viewer could play back a TV news account to catch something that was missed. "The viewer is a virgin," a later consultant named Willis Duff would state.[7] "Viewers believe that television editorials can supply and explain issues in terms which can be more easily understood," SRI had learned. "[T]he editorialist is talking directly to them and [can] talk in a language the average viewer can understand."[8] Further, "The pitfall of assuming a professorial/education stance should be avoided at all costs. Instead of a 'pontifical' approach, the editorial should . . . be concerned with local issues which are of greatest interest to the mass audience; i.e., the grass roots or 'gut' issues of the community."[9]

The remainder of the early action plans related to promotion. Entering WJBK, McHugh had been aghast to find out that the station was spending its own money to promote CBS programs, a task CBS itself was fit to perform. New ads downplayed CBS and touted "the loud, clear voice of WJBK" instead.[10] Also baffling was McHugh's discovery that WJBK never advertised on WJBK. Everything was in print. Storer had refused to sacrifice its own airtime and the ad revenue it generated. So like a football referee signaling an incomplete pass, McHugh told Michaels this thinking had to change. Television was unsurpassed as an advertising vehicle; to maximize revenues in the long run, Storer must advertise on its "own air."

McHugh next articulated the first innovation to ruffle the media elite, when the Storer stations abandoned their call letters and identified themselves by their channel numbers. Guardians of broadcasting basked in the tradition and ambiance of call letters, endemic in radio, and were put off by artless numbers that were the same all over the country. A special SRI study had just shown that middle majority viewers did not relate to call letters and got them mixed up.[11] McHugh told Detroit's Larry Carino, the general manager of WJBK, "People can't find a 'WJBK' on their clickers; all they see is a 2."

Viewers from coast to coast also would recognize another McHugh invention, the "ID promo." Under FCC rules, every station had to provide a three-second station identification every hour. To McHugh it was ridiculous to have an announcer endlessly repeat "This is WJBK, Channel 2, in Detroit," when all this could be squeezed into the bottom of a TV screen—in a free promo advertising the next newscast. During prime-time, three seconds were worth tens of thousands of dollars. When McHugh explained the payoff of this simple tactic at a Storer managers' meeting where other attendees had stayed mum, president George Storer, Jr., shot up out of his chair and started clapping by himself. "Even the shortest periods of time could be used for station promotion," Storer exclaimed.12

November 1962 marked the first ratings "sweep" following the entry of the consultants. It had worried them and Storer. Ominously, they arrived just before Christmas as fall ratings always would. "If the ARB bears out the Nielsen . . . [we need] to make an evaluation," Michaels told McHugh. "Cleveland," Michaels emphasized, "is the big area of concern."13

The loss of viewers at Cleveland's WJW had been glaring indeed. With a 20 percent share then the rock-bottom, WJW's 11 o'clock newscast had just fallen to a "19."14 WJW's dinner-hour combination of "Sohio Reporter" and "City Camera," separate newscasts with different sponsors, had dropped to a "20." WJW had been blistered by a WEWS news block featuring popular commentator Dorothy Fuldheim and a news segment hosted by WEWS's young news director Joel Daly.

Michaels brought in a new station manager named Robert Buchanan. At 29, Buchanan was one of the youngest people ever to head a major market television station. Then, Michaels ordered McHugh & Hoffman to make WJW "the first priority." McHugh cautioned Michaels to expect a much larger consulting bill. Michaels replied that money was "no obstacle."15

Eventually, Buchanan would hire a news director named Norm Wagy, part of a new breed of news manager who worked the job full-time and did not double as the news anchor. Wagy later would coordinate McHugh & Hoffman's activities.

Yet the person who initially served as news director was a young newscaster named Doug Adair, about to become the first TV journalist to meet and then actively work with research-based news consultants. Adair felt a strange sensation. "We kept hearing rumors about this 'McHugh-Hoffman,' but no one in the news department knew what that was." Just the same, he would relate, "We could tell something was up."[16]

Enduring concepts in people's news would spring from several cities. From New York had come "Telepix Newsreel," and more was ahead. Los Angeles had contributed Klaus Landsberg, the first "million-dollar" anchor in George Putnam and "The Big News." Detroit and Chicago shortly would be in the spotlight, and Philadelphia would join them in a big way. But if local broadcasting had a cradle of innovation it was Cleveland, the nation's eighth-largest television market and crucial to the sixth-largest broadcaster.

The station where all this was happening, WJW, had just ignited the nation's rock-and-roll music craze. A WJW radio disc jockey named Alan Freed was one of the founders of the rock music genre. Years later Freed would be immortalized in a Rock-and-Roll Hall of Fame that, because of Freed and WJW, was located in Cleveland. Also from Cleveland would come several TV news figures later to assume national prominence, including Carl Stern, Bill Beutel, Jack Perkins, Don Oliver, Bill Jorgensen, Tom Snyder, and Phil Donohue. The most popular syndicated program of the 1960s, "The Mike Douglas Show," also had begun in Cleveland.

Meanwhile, the hopes of McHugh & Hoffman greatly rested on the individual who sat in the WJW control room and directed Doug Adair's "City Camera" newscast. His real name Tom Conway, he was the person millions would know as "Tim Conway," whose comedic career took off when WJW let him double as a movie host. The person who sat in the audio booth across the glass from Conway and who voiced introductions for "City Camera," was Ernie Anderson, a figure who had already gained national notoriety, in *Time* magazine and elsewhere.

Anderson was a freakish, irreverent WJW movie host named "Ghoulardi."[17] McHugh could not stomach this "Ghoulardi" character, and neither could many Storer executives. Yet it was chiefly because of McHugh that "Ghoulardi" became an institution in Cleveland. The data from parents indicated an overpowering following among teenagers of baby-boom age. Anderson followed Conway to Hollywood and for three decades as the "voice of ABC" was a presence unmistakable to American TV viewers. Anderson's voiceovers in the 1970s for ABC's "Love Boat" series, in which he drew out the word "love," were parodied again and again.

Moreover, Cleveland became the first crossroads of people's news. It was a hotbed of local news, with events ranging from the nation's first major civil disturbances to the expected departure of its baseball team, the Indians, of great concern to its middle majority residents. In 1965, escalation of the Vietnam War would push news interest to unparalleled levels, with downtown draft boards and a budding protest movement in Ohio the focal points of local coverage. According to the research, the Vietnam War initially was passed off by upper-middle class individuals. At first, it was followed only by lower status families, who knew they were vulnerable to the draft and likely to be sent to Vietnam to fight.[18]

Yet more than just hot news had set Cleveland apart. Cleveland residents had been forced to use television because of recurrent newspaper strikes in the 1960s.[19] Further, after Boston, Cleveland was the largest market not to have any of its TV stations owned by a network. This heightened creativity. It mattered greatly that Cleveland was the first market to open itself to news consultants and audience research. Cleveland had a small upper-middle class grouping. At about 15 percent nationally, Cleveland's upper-middle class was only 10 percent. It was an area predominated by blue collar working class families. Seventy-one percent of those sampled in Cleveland were part of the middle majority. Of this, 42 percent were in the upper-lower class. Cleveland had one of the largest concentrations of upper-lower class residents of any U.S. locale.[20] "The way McHugh & Hoffman saw the world was perfect for Cleveland," Storer's Ken Bagwell observed.[21]

Cleveland's single most widely emulated contribution to television news was in abandoning the traditional man-on-camera format in favor of a new concept that purposely made news presentation a shared experience between two newscasters. Soon a hallmark of news consulting and a defining feature of local TV news, the "co-anchor" format owed its creation to McHugh & Hoffman's class-stratified behavioral analyses, namely tracking studies in the winter of 1963 and a 500-respondent formal survey in late spring, each suggesting that preferences for WJW roamed all over the social class diamond. Although comments from WJW's own loyal viewers widely varied, an impression had formed among non-WJW viewers that this station was too "uppity." For some yet-to-be-determined reason, its "Sohio Reporter" had a marked appeal in the tiny upper-middle class. WJW's competitors had appeal where it needed to be: smack in the middle of the diamond. Attention was given to Westinghouse-owned KYW, which had been expanding its on-the-scenes coverage and gaining blue collar viewers.[22]

However, as KYW was in second place, the consultants most wanted to learn why first-place WEWS was the middle majority's clear favorite. The best answer was the 27-year-old newscaster Joel Daly. The research emphasized that "Joel Daly at WEWS . . . is warm, friendly and a pleasantly competent newsman" with a "personal attraction."[23] From a small station in Rock Island, Daly had been brought to WEWS as a news director-newscaster only a year earlier to replace anchor Bill Beutel, who had left to start the first local newscast on a weak TV station in New York called WABC. At first glance, it had appeared Daly stood out because of his youth. The market was dominated by figures twice Daly's age.

While youth did factor, it was evident Daly, in the words of a 1963 monitoring report, was "more than a person who just read the news." This had started McHugh & Hoffman thinking. In those network news studies, middle majority respondents had gone on and on about "stilted" and "stone-faced" newscasters and their extreme preference for "real people." After monitoring Daly several times from Cleveland hotel rooms, Hoffman theorized that Daly, being so young, had only vague memories of the Great Depression and World War II. Thus, Daly did not go on TV and project "gotterdammerrung," as older newscasters did. "He smiled," a disbelieving Hoffman had noted.[24] Few could savvy this better than Buchanan, WJW's general manager. He and Daly were only two years apart.

Originally, WJW management had not contemplated what was to come, a co-anchor arrangement that would place Daly alongside Adair. The essential step nevertheless occurred when with further input from McHugh & Hoffman, Buchanan pulled off the first ever talent raid on a competing TV newsroom. Although news consultants would be in the thick of many more raids, McHugh & Hoffman had been sheepish about this first go-around. Impressed by Daly, McHugh & Hoffman had only told Buchanan to find "someone like him."

Buchanan had read right through the code. Using back channels, he contacted Daly and facilitated the jump by offering an annual salary of $30,000, an amount that in 1963 could have purchased a five-bedroom house, 10 new cars or a small airplane. Daly was dumbfounded. "I honestly couldn't believe WJW would do something like this. At the time, taking another station's talent completely defied the principles of news," he recalled.[25] When Daly came aboard in August 1963 and finally met McHugh and Hoffman, the consultants saw a quintessential people's newscaster. He was a magna cum laude graduate from Yale, and yet he rarely showed this in public. What viewers perceived was a person who had grown up in a working class section of Spokane, had served in the Army and was an accomplished country-western singer. Daly also was a pilot, and later an actor and a lawyer, and he had a lifelong fascination with the wanderlust of long-haul truckers,[26] the reason Daly's "real person" appeal had been easy to figure.

Yet the co-anchor format had required more than the raid on WEWS. Now at WJW Daly was supposed to host a five-minute feature segment at the end of "City Camera," anchored by Adair. But Daly's pairing with Adair materialized after WJW's next TV first. In a move so controversial that it cost Buchanan his job, WJW became the first consulted station to fire a main newscaster.

It was certain from the research that another WJW newscaster, Warren Guthrie, had to go. Guthrie was the patriarch of Cleveland television and WJW's "Sohio Reporter." Behind the scenes he was a much-loved individual. Possibly with the highest IQ of anyone ever to step before a news camera, he had dazzled associates by memorizing his entire news script and then reading it back into the camera without ever breaking eye contact. Still, Guthrie's appeal was class polarized. The small number in the upper-middle class approved Guthrie's style and delivery, but the huge blue collar working class did not. It was all over when McHugh & Hoffman had found out that Guthrie had a second career. He was a college professor! For years he had taught speech courses at Case Western University. "In proposing news talent we are going in a different direction," Hoffman exhorted to Buchanan.[27] "[Guthrie] lacks appeal. . . . The public [is] experiencing a personality clash" between Guthrie and the others. "The one person they want to see more of is Doug Adair; and since this is a finding of two studies in a row, we believe his function at WJW-TV should be expanded."[28] The matter was resolved, although in the wake of a firestorm, when Guthrie was axed.[29]

The tempest was so intense that George Storer, Sr., personally came to Cleveland to clear the air and demote Buchanan. In this atmosphere, few could imagine how either Adair or Daly could fill Guthrie's shoes, including Adair and Daly themselves. Teaming Adair and Daly was an idea Adair and Hoffman had discussed to get WJW back on track. Besides both being in their twenties, Adair and Daly had just started families. And previously while competitors, but as the two youngsters in a TV market some recalled as looking like "the Alps"—promontories of white hair on every channel—they had formed an intimate out-of-the-studio friendship.

Finally, on September 2, 1963, Adair and Daly sat side-by-side on a hurriedly rebuilt WJW news set and introduced the co-anchor

concept. It was so radical that WJW in a ream of publicity had announced a "magazine," not a real newscast.[30] Although WJW had
been aware of the success of the Huntley-Brinkley combination on
NBC, the WJW co-anchor format barely resembled it. WJW's venture
was a half-hour in length, the "Huntley-Brinkley Report" still only 15
minutes. Meanwhile, a light to the whole idea was research showing
that Huntley and Brinkley were not perceived as a team. The NBC
newscasters had sat in different cities and were electronically switched
onto the screen, Huntley in one segment, Brinkley in the next. This
was precisely the effect WJW most wanted to avoid. The goal was an
open environment allowing the newscasters to spontaneously react to
one another. No longer a medium of record, TV news now would be
redefined as the goings-on in the studio at the moment a newscast was
on the air. Adair and Daly appeared together at the beginning, in exchanges leading into commercials, in exchanges with sports and
weathercasters and in additional exchanges at the end of the program
that introduced a light story called a "kicker."[31] Hundreds of thousands of succeeding local newscasts would follow the same pattern.

It looked effortless to viewers. Nevertheless, the co-anchor format
was one of the most arduous of all people's news practices. "You had
to have chemistry," explained Adair. "Joel was one of my best friends.
I wanted to share the news with him for personal reasons but also because I knew the audience would appreciate seeing us together as a
team."[32]

Adair was right. Ten months after the debut, SRI's research had
shown a "uniformly favorable response" to the new format.[33] In the
May 1964 ratings, WJW's share of the audience was up to 29 percent,
a gain of nine points and good enough for second place.[34] To
Hoffman, the Adair-Daly duo clearly was one of the few bright spots
on a darkening American urban landscape. "Things are really going
to pot here in Cleveland," he wrote in a monitoring report after
watching on the news "beatings, murder indictments, fraud indictments" and aftershocks from racial violence that had erupted in the
city's Hough district. "Doug is more of a straight man, whereas Joel
has more of a smile. . . . [They have] brought sanity [to] some very de-
pressing television," Hoffman reported.[35]

Yet WJW was not No. 1, something that in the new climate of TV
news it absolutely had to be. There was no mood for celebration with
WJW still trailing its main rival, WEWS. Then, McHugh & Hoffman
informed Storer of a new threat, the newscast on the third station,
KYW. In his monitoring trips in January 1964, Hoffman had noticed
on KYW the heaviest film coverage he had ever seen. But the films

were not the traditional talking heads of government officials. Instead, KYW was showing real news; if a fire, strike, protest demonstration or police manhunt had taken place, the viewer actually saw this. Not knowing what else to call it, McHugh & Hoffman had started referring to KYW's new style as the "you-are-there" approach.[36] Very soon, however, they would be consumed by the name KYW had given it. It appeared in Cleveland TV listings as "Eyewitness News."

"Eyewitness News" had begun two years earlier as a promotional handle for KYW's conventional man-on-camera newscasts. Because all that was new was the name, the debut of "Eyewitness News" in Cleveland in August 1962 caused few to take note.

However, changes had come rapidly beginning in January 1964 after Westinghouse brought to KYW a new news director named Al Primo. At KDKA in Pittsburgh Primo had been a backup newscaster and might have ventured into an on-air career, his affairs boosted by managers attesting to Primo's flair and charisma. Yet Primo was one of the few personalities to opt for the news director route. Primo's last duty at KDKA had been helping newscaster Bill Burns host four days of local coverage of the Kennedy assassination in November 1963. "I got to Cleveland just after Christmas and we started working on the newscast [with] shorter stories, more graphics, and a faster pace," Primo related. "It was the start of everyone saying, 'Something's happening.'"[37] Already in Cleveland, McHugh & Hoffman was intrigued, and the event marking Primo's exit from Pittsburgh was the reason.

Primo's "Eyewitness News" had been introduced at the very moment McHugh & Hoffman had been analyzing that study by SRI on the assassination, the one that had told of average people being spellbound by the TV news coverage the tragedy had inspired. Soon after this, in the next major Cleveland study in July 1964, the first findings on "Eyewitness News" arrived. Sparks flew up. It was plain that the four days of assassination coverage and Primo's "Eyewitness" concept were perceived much the same way. Indeed, in both studies the words "seeing it," "pictures," "real," "action," and "on-the-scenes" had been volunteered dozens of time. "Viewers remark with considerable frequency that the 'Eyewitness News' on Channel 3 [KYW] has been interesting." As one upper-lower class respondent put it, "They seem to do anything to get a good picture." "Seeing for yourself," another commented, "makes it easier to understand."[38]

Thus, just when the Adair-Daly combination had begun to take flight, WJW had another predicament. There were "complaints that Channel 8 [WJW] film has not had an appropriately dramatic effect," the July 1964 report continued. "I'd rather not comment on Channel 8," swore an upper-lower class male. "I want to say: I think their program could be a lot more interesting with more pictures."[39] With only one sound-recording film camera, Adair had tried to compensate by passing out Polaroid cameras. The photographs, as many as 50 per night, were then tacked to a large board. During the news, a studio camera panned from snapshot to snapshot.[40] Yet it was obvious from the research that this could not substitute for the action effect of taking viewers straight to the scene.

In 1964 "Eyewitness News" was a long way from what it later would become. Nevertheless, WJW had no choice but to "out-Eyewitness" the KYW effort, and Storer purse strings that kept getting looser greased the cause. "Cleveland is a city that responds to excitement in television and WJW-TV *must* be a more exciting station to watch," McHugh told new station manager Ken Bagwell.[41] In late 1964, Bagwell ordered a major staff expansion and sent Wagy, the new news director, on an equipment buying spree. The newsroom doubled to 20 people.[42] Previously, with only one film camera, WJW immediately had three. More cameras and a lot more people were on the way.[43] Bagwell rightly called it a "full court press."[44]

Yet one thing was unclear. Both KYW and WJW had just hired a half-dozen trained journalists who carried the title of "reporter." But under time-honored conventions of television they could not be seen on the air. Managers were skittish about exposing newsroom rank-and-file. To be on TV one had to be rich of voice, polished in appearance and look like a star. Another deterrent was the American Federation of Radio and Television Artists, a labor union that protected the then-very small fraternity of on-air talent.[45] In early 1965, Primo finally hired the first local field reporter, an out-of-work newscaster formerly of KTLA in Los Angeles named Tom Snyder. Yet even Snyder, who had an AFTRA card and later became a network personality, had to endure a battery of on-camera auditions.

The consultants pushed and pushed to get more reporters on the air. The research showed that average people didn't care what reporters looked like as long as their reports were interesting and believable. "For many viewers, particularly Lower-Middle and Upper-Lower class people," a 1967 study would state, "the most facilitating way to become involved in a news story and understand it, is to see and identify the people directly concerned." The report went on to point out, "The ability to relate and absorb information presented 'in the abstract' is generally dependent upon the degree of education . . . a person has had. Most people are simply not equipped to deal extensively with abstract material. They become interested in and understand things better by observing other people."[46] No practice would be deemed more integral in people's news than this technique called reporter involvement. WJW helped pioneer this by having Adair, Daly and soon several other reporters file filmed stories from the field.

Because WJW's was the first consulted newsroom, its staff had a rare amount of direct dialogue with the consultants. Later, in the 1960s and until the mid-1970s, consultants were known for communicating only with top managers. Adair and Daly liked the McHugh & Hoffman figures personally. According to Adair, "they tried to be one of us, not the stuffy social scientists we thought they were." Adair recalled hitting it off with both McHugh and Hoffman at a WJW social function.[47] Hoffman and Daly were Ivy Leaguers and from their experiences in the Army had many stories to tell.

But when sizing up the consultants from a professional standpoint, different feelings were aroused. "Quite honestly," in the view of Daly, "they didn't say anything Doug or I didn't already know. I think McHugh-Hoffman went out and sold a lot of our ideas."[48]

Storer's first major stride in news, and McHugh & Hoffman's first rags-to-riches TV news success story, culminated in a most unusual way. In June 1965 its rival, KYW, literally packed up and left town. This never-to-be-repeated episode, which many felt reflected the arrogance of big television, had begun in 1956. That year the Westinghouse station KYW actually had been located in Philadelphia, while the Channel 3 station in Cleveland had been owned by NBC. Because Philadelphia was a larger market, NBC had wanted Westinghouse's Philadelphia channel. The network held a gun to the head of Westinghouse and told that company it must either agree to trade the stations or lose its NBC affiliations. With no choice but to do as NBC said, Westinghouse moved KYW to Cleveland, while NBC bolted for Philadelphia. Incensed by this bullying tactic, Westinghouse took the matter to court. Finally in June 1965 U.S. Attorney General Nicholas Katzenbach signed an order allowing Westinghouse to reassume the station in Philadelphia.[49]

In a seemingly inexplicable scene, the management and main staff of Cleveland's KYW moved to Philadelphia. They included Primo, Snyder and an immensely popular weathercaster named Dick Goddard. The KYW call letters also transferred to the Pennsylvania city. In turn, a cadre of new news people who had been based in

Philadelphia came to Cleveland—to work for a TV station that after 1965 was owned by NBC. Much of this move had occurred in the span of a single weekend.

Although unheralded by the many opinion leaders who lavished the big networks, the Philadelphia-Cleveland station switch had been a milepost in the affairs of American television. All over the country local broadcasters were disillusioned by NBC's act and sympathetic to Westinghouse. Many felt that if a major network like NBC could beat up on one local broadcaster, it just as easily could beat up on another. It had been obvious NBC had ignored the needs of one of its local affiliates and had acted solely in its self-interest. Because it had taken the Justice Department to settle the dispute, broadcasters sensed for the first time that big television was not their friend.

Westinghouse was livid. That company's contempt of the network system would know no bounds. After winning this key battle with NBC, Westinghouse president Don McGannon immediately launched a campaign to limit the networks' domination of prime-time. McGannon's Prime-Time Access Rule, enacted in 1970, would be a bombshell for network newscasts because it gave local stations control of all but three hours of evening airtime. Not stopping with this, the angry yet energized Westinghouse would do even more damage back in Philadelphia by continuing to tinker with its "Eyewitness" concept until it became a clear alternative to network news.

In Cleveland, Storer was ecstatic. A memorable event for those at WJW was an all-night party Bagwell had thrown when word officially came that NBC was coming back to Cleveland. Westinghouse had been an imposing foe. WJW had learned through McHugh & Hoffman that, although blue collar Clevelanders sometimes had troubles understanding the news, they had a riveting impression of NBC from what had happened nine years earlier. It was "NBC to Cleveland: Go to hell." Because of the Justice Department, NBC had to return to the place where everyone knew it did not want to be. Viewers once loyal to Channel 3, renamed WKYC, flocked to WJW.

McHugh & Hoffman would prove its worth once again. Following two years of appeals to Buchanan and Bagwell that KYW's boyish Dick Goddard "is one of the most popular weathercasters we have ever seen," McHugh & Hoffman guaranteed that WJW, not his former station, the one now owned by NBC, would be Goddard's new home.[50] Sure enough, after six months in Philadelphia, Goddard wanted to return. New to Cleveland and without research to show Goddard's sweeping appeal, NBC just let him sign with WJW. The impact of eyewitness-style news coverage, the Adair-Daly combination and now Goddard was visible in the fall ratings of 1966. "City Camera" soared to a staggering "52" share.[51]

———————————————————————————

By the end of 1967, all of the Storer stations were headed for comparable ratings. Even WAGA in Atlanta would equal the "blowtorch of the South," WSB. Yet as had been the case in Cleveland, efforts elsewhere had been bathed in concerns. One morning in Detroit, McHugh received a telephone call from Storer executive Terry Lee, who did nothing but vent that "last night's news on WJBK was 1952 television, with its large Standard Oil signs [all over the set] . . . and no visuals for the first six minutes."[52] McHugh & Hoffman imported into Detroit WJW's plan from Cleveland. This included careful examination of one part of the FCC community ascertainment research, the ranking of community problems, which translated into the news content that was most on the minds of Detroiters. Because crime, violence and race relations were 1-2-3 on the Detroit list, WJBK was wired into those issues.[53]

Setting sights on the *Detroit News* TV station, WWJ, McHugh & Hoffman had WJBK adopt the name "Eyewitness News" and then introduce co-anchors. Using the research, McHugh & Hoffman then found out that the Walter Cronkite of Detroit, WWJ newscaster Dick Westerkamp, had serious liabilities. Detroit had a working class as large as Cleveland's. In it, Westerkamp was perceived as another Warren Guthrie, more as a professor than as a newscaster. Even though he was not as familiar, WJBK's own Jac LeGoff was better liked. To dramatize LeGoff's real-person appeal, he was paired with another likeable figure named John Kelly. Kelly, too, had more latent appeal than Westerkamp.[54]

The stage was set for the consultants' next blockbuster, although the pivotal event had historical importance far exceeding WJBK's affairs and those of television news. WJBK became Detroit's No. 1 station during the Detroit riots in July 1967. They were the worst civil disturbances in U.S. history up to that time. Forty died on the streets of Detroit, and thousands were injured and left homeless. McHugh & Hoffman had never let up in its demands that WJBK invest in more and more personnel and cameras, and these were deployed continuously, much the way the networks had covered the Kennedy assassination, for almost eight days.[55] WJBK's facilities were so sophisticated and its riot coverage so complete that Great Britain's BBC placed its satellite hookups at the Storer station. The coverage seen in Europe had come from WJBK.[56]

Then, incredibly, WWJ opted not to televise the event. WJBK and WXYZ, the last-place ABC station, had a scoop on the biggest story in Detroit history. "You had to hand it to [W]JBK for getting its act together," recalled Bob Bennett, a reporter at WWJ.[57] As it turned out, Bennett and his WWJ colleagues did film the riots, but they had been ordered by executives to keep this material off the air. According to some, those in executive suites had found the riots too disturbing. Later, though, WWJ did relent, and some coverage of the riots was seen.

Nevertheless, WWJ would pay dearly for this attempt to stay country club clean and above the fray. That average people had noticed was a main theme in the next SRI study. "I don't watch Channel 4 [WWJ] at all [any more]. They didn't do a complete job with the riots. Now we watch Channel 2 [WJBK]," an upper-lower male later told SRI. According to a lower-middle female, "I used to watch Channel 4, but I don't think their news is complete." According to a lower-middle female, "I changed over from Channel 4. They don't say if the person is colored or not. . . . If they are biased in this way, what about the other news." Glowing, though, was the middle majority's new-found acclaim for WJBK. "For any emergency, I'd go to Channel 2. I have confidence in them," an upper-lower female stated. "For anything about Detroit, Channel 2 is the best one. They tell you who you can call for help," stated another, while yet another volunteered that "Channel 2 is the best for news. They did a lot of on-the-spot interviews [during the riots and] I feel like I know all of the personalities."[58]

Interestingly, what was new to the middle majority meant little to the nation's media elite. WJBK and WXYZ were thanked by both Detroit's white and minority communities for their non-judgmental portrayals.[59] LeGoff and Kelly and WXYZ's Bill Bonds had remained in the studio around the clock for bulletins and special reports; locally, they were lauded for their calm and stabilizing demeanor.[60]

Even so, when the National Academy of Television Arts and Sciences decided the 1967 national Emmy Awards, WWJ was a winner. Based on a documentary on the riots produced long after the violence was quelled, WWJ received a citation for news excellence. Detroiters, though, wondered what these New York media experts had been smoking. "Far eclipsed was the effort . . . of WWJ," the Emmy Award winner, wrote Bettelou Peterson of the *Detroit Free Press*. Remarkably, all through the riots the station honored by the

TV Academy had run an "entertainment guide" in which an announcer had kept saying "Detroit is a swinging town."[61]

While only 8 percent of SRI's respondents felt WWJ had had the fairest coverage of Detroit, more than 50 percent had given this distinction to WJBK.[62] In the first ratings sweep after the riots, in November 1967, WJBK registered a 39 percent share, almost double the "23" it had just one year before. With ratings in the teens, WWJ was in ruins. Although they had just won a national Emmy award, numerous WWJ anchors, reporters and producers lost their jobs because of the plummeting ratings. Until LeGoff, Kelly and a host of WJBK news people were raided by WXYZ in the mid-1970s, the Storer station would command close to one-half of the Detroit news audience. Insiders knew it as "The Big Deuce."[63]

WJBK's approach differed not only from WWJ. Detroit viewers who had followed WJBK's reporting and had then stayed tuned to that same channel for the "CBS Evening News" weren't sure whether the same story was being treated. On July 28, 1967, the riot's fifth day, CBS covered Detroit from everywhere else, with 20 minutes of talking heads mostly from Washington, D.C. Attorney General Ramsey Clark, New York Mayor John Lindsay, Atlanta Mayor Ivan Allen, Illinois Governor Otto Kerner and Kentucky Senator Thruston Morton explained what the riots meant. Only a three-minute report late in the broadcast had gone to the streets and shown what had actually taken place.[64]

As a Detroiter himself, and as a person who during the riots had watched plumes of smoke from his office window, McHugh couldn't believe that CBS would cover the fracas in such a nebulous and detached manner. He stiffened. "The strength of [television news] is the drama of on-the-spot coverage," he would tell clients. Because of its "unwillingness or inability to accept the movement of television news programs out of their traditional mold . . . [n]etwork news viewing will suffer." Or as a lower-middle class research respondent had observed, "The most improved change [in television news] is the detailed news coverage and they have pictures of most local news items instead of having a guy sit at a desk and tell you about it."[65]

At Storer, the intervention of McHugh & Hoffman had had nothing short of a blast effect. With No. 1 local news ratings, Storer would report profits of $11.5 million on earnings of $65 million; its earnings-per-share of $2.75 in 1968 compared to $1.12 in 1962, the year McHugh & Hoffman and SRI joined.[66] "McHugh & Hoffman is considered by Storer a major asset," Terry Lee would affirm.[67]

It was good for McHugh & Hoffman that it wound up in the winner's circle. This was because its relationship with its only other clients, the CBS local TV stations, had soured. McHugh had hoped this local assignment would lead to a network-level contract, particularly because the research had begun to track middle majority restlessness with CBS's elite style of news. McHugh & Hoffman proposed to CBS the same innovations proven at Storer: co-anchors, visualization, more eyewitness coverage and even the "Eyewitness" name.

But CBS cast them aside. Tensions reached a breaking point at CBS's WBBM in Chicago, where McHugh had insisted on peopleizing aging yet potent newscaster Fahey Flynn and CBS wound up firing Flynn.

Finally, CBS terminated McHugh & Hoffman with a promise never to use news consultants again. McHugh exploded. A "gut-level approach is the antithesis of what CBS says it stands for," McHugh told CBS executives. "You've got a majority of the audience seeing the world and perceiving news differently than those trained to prepare the news. Generally, [a] decision is made by a group of upper-middle class people . . . who do not find out what the audience thinks. So a lot of martini drinkers [like you] decide what beer drinkers are supposed to like. It doesn't work out that way."[68]

Out in the street on network row, McHugh & Hoffman still wanted that network opportunity, which, fatefully, was just another door-knock away. With the two big networks turning their backs, an almost-network angel was waiting in the wings.

6

Eyewitness News (1967–1971)

The watershed development in the movement of people's news began just weeks after the Detroit riots, when McHugh & Hoffman entered another beleaguered domain: the local stations owned by ABC. A broadcast brimming with mass audience sparkle, one which stood out against newscasts stamped in the network tradition, again would propel a tremendous audience upheaval. This time, though, the impact was vastly more profound.

Introduced in Cleveland and matured in Philadelphia, the concept of "Eyewitness News" was finally defined in the nation's two largest cities, New York and Chicago, where viewers saw everything from action video and story-telling reporters to space-age studio sets and Madison Avenue razzle-dazzle. One of the most sweeping innovations ever to affect television news, that of having anchors abandon the serious newscaster pose and appear as real people—a technique that when first seen was labeled "happy talk"—gave this people's newscast inordinate mass audience appeal. Because it broke in New York and was identified with one of the big networks, news of its success spread rapidly. By 1971 more than 100 cities had "Eyewitness News." Eventually, because of news consultants, every city and virtually every station would have "Eyewitness News" whether they used that name or not.

Even Walter Cronkite, who had practically had to cover his eyes to watch, would conclude, grudgingly, that "Eyewitness News" had been a "seminal moment" in the history of broadcast journalism.[1]

This was true not just because, in form and substance, it was the new paradigm for television news. "Eyewitness News" drew together one of the most diverse and colorful groups of individuals ever to come forward in the TV field. Among them was Marshall McLuhan, who was captivated by "Eyewitness News" and considered what he called the million-person "news of the neighborhood" the fulfillment of journalism on the "cool" medium of TV. Meanwhile, "Eyewitness News" was a determinant in do-or-die corporate stakes; this at what experts then called the "Almost Broadcasting Company." "Eyewitness News" rescued an ABC on the brink of bankruptcy. No venture in television news, network or local, ever made more money. That news consultants were involved cemented their stature in the industry.

The main event, though, was the beginning of the end of the broadcast news establishment. "Eyewitness News" fed off the energy of ABC insurgents full of contempt for the big and great figures at NBC and CBS. They were baby boomers entering adulthood during an epic period of dissent, protest, and generation gap. They were convinced the prevailing model of television news had been ordained in NBC and CBS news divisions by comfortable and out-of-touch old men. As baby boomers in the contentious late 1960s they savvied the phrase "power to the people," which pleased the consultants. From a trajectory that had taken them from Bugs Bunny to newsrooms, they knew TV; "Eyewitness News" was, literally, the TV news of the TV generation.

The synergy from these varied elements created in ABC local newsrooms a revolutionary esprit d' corps. It soared the moment the insurgents realized they had the establishment in a rout. The ABC-owned stations went on to score not measured but Carthaginian ratings victories over CBS and NBC. Nothing in the annals of television had been more inexplicable, decisive, and influential.

All this had taken shape in the 1960s, a decade celebrated for the many spirits who hadn't just seen things the way they were and asked "Why?" They were moved by Irish playwright George Bernard Shaw and John and Robert Kennedy who in using Shaw's words had seen things "that never were" and asked "Why not?" A fellow Irishman named Richard O'Leary had been among them. The general manager of ABC's sputtering Chicago TV station, O'Leary questioned why television news always looked like a liturgical rite. With Americans polarized by the war in Vietnam, urban areas in ruins and students in a state of revolution, O'Leary could not fathom how newscasters could sit in a TV studio stone-cold, solemn and emotionless while the nation was falling apart. The networks were beyond figuring.

But even in Chicago, CBS-owned WBBM and NBC-owned WMAQ had newscasts that almost seemed surreal. Just two minutes of WBBM news, with stone-faced Fahey Flynn, was enough to give O'Leary the creeps. Even the young Floyd Kalber, who had just brought ratings gains to WMAQ, looked to O'Leary like a Delphian oracle. As he studied Flynn and Kalber, O'Leary could not escape an image of ancient Greece. "Everybody watched CBS and NBC, and what you saw were newscasters who communicated to the people as if they were standing on the top of Mt. Olympus," O'Leary observed.[2] O'Leary was conjuring what no one had: completely level communication in which the newscaster and the viewer were equal.

O'Leary's station, WBKB, was part of an outfit that really was an almost broadcasting company. Having started as the cast-off NBC Blue radio network in 1943, ABC had foundered ever since. O'Leary had joined WBKB in 1966 at the beginning of ABC's darkest period. A cipher in the Nielsen ratings, ABC had just been saddled with a $100 million conversion to color TV. It didn't have the money.

While O'Leary had been sizing up the situation in Chicago, a development that would be intertwined with "Eyewitness News" had been unfolding at ABC headquarters in New York. To raise desperately needed cash, ABC chair Leonard Goldenson had begun negotiations with the giant International Telephone and Telegraph corporation for the sale of ABC to ITT. To Goldenson, who knew ABC was vulnerable to a hostile takeover and that the company would be dismembered should such a raid take place, the proposed ITT merger was crucial. Goldenson had extracted a commitment from ITT that his own job would be preserved and that ABC would remain completely intact. Further, the negotiations had confirmed for Goldenson that ITT had its priorities straight.

ITT had little interest in ABC's hapless network operations. What the big firm wanted were the licenses to ABC's five local TV stations, which in addition to Chicago's WBKB had included WABC in New York, KABC in Los Angeles, KGO in San Francisco, and WXYZ in Detroit. Although these stations numbered only five, they were, on paper, one of the greatest engines of profit in the entire broadcast industry. Not even CBS and NBC had a more promising local station group. ABC's television stations were located in five of the six largest markets. Their book value carried a premium because they all operated on Channel 7. ITT was hesitating because they were under-performing where it counted, at the bank.

Indeed, despite their immense potentials, the ABC-owned stations were considered an industry joke. The Chicago station was the worst of the lot. Not only was WBKB a distant No. 3 in most time periods, WBKB's newscasts, anchored by the strict Frank Reynolds, had been No. 4 in the Chicago ratings, behind even independent station WGN.[3] O'Leary realized that with the exception of "Bewitched," ABC had no hit shows and that local news was the only program that allowed a solution. Under his close friend and mentor Elton Rule, the general manager of KABC, O'Leary had risen at ABC's Los Angeles station by selling advertising against KNXT and its "Big News." O'Leary had been awed by "The Big News" and, like Robert Wood, its inventor, felt local news was the best way for a local station to leave its mark. Shortly after arriving in Chicago and discerning the mess at WBKB, O'Leary befriended Morry Roth, a lead writer for the influential trade newspaper *Variety,* which in March detailed O'Leary's first planned step, "two newscasters instead of one."[4]

Immediately, O'Leary was opposed. The news director warned that co-anchors had been attempted without success at WGN. Meanwhile, since the recent departure to ABC News of Reynolds, a saint to those inside WBKB, the station had continued with a single newscaster. Many clamored that it should stay that way.

O'Leary could not be dissuaded. On O'Leary's mind was his "Olympus" metaphor and his disdain for anchors like Flynn and Kalber who seemed to be preaching from a mountaintop. "We are going to have a newscast that gives you the core of the family" with "two average guys who can project their own reality and reflect the tenor of the times." He went on, insisting, "The average person is disoriented by war, violence, unresponsive politicians and rebellious, drug-loving youth." And "Who are these 'hippies'?" O'Leary wanted to know. The point being that "CBS and NBC are stuck in the cement. But we have the chance to face the new world."[5]

A young news director more on O'Leary's wave length, Bill Fyffe, was hired.[6] O'Leary then went ahead with the construction of a modular studio set that would fit not just the two newscasters but eventually the weather and sportscasters. It was small but because of its modular form had sort of a "space age" look. It was a stark contrast to the everyday office furniture that WBBM and WMAQ were still using.

At first Chicago viewers saw empty chairs. According to O'Leary, "I was of no mind to put just anybody in those seats. We needed two regular guys who could communicate the news like a family," requirements not easy to fulfill as O'Leary found out during nationwide talent searches. Holed up in hotel rooms with rating books in one hand and a TV remote control in the other, O'Leary scrutinized three dozen local newscasters, finding them all as cold and distant as the ones on CBS and NBC. Then his fortunes changed. O'Leary happened onto a television station whose newscasters looked different, as if someone was instructing them to keep off Olympus.

Someone was. The newscasters O'Leary discovered were the ones at WJW in Cleveland. It had been at WJW in 1963 that Doug Adair and Joel Daly, behind the urging of McHugh & Hoffman, had instituted TV's first co-anchor news format. O'Leary escaped from Chicago to Cleveland on more occasions. On one of the reconnaissance trips, WJW had carried a "mini-documentary," a night-after-night series, this one showing Adair and Daly in each other's homes and demonstrating how "bachelors" could take care of their families while their wives were away.[7] O'Leary had seen enough. "What you had were these two young men, both products of the genuine Midwest, who were like your brothers," he related.

O'Leary finally invited Adair and Daly to Chicago. What amounted to an audition consisted of informal chatting in O'Leary's office. Amazed to discover that Adair and Daly were as personable in real life as they were on television, O'Leary offered them the vacant anchor chairs right on the spot. Daly accepted the offer but Adair didn't, believing the move too risky.[8] In August 1967, Daly took over at WBKB and for six more months hosted the news next to a still-empty seat. "For awhile, I didn't think they were ever going to find anybody else," Daly related.[9]

When they did, it was part of a tempest the likes of which Chicago had seldom seen.

O'Leary's missing link turned out to be Fahey Flynn. In another landmark episode in people's news, Flynn left CBS-owned WBBM and joined Daly at WBKB when CBS refused to permit Flynn to appear on camera with a bow-tie. Flynn had worn them for almost 15 years. Bow-ties, though, ran afoul of CBS decrees that conventional ties were best. To keep his job at WBBM, Flynn relinquished the bow-ties. This did not stop thousands of viewers from calling both WBBM and CBS headquarters. These complaints made no sense to the CBS experts in New York.

But to the people of Chicago the removal of Flynn's bow-tie was as if someone had come in and torn down Wrigley Field. Press reaction that had begun in gossip columns gradually made its way to the front pages of Chicago newspapers. As the controversy intensified, reporters learned the truth, that Flynn had not willingly given up the bow-ties but instead felt naked without them.[10]

It didn't matter that Flynn was a rival and, worse, an Olympian. At WBKB, O'Leary detonated when he read about Flynn's emasculation by WBBM. "CBS is the epitome of snobbism," O'Leary raved. He telephoned Flynn at his home "to tell him, one Irishman to another, that if he came to WBKB he wouldn't have to suffer any more humiliation." All of a sudden, O'Leary had a new take on Flynn, as a human being, not the on-air automaton CBS with its codes and policies obviously was forcing him to be. Poignant conversations, including one in which Flynn disclosed that his only reason for staying at WBBM was to provide for his large family, moved O'Leary. Still, it seemed unlikely that Flynn "would leave the mighty CBS and come to our gnat of an outfit," or that he could. Flynn was tied to a six-year CBS contract with a renewal option.

Ultimately, events turned not on WBBM's snobbishness but its naiveté. With public opinion on his side, Flynn and his agent approached WBBM about reassessing the bow-ties. Then, according to Flynn's wife, the WBBM general manager just "showed him the door."[11] Flynn's account of this meeting imparted a lasting impression on O'Leary, who grew determined to "bring those CBS s.o.b.s to their knees." CBS gave O'Leary the means for doing exactly that. In its rush to dump Flynn, WBBM voided Flynn's contract including a "noncompete" provision that would have required Flynn to stay off the air in Chicago for one year should he be hired by a competitor.[12] WBBM's hasty action meant Flynn could start at WBKB immediately. There was a stir in Chicago and more glowing publicity on February 12, 1968, when viewers no longer could find the veteran newscaster on Channel 2, but instead saw him utter his signature "How do you do, ladies and gentlemen. I'm Fahey Flynn" alongside Daly on Channel 7.[13] The bow-tie was back.

By this time, the contract between ABC and McHugh & Hoffman had been signed. In chapter and verse, O'Leary wanted to know everything McHugh knew about Flynn. McHugh turned over SRI's private work-up on Flynn, current as of 1967. "While weak in the 'under 30' group," it read, "Fahey Flynn holds a substantial lead [over Kalber] in the following categories: 'most informed about national news,' 'most informed about local news,' 'knows most about Chicago,' 'best personality,' 'most sincere,' and 'most interesting to listen to.'"[14] In short, Flynn was one of the most powerful newscasters McHugh & Hoffman had ever examined. Indeed, in an interview 11 years later, Flynn recalled being besieged by telephone calls and letters from jubilant Chicago TV viewers incensed at CBS, who told him, "You have struck a blow for freedom."[15] Two weeks after moving to WBKB, Flynn permitted Clay Gowran of the *Chicago Tribune* to look through his four-inch-thick stack of letters. "This is the nicest break the people of Chicago have had in a long time," someone wrote. According to another, "I have switched to 7 after years with 2." Yet another told Flynn, "The bow-tie looks great on channel 7. Long may it wave."[16]

O'Leary wasn't finished. After recruiting another WBBM reject, weathercaster John Coleman, O'Leary put on a finishing touch by dressing Flynn, Daly, Coleman, and sportscaster Bill Frink in blazers, each adorned with WBKB's logo, a simple white "7" on a blue field outlined in white by a circle. Borrowed from KGO, the circle-7 logo would become an emblem of "Eyewitness News." O'Leary claimed to have never coached them. Yet throughout the ABC stations newscasters would recall "prayer meetings" with O'Leary. "I told each of them to 'be yourself' [and] not worry about structure. 'The classic core of society is the family,'" O'Leary instructed. "'That is what I want you to be.'"[17] The WBKB news team gelled and surpassed even O'Leary's expectations.

To an extent never before seen in a television newscast, the four figures chatted with one another, shared parts of their daily lives and informally reacted to the events they reported. Smiles and levity were displayed with abandon. One of hundreds of early examples occurred on the very first night, when Flynn and Daly appeared in tuxedos so they could jab CBS and its oppressive dress code.[18]

Again dressed in tuxedos and with champagne and cakes, the news team would mark each anniversary of their first newscast. In one celebration that caught Coleman without this attire, Flynn opened the newscast by remarking, "We're all wearing tuxedos except John. He overslept." It was ten o'clock at night. After a pregnant pause in which Flynn looked over and glared at Coleman, laughter could be heard off screen among the technicians in the studio, a trademark of the concept.[19]

A different gambit materialized when *Life* magazine carried a picture from Chicago's raucous 1968 Democratic convention mistakenly identifying members of a WBKB news crew as an "Army surveillance team." Daly held up the magazine, pointed to the picture, and spoofed, "That crew has been placed under house arrest and advised they are required to give only their name, rank, and serial number!"[20]

Ongoing were the barbs of Flynn, Daly, and Frink relating to Coleman's apparent troubles in spelling words correctly on the weather maps. Actually, Coleman was a master with these maps and an originator of a device called "chroma-key," which allowed him to superimpose his own image over them. Nevertheless, Coleman's spelling disability came to light in October 1968, when one of the

news items was WBKB's name change to "WLS." O'Leary had decided that WBKB "were bad call letters from a bad era at Channel 7."
The station was known as WLS from then on. "Three letters, John,
should make it easier for you," Flynn intoned.[21]

Flynn maintained that nothing was artificial. "With one sentence
on television, you can sometimes do what it might take a minute and
a half elsewhere," he would sum up. "It's the McLuhan factor, that is,
the extension of the media. The reality to the guy at home."[22]

The on-set conversation, unimaginable in TV news up to this
time, had offered Chicago viewers a transparent alternative to
Kalber's approach on WMAQ. Once pegged as a lively new force in
Chicago journalism, Kalber, according to the research, now was per-
ceived as delivering news in a paleozoic fashion. "Channel 5
[WMAQ] appeals to those who would not feel comfortable with the
youthful exuberance of Channel 7," an SRI report had confirmed.[23]
Flynn was 52 years old.

WLS had 12 percent of the audience in November 1967 on the
eve of the Flynn-Daly debut. One year later WLS was up to a "25"
and would hit "29" in November 1969. Kalber's numbers had gone
from "45" to "41" and then to "36." In February 1970, after another
gain by WLS and another five-point loss by WMAQ, the two stations
were even at "31." Finally in 1971, Chicago's "Eyewitness News"
would claim undisputed leadership with shares eventually in the for-
ties.[24] As NBC continued its nosedive in Chicago, the CBS station,
WBBM, plummeted into the teens.[25] Flynn was delighted; the CBS executive who fired him would be starting a new career—in
condominium conversions.[26]

In the February 11, 1970, issue of *Variety*, O'Leary's friend Morry
Roth wrote, "'Happy talk' news on WLS-TV—purposely treating
news in a light-handed manner—is creating a massive news rating
dustup in Chicago that could have reverberations throughout the
country." It would, and Roth's phrase christening this concept—
"happy talk"—was permanently affixed in TV news lexicon. In the
same article, Roth trumpeted the tripling of the WLS audience and
linked this to the same "silent majority" Vice President Spiro Agnew
in 1969 attacks on network news had claimed the networks totally ignored. Roth felt Agnew was on to something. While "NBC News
prexy Reuven Frank . . . was still defending the tradition of Good
Gray 'do-gooder' News, [ABC] has shrewdly managed to steer the
shoals between sobriety and silliness. . . . [I]t is not that Flynn-Daly
are so much more giddy than their competitors, but that they are so
much less dull."

Immortalizing not just his term but also O'Leary's, Roth proclaimed, "They [have] shattered the Olympian approach."[27]

ABC's two-city people's news advance had an unusual geographic symmetry. In Chicago, a broad-shouldered hard news locale, WLS had struck with personalities. Yet in New York, a mecca to the stars, WABC would pull the newscast's other developmental lever, content and structure.

Events in New York began the first day of 1968, with a bombshell delivered to ABC headquarters. ITT wanted out of that merger. O'Leary's initiatives in Chicago were not going to be enough. To avert a hostile takeover by billionaire Howard Hughes, ABC had to show improvement in New York, where the financial community was located. With ABC now cutting every budget and laying off staff, it was another desperate situation. Because ABC's network shows were still being whipsawed in the Nielsen ratings by CBS and NBC, local news again offered the only solution.

Nevertheless, ABC executives shivered to think their survival would depend on a WABC newscast. WABC had gone 14 years without a local newscast and would not initiate a news program until 1962, when Bill Beutel arrived from Cleveland. In 1968 WABC trailed two independent stations, including pioneer WPIX, and was in fifth place. In a different league and solidly in second place was the WCBS local newscast, anchored by radio-age news veteran Robert Trout. Yet since the 1950s, NBC's WNBC had towered over this market. WNBC's "Eleventh Hour News" with Frank McGee was reaching 35 percent of New Yorkers. On a good night, WABC hit "12."

Drawing a deep breath, WABC general manager Richard Beesemyer began that winter by giving a hearty welcome to McHugh & Hoffman and then by postponing its first research study. Too much had to be ironed out. One issue stemmed from the departure of Beutel, who had transferred to London as a correspondent for ABC's network news. This had meant the hiring of a new main newscaster, Roger Grimsby, who had been the news director and the newscaster at San Francisco's KGO. Grimsby took the job in New York as not just the new anchor but, as he recalled, the next news director of WABC. Beesemyer, though, had penciled in someone else.

It was Al Primo. In July 1968, Beesemyer flew to Miami and upon telling Primo "save my ass" offered him the job. The moment was

989898989898989898989898989898989898989898989898989898989898989898989898989898989898989898989898989898 Chapter 6

awkward. Primo was in Miami coordinating coverage of the Republican national convention for stations in the Westinghouse group. Westinghouse had committed more resources to the 1968 conventions than the entire ABC network. Primo turned Beesemyer down. The only advantage Primo could see was the chance to work in New York. Yet it was not worth $15,000 per year, Beesemyer's paltry salary offer.[28]

By 1968, Primo knew he was worth more. A lot had happened in the three years since he'd taken "Eyewitness News" from Cleveland to Philadelphia in the Westinghouse-NBC switch of 1965. Still the news director of KYW, Primo's big feat was breaking resistance and unveiling TV's first on-camera reporting team, with reporters allowed to actually appear on TV. The Philadelphia station had been No. 1 in every rating book since 1959, a year after newscaster Vince Leonard was recruited from WISH in Indianapolis. Although a competing newscaster named John Facenda had had a larger public profile in Philadelphia, Leonard's newscasts had never relinquished first place.[29] Primo got his way with his "team reporting" idea after finding a loophole in KYW's AFTRA union contract. An obscure clause in this contract had stated that any KYW employee could perform if there was an "important" news event. Primo simply defined every news event as "important" and then put the reporters on the air.

The morale boost was exceptional and historic, as for the first time the newsroom's little guy—the person with an unvarnished voice and rustic face—was seen. Yet contretemps were ongoing. Only veteran Tom Snyder, who had had anchoring experience, could look into a camera and communicate extemporaneously. The others, noted Primo, "all went out and got clipboards." After watching the fledglings read their prepared copy from these clipboards, Primo ordered them banished. "What we want is you talking to the viewer, not to your clipboard," Primo said. The KYW reporters took to this and soon were turning scoop stories.

Just before his contacts with Beesemyer, Primo's newscast had a "38" share and had seriously destabilized Facenda's station, WCAU, which was owned by CBS.[30] That was meaningful to Beesemyer. When the July 1968 ratings showed KYW's "Eyewitness News" with close to a "40" and WABC with a "10," Beesemyer made another pitch. "We had a terrible local news in New York," he conceded, whereas in Philadelphia, "'Eyewitness News' was creeping into their [CBS's] knickers." Beesemyer's hope was that if CBS could be stopped in Philadelphia the same might happen in New York. As for Primo, "I liked his youth, I liked his aggressiveness, and I liked his looks. He was dapper and had an air about him," Beesemyer observed. "We needed someone with no loyalty to the establishment who could come in and tell everybody, 'Let's quit being the other guys.'"[31] Beesemyer got his man by doubling the salary offer.

Still, as Primo expected, facilities at WABC were ramshackle. Meanwhile, a confrontation came when Primo passed out matching blue blazers with the circle-7 logo. The blazers meant that Tex Antoine, one of the great gimmick weathercasters formerly of WNBC—and who with sportscaster Howard Cosell were the only well-known personalities WABC had—had to give up his artist's smock. Antoine protested until Primo announced, "Either we all wear blazers or we all wear smocks."[32]

Left after a housecleaning was a contingent of young people seeking leadership and who were touched by the period's social upheaval. They were certain CBS and NBC were reporting the 1960s from an ivory tower, and that despite its "big" and "great" image, the establishment did not understand television or news.

Don Dunphy, Jr., and Al Ittleson had been drifting at WABC. The same was true of Melba Tolliver, one of New York's first minority reporters who a year earlier had been a WABC secretary. Steve Skinner, Ron Tindiglia, and Peter Jacobus particularly reeled against the comfort and conformism in New York TV news, local and network. In Skinner's opinion, "They were just throwing up newscasts night by night."[33] According to Tolliver, "We were a group of people who were at an age when we wanted meaning behind the experience of being in television. We didn't just want to go through the motions."[34] Ittleson felt this ensemble was not rebellious, just untarnished. "We weren't tainted with the New York-NBC-CBS way of doing things," he would note.[35]

Nor in their minds could they have been. Because they were in their twenties, wore long hair and identified with the Rolling Stones, not Mitch Miller, they knew they had no chance of getting a job at CBS or NBC. Some, including Tolliver, felt this way because they were women and minorities. "'Eyewitness News' was not a political statement," Primo would state, "but it was running along the same path. It was rocking the traditional boat. . . . The time for 'Eyewitness News' was then."[36]

The impetus behind WABC's "Eyewitness News" was the image these newsworkers had of hordes of New Yorkers disenfranchised by the type of news then on the air. The reporters accepted the *New York Daily News*—not the *New York Times*—as must-reading. The tabloid newspaper was a link to New York's disaffected masses. Dunphy, Ittleson, Tindiglia and Skinner directed the effort. Milton Lewis covered government; Bob Lape, politics; Bill Aylward, the draft and military activities relating to the Vietnam War; Bob Miller, New Jersey events; and John Schubeck, the entertainment scene. All saw themselves as ombudsmen for New York's working class.

Reaching out from the Bronx to Brooklyn, it was as if the middle part of Manhattan, where power concentrated, had been airbrushed off the map of New York. "The people of New York had no voice," Tindiglia stated. Institutions were breaking down, government was indifferent and politicians cared only about reelection. "We modeled our appeal on the *New York Daily News*," only with television "we [could be] people speaking to people." In the newsroom, minds met and a philosophy of people's news ascended. "We knew what 'Eyewitness News' was and what it was not," Tindiglia related. "It had to be people. We looked at our own work" and during self-criticism sessions, when a WABC story had an establishment tinge, "we would sit in the newsroom and say, 'That's not Eyewitness News, is it?'"[37]

"Eyewitness News" premiered in New York on November 28, 1968, and not just the content was different. Against a budget of nickels and dimes, and like high school students building a homecoming float, Primo's crew fashioned a sophisticated studio set. Wanting an upbeat and spacious musical theme but with no money to compose one, someone located appropriate sounds in the 1967 motion picture *Cool Hand Luke*. A WABC audio engineer cut up several components and then spliced them back together into a moving rendition. *Cool Hand Luke* soon would become another signature of "Eyewitness News" not just in New York but all over the country.

Grimsby opened with his "Here now the news" on a huge set, to his left the weather maps and apparatus used by Antoine and the seat where Cosell delivered the sports. To Grimsby's right was a three-tier platform that seated the reporters. In full view of the audience, they walked onto the set while the music played. Grimsby introduced the reporters, who in turn introduced their filmed stories. Then, Grimsby asked followup questions. At the end, while the theme music again was heard, studio cameras captured the personalities interacting with one another.[38]

Rarely was there a report on a governmental board or commission that did not also show the reactions of the average people affected. Reporters who let politicians dominate their reports were told by Tindiglia and others to "go work for CBS or NBC." The first year of "Eyewitness News" had featured the first known films of an actual auto theft shot by photographers hiding in parking lots, an interview with an accused murderer just minutes after her acquittal and a seven-part series on medical fraud recorded with hidden cameras.[39] In February 1969, "Eyewitness News" went undercover for the first video look at New York's 25,000 working prostitutes and how an above-the-fray attitude by politicians was inducing not just vice but a burgeoning narcotics industry.[40] WABC exposés led to the jailing of an assistant to the borough president in the Bronx, while endless coverage of sordid housing conditions regularly led to improvements.

Lacking resources, few of the reports were polished. Sometimes reporters let the film roll and just talked the viewer through the event being seen. *New York* writer Paul Klein called it the "wind-in-the-hair" technique. "The reporter stands on the Brooklyn Bridge, where the police emergency squad has just wrapped a bowline around a would-be jumper, and the reporter leans into the breeze to tell you what the cops told him."[41] In late 1969, "Eyewitness News" would exclusively telecast extended courtroom testimony of Joseph Serpico, who exposed corruption in the New York police department.

The most unusual feature of "Eyewitness News" was the visibility of women and minorities. While WABC would not appoint a female main anchor until 1978, Primo and WABC were the first in TV news to give women and minorities definitive on-air exposure. Gil Noble anchored the weekend "Eyewitness News," while Tolliver and colleague John Johnson were pivots in the newscast with Grimsby. Primo's best-known "Eyewitness" reporter would be Geraldo Rivera, who had worked for a legal aid service in Harlem and like most of Primo's employees had no news experience. "With the rest of the business comfortably white bread, Channel 7 decided to become seeded rye," Rivera recounted. "I never thought of Al Primo as a champion of social change and equal opportunity . . . but his hiring practices undeniably made him one."[42]

Eventually better known in New York than even Rivera was a former human rights commissioner with a master's degree in sociology named Rose Ann Scamardella. "Social class was not [just] something I studied in school but was my whole experience. I was an Italian woman from Brooklyn . . . [and] that's how I got to be a commissioner," she would relate. "Primo knew I was someone Italians would trust." Moreover, "I was a total liberal" and joined WABC "because I hoped to change things." Still, recalling "incredible energy" and "everyone . . . giving 100 percent," Scamardella "didn't expect it to last."[43]

It almost hadn't. WABC had had a "9" when "Eyewitness News" started in November 1968. It was up to an "11" one year later.[44]

Whether it should continue suddenly became an issue that would divide the highest echelons of ABC. Starting a people's newscast in Cleveland or Philadelphia was one thing. Much different was bringing this oddity to New York, the capital of American television, where feeling ran high that ABC was making a fool of itself.

Because it was sending the wrong signals to the financial community, Goldenson, the ABC chair, did not favor the broadcast. Goldenson, though, had just named Elton Rule as ABC network president, and the young Rule liked "Eyewitness News." Beesemyer as well had just won a promotion to the network level and would urge Goldenson to let WABC press on.

The opposition was formidable and was led by the person in the best position to pull the plug, Theodore Shaker, the president of the ABC-owned stations. A former sales wunderkind at CBS, Shaker had come to ABC in a move that most thought would land him the company's top spot. Yet as owned-stations president, Shaker's ambitions collided with those of Rule, the network president. When Goldenson intervened and sided with Rule, Shaker resigned. For those backing "Eyewitness News," it was as if the wicked witch was dead. "Elton, Leonard, O'Leary—we all knew you had to be different," Beesemyer explained, but "Shaker tried to be disruptive. . . . He loved CBS [and] said, 'That's what we have to be.' . . . I want to emphasize: Al Primo was skating on thin ice. Whenever Ted saw 'Eyewitness News,' it drove him crazy."[45]

Even so the low ratings could not be ignored. When Beesemyer advanced to the network level, Ken McQueen became the WABC general manager. Although another supporter of the broadcast, McQueen had begun pondering alternative plans should "Eyewitness News" not pan out. Then in mid-1969 attitudes changed. Good news had struck.

It came in the arrival of McHugh & Hoffman's first research on "Eyewitness News," which Beesemyer, fortuitously as it turned out, had delayed. McHugh & Hoffman's 210-page report, circulated at the peak of the dispute, was a ringing endorsement of "Eyewitness News." McHugh & Hoffman had placed interviewers in more than 800 New York homes. It was apparent from what the respondents had said that a ratings tempest was about to catapult WABC. "'Eyewitness News' brings you into the news. They take me through New York via pictures. It's interesting and easily understood," an upper-lower class female stated. Stressing that "seeing is believing, . . . I like the way they operate on this channel," another volunteered. According to an upper-lower male, "'Eyewitness News' is good because it isn't second-hand information. They take you there so it's more informative." Fifty-one percent had noticed "positive" changes, and 30 percent had identified them with WABC. These numbers were exceptional. "Eyewitness News" had been on the air for only six months. Nine out of 10 New Yorkers had not watched WABC's news when the "Eyewitness" experiments had first begun.[46]

Shaker's departure as president of ABC's owned stations had not just resolved ABC's executive suite battle for power between Shaker and Rule. For local TV news it had even greater consequences because Rule got to pick Shaker's replacement. The person Rule selected was his close friend O'Leary.

O'Leary's move to ABC headquarters, as the progenitor of "happy talk" at Chicago's WLS but now as the company's third-in-command, heralded a momentous period in American television. Under O'Leary and with Primo's hand, ABC would brand the people's newscast. It was installed at the other ABC-owned stations, and all would become No. 1. With only break-even net revenues in 1969, the five ABC stations would generate more than $1 billion in profits between 1970 and 1983, the 13 years O'Leary was in charge. Around 60 percent of these profits had come from local news. According to Goldenson, this was what finally saved ABC. "Without the success of our owned and operated stations," Goldenson explained years later, "we never would have had any chance."[47]

As O'Leary recalled, "Leonard and Elton told me to do at the other stations everything I'd done at WLS." He would not let them down.

O'Leary had arrived at "1330," ABC's headquarters on New York's Avenue of the Americas, in February 1970. He immediately began what was called a "cross-pollenization" of the techniques from WLS and WABC. It was at this point that WLS adopted the name "Eyewitness News," originally known as the "Flynn Daly News." With McHugh & Hoffman's assistance, Chicago viewers of WLS also saw the team reporting concept of Primo.[48] Then O'Leary delivered the "real person" newscaster model from Chicago to New York.

O'Leary's down-from-Olympus design proved a major development at the New York station, and the one which finally lifted the ratings. The New York research had been critical of WABC anchor Roger Grimsby. To viewers, Grimsby had allowed himself to be overshadowed by the many reporters. Some felt he was "bottled up." Rather than proposing that Grimsby be replaced, the consultants urged a showcase co-anchor arrangement. McHugh's recommendation was to recruit a new anchor who could be a "straight man" to Grimsby and, thus, relieve Grimsby of some of the pressure.

"Anything less than strong personalities would mean an effective non-news status for Channel 7," McHugh & Hoffman insisted.[49]

Knowing of no other anchor in New York, network or local, that they wanted on their news, O'Leary, McQueen, and Primo hit on the idea of pairing Grimsby with Beutel, the original anchor of WABC. Beutel came back from London. Then the prayer meetings began. Thinking O'Leary a crazy man, Grimsby and Beutel listened as intently as choir boys as O'Leary preached person-to-person communication, conversational delivery and informality. Antoine, the weathercaster, was so loose that he easily went along, and Cosell and O'Leary instantly clicked. Cosell, one of TV's most controversial figures, always showed his real side.

Yet for old-school news veterans like Grimsby and Beutel, one a former news director, the other a former foreign correspondent, resistance was instinctual. "He wanted you to get down off Olympus and give up your elitism as a newscaster," Grimsby would recall. "You were supposed to see one of your neighbors and give the news in a way that showed you cared. He'd talk your ear off about this."[50] Beutel was downright suspicious. "People didn't appreciate how hard it was for us older anchors to adapt to being yourself," Beutel recalled. It was not long, though, before they realized O'Leary was right. Beutel felt "local news [was] special because each day you lived the events along with every person in the audience. It took us a long time to understand that if there was a snowstorm, you shared that experience with the viewer. There was no need to pontificate like the networks because you weren't a thousand miles away."[51]

Grimsby and Beutel conquered happy talk and as fixtures in the nation's largest market for 16 more years, and as the people who would bring down Olympus in the city where it soared, they were the two most influential newscasters local television ever would produce. O'Leary's directives had their greatest effect on Grimsby, who had had a reserved and thorny personality that conformed to New York. He was the closest any newscaster ever approached to the Howard Beale character in the 1976 motion picture *Network*. He saw life as unfair and was as "mad as hell." But rather than saying "I'm not going to take this anymore," Grimsby reached the audience by signalling "We're in this chaos together." Also liberated was the stiff and pompous network persona of Beutel, who revealed an easy-going real-life side. The altered dynamics of "Eyewitness News" were irresistible across the many diverse communities and within the complex cosmopolitan working class that characterized New York.

There was little of the homespun interaction seen in Chicago. "What came natural for me were comments," Grimsby related. Genuine, for example, was the disdain Grimsby felt for Cosell, who had cold-shouldered Grimsby as a speck from San Francisco and unworthy of a position in New York, when Grimsby had arrived from KGO. One night Grimsby struck back by pretending to be asleep on the news set when Cosell finished his sports report. In another episode Grimsby remarked, "You know, Howard, I don't mind being your pigeon since you are such a big statue in the sports world."[52]

The barbs were not limited to exchanges between Grimsby and Cosell. After saying "Secretary of State" in a story about the Middle East, Grimsby's teleprompter broke down. When from off camera Beutel finished Grimsby's sentence by whispering "Henry Kissinger," the studio erupted. But it was rare when Grimsby didn't get the last laugh. After a story about a two-headed turtle that concluded with Grimsby's line, "And both heads like each other off camera as well as on," the others howled. Grimsby was making fun of a WABC promotional campaign, being seen all over the city, that conveyed the same message about him and Beutel, that "they liked each other off camera as well as on."[53]

Following a story about a boy who died from a disease that made him age at eight times the normal rate, Grimsby quipped, "At that rate he must have been frustrated by the time he was two and a half."[54] On his twenty-fifth anniversary as a New York weathercaster, Antoine was stopped in the middle of his forecast and presented a cake in the shape of a weather map. To complete the ceremony before the newscast ended, Grimsby demanded, "Hurry up! Tex wants to eat Florida!" Antoine was so vanquished by laughter than an obscenity slipped out and hundreds of phone calls came in.[55] While Grimsby's remarks offended many, it was Antoine who finally crossed the line. His career ended the night of November 24, 1976, when Grimsby finished a story about the rape of a eight-year-old girl, and Antoine said, "Confucius once say: If rape is inevitable, relax and enjoy it."

In the first research after the hiring of Rivera and the pairing of Grimsby and Beutel, in July 1971, McHugh & Hoffman had used a procedure called factor analysis. From it emerged 10 factors that the public said were the leading components of newscast image: news team, personalities, weathercasting, news about New York, field reporters, on-scene coverage, film, human interest features and sports. WABC was first in every category. That November, when "Eyewitness News" hit "26" in the ratings, champagne bottles were uncorked as for the first time in broadcast history, in the nation's TV capital,

ABC's news was No. 1.[56] Even with this, the big numbers were still to come.

"Eyewitness News" never would have succeeded had it not also ushered in modern news promotion. The first wizards of this art were WABC's George Rodman and his two counterparts at WLS, Chris Duffy and Brandon Tartikoff, who eventually became the president of NBC. They were O'Leary's inner voice. Many times, Duffy recalled, "I watched the sun come up in Dick O'Leary's office," the two of them having worked all night brainstorming the next promotional scheme.[57]

On-air news promotion had been virtually non-existent. "News was too sacred to promote," especially at the networks, where "the idea of promoting a [nightly] newscast was unthinkable," Rodman recalled.[58] And "hitting them over the head with a hammer was not what we wanted to do," Duffy would add. "Everything came down to image and perception. We wanted to give [the viewers] an image and feeling about our news [that] they would carry with them" and which would put CBS and NBC in the worst possible light. Two more visionaries later of international stature, Joe Sedelmaier for WLS and Jerry Della Femina for WABC, would drive this "responsive-chord" technique straight into news. Both WLS and WABC would win Clio Awards for their "Eyewitness News" promotions. They were two of only a handful of local stations ever to be accorded advertising's highest honor.

Duffy hit the jackpot in his very first outing, when a barrage of ads asked Chicago viewers, "Will Success Spoil Fahey Flynn and Joel Daly?" In this famous campaign, Duffy wanted to slap, and hard, the stone face of CBS. After Flynn's firing in the bow-tie incident, Duffy could not wait to exploit the public backlash against CBS. In set-ups on the streets of Chicago, Flynn and Daly were seen waving to throngs of people and behaving like Eisenhower after World War II, even though they were still behind in the ratings.[59]

Duffy's "Will Success Spoil?" campaign ended the taboo on creative news promotion. It was in a more liberal environment that WLS turned to the creative genius Sedelmaier. In 1984, Sedelmaier would become the darling of the ad industry for his spots touting a hamburger chain, in which an elderly woman went to a competitor, bought a hamburger, and said, "Where's the beef?" "Where's the interest?" was the question Sedelmaier would provoke in TV news.

Sedelmaier's first "Eyewitness" promo was made to look like a grainy 1930s newsreel. "Chicago—a new concept in news reporting flashes across the night sky bringing awards and legions of new viewers to Channel 7," a narrator began. "The principals in the drama" included weathercaster John Coleman, who was "using words years ahead of their time—words like 'hot,' 'cold,' 'wet,' 'dry.'"[60]

In another Sedelmaier promo, an announcer opened, "In view of their phenomenal success, the question was inevitable: How did Channel 7's great news team Flynn, Daly, Frink, and Coleman first get together?" The make-believe spot followed the lives of the four men as they met in chance encounters, in a maternity ward at the turn of the century, as soldiers under siege during World War I, and finally in a four-vehicle collision during the 1920s, with Flynn dressed as mobster Al Capone.[61]

After this the WLS anchors were seen in encounter therapy at the "world-famous Klopfmann Institute."[62] Chicago viewers thought this promo, too, was fictional. Actually, it started as an inside joke—a takeoff on O'Leary's prayer meetings.

Although funny, these promotions imparted the intended message, that news did not have to be a sermon from the mount. Finally through Sedelmaier, O'Leary's image of Olympus took physical form in a promo showing a newscaster who looked like Walter Cronkite. "This is H. P. Vandakott taking the pulse of the world," the man said. Only Vandakott took this pulse from inside a small hatch recessed into a giant globe that spun around and around as he delivered the news. To further mock Cronkite, whose signature line was "That's the way it is," Sedelmaier had Vandakott, still spinning, finish his newscast by signing "Good night, good night."[63]

With Chicago in stitches over this promo, another would show Flynn and the others auditioning a new "Eyewitness News" reporter. They sneered when an applicant with a British accent stepped to the microphone. Then, after another stuffy candidate stepped up, Daly held his nose while Flynn hit a bell that signalled, "Get rid of him."[64] This candidate looked so much like NBC's David Brinkley that many called in to find out if it really was.[65]

The promotion in New York had had just as much of a flair. One of Della Femina's best known later ads was a 1988 spot for Isuzu automobiles, in which a self-interested and crooked character named "Joe Isuzu," who sold competing cars, irritated and unsettled viewers. At WABC, Della Femina's ad used the same tactic against CBS and NBC. The idea was to khartoum CBS and NBC as both above the fray and as champions of darkness. One promo that showed a government official making a dreary speech started off looking like

typical establishment news coverage. Suddenly, a WABC microphone
was thrust at the official as an "Eyewitness" reporter asked, "Did you
see what Seven said about your campaign?" Exposed as a crook, the
official who was supposed to cut a ribbon cut the microphone cord instead.[66]
Meanwhile, a recurring symbol was a frightened bird. "Does
Chicken Little scare you every night on the 11:00 p.m. news?" WABC
asked. "And make good news sound bad and bad news sound even
worse? We do it with a little more warmth. And a lot more understanding for the viewer."[67] The next "frightened bird" was an NBC
peacock, which WABC showed with its feathers being clipped off.[68]
WABC's counter-image of warmth, understanding and hope was
instilled time and time again. One of the most effective promos in TV
news showed Rivera inviting Grimsby, Beutel, Antoine and other
WASP "Eyewitness" team members to a huge Puerto Rican wedding.
Unforgettable was a scene in which a woman, presumably Rivera's
aunt, shouted "Roger Glimsby!" and then persuaded the visibly re-
luctant Grimsby into a dance marking the occasion.[69] Although the
wedding spot had a very large cast, it was outdone the day WABC
filmed an "Eyewitness News" promo in Central Park, in the setting
that had inspired the popular Broadway musical *Hair.* What looked
like 200 people held hands and sang "Let the Sunshine In."[70]

But in the citadels of the big media, big journalism shook its head.
Attacking the warm and friendly antics of Grimsby and Beutel, Joseph
Morgenstern of *Newsweek* tabbed "Eyewitness News" as the "perfect
news show for people who can't stand the news anymore."[71] *New
York Times* critic Jack Gould acknowledged "Eyewitness News" in
1969 by assailing as "ratings bait" that mini-documentary on prostitution.[72] *Time* reprimanded WABC for ignoring Gould's newspaper;
on one night, *Time* criticized, only two WABC stories had been in the
New York Times.[73] "People who defined journalism as words on a
page," Primo remarked, "could look at 'Eyewitness News' and never
be able to figure it out."[74]
But the middle majority could. "Viewers feel that they are not
only being well-informed, but are being entertained by men who can
be serious when it's warranted and cheerful whenever possible."
Viewers feel this approach "relieves [the] depression that most of
today's news holds," the researchers would underscore.[75] "That's
Eyewitness News," a lower-middle female would relate, "[when] they

cover the city, all over. They show the dirty city, rat problems, slums, housing programs [but] I like the way the news people talk to each other [about it]." As a lower-middle male would observe, "They have this eyewitness news and they are right on the scene. Before [Channels] 2 and 4 seemed to have all the news." In concurring that "Channel 7 now did," a lower-middle female simply stated, "I like to watch it because they have eyewitness news."[76]

Research on the personalities also had made a statement. Excoriated by experts as a plague on TV journalism, Rivera's research in New York's 69 percent middle majority was through the roof. "He is beautiful. If all Puerto Ricans were like him, we would have no problems," a lower-middle female had volunteered. "He cares about poor people like me," another offered. "He manages to get into places that others don't get, places that interest me," a lower-middle class male likewise had stated. An upper-lower class female commented, "I like him. I think of him as young, in my age group. I saw him do something from Italy and he was dancing and having a good time." Another viewer said of Rivera, "He cares about people [and] is always helping poor people. He found a little girl who was missing and took her home. I like him." Only upper-middle class viewers, such as one who remarked "It seems he has empathy for his type of people in the city of New York," had doubts.[77]

As revealing as the volume of verbatim testimony were numerical Q scores. Using a nine-point system, a 1977 McHugh & Hoffman ranking for New York would be topped by Grimsby at 7.3 and Beutel at 7.2. With 7.0s and tied for third and fourth place were WCBS anchor Jim Jensen—and network anchor Walter Cronkite. ABC anchor Harry Reasoner was fifth at 6.9, with NBC's David Brinkley and John Chancellor in a ninth-place tie at 6.6. A year earlier in a poll by *U.S. News and World Report* Cronkite was named "the most trusted man in America." Yet in New York, this distinction would have gone not to Cronkite but to Grimsby. "Eyewitness News" was expressly preferred by 34 percent of New York Jews, 40 percent of Catholics, and 54 percent of Blacks. "The concept almost completely envelops the experiential viewer," Phil McHugh would sum up.[78]

In 1972 O'Leary would lift Primo out of the WABC newsroom and bring him to the network level as a vice president of the owned stations. Primo's job would be transplanting the "Eyewitness News" concept to ABC's three other stations, KABC, KGO, and WXYZ. All became No. 1. KGO, with anchors Van Amburg and Jerry Jensen, and WXYZ, with Bill Bonds, would have shares close to "60."

As this happened, station managers and news directors from every point on the map were converging on O'Hare Airport merely to sit in TV lounges and watch Flynn and Daly execute the down-from-Olympus concept on WLS. They had had to make the trek to Chicago because satellite relays were not then available and videotape cassettes, which later did permit the recording of newscasts, had not yet been invented. "I lost track of the number of phone calls I got from the airport," Daly would note.[79] One of those who had been there was Frank N. Magid, the head of a data company in Cedar Rapids, Iowa, that had just started a news consulting unit. "I didn't know anything about this Magid," O'Leary revealed, "but I knew that if he could do anything like McHugh & Hoffman I didn't want him anywhere near our competition."[80] O'Leary hired Magid so ABC would have a lock on both consultants.

In the midst of this groundswell, it was obvious big television had a problem. Between 1968 and 1971, CBS local newscasts in just New York and Chicago lost around 300,000 homes; NBC, more than a million homes. In *Newsweek,* Morgenstern had commented that "Eyewitness News" had "cut cruelly" into the local ratings of the two big networks. This had been putting it mildly. In New York NBC tried to fight back by installing its top network correspondents as anchors of its local news. Yet one after another, Robin MacNeil, Jim Hartz, Lew Wood, John Palmer, McGee again and Sander Vanocur were chewed up in the ratings by Grimsby and Beutel. In a September 1971 article detailing "the anatomy of the disintegration," *Variety* writer Bill Greeley reported that morale at WNBC was so bad that those in the news division "were actually cheering when the low ratings came in." Fearing for their jobs, WNBC staffers wanted their bosses to wake up. Yet according to Greeley, "NBC News top management seemed gapingly removed from their troubles." With WNBC down to an "18" and WABC on some nights hitting "44," NBC News president Reuven Frank felt the time was right to circulate a three-page memo on the subject of "words." "Every dictionary I trust says 'paddy' is rice in the husk. A 'paddy field' is a field of unharvested rice. A 'rice paddy' presumably is different from other paddies, since that is what adjectives are for. Would you say 'wheat paddy?'" Frank queried his news department.[81]

What others at NBC feared might happen finally did in the July 1972 ratings. WNBC's local news with Vanocur finished with a "0."[82] Although some viewers probably had tuned in, officially nobody was watching WNBC.

Dazzled by all this was Marshall McLuhan, the guru of the electronic age and the person who had envisioned a "global village." "Eye witness . . . is the 'I' as witness," McLuhan would write. "It is a wholly new ball game in a brand new ball park."

McLuhan celebrated "Eyewitness News" in an essay entitled *Sharing the News,* which ABC used in still more of its promotion. McLuhan observed: "For ages men have heeded only the inputs in communication. The *effects* have been ignored." But in TV "there are no distant perspectives and no remote events. What Orson Welles discovered about the close involvement of even the radio public, concerns the TV public much more. . . . ABC's 'teamness' news has put to work the fact that TV is not just a visual medium. Since the TV audience is part of the action, TV can not present a distant perspective or the detached outlook of a mere spectator," like those McLuhan saw on network news each night. "When the [ABC] news team explains 'we've always tried to be ourselves,' they are quite naturally expressing their response to people and events." By contrast, "press type of stories are detached ways of saying," as CBS's Cronkite said each night, "'And that's the way it is,'" the hallmark of the "old news game."83

McLuhan was not alone in forecasting the demise of this "old game." A new research-consulting firm had heard McLuhan's call. Like McLuhan, it was convinced that "that's the way it is" was not the way it would be.

7

Action Plan
(1969–1972)

"Eyewitness News" had a glitch. Like automobiles of the day, it was a gas-guzzler. From its teams of anchors and armies of field reporters to its undercover coverage and wind-in-the-hair visuals, "Eyewitness News" was a self-contained energy crisis in getting it all to move. While Primo and the others had trammeled many traditions, one rule, the medium's first, still stayed. It was the one that stated that the best 30 minutes of television were those that seemed to go by in 15. Yet outside the "Eyewitness" domain, this pacing had been accomplished years earlier, with a newscast Dr. Johnny Fever might have devised.

Since 1961, viewers in Cincinnati had flocked to a broadcast that had done for TV news what MTV did for pop music. A confident CBS affiliate named WCPO had decided it had enough of its network's three-minute reportorial sagas. WCPO perfected the first newscast to compress news stories into 20 and 30-second increments. Stories this short enabled WCPO to triple the number of items it could carry. The effect had been a whirlwind of news. In the words of its plainspoken architect Al Schottelkotte, "The networks thought they owned the world. . . . [CBS] hardly ever covered anything west of Washington. Everything you saw was an epic from Timbuktu. I was not interested in having the people of Cincinnati waste their time with that kind of news."[1]

So for many years they didn't. During the early 1960s the "CBS Evening News" wasn't shown in Cincinnati. With Walter Cronkite a stranger in the nation's twentieth market, CBS executives began courting Schottelkotte, who was not just the news anchor but also a vice president for Scripps-Howard, the owner of WCPO.2 In one overture, CBS News president Richard Salant flew Schottelkotte to New York for a preview of the first half-hour CBS newscast. According to Schottelkotte, "I told Salant it was twice as much of the nothing they already had." And he flew back home.3

"I began what we created as a completely visual format, quicker and immediate," he said. "I wanted to make the news, not the newscaster, the star." Thirty-second time limits were rigidly enforced as slides and films raced by. One of the onlookers then living in Cincinnati was cable TV pioneer Ted Turner, who in 1982 would model his "Headline News" on this "Schottelkotte format." Sustaining the fast pace was so crucial that no obstacle, not even incongruities between different news items, stood in the way. Transitions took the form of "opticals," the figure "9," WCPO's channel number, spinning like a top on the screen. Another optical was an animated spotlight beam.4 When these were too slow, Schottelkotte changed the tone by altering the color of the studio background with foot pedals underneath the news set. "It was sort of like driving a car," he reminisced.5

WCPO's broadcast became an institution in the Queen City. Schottelkotte was better known on the streets of Cincinnati than Oscar Robertson and Pete Rose.6 WCPO didn't even need a name like "Eyewitness News." WCPO simply called its news "Schottelkotte."7 In the copy-cat business of TV, more than a few were intrigued. But Schottelkotte had a habit of overwhelming the curious—even those from WCPO's sister stations WEWS in Cleveland, WMC in Memphis, KJRH in Tulsa and WPTV in West Palm Beach. John Haralson, the executive news producer of the Memphis station, recalled being summoned to group-wide seminars at Scripps-Howard headquarters convened by Schottelkotte, who told them his special formula required so much technical complexity that other stations "dared not copy it." According to Haralson, "His whole idea in flying you to Cincinnati was to tell you, 'You'll never be able to go back to your station and do anything like this. . . . It won't work anywhere else. It can't be done.'"8

But up the Ohio and across the Alleghenys, Schottelkotte was about to be proved wrong. With people's news fervor simmering in a half-dozen major markets and with that many places to look, broadcasters would next fix their gaze on Philadelphia, and it wasn't because of "Eyewitness News." A new type of broadcast with a Cincinnati stripe had broken out in Philadelphia. And it mattered everywhere else because it marked Frank Magid's journalistic debut.

It was called "Action News," and it premiered on Philadelphia's WFIL the night of April 6, 1970. "Action News" was a new beachhead in the anti-establishment people's news movement. Eventually, it would synthesize with "Eyewitness News" until the two couldn't be distinguished. Like the "Eyewitness" concept, "Action News" had deep roots—all the way back to the period in the 1950s when applied research was changing American enterprise. In 1957 applied research had beckoned a restless 25-year-old doctoral candidate named Frank N. Magid.

A native of Chicago, Magid had been finishing his Ph.D. in psychology at the University of Iowa while teaching courses there and at Coe College in nearby Cedar Rapids. Not keen on the low stakes and low pay of an academic career, he opened Frank N. Magid Associates as a dollar-a-collar applied research firm catering to local Cedar Rapids businesses. The similarities between Magid and McHugh & Hoffman were striking. In the same orbit as the University of Chicago and not far from it, Magid's alma mater, the University of Iowa, had been one of the first Big Ten campuses to welcome private sector research projects. It also was known for its qualitative expertise. Magid's academic mentor, David Gold, had earned his Ph.D. from the University of Chicago and was part of same "Chicago School" given fame by Lloyd Warner and Burleigh Gardner. Inspired by the potentials of qualitative analysis, Magid also had been moved by the flood of literature on social class stratification. He knew the social class diamond as well as anyone.

With the support of his wife, also a teacher, Magid had gone door-to-door in search of a first client. Months passed without Magid finding one. He called his firm "Frank N. Magid and Associates" even though it was not until 1958, when he hired an assistant named Naida Helm, that any associates appeared. "In the early years, it had seemed that few were receptive to qualitative research," Magid would recall, "as much as we told them that 'why' people did what they did, not 'what' they did, was important to them." His problem turned out to be a sales pitch that sounded like a presentation at an academic convention. Magid happened onto a new mentor, a Cedar Rapids real estate executive who took him aside, told him he sounded like a

college professor and revised Magid's spiel so businesses would listen.[9] Eventually, with consequences for all of TV news, Magid, the
researcher, emerged as a super-salesman, a rare individual who could
not just interpret a random sample but persuade as well.

No less formative was Magid's first research encounter, at Iowa's
Merchants National Bank. After studying the bank, Magid submitted
a snappy final report and to his amazement nearly lost the account.
The manager of the bank tried to get rid of Magid because the findings reflected poorly on his work. Fortunately for Magid, a
higher-ranking bank officer intervened and kept Magid on board. The
incident taught Magid resolve, which he later applied when critics of
local TV news tried to destroy him. "People who are in a position to
have their own ox gored will never like what you [the researcher] are
doing," he had learned. Not long after this, Magid would spot a little
sign in an office at KSL-TV in Salt Lake City, which read: "New ideas
are always in danger of being beaten to death by either those with in-
sufficient knowledge or those whose applecarts they would upset."[10]
Magid would repeat this "applecart" aphorism everywhere he went.

Magid enjoyed success at the bank and won over several additional Cedar Rapids businesses, including the Iowa Public Power
Company. Also on Magid's client list was Bill Quarton. Headlong into
dealings with a dozen downtown merchants, Magid's first meeting
with Quarton did not shape up as anything special.

Yet Quarton, the general manager of WMT, was Magid's springboard into broadcasting. Magid had had to work for this chance,
since Quarton was more skeptical than the others about spending
money on research. "I visited with Frank, and he showed me this
open-ended questionnaire he said could help WMT," recalled Quarton, who still told Magid, "It looks a little thin." WMT did not seem
to need help.

Magid's timing, though, was fortuitous. WMT had barely started
its TV operation in 1953 before a second station was on the air, this
in a town with only 72,000 residents. Quarton asked Magid to find
out how WMT could attract audiences not just in Cedar Rapids but
also in Waterloo and Dubuque, as well as all over eastern Iowa. Because of Quarton's move, Cedar Rapids-Waterloo-Dubuque did
become the first official multi-city market. The research problem had
hinged on WMT's daily farm programs, big in the rural Midwest. Two
WMT personalities, a hard-working agriculture expert who was "very
popular inside the station" and another who was "careless" and not
highly regarded internally, were put to the test. Magid's survey contained a major surprise. "The farm fellow that we liked [did poorly],"
Quarton related. "The boys out on the acres liked the other fellow

better." Magid's first TV research "changed my whole way of management," Quarton would attest. "From then on, I didn't give a damn about what I thought. It was what they thought out there [that mattered]."[11]

Then Magid made a fateful discovery. Having pegged Quarton as just another man-about-Main Street, Magid was struck upon finding out that his client was a broadcast king-pin. WMT, owned by the Gardner Cowles family, had once centered a group of radio stations stretching from the Twin Cities to Kansas City. In 1946, Quarton had urged this company to recruit a correspondent in Washington. The person Quarton screened and later recommended was Walter Cronkite, then a reporter for United Press. Many years later, after becoming Magid's fiercest adversary, Cronkite would make his own astonishing discovery about Quarton, that the man who had given him his break into broadcasting also was Magid's first TV client.[12] Eventually, Cronkite publicly denounced broadcasters who had hired Magid, not aware that Quarton had been the first.

More important to Magid was that Quarton was the past president of the National Association of Broadcasters and currently sat on the CBS affiliates board.[13] Quarton had contacts all over the United States, and Quarton's name looked impressive on Magid's resumé.

At Quarton's encouragement Magid expanded his quest for clients beyond Cedar Rapids. With no air service in Cedar Rapids, he boarded a Union Pacific train and railed to Denver to meet Hugh Terry, the general manager of KLZ. Magid subsequently signed his next three clients, KLZ, KOGO in San Diego, and WFMB in Indianapolis, all owned by Time-Life. On a followup visit to Denver, Terry urged Magid to extend his trip further west to Salt Lake City. There Arch Madsen, the general manager of KSL, needed serious help. Madsen signed in 1964 as Magid's fifth TV client. The same year Magid added KSL's sister station, KIRO in Seattle.[14]

While small, the Magid firm was growing. It departed a tiny startup office and moved into a new facility that by 1967 occupied the third floor of the Dows Building in downtown Cedar Rapids. Magid continued with a diversity of clients, including several regional firms then seeking national niches in the working class consumer market. Two of them, Coors beer and Harley-Davidson motorcycles, ascended from regional status into nationally known names in part because they had relied on Magid's research.

Still, television and especially TV news grew as Magid's first love. The FCC's community ascertainment requirement, which expedited his first TV contracts, was ample assurance that broadcasters would need research in the years ahead. Meanwhile, Magid's first studies of

TV viewing behavior had turned unexpected findings, just as had those of SRI and McHugh & Hoffman. While interested in live news spectacles, average viewers rejected the aloof and pontifical network newscasts seen night after night. Magid had reacted to this result with amazement. Further, "people were interested in local news happenings. . . . To them, news was local," Magid would relate. This, too, had been compelling. At the time, Magid recalled, "the networks were getting all of the attention." When in Seattle Magid had found "viewers . . . of the opinion that [no] any station offers any real reason" for watching, he knew that in local TV news a great deal needed to be learned.[15]

As of 1967 Magid had not engaged in consulting. His firm had specialized strictly in data gathering. Once Magid had finished a project and given the results to a client, the firm's job was done. Thus, in function, Magid differed from McHugh & Hoffman. Phil McHugh's firm did not specialize in research and had relied on SRI for its data. As a consultant, McHugh & Hoffman interpreted the data and then formulated directions. Bearing these directions, McHugh & Hoffman had then gone into newsrooms and through interactions with managers and newsworkers made sure they were followed. The two companies were sufficiently distinct that in 1966 Peter Hoffman met with Magid to discuss the possibility of having the Iowa firm conduct some of the McHugh & Hoffman studies.[16]

By this time, though, Magid was eyeing a McHugh & Hoffman role for himself. Associates kept hearing him speak of the need for an "action plan." An action plan was a summary of research followed by a numbered set of recommendations. Every McHugh & Hoffman project had contained one of these plans. They were the heart of the consulting process. "Some stations had action plans; others did not," stated Magid. "Those that did not have action plans bothered us," he explained, because research was an academic exercise unless the data were put into play. "[Clients] would ask, 'Why should I pay more for this?' which we answered, 'We want to be sure there's a plan to make sure you're taking appropriate action.'"[17] Even though Magid had never worked as an employee of the media, an experience at the Salt Lake City station would demonstrate Magid's sense for the kind of action broadcasters deemed necessary.

KSL had been the only client Magid had been leery of joining. "At a time when CBS was number one in the nation overwhelmingly, this station was number three," Madsen, its manager, admitted. Worse yet, "CBS was trying to cancel the affiliation [because] we were a joke."[18] KSL was so low that Magid fingered this operation as "eighth in a three-station market." The plight of KSL was not so much a joke, though, as an anomaly. KSL was owned by the Church of Jesus Christ of Latter Day Saints in a city 60 percent Mormon. Magid dispatched a research team and determined that KSL's dilemma was its poorly perceived newscasts. Then, Magid volunteered a semblance of an action plan. Knowing what it contained, Magid was ready to have Madsen throw him out the door. But Madsen listened as Magid told him the KSL news anchor had to go. The problem, said Magid, was that viewers identified this anchor not as a news person but as the son of a leading figure in the Mormon Church. With Magid's input, Madsen persuaded the Church to approve this change and others. In one year, Madsen would bring KSL to a first-place position.[19]

Magid moved further after a similar experience at another church-owned station, the Jesuits' WWL in New Orleans. While WWL's ratings problems were not as tenuous as those at KSL, they were bad enough. In last place and likewise fearful CBS might strip the affiliation, a perplexed Mike Early, the WWL general manager, actually asked Magid for an action plan. Early also purchased one of Sony's first portable videotape recorders and helped Magid acquire a compatible machine. Beginning in early 1968, Early recorded WWL's newscasts and those of competitor WDSU and sent the tapes to Cedar Rapids. Magid compared what he saw to what he read in the research and proposed major revisions, including friendlier, down-to-earth news anchors.[20] WWL pulled even and then further and further ahead.

Magid remembered the Salt Lake City result "as one of the most fantastic turnarounds ever." Yet the result in New Orleans meant more because "Early opened our eyes to what should be done: the carry through, the follow through, the action plan" all keyed to the research.[21]

It was not clear how these events became known to Eugene McCurdy, the general manager of Philadelphia's WFIL. Magid had been a Western firm, with all of its clients but one, the Indianapolis station, on the Cedar Rapids side of the Mississippi. Magid never advertised. Eventually, Magid would preside over a multi-million-dollar clientele—all generated by word-of-mouth. McCurdy said it was "a case of having decided on research and knowing Magid was available. . . . Our newscast was not competitive in the ratings"—an understatement. In January 1969, McCurdy invited Magid to pitch WFIL. Before even meeting Magid, McCurdy was ready to sign.[22]

Walking into this TV station, Magid saw a living shrine of Americana and broadcast history. Owned by Walter Annenberg,

Philadelphia's Channel 6 had been the first ABC affiliate. As a base of Annenberg's Triangle Communications, it was at WFIL that the nation's most popular magazine, *TV Guide,* had been conceived in 1952. Meanwhile, WFIL radio was known all over the country as a bastion of the top-40 rock-and-roll music craze. In 1957 WFIL would launch an afternoon teenage dance show called "American Bandstand," beamed coast-to-coast on ABC from the WFIL studios. WFIL radio disc jockey Dick Clark, like "American Bandstand" itself, became a national institution. If this had not been enough to impress Magid, the day he arrived Annenberg was named as U.S. ambassador to Great Britain. Annenberg was a close friend of President Richard Nixon.

Annenberg's wealth and influence were immense. According to Al Primo, who worked in Philadelphia between 1965 and 1968, "WFIL was a sleeping giant. It could have done anything it wanted."23 But since signing on in 1948, WFIL had done nothing in news.

WFIL's newscast called "News Time" had a "3" rating and a "7" share. This compared to roughly "35" shares each for "Eyewitness News" on Westinghouse-owned KYW and "The Big News" on CBS-owned WCAU. WCAU not only was owned by CBS; it had historical significance as the station that had started the entire CBS network under William Paley in 1927. After Primo's departure in 1968, "Eyewitness News" had fallen back, although WFIL was still far out of the race. George Koehler, the head of Annenberg's TV division, recalled that "after McCurdy mentioned Magid, I felt we had nothing to lose by having him come in and conduct a research project." Money plainly was no deterrent.

Koehler also knew that neither KYW nor WCAU had a research program. WCAU had rid itself of McHugh & Hoffman in 1966, CBS vowing never to use news consultants again. "Magid's first research study told us everything we needed to know to move ahead with 'Action News,'" Koehler would describe, and this report made interesting reading. It told the extraordinary story of a million TV viewers tuning to the news on KYW and WCAU and not knowing why.24

Informal panels called focus groups alerted Magid to areas needing coverage in the actual survey, in which data were collected from 820 two-hour in-home interviews. The dynamics of the Philadelphia media revolved around 51-year-old John Facenda, the anchor at WCAU since 1948. Facenda was "Mr. Philadelphia," and Magid could see the reason. Facenda had an astounding 96 percent familiarity rating. But viewers also liked the sparkle and organization of KYW's "Eyewitness News." "[T]hose who prefer KYW are more likely to note that the news is unusually well presented on that station and that they prefer what they refer to as the news 'format,'" Magid's report began.

The same report also teased out a long list of KYW liabilities. "Eyewitness News" was slow paced and starting to seem worn. Those most likely to complain about "Eyewitness News" were the target audience of working-class viewers. Ironically, Philadelphia's "Eyewitness News," one of the forerunners of people's news, had become the choice of the elite. Overwhelmingly, "Eyewitness News" was favored in Philadelphia by the socio-economic group Magid had labeled "high," exactly 26 percent of all respondents and roughly equivalent to McHugh & Hoffman's 20 percent upper and upper-middle class. Respondents complained about specialty reporters who covered the arts and society and concentrated on Philadelphia's upscale suburbs. Magid emphasized that "KYW draws more than three times the viewership among members of the high socio-economic status group than does WCAU, . . . is particularly strong among residents in the counties outside Philadelphia proper, . . . [and is] weak among Negroes."[25]

Clearly, WFIL had nothing to gain by directing its efforts at KYW's "Eyewitness News." Thus, according to WFIL news director Mel Kampmann, "We took dead aim at Facenda."[26]

"Mr. Philadelphia" did have personality. He owed his popularity to community activities and to reading stories to children on TV each Christmas.[27] But when the news came on, Facenda turned into a classic Mt. Olympus newscaster. He was the lord of the stentorian voice and read the news the way Keats or Shelley would have read long epic poetry. After his firing by CBS later in 1973, Facenda would accomplish the seemingly impossible, mocking his own mock heroic tone as the narrator of NFL Films. Millions of American football fans would hear Facenda make every football game seem like Spartacus versus Ben Hur. Long after he died in 1984, Facenda would remain synonymous with professional football. His approach was much loved by fans of the NFL.

Nevertheless, Magid's research had brimmed with discomforted comments about this characteristic as seen on the news. "He reminds me of a college professor," one respondent stated. Oddly, there were more positive comments on Facenda's grooming and attire than his news capabilities. Worse, his style showed little spark or imagination. "He's like an old glove," one person noted. Ahead, WFIL would need to select a new anchor. The research on Facenda practically drew a picture of who not to get.

Yet it had not been Facenda's vulnerabilities as a newscaster that had initially caught Magid's attention. Magid had isolated in the research an explanation for why none of Philadelphia's local newscasts were stirring excitement among viewers. His discovery would clear the way for the defining characteristics of "Action News," its abundance of short news stories and, in turn, its rapid-fire pace.

In the focus groups viewers had complained of too many long items and had urged the addition of more stories. During the formal study, "more stories about [the] local area" was one of 15 items given to viewers in a question that had asked them to rate factors that influenced their selection of a local news station. After personalities, a factor affirmed by 68 percent of the respondents, "more stories" had been the most-often volunteered criterion. Close to 50 percent of middle and lower status respondents had named "more stories." Around 40 percent said that they wanted broader news coverage and more pictures. In the view of more than one-half of the respondents, none of the Philadelphia stations were satisfying the "more story" need. Further, another item had shown that 78 percent preferred no expansion of the city's existing half-hour newscasts.[28] It was apparent that viewers not only wanted more stories but that they wanted them to appear within the span of 30 minutes. From Magid's research had come the formula for "Action News."

After discussions about this with Magid, Koehler sketched a new news format in a seven-page memorandum. "I had never seen Al Schottelkotte's newscast, although I certainly knew how popular he was in Cincinnati," Koehler recounted. "For me, the thing just happened like a light bulb." Inspired by Walter Winchell, whose NBC radio newscasts had "chased the red hand around the clock," Koehler envisioned a televised "front page."[29] "We skim across the news the way the reader skims across the newspaper. Moving from left to right," Koehler directed, "we have one story, then another story, then another story. Then we say, 'But the Big Story is . . . .'" Having the viewer skim an abundance of short news stories, at lightning-quick pace, answered the main need in Magid's research.

Koehler, though, overruled Magid on two key points. One was naming the newscast. In the research, 41 percent of respondents favored "News Final" compared to only 8 percent who liked "Action News."[30] Even "News of the Night," "Twentieth Century News," and "Report to Pennsylvania," did better than "Action News." "The title I really wanted was 'Eyewitness News,'" Koehler revealed years later. Because the broadcast became a ritual in Philadelphia, considerable legend centered on how "Action News" finally was picked. Some felt it was derived from a top-40 radio format called "Action Central News," while others had heard that Magid proposed it after seeing "action" blazoned all over billboards promoting a brand of beer. "None of those stories were true," Koehler would maintain. "The title came to me as I was driving across the Benjamin Franklin Bridge and saw the pace of the city. I said 'Action News' is it.'"[31]

The other disagreement was over anchors. WFIL had two news-casters, radio-age veteran Gunnar Bock and another figure distinguished in the research by the number of times respondents had commented on his toupee. Magid also studied 27-year-old WFIL radio newscaster Larry Kane. However, only 21 percent said they'd accept a newscaster "Below 40."[32] This excluded Kane and everyone else WFIL had available.

As a result, for six months Kampmann, the news director, was consumed by a nationwide talent search. A curious Frank Magid looked on. One blessing eased the pain. Rather than flying on a com-mercial airline, Kampmann used the so-called "Annenberg Air Force," the fleet of private luxury jets that ferried Walter Annenberg and his staff around the world. Kampmann traveled almost 100,000 miles, sat before innumerable hotel room TV sets and had nothing to show for this effort. Making matters worse, he had had to arrange videotapes of all the anchor prospects so they could be shown to more focus groups back in Philadelphia. With video cassettes years away, Kampmann could not make these recordings himself. Nor, obviously, could he call a manager at a TV station whose anchor he might steal. Most of the tapes Kampmann did use were recorded at WFIL and fea-tured candidates who had had to travel to Philadelphia for a personal audition.

As Kampmann seethed over this confusion, Magid's saw oppor-tunities. Meanwhile, ignoring Magid's red flag about young newscasters, McCurdy finally ended the mess and said, "Hire the kid."[33]

Larry Kane thus became the youngest person ever chosen to an-chor a main newscast in a major market. "When they told me I was going to be the anchor I just about fell out of the chair," Kane re-called. "Nobody put a person my age in an anchor position. . . . I never felt 'Action News' was about Larry Kane. To me, it was a vic-tory for a whole younger generation."

Others hired were even younger than Kane. Howard Glassroth, the "Action News" executive producer, was only 25 years old.[34] Like the one at WABC, the "Action News" team prided itself on the fact that almost no one had any newspaper experience. That they were first-generation "television" journalists, not tainted by a words-on-paper mentality, was a point of pride. The contrast between the "Action News" contingent and the news staff at WCAU was read-ily apparent. While WCAU opened its "Big News" with a montage of Facenda's news-gathering feats from foreign capitals, Kane's achievement had been his exclusive interviews with The Beatles when the British band first toured the U.S. in 1964.[35]

The misread of Kane would endure as Magid's best-known mistake, even though it had been unavoidable. The Larry Kane assessed in the research was not the Larry Kane eventually seen on "Action News." The "before" Kane as captured in a 1969 "News Time" broadcast appeared to have a wardrobe assembled at a second-hand store, with hair that looked like he cut it himself.[36] With the first broadcast just weeks away, Kane slipped out of sight at WFIL. Only the managers and Magid knew that Kane was in New York and under the tutelage of famed Broadway talent advisor Lilyan Wilder. The founder of a future society of news anchor coaches, Wilder had promised Kane, you will be "helped to [your] most magnetic self."[37] When "Action News" began, the "after" Kane looked like a cross between a Philadelphia lawyer and a teen idol.[38]

Magid's research and guidance was followed all the way through to the first broadcast. Besides exposing the mass audience's preference for "more stories," the research had helped determine what these stories should be. By a four-to-one margin, middle and low status respondents preferred more local content over more national and international content; in the high status group, the preference was two-to-one in the opposite direction.[39] Among the most sought local topics were weather, transportation, breaking stories, sports and crime-related coverage. While these preferences were uniform across socio-economic divisions, twice as many middle-low status respondents preferred racial news as did those of high status. Political news appealed to only 2.4 percent of the total respondents.[40]

"Many months of extensive research by highly regarded analyst Frank N. Magid has provided the strategy that is going to make WFIL-TV the Number One News station in the city," a promotional brochure read. "Channel 6 realizes that . . . filling an hour [of news] is just that. Filling. And padding and making much ado about practically nothing. And wasting your valuable time." Thus, "We at WFIL-TV are ever-conscious of the public's need and interest to know what's going on in this shrinking world, . . . where the stroke of a governor's pen can determine how much bread we put on the table tonight. . . . You come over to our new news and we promise, first, that you'll like it, and second, that you won't miss a thing."[41]

With this fanfare and Kane at the helm—his "voice throbbing with excitement, [and] looking down the electronic tunnel into your living room," in the words of *Philadelphia* magazine's William Mandel—"Action News" finally premiered in April 1970, the same week in which Americans had been gripped by the drama of

Apollo 13, when astronauts had almost lost their lives on their way to the moon.[42] Reading the next set of Philadelphia audience ratings was like witnessing the launch of the rocket that had blasted the astronauts into space. Starting with a "7" in May 1970, "Action News" thundered to an "18" share in November 1970. It was up to a "23" in February 1971. Then in May 1971, "Action News" amassed a "31" share and took over first place. In just 12 months WFIL had more than quadrupled its news audience. This was the greatest ratings expansion, network or local, in the history of television news. Fifty shares were ahead.

In Philadelphia "Eyewitness News" was reeling and in need of redefinition. CBS, which previously had done nothing to respond to "Eyewitness News," was immobile again as "Action News" appeared. Already overcome by people's newscasts in New York and Chicago, William Paley's first station, WCAU, with audience shares in the teens, had been dealt a bruising blow.[43]

As it turned out, the triumph of "Action News" was not the "Big Story." In February 1971, with "Action News" assured of that No. 1 rating, Annenberg came back from England and shocked the media establishment by announcing the sale of WFIL to an obscure company from Albany called Capital Cities.[44] The success of "Action News" had enabled Annenberg to jack up the sales price to a then-record $62 million. Because Annenberg was still part of the Nixon administration and well-known, his sale of WFIL received national publicity. Experts who had followed only the affairs of the major networks and who had analyzed the sale had concluded that $62 million was too much and that novices from Albany had been robbed. Yet Capital Cities had shrewdly paid a premium for the station it renamed WPVI because it knew that major market TV stations with powerful local newscasts could turn as much profit as a network. Fifteen years later, swimming in profits from "Action News," tiny Capital Cities again would make news on network row. This was when Capital Cities went there to buy part of it in its 1986 takeover of ABC.

"Action News" had looked ahead in many other ways. It had been another victory of youth culture over the broadcast news establishment. In addition, "Action News" had spelled out the imperative of visualization in communicating the news to middle and lower status groups. Above all, "Action News" had dramatized that average people were not news "junkies" and preferred news with only a smattering of details. The attraction of "Action News" had been its relentless quick-cut, action video clips. Because "Action News" had institutionalized everything short and brief, it helped mark the beginning of a new information environment in the TV age. No "Action News" innovation would be more influential than a device called the "soundbite." It was at WFIL that this term was first used, when Kampmann had ordered reporters to pluck from extended interviews 10-second "bites."[45] Typical "Action News" newscasts had as many as three stories every 60 seconds.

Yet not all of the original concept had remained intact. Unexpectedly, "Action News" became a lesson for idealists who felt, as Schottelkotte and Koehler had, that news content could supersede newscasters and be "the star." In the first Magid studies after the 1970 premier, middle and low status viewers said they could not accept a TV newscast as merely a news machine. They still insisted on strong anchors. When it became evident that "Action News" would have to project personalities and emulate that aspect of "Eyewitness News," the concept no longer was unique.

Charismatic personalities would finally give "Action News" its insuperable advantage in the ratings. The station settled into a three-person anchor team of Kane, sportscaster Joe Pellegrino, and weathercaster Jim O'Brien. They had the three highest Q scores in Philadelphia. The perceptions of Kane and Pellegrino were imposing. Yet the data on O'Brien, formerly Philadelphia's dominant top-40 radio disc jockey and the "Boss Jock" of WFIL, were off the sheet. By 1977, O'Brien would have a familiarity rating of 98 percent and a likability rating of 79 percent.[46] According to research performed by both Magid and McHugh & Hoffman, the Q scores achieved by O'Brien were the highest ever recorded by any television news personality, network or local.

As viewers warmed to the "Action News" anchors, they were moved by the rhythm of WPVI's accompanying mosaic of news promotion. The distinguishing feature of WPVI's image campaign would be an original musical theme, the first ever developed in television news. Even before the music was composed, promotion manager Ned Armsby and his associates Mike Davis and Walter Liss had made Philadelphia the next laboratory of soft-sell promotional techniques. They spent more than a million dollars on the promotion of "Action News" in the first year alone.[47] Like WLS in Chicago and WABC in New York, the objective in Philadelphia was to make viewers uncomfortable with competitors, notably the stuffy CBS station, and make "Action News" seem like a family friend. Besides an open checkbook, WPVI's image-makers had no competition. As McCurdy, the general manager, recalled, "Neither of the other two stations reacted at all to what our station was doing. . . . They just let it sit, so the field was [ours]."[48]

During the November 1970 ratings, Philadelphians opened their newspapers to find gigantic display ads showing downtown, with comic strip balloons emanating from the windows of buildings. "It moves," someone said. "What comprehensive coverage!" was a comment from across the street. A surprise tactic was having one of the characters confuse Larry Kane's name. "I think Frank Kane is great," this person exclaimed.[49] This much-talked-about ploy had been inspired by Page 244 of the Magid research report, in which an actual respondent had gone on and on about Kane and then called him "Steve."[50] In the ad, rather than "Steve," they used Magid's first name instead. "It was a way to show the public we were real, not caught up in our own importance. That we could laugh at ourselves," Davis explained.[51]

WPVI's barrage of on-air spots carried the humor further. One showed workers unloading box after box, each marked "Film." At the end, the truck pulled away with two tiny boxes remaining. "Those are for our competitors," a WPVI worker remarked.[52] In another promo, Kane was writing his script while his producer kept announcing "new film." As the films piled up, Kane had to eliminate one story after another from his script. Finally, nothing was left. When the producer said, "Let's hear all your copy," Kane said, "Good evening, I'm Larry Kane. Thanks for being with us." As the newsroom burst into laughter, an announcer intoned, "Sometimes it's tough to find room in the show for Larry."[53]

Emulated in many other cities was WPVI's so-called "elevator" ad. The suave Kane and Pellegrino were met in an elevator by a person off the street, actually an actress regularly seen on Alan Funt's "Candid Camera" show, who WPVI dressed as a housewife with a handbag and gloves. Dazed in the presence of the two celebrities, the woman kept striking them with the gloves. "Oh. Ho-ho. I know you (whap). I watch you (whap). Television. Channel 6. Action News! You're Larry Kane (whap). And you're Joe Pellegrino (whap). And you're hip!"[54]

Another person-on-the-street promo was simpler yet no less effective. Near the Liberty Bell it captured two radiant and young African-American women. As one gleamed in agreement, the other said, "Action News is the show for the people. We love Action News."[55]

While backers of "Action" and "Eyewitness" news would argue over whose ads broke the most ground, all hailed the "Action News" theme music as a stride in people's news. In time, music would be a "calling card" for local TV newscasts. Yet in the early 1970s, no one had thought of this. In big journalism, sentiment reigned that music was a show business overlay and that was why viewers who tuned to ABC's network news heard the shrill screeches of snapping cameras. CBS opened its news with the raw noise of clattering teletypes. Only one network permitted music. The draconian sounds of Beethoven's Ninth Symphony, heard each night on NBC, were perfect for network news. At the local level, thinking had advanced only as far as movie soundtracks. "Eyewitness News" on competitor KYW borrowed from the 1964 film *From Russia With Love* and the 1966 film *Kaleidoscope,* while the current local news standard for theme music remained those spliced-together passages from *Cool Hand Luke.*

With a much larger vision and budget, Liss located a composer named Al Ham, who had just written a popular Coca-Cola ad and later hit tune, "I'd Like to Teach the World to Sing." "I worked with Walter to create a melody . . . which could get across the humanity of news," Ham recalled.[56] Liss, Ham and an ensemble called the Hillside Singers then flew to London to join the London Symphony. Several days of recording produced two hours of music in 65 parts; this composition, entitled "Move Closer to Your World," differed dramatically from any preceding news music and had persuasively signalled "news down from the mountaintop."

Opening with timpani drums and building to full orchestration, "Move Closer to Your World" began with an 18-second prelude that became the theme for each "Action News" broadcast. It went on to depict the highs and lows of news, and life, its different motifs used as interludes in the newscast but mostly as background for WPVI promos. As the music played, viewers saw people in parks, people on the job, people in schools and churches and people at home with their families. As the scenes were shown, lyrics written by Liss were sung by a female chorus: "Move closer to your world, my friend. Take a little bit of time. Move closer to your world, my friend. And you'll see. . . . Your world needs you to care, to share it. Take the time. Join hands my friend with all the people in your world. Move in close, move on in. And you'll see. . . . "[57]

During the 1970s "Move Closer to Your World" became, in effect, an anthem for local TV news. There were few people in Philadelphia who did not know the words and who could not hum or whistle the music. It was released on records. High school bands performed it at football games. Mayor Frank Rizzo used it at out-of-town appearances. Through syndication "Move Closer to Your World" became the theme for local newscasts in 92 other cities, while dozens of newer composers would thrive by writing similar versions.[58]

Although Kane would leave for WABC in 1977 and O'Brien would be killed in a parachuting accident in 1983, "Action News" would continue to dominate Philadelphia local news. What began in 1970 went on to become a ratings dynasty. Headed by the new "Mr. Philadelphia," WPVI anchor Jim Gardner, "Action News" would remain the nation's highest-rated major market newscast for nearly 30 consecutive years.[59]

But by 1972 it was time for Frank Magid to move on to other locales. Magid's spoils were not in the City of Brotherly Love but every place else. The ratings successes of WPVI became grist in national trade publications such as *Broadcasting* magazine.[60] All over the country local station managers had wanted to know how WPVI had quadrupled its ratings in one year. Magid could tell them.

Thus, Magid entered news consulting on a national basis and as a direct competitor to McHugh & Hoffman. Magid had a bigger vision for the consulting field. More intimately connected to "Action News" than McHugh & Hoffman had been at "Eyewitness News," Magid realized that television news had numerous unmet needs. Indeed, while only a background element in the "Action News" story, no part of the encounter would be more meaningful to the TV industry than Magid's service as Mel Kampmann's sympathetic ear during that 100,000-mile travel odyssey. This was when WPVI had needed to recruit a new anchor and had no ready access to resumés and audition tapes. After witnessing the frustrations over this, Magid knew that a centralized talent system, in which one company could screen and recommend anchors and reporters and coordinate the tapes, would be considered a masterstroke by local broadcasters. Soon, Magid's move into talent recruiting would give his firm a voice in the hiring and firing of journalists all over the country.

By 1971 Magid had signed most of WPVI's past and present sister stations, WLYH in Lancaster, WFBG in Altoona, KTRK in Houston, WKBW in Buffalo, WTNH in New Haven-Hartford and KFRE in Fresno, and then had converted them to "Action News." A dozen additional clients were signed in 1972. "Magid just took the idea and ran with it. It provided him fairly easy consultation," Koehler sighed.[61] Kampmann, though, was having a ball, finding he could track Magid's travels all over the country. "The phone would ring and it was a news director from somewhere wanting a dub of our newscast," Kampmann explained. "I knew Frank had been in their newsroom trying to tell them how to do 'Action News.'"[62]

Unable to copyright "Action News," Capital Cities did try to out-maneuver Magid. On the front cover of *Broadcasting's* January 24, 1972, edition, Capital Cities announced, "Private consultations of all aspects of the Action News format are still permitted."[63] Yet by then, the real consultant had the upper hand. While Capital Cities had newsrooms and transmitters, Magid had travel itineraries, hand-shakes, and action plans.

All of this meant a new way of life for McHugh & Hoffman. Coming from different directions, Magid and McHugh & Hoffman had reached the same point. Their research procedures were identical, and so were their commitments to people's news. A fierce rivalry was inevitable. "Action" and "Eyewitness" news had swollen into a snow-ball. Now to be pushed across the country by consultants, this juggernaut would flatten for good Mt. Olympus and change the face of TV news.

8

The Long March, Women, and News War (1971–1976)

The culmination of the people's news movement was a long march by the news consultants beginning in 1971. Over the next five years, Frank N. Magid Associates and McHugh & Hoffman would push from one end of the country to the other, along the way to enter 150 new local newsrooms and seed people's news in every major, large and medium-sized city. New news anchors, innovative promotions and expanded newscasts arrived, as did tricks and gimmicks at ratings time. They were so noticeable that they often were topics in people's everyday conversation. But few knew what was propelling all this. Unseen was the formation of two new television networks, Magid and McHugh & Hoffman, which would nationalize local news and bowl over traditions left from the real networks, ABC, NBC, and CBS.

Two versions of people's news, "Action" and "Eyewitness," would synthesize into the fast-paced, personality-driven newscasts all Americans would know as the consultants helped blaze another trail. They would expose hundreds of station managers and news directors—almost the entire TV news industry except for network news—to professional audience research. The most meaningful consequence of the research would be a mass movement of women into visible on-air positions, at a time when television news had been virtually all male. The consultants had commercial motives in helping women advance. Yet they also knew this was a fait accompli. Once research had been unleashed, and the one-half of viewers who were women finally had a voice, males no could longer control TV news. Women had wanted to see more women on the air.

Had the long march been recreated on a lighted map of the United States, it would have looked like a Fourth of July display with flash-bulbs popping from coast to coast. Yet the outcome was more radiant for middle majority TV viewers than for both men and women behind the screen. As the proliferation of people's news translated into record audiences, expectations for top ratings and more profits became manic, with no city immune. The end of the long march would leave television news in a perpetual station of news war. Regardless of gender, no one was secure without being No. 1.

This warfare bore the imprint of a bitter rivalry between Magid and McHugh & Hoffman, their hostility primed with Magid's entry into news consulting at Philadelphia's WPVI. At this crossroads, the two firms had not been alone. Seeking action and money, eight other companies had declared themselves as news consultants during 1971.[1] Phil McHugh had tabbed not Magid but a firm called TelCom Associates as his probable foe. Melvin Goldberg's MAGIC, Inc., also showed promise.[2]

These upstarts had been able to consult, but they didn't have research, the pipeline to the people. Consultants who relied on past experiences and gut-level advice did not remain consultants for long. To survive as a consultant, research was a must. As the only consultants with deep research capacity, Magid and McHugh & Hoffman took a vital first step in the long march by running off TelCom, Goldberg, and all of their competitors. They couldn't run off each other, though; their battle for bragging rights stoked competitive fires in every TV market. McHugh & Hoffman had been the first news consultant, and *Broadcasting* magazine would acknowledge its longevity and positive image.[3] However, Magid had the preemptive claim, clients. Between 1971 and 1976, McHugh & Hoffman's clientele would quadruple, from 12 to 44 newsrooms. Yet Magid's would balloon from 15 to 100.

Both firms acknowledged years later that much of the fervor of the 1970s had been unnecessary. Indeed, Magid and McHugh & Hoffman had written their own tickets. Not only were they the gurus of "Action" and "Eyewitness" news; they had just received an enormous boost from the FCC, which in early 1971 held hearings on the community ascertainment policy. Stations that had used Magid and McHugh & Hoffman for ascertainment studies had submitted testimony and materials. The commission was so impressed that it discussed whether all TV stations should use professional research. "[A] professional service . . . [is able to] provide the applicant with [all] background data, including information as to the composition of the city of license," the FCC concluded.[4]

With so many factors in their favor, the consultants prepared for big bank accounts. A sign of the times became new command centers. Anticipating its first million-dollar year in 1971, McHugh and partner Peter Hoffman left Detroit to settle in a plush complex with a schnazzy address along "consultants row" in the Washington, D.C. suburb of McLean, Virginia. It was an appropriate address, too. Situated on Virginia State Route 123, McHugh & Hoffman was about a mile up the road from the headquarters of the CIA, the intelligence agency to which the consultants were constantly compared.

At the same moment, moving vans pulled up in front of the Dows Building in downtown Cedar Rapids, where Magid had been based. Magid's move was short—a seven-mile caravan to the southern outskirts of Marion, a Cedar Rapids suburb. Its new headquarters, on a six-acre campus surrounded by trees and rolling cornfields, was called One Research Center. It eventually would house a 1,500-square-foot telephone center and satellite receivers hooked up to clients not just in the U.S. but all over the world.[5] While there were no CIA agents around, many who lived nearby were not so sure. "People from town would drive out here, and it was interesting to see the looks on their faces," Magid's Naida Helm would relate. "There always was a mystery about what we were doing."[6]

One Research Center reflected Frank Magid's vision for total news consulting. Basic components of the TV news process, things millions of viewers would recognize, were to form in that building. Endlessly, viewers would wonder why familiar local news anchors would be taken off the air and replaced by new anchors that had just arrived from a distant city. This was because Magid, learning from Mel Kampmann's frustrations during the Larry Kane hiring episode at WPVI, finally formed the first national talent bank. By 1975, Magid had a recording of every significant local news personality.[7] Broadcasters no longer had to search for talent, and this accelerated anchor turnover. If a news, weather, or sports anchor had a low Q score, station managers willingly removed this person knowing they could go to Marion and one-stop shop for a replacement. As for the WPVI experience, another stride in news consulting had come from those secret sessions between Kane and Broadway talent coach Lilyan Wilder. Magid formed the first talent school. When viewers heard a local newscaster say "So-and-so is off tonight," it often meant the missing person was in Marion learning how to be a better anchor.[8]

Another Magid innovation was the news director-turned-news consultant. McHugh had not been keen on hiring news directors because he didn't think they understood research. In 1972, Frank Magid, with larger priorities at his firm, bowed out as its chief news advisor and put in that role Leigh Stowell. To get Stowell, Magid had raided McHugh & Hoffman. Stowell had been one of the first McHugh & Hoffman consultants and had worked directly under McHugh. Stowell's surprise move underscored a competitive kinship between the small number of consultants and the even smaller number of competing firms.

At Magid, Stowell would bring trained journalists into the research-consulting domain for the first time. "It was important to us then that probably ninety percent of newsrooms had not been exposed to our concepts," he related.[9] The first Magid traveling consultants included Duluth news director Mitch Farris, Boston's Dick Mallory and Miami reporter Rich Sabreen. But then Stowell hired Ed Bewley, an anchor-producer at WTVN in Columbus, and Bill Taylor, the news director at WISN in Milwaukee. In 1978, Taylor and Bewley would leave Magid and with Willis Duff form the third major consulting firm, Audience Research & Development.[10] During the 1980s, AR&D would enter another 100 newsrooms. Although local TV news would continue to expand, almost the entire field would be linked through a long grey line of pioneer news consulting figures, from McHugh to Stowell to Magid, and then from Magid to Taylor, Bewley and Duff.

A first challenge was making sense of the alphabet soup of station call letters. It was mind boggling, especially for the many people who worked for the consulting companies but had never worked in TV. In some cases consultants discovered they could remember the names of their clients because they spelled out or suggested key words. McHugh & Hoffman had just entered a station called "KING" in Seattle, and this was easy because Seattle was located in Washington state's King County and its stadium was called the Kingdome. Even easier was the firm's client in Phoenix, a station called "KOOL," just what one needed in the Arizona city especially in July. Magid had entered at "KRON," owned by the *San Francisco Chronicle,* and at Dayton's "WHIO," which sounded like "Ohio." Sometimes, anagrams did the trick, such as Magid's KCMO in "Kansas City, Mo."; WTMJ, which spelled out *The Milwaukee Journal;* or Washington's

WJLA, the initials of the person who had just signed McHugh & Hoffman, owner Joseph L. Allbritton.

Because most were having ratings difficulties, the consultants soon learned all the rest. McHugh & Hoffman would enter Philadelphia's KYW, Boston's WBZ, Dallas's WFAA, Minneapolis-St. Paul's WCCO, Miami's WPLG, Pittsburgh's KDKA, Houston's KTRK, Indianapolis' WRTV, Baltimore's WJZ, Denver's KMGH, Kansas City's WDAF, Portland's KATU, Sacramento's KXTV, San Diego's KGTV, New Orleans' WDSU, Charlotte's WBTV, Nashville's WSM, Orlando's WCPX, Louisville's WHAS, Memphis' WBEQ, Buffalo's WBEN, Little Rock's WTVK, Richmond's WRVA, Mobile's WALA and Huntsville's WAFF.

A portion of Magid's new clientele would include Boston's WNAC, Cleveland's WEWS, Miami's WTVJ, Pittsburgh's WIIC, Houston's KPRC and later KTRK, Minneapolis-St. Paul's KSTP, Atlanta's WSB, St. Louis's KSD, Baltimore's WBAL, Portland's KGW, Indianapolis's WLWI, New Haven-Hartford's WTNH, Buffalo's WKBW, San Diego's KFMB, Charlotte's WSOC, Louisville's WAVE, San Antonio's KSAT, Oklahoma City's KWTV, Charleston, West Virginia's WCHS, Little Rock's KATV, Tulsa's KTUL, Des Moines' WHO, Green Bay's WFRV, Greensboro's WFMY, Albuquerque's KOB, Evansville's WTVW, Fresno's KFRE, Spokane's KREM, Tucson's KVOA, Chattanooga's WTVC and Baton Rouge's WBRZ.[11] Viewers of these stations were about to see something different. "Around the country everything was changing. All of the old rules were out the window," Magid's Stowell observed.[12]

Nothing more dramatically indicated this change than the hundreds of women about to join the all-male kingdom of television news. In 1970, equal opportunity employment regulations became criteria in FCC license renewals, and while this accounted for the stepped-up hiring of women, another force—news consultants—would explain the truly inexplicable, why they were seen on TV in large numbers. The FCC had not required broadcasters to name women as lead anchors. Yet this would happen in city after city as the news consultants fanned out.

The consultants were sympathetic with the women's movement to the extent it represented a fight against the establishment. Headlong into a similar anti-establishment fight, the consultants' ability to sign clients depended on innovative tactics. Even though the consultants were all male, the egos of their similarly all-male clientele were irrelevant if change was possible and, above all, money could be made.

Picturing an opportunity, the consultants had been noting an absence of female anchors and a dearth of female reporters on the network newscasts. Because the network news divisions were still considered the trend-setters, opportunities for women were not foreseen until the networks acted first. Yet in finally providing these opportunities the networks would remain years behind local TV news. Not licensed by the FCC, the networks could do—and say—as they pleased. In August 1971, one of the giants of network news had said a lot. Magid and McHugh were inspired after picking up a copy of *Newsweek* and reading statements made by Reuven Frank, the president of NBC News. In defending all-male TV news, Frank belittled the potential contributions of women and went on to declare, "I have the strong feeling that audiences are less prepared to accept news from a woman's voice than from a man's."[13] Women were aghast by Frank's remark. The consultants were ready to prove Frank's statement wrong.

Until the 1970s, the only true inroads of women had been the weathergirls of the 1950s. The first woman to assume a showcase role was Dorothy Fuldheim, a fixture on Cleveland's WEWS, although not as an anchor but as a commentator.[14] Technically, the first woman to anchor a TV newscast was an eventual network reporter named Diane Sawyer. Sawyer's brief assignment in 1968, however, had been as a half-anchor, half-weathercaster at a weak ABC affiliate in Louisville.[15] While they were not anchors, NBC News once had had two female correspondents, Pauline Frederick and Aline Saarinen, and CBS had had a third, Nancy Dickerson. Dickerson moved to NBC and did become an anchor—of a five-minute news brief sandwiched between game shows each weekday afternoon. In the same article quoting Frank, ABC's woman, Marlene Sanders, sighed, "They will always come up with some theory about why it cannot work."

Exactly the opposite theory was growing in the minds of the consultants. They felt female newscasters might answer a supreme need, differentiating newscasts. With news wars ahead, news content wouldn't be enough. Because competing newsrooms covered the same news, women anchors and reporters were a means for getting newscasts to stand out. Yet following through was a risk because of the certainty that existing male newscasters would fight such a move. It took research, the voice of the people, to finally show the way.

Significant had been Magid's research in Philadelphia, where, stunningly, 38 percent said gender made no difference and 21 percent said they'd immediately accept female newscasters. This was meaningful because there were no female newscasters on the air in Philadelphia at the time.[16] More auspicious had been the handful of cities where researchers could name specific women. An example had come in Indianapolis, a city where a few female field reporters had been employed. McHugh & Hoffman succeeded in steering the promotions of two second-string WISH reporters, Faith Levitt and Kay Field, after quizzing viewers about them specifically and not about women in general.[17] Another example had come in Cleveland. Fuldheim's extreme presence there had cleared a path for WJW reporter Jenny Crimm. Because Crimm could be isolated in surveys and focus groups, her positive traits could be assessed. Levitt, Field, and Crimm remained as reporters, though. Crimm did finally advance to main anchor status at WJW only after male opposition had been surmounted.[18]

The more the consultants pondered this confirming data, the more logical women's on-air roles had seemed. "Half of the viewers and half of the people in the research were women, and women naturally wanted to see more women on news," Hoffman explained, adding that "this was something you'd never know if you sat in an ivory tower," did no research, "and pretended the people didn't exist."[19] McHugh, not a person anyone would term a women's libber, suddenly became consumed by the idea of installing women as anchors. In part to help diffuse opposition, McHugh would circulate to clients something he called the "family concept." "Somebody in your family dies," McHugh proposed. "The first question is, 'Who's going to tell mother?' The communicator of the sad news must be a very special kind of person who somewhere along the way can find something to brighten her up."[20] Common sense told McHugh that a typical woman was better qualified to "tell mother" than a typical man.

The logjam finally was broken in 1971, in the first direct confrontation between Magid and McHugh & Hoffman. In Seattle Magid had just implemented co-anchors—two men—in initiating "Eyewitness News" at KIRO. Middle and lower status viewers started shifting to KIRO from long-dominant KING, a station with several Peabody and Emmy Awards and, then, a single-male Olympian newscast. In ratings trouble, KING brought in McHugh & Hoffman, which insisted that KING "peopleize" with two anchors. McHugh and KING general manager Eric Bremner saw potential for putting a woman in one of the two seats. Of all the cities yet studied, Seattle was the most receptive to female newscasters. Magid, just finishing a workup on the subject, showed that one-third of Seattle-Tacoma respondents expressly wanted to see women, 55 percent said gender made no difference and only a small number expressly wanted to continue seeing only men.[21]

The pivotal development in Seattle was a 1971 McHugh & Hoffman study that had locked on to a specific candidate. She was a KING weekend reporter named Jean Enersen. "Before the research," Bremner noted, "we didn't know she was so well liked."[22] Despite low familiarity ratings from the obscure weekend assignment, Enersen ranked seventh among all Seattle personalities in likability. Among the dozen male newscasters who had ranked behind Enersen had been one of the new KIRO co-anchors, Jim Topping.[23]

In August 1971, Enersen was teamed with a newscaster named Jim Harriott and thus became the first woman ever to permanently anchor a main newscast. She would become a Seattle fixture as identifiable as the Space Needle to the people living there. Enersen credited her success to Harriott, her partner, who rather than resisting Enersen had given her tips and made her feel part of the team.[24] Numerous other women would not be so fortunate. Enersen's blast through the gender barrier was so thorough that by 1975, after Harriott had left, McHugh & Hoffman actually wrote of her "token male" co-anchors.[25]

Enersen ended the anchoring career of Topping, who in 1972 became the news director at KDKA in Pittsburgh. Topping's lesson on the impact of female newscasters foreshadowed more. With Topping gone and KING's ratings going up, Magid wasted no time proposing a female anchor at KIRO. KIRO conducted auditions and Magid focus groups on 102 candidates. The winner was a former Miss Washington named Sandy Hill. "I got lucky and was hired," she said.[26] Hill started at union scale, labor's minimum wage, about $9,400 per year, although soon she would be earning 30 times that amount. Hill, too, was instantly accepted by Seattle viewers and by 1973 was the centerpiece of KIRO's news promotion. One KIRO ad had mentioned Magid's research and how KIRO was "listening to the public." The same ad had touted Hill's status as "the most popular woman on Northwest television."[27] Actually, Enersen still had that distinction.

Momentum gathered. A repeat of the events in Seattle next played out a short distance away in Portland, where KING's sister station, Magid client KGW, hired an anchor named Rose Marie Scott in early 1972. Competitor KATU then enlisted McHugh & Hoffman, which recommended an anchor seat first for Beverly Byer, then for Linda Yu, then for a newcomer named Kathy Smith. Magid played its hand by having its Seattle client, KIRO, steal Smith from the McHugh & Hoffman client in Portland, but not before McHugh & Hoffman had struck again in Seattle with the first female sportscaster, Ruth Walsh, at new client KOMO.

After that it was dueling women all over the country. In 1973, Dallas greeted its first permanent female anchor, Iola Johnson, after McHugh & Hoffman had urged WFAA news director Travis Linn to promote her.[28] A double beneficiary of these maneuvers was a reporter in the Southeast named Monica Kaufman. After McHugh & Hoffman's research helped Kaufman win the main anchor position at Louisville's WHAS, she then went to Atlanta's WSB, a Magid client, on the strength of Magid's Louisville research at WAVE.[29] But in Atlanta, McHugh & Hoffman already had moved. Its 1974 research confirming that Atlanta was "ready for women," McHugh & Hoffman cleared the way for that city's first female anchor, Judy Woodruff, at WAGA.[30] The same year, Bay Area viewers saw their first female anchor, Kirstie Wilde at KRON, after a Magid study in Louisville, where Wilde had begun, had singled her out.[31]

The consultants took heavy flak. Magid lost its contract with Miami's WTVJ after recommending that veteran Ralph Renick be paired with a female.

Still, the consultants spent far more time recruiting rather than defending women. There weren't nearly enough, and almost none excelled in credibility perceptions because they hadn't been seasoned. An example was Indianapolis's first woman main anchor, WISH's Jane Pauley, who repeatedly drew responses to the effect that "I'm glad they finally put a girl on." In Indianapolis, though, the novelty did wear off. Pauley became the third best-liked personality there.[32]

The consultants, more and more fearful of alienated male factions in newsrooms, had to armor their research and strike from new angles. With the networks' single-male paradigm increasingly perceived as passé because of co-anchor arrangements at the local level, the question in 1974 was whether future anchor teams should be male-male or male-female. That year McHugh & Hoffman ran a study on this issue. It was conducted in the Twin Cities, where McHugh & Hoffman had just been strafed by Magid's biggest success since "Action News." In 1974 Magid client KSTP brought down WCCO, a station that had been No. 1 in the Twin City ratings for 25 consecutive years. Magid had insisted that KSTP recruit an anchor named Ron Magers and pair Magers with Stan Turner.[33] Respondents did not merely allude to a "family." In open-ended items they had come right out and volunteered that Magers and Turner "were just like part of the family." This was vital to both consultants, whose research had shown unusually strong family values in the Twin Cities.

Thus, in the McHugh & Hoffman project for WCCO, viewers were asked whether a male-female combination would do a better job of fostering a family characteristic. Fifty-four percent said they favored Dave Moore, the existing WCCO anchor, "with woman," against only 18 percent who preferred Moore "with man."[34] The woman tapped, Susan Spencer, later joined several former WCCO colleagues at the networks.

Another tack was experimental research, in which respondents were brought into auditoriums to view test tapes of female prospects. Los Angeles became the proving ground of this soon controversial technique after CBS-owned KNXT allegedly used it to fire Sandy Hill, who'd been brought in from Seattle. The other KNXT anchor, "Big News" mainstay Jerry Dunphy, would succumb to the same tests. In the meantime, using a combination of surveys and screenings, rival KABC had plucked from the pack a figure named Christine Lund.[35] Eventually, Lund would be paired with Dunphy on KABC's "Eyewitness News" and in the ratings would virtually lay waste to KNXT and that station's next woman, Connie Chung, in the ratings.

Yet another experiment would illustrate how managers teamed with consultants to create special research opportunities. In New York WABC anchor Roger Grimsby took time off, this so the station could field test a reporter named Joan Lunden. For two weeks, Lunden co-anchored "Eyewitness News" with Bill Beutel, with a research team already in place. Only 8 percent felt Lunden was right for a main anchoring role.[36] Although this thwarted WABC's plan of elevating Lunden, the station's interest in introducing New York's first female anchor grew. As it turned out, the consultants had been running studies on a different female, Rose Ann Scamardella, the activist and former human rights commissioner from Brooklyn that Primo had hired as one of the first "Eyewitness News" reporters.

In telling WABC flat out that it had "to find a woman," McHugh & Hoffman urged that "Scamardella is outgoing, professional, vivacious [and] a diamond in the rough."[37] She indeed was rough. She pronounced "news" as "noose" and did not savor prissy wardrobe guidelines. Sent to Lilyan Wilder, Scamardella came back saying, "She wanted me to buy blouses with flowers. Everything I bought with her I haven't worn."[38] But in New York roughness was a virtue. Finally named to WABC's 11 p.m. news, Scamardella became a sensation not just in New York, where she did become the first woman anchor, but all over the country. Viewers elsewhere knew her as "Roseanne Roseannedanna," Scamardella's impersonation by comedienne Gilda Radner on NBC's "Saturday Night Live."

Surveys and focus groups had drawn attention to the public's need to see more women. Public input helped persuade indifferent broadcasters to put more minorities on the air as well. Broadcasters were slower to elevate non-white individuals. Still, consultants did encourage minority anchors and reporters. Research showed that middle majority Americans were ahead of the news establishment in accepting them.

Atlanta's Kaufman and Dallas's Johnson, for example, had been overlooked until research had demonstrated their appeal. Another case had been that of Washington's Rene Poussaint, who in her first research in 1978, a 10-point perception index, had registered a striking "8.3" among blacks and a still extremely high "6.4" among whites. Poussaint had topped 20 other mostly white male news personalities. That 1978 Washington study had given another indication of public acceptance of minorities in the findings on WTOP's Max Robinson and J. C. Hayward and WRC's Jim Vance, who had been promoted to main anchoring positions a few years earlier. These minority anchors, all with 7.5s on the 10-point scale, were the second, third and fourth best-liked newscasters among Washington's white viewers.[39] Yet another example had been KOA's Reynelda Muse, who became the No. 1 news personality in predominantly white Denver.[40] As McHugh & Hoffman's John Bowen recalled, "Our findings on women and minorities were persuasive . . . . It wasn't the viewer who was resisting [minority newscasters]. It was the old guard in newsrooms who didn't understand what the viewer perceived."[41]

Those first across the gender line had mixed views about the consultants. "[T]hey will normally opt for bland programming and bland personnel," Poussaint would comment.[42] Linda Yu, who would advance from Portland to San Francisco and then to WLS in Chicago, shared a similar concern. "The one aspect of consult[ing] we all suffered from was having to be cosmetically correct. Be blonde. Do your hair a certain way. I don't know how many times we heard that," Yu pointed out.[43]

Yet while bothered by insensitive advising, these women welcomed research. Their reactions to research would differ from those of many white male news directors and anchors, such as Renick, who tried to have it banished. "I owed everything to McHugh & Hoffman," KOOL-TV's Mary Jo West would relate. West recalled brutal internal opposition when she became the first female anchor in

Phoenix and felt that had there been no vote of confidence from the public she never would have survived.[44] Yu finally conceded that to the extent they "communicated to broadcasters the public's wish to give everyone a chance" the consultants were a "good thing."[45]

In countering the network news paradigm, local TV news had given two in return. One was the fire-blazing "Action News," with its whirlwind of video and 10-second soundbites. The other had been the chummy "Eyewitness News," distinguished by legions of the warmest and friendliest anchors and reporters the research could find. At the beginning of the long march, they were poles apart. Illustrating the distinction had been Jacksonville's WTLV, which in promos had used stock market charts to show how its "Action News" was far ahead of the Brand X "Eyewitness News."[46]

Soon, though, "Eyewitness" and "Action" news became stalemated in the research. The public had found benefits in both. The people's newscast raced to its ultimate form when under the pressure of competition the two concepts merged. Left at the end was a distinctive style of local TV news—and something else: a tradition for still more competition. By 1976, the synthesis of "Eyewitness" and "Action" news was the main event in television's first classic news wars.

One of them was in Boston, where Magid had converted granite CBS affiliate WNAC into the rapid-fire "Action News" concept in order to challenge "Eyewitness News" on WBZ. The "Eyewitness" format revolved around an unusually strong WBZ anchor named Tom Ellis. Helped by Ellis, personality projection gradually ordered the dynamics of the market. The Boston battle raged for three years and was climaxed when the "Action News" station absorbed the warm-and-fuzzy approach. In WNAC's Chuck Scarborough, Sara Ann Shaw and Jacqui Adams, the research had found "beautiful people."[47] Thus, in Boston, the original "Action News" concept on WNAC had faded away.

In Atlanta, though, "Action News" had the upper hand. Using the "Eyewitness" formula, McHugh's client, WAGA, finally passed long-dominant WSB—but only until Magid converted WSB to "Action News." Dropping in the ratings, McHugh & Hoffman told WAGA to back off on the "warm and friendly" and start incorporating "excitement"—shorter stories, more pictures, and "action."[48] Another synthesis of "Eyewitness" and "Action" then occurred.

In Baltimore, the "Action" format on Magid client WBAL and the "Eyewitness News" on McHugh & Hoffman's WJZ had battled in the ratings with no resolution. Not even WJZ's Oprah Winfrey, yet another new female news anchor and a then symbol of "Eyewitness News," could break the competition from WBAL, this as the styles of the two newscasts converged.[49]

As these "Action-Eyewitness" news wars played out, it became increasingly clear that the consultants no longer were loyal to either idea. Revealing this had been a Magid tactic at its successful Twin Cities station. All along Magid had been known as the "Action News" consultant. Nevertheless, Magid acted fast when the third-place station in the Twin Cities cut back its newscasts and dropped the "Eyewitness" moniker. This had happened on a Friday. By Monday, Magid client KSTP had grabbed the title and had re-christened its existing broadcast "Eyewitness News." In the span of a single weekend Magid consultants had entered KSTP and had had the station change the program schedule, reletter its news set, alter the newscast opening and produce new promos, all this so viewers would know KSTP's news as "Eyewitness News."[50]

Another important battleground had been Detroit, where Magid had entered at last-place WXYZ. It achieved success by having WXYZ's "Action News" out-eyewitness the existing "Eyewitness" station, Storer's WJBK. Because the "Eyewitness" concept depended on personalities, Magid helped WXYZ engineer what became the biggest talent raid in TV news history. It involved the entire WJBK anchor team, the contingent that had helped pioneer people's news a decade before. One by one, Jac LeGoff, John Kelly, weathercaster Jerry Hodak and sportscaster Al Ackerman joined lead anchor Bill Bonds at WXYZ. After signing these popular figures, WXYZ next enlisted the J. Walter Thompson ad agency for a million-dollar campaign that exclaimed to Detroiters "We Got What You Wanted."[51] The phrase, anti-elite and purposely ungrammatical, had the intended effect. Within one year, in May 1975, WXYZ had doubled its audience to a "44" share.[52] According to news director Phil Nye, "Magid's research had led to that. We had proof that what we did get was what the people wanted."[53]

The merger of the two concepts finally was consummated in what consultants had called the "mother" of the 1970s TV news wars. Symbolically, this had occurred in Philadelphia, where both "Eyewitness" and "Action" news had begun.

This conflagration took shape in early 1973 when CBS's once proud WCAU fired "Mr. Philadelphia," John Facenda. At CBS Facenda's "18" share had been unacceptable. A memorable day in

Philadelphia television was March 26, 1973, Facenda's last broadcast. CBS's decision to remove Facenda just short of his silver anniversary at WCAU had been painful. With him and others holding back tears, Facenda bowed out with dignity, saying, "A fellow can hardly be expected to just walk through the door. A quarter of a century is a hefty chunk of one's life, and I want you to know what your loyalty and your friendship have meant to me . . . . Be happy for me because I am content."[54]

The person who had given Facenda the news of his firing, WCAU news director Robert Morse, saw this as a turning point in television news. Facenda had been the last local defender of a dying Olympian news cause. Yet to Morse the moment had been important for another reason. "It told a lot of people that if somebody like John Facenda was expendable nobody was safe, not Cronkite or anyone else," Morse explained.[55]

Facenda's departure created a void that Westinghouse's KYW was determined to fill. Almost as much as Facenda's station, KYW had been reeling because of "Action News" on WPVI. That November, while KYW's "Eyewitness News" had a "25" share, WPVI's "Action News" had a "40." The original "Eyewitness" anchor, Vince Leonard, had just been paired with Mort Crim, a person McHugh & Hoffman had anointed as a rising star from Crim's spectacular research at Louisville client WHAS.[56] But at KYW's "Eyewitness News" morale had sunk. Declining ratings that had troubled the news staff coincided with research that managers had had to force themselves to read. The research revealed the obvious. As McHugh & Hoffman reported, "Eyewitness News pale[s] next to Action News. . . . Channel 6 [WPVI] local newscasts are fast-paced. It is the rapid pace that attracts many of its fans."[57] Leonard submitted his resignation.

KYW not only was the flagship station of the Westinghouse group; its fortunes were crucial to Westinghouse president Don McGannon, still engaged in his battle to reduce the power of the New York networks. McGannon wanted the problems sorted out. A close relationship formed between new general manager Alan Bell and a new news director, Jim Topping, the man whose on-air career had been upended by Seattle's Jean Enersen two years before. McHugh & Hoffman's John Bowen then joined this circle after studying the research and reaching a surprising conclusion.

According to Bowen, while WPVI's whirl of short stories did attract viewers, that station's personalities better explained the high ratings of "Action News." But despite the remarkable Q scores of Larry Kane, sportscaster Joe Pellegrino and weathercaster Jim O'Brien, they had ascended separately and were not perceived as being a family. This, said Bowen, was the Achilles heel of "Action News," for much like the Twin Cities, Philadelphia was strong on family roots.[58] Particularly, O'Brien, who had the very highest Q scores, had not risen as a "family member." "Women find him cute and attractive, and they respond to him almost as though he were a mischievous but delightful child," the research read.[59] Leonard, Crim, weathercaster Bill Kuster and sportscaster Al Meltzer actually were ahead of WPVI in family-image criteria. On the strength of this finding, Bell not only rejected Leonard's resignation but gave him a raise.

The thinking escalated. As Bowen recalled, "KYW felt the time had come to name a woman as one of the anchors, and this was something the research indicated. We needed to build up the family characteristic of 'Eyewitness News.'"[60] Topping rose as the main advocate of having a woman on the news team, and he was so determined that he had demanded no opposition in the newsroom. Having been the chief victim of the Enersen phenomenon in Seattle, Topping had wanted to be on the right side of the matter this time. Topping confronted the leaders of the resistance, Leonard and Crim. Next, Topping tried to stir the family dynamic by encouraging more interaction between the anchors. The four men made visible progress. Characterizing Leonard and Crim as the fathers, Kuster and Meltzer the uncles, Bowen was convinced KYW was on the right track. Nevertheless, sentiment reigned that "Eyewitness News" had to have a mother.

She virtually flew off the pages of the next research report. The person selected was a 27-year-old KYW reporter-weekend anchor with a polished voice, shoulder-length blonde hair, and striking features named Jessica Savitch. Savitch's life would change because of the convergence of two research variables. She had a very low familiarity rating of 20 percent, no surprise because she worked on weekends and was not widely seen. But Savitch's likability rating had turned heads. Quantified at "13," Savitch was the fifth best-liked personality of the two dozen anchors and reporters then on the air in Philadelphia.[61] Achieving such a score in an obscure position meant that almost every respondent who knew her liked her. By routine, consultants scoured their analyses for just this pattern, low familiarity and high likability, for this was evidence of a star in the making. Without delay, Savitch joined Crim as co-anchor of KYW's 5:30 p.m. newscast.[62]

The research proved true, as Savitch, now in a frontline role at KYW, proceeded to redefine Philadelphia local news. The addition of the "mother" had so dramatically altered the perception of "Eyewitness News" that in the next rating period, November 1974, KYW had bounded from its "20" to a "31" share.[63] After proving herself in numerous reporting assignments, she won over her male adversaries, most notably Crim, who was her co-anchor.[64] Their chemistry was plain to the middle majority. "With Jessica on, I feel I can relate to the news a lot better," one respondent observed. Against fears Savitch would be accepted by male viewers only because of her good looks, data consistently showed credibility among both men and women. "She's interesting, good, and adds something extra," a lower-middle class female commented. A male in the same strata stated, "She seems like a pleasant person, not a women's libber at all."[65]

KYW followed through with a rebuild of its then tired "Eyewitness" format. By late 1974, it was indistinguishable from "Action News." "'Action News' was the rock 'em, sock 'em format [and] our counterpoint," Topping recalled, but "the research pointed to an adjustment we had to make."[66] McHugh & Hoffman monitored the stations for story count, making sure KYW had as many short, quick items as WPVI. Three-sentence soundbites were instituted; gone were the onerous talking heads. "Talking heads are not fundamentally good for television," McHugh & Hoffman had stated, "and they are not fundamentally good for television news."[67] Stories on politics and government were balanced by lifestyle, crime, and consumer news. Three showy features, "Energy Warden," "Consumer Cop," and "I-Team," the latter an investigative series, reflected the souped-up look.

In November 1975, KYW was No. 1. WPVI's ratings had declined, although only temporarily.[68] This began what many recalled as the "eyewitnessization of 'Action News.'" WPVI hired a new news director, Ron Tindiglia, one of the "Eyewitness" insurgents from WABC in New York. "It was apparent we were going to have to meet the competition from 'Eyewitness News,'" he would note. Working with Magid, Tindiglia changed the format so Kane interacted with Pellegrino and O'Brien. In the original "Action News" format, package stories by field reporters had not been allowed. For the first time in "Action News," reporters were seen.[69]

Some of these WPVI field reporters were being televised with new portable video cameras that unlike existing film cameras created a vivid, all-electronic picture. According to Magid's research, Philadelphia viewers already had noticed this innovation on WCAU. It was something the CBS station was calling "electronic newsgathering."[70] "You absolutely have to have this if you are going to keep up," Magid told WPVI.[71] Because at first these cameras could only be used for live reports, which ran for two minutes, "Action News" slowed to an "Eyewitness" pace.[72]

With WPVI's final step, it was clear to all that "Action" and "Eyewitness" had been fused. This was in mid-1976 when WPVI introduced a co-anchor arrangement. Larry Kane's partner was a woman, and she had a polished voice, shoulder-length blonde hair, and striking features. The new Jessica Savitch was a former school teacher named Gwen Scott, who'd been selected in a public talent search. Some at KYW were offended, but more were amused. Savitch would write of "Action News" as an "Eyewitness" clone.[73]

WPVI would prevail, though. KYW could not keep its imposing anchor team intact. After Savitch, Crim and Leonard departed, "Action News" with Jim Gardner again would soar to dominance. Yet back and forth, WPVI and KYW had seesawed for the top spot. There were scoop stories, more investigative I-Teams, newer technical gimmicks and promotions morning, noon and night.

In 1977, Savitch became the first permanent female network news anchor when she joined NBC as a backup to John Chancellor. Nothing would better underline the differences between network and local news than Savitch's six years of agonies in the NBC newsroom. Having excelled in local news, Savitch was shunned by what she felt was the "old boy" network at NBC. After failing to meet expectations in her coverage of Capitol Hill, NBC News revoked her correspondent status and used her only in anchoring roles. Just before her untimely death in 1983, in a freak car accident, Savitch anchored an NBC prime-time news brief with slurred and fumbled words. Many felt this incident had resulted from Savitch's acknowledged drug problem, brought on by the stresses she had felt at NBC.[74]

After Savitch left Philadelphia, Kane and Tindiglia went to WABC, Leonard to Phoenix, Crim to Detroit and Kuster to Denver. Topping became a McHugh & Hoffman consultant. Passions vanished when these once-fierce competitors began showing up at each other's going-away parties. Appearing on a "stag" videotape with Savitch, Crim had wished Larry Kane good luck by joking, "The main reason Jess and I are getting out of town [is because] we can't bear to stay here without you on the screen."[75] The real reason, though, was the first hint that people's news was a breeding ground for professional disillusionment. News wars could never be won, and as long as they had to be fought everywhere, it was just as good to leave Dodge and seek the best deal. A problem for Savitch had been that antagonism between Westinghouse and NBC. Even though Savitch had been offered a network position prior to 1977, Westinghouse refused to release her from her KYW contract.

Nevertheless, they left in Philadelphia the essence of modern television news. An example was the October 27, 1976, edition of

"Action News." The first item showed reporter Judi Bloom relaxing in an office chair used that day by President Gerald Ford, who had travelled to Philadelphia in his reelection campaign. Later, reporter Mike Strug used people's news techniques to simplify an analysis of the referendum that brought casino gambling to Atlantic City. He talked to average people and illustrated key points with pictures. Also visible was the happy talk element. Kane conversed with O'Brien and then chided Pellegrino for being late with his sports segment. In response, Pellegrino connected the celebrity status of visiting President Ford to that of his partner. "I haven't seen this much security," he wise-cracked, "since the last time I went to Larry's for a cookout."[76]

KYW's "Eyewitness News" had the same trappings. An example was the newscast on February 11, 1977. It had trim and snappy stories, some 15 seconds long. Statements from public officials and politicians often consisted of one sentence.

Meanwhile, KYW had refined the happy talk and used it, like WPVI, only in transitions between the anchors. It was during these transitions that Savitch had stood out. After announcing the winner of a KYW kid's picture-drawing contest with a very squeaky "ta da," Kuster had turned to Savitch to find out what she thought of the successful entry. "It's better than that 'ta da,' I'll tell you," she said while turning to the camera and smiling at the audience. At the end Savitch appeared with Crim, who had tried to ad-lib a light show-closing pun but had gotten his words tangled. After Crim tried to hurriedly sign off by telling viewers he and Leonard would be back for the next newscast, Savitch cut in and said, "Fortunately, I won't be here at the time."[77] Everyone on the news set broke into smiles. In her element, local news, Savitch had shined. Television would never produce a more effective people's newscaster.

Never before had any sector of the American news media witnessed so much upheaval in such a short period of time. In nearly 100 cities there had been at least one weak and obscure television station converting to people's news and then surging in the ratings, often to a first-place position. Venerable stations like WCAU, whose names had been synonymous with broadcasting since the medium's inception, usually kept their Olympian newscasts and were turned into also-rans. It was like a football season in which the nation's No. 1 team was upset every week.

Even skeptics were struck by the litany of struggling local TV newsrooms that consultants had carried all the way to the top. They had included New York's WABC, Los Angeles' KABC, Chicago's WLS, Philadelphia's WPVI and KYW, San Francisco's KGO, Detroit's WJBK and WXYZ, Cleveland's WJW, Washington's WJLA, the Twin Cities' KSTP, Dallas' WFAA, Houston's KTRK, St. Louis' KSD, Baltimore's WBAL, Milwaukee's WITI, Phoenix's KPNX, Nashville's WSM, Louisville's WHAS, Charlotte's WBTV, Buffalo's WKBW, New Orleans' WWL, Orlando's WCPX, New Haven-Hartford's WTNH, Dayton's WHIO, Oklahoma City's KWTV, Toledo's WSPD, Little Rock's KATV, Greensboro's WFMY, Evansville's WTVW, Green Bay's WFRV, Mobile's WALA and Tucson's KVOA. A glimpse of the future had been Magid's first steps into the very smallest newsrooms, beginning with WTWO in Terre Haute, Indiana, the 116th market, "We never moved a station faster than [in] Terre Haute," Magid's Jeff Davis had beamed.[78]

No longer did local broadcasters have reason to follow the network model. Nor could the new trend-setters, Magid and McHugh & Hoffman, keep the magic to themselves. By 1976 their success had spawned a second generation of news consultants, this time rival firms grounded in research, which had seized an important moment. This was when losing stations like WCAU realized they, too, needed people's news. Reymer & Gersin, ERA Research, Audience Research & Development and Al Primo's Primo Newservice were more companies obscure to the public whose handiwork nevertheless would be recognized by millions.

As ratings and research data kept pouring in, the public's latent distresses with network news, which the consultants had detected as far back as the early 1960s, began to roost. In local TV, much attention was given to Nielsen national ratings summaries showing a network-to-local flip-flop in the public's news viewing preferences. In 1969, network news ratings had exceeded those for local news. Just three years later, dinner-hour local news commanded larger numbers.[79] In December 1974, *Broadcasting* reported that in 33 of the top-50 markets, local newscasts were "Top 25" programs. This meant that in most major and large markets local news, once a license renewal throwaway, was more popular than many of the network's prime-time entertainment shows. It was estimated that between 15 and 20 million Americans who had never regularly watched television news were now part of the local news audience.[80]

Ironically, it was just then that local broadcasters were hearing of plans by both CBS and NBC to expand their network newscasts from

30 minutes to an hour or more. For the networks, expansion was the only way to sell more advertising and keep afloat their humongous news divisions. After 30 years network news had yet to turn a profit. Schedules, though, were packed, and it was not clear at what hour these longer national newscasts would appear. One person, CBS anchor Walter Cronkite, had an easy solution. He told local station managers that if they canceled some of their local news a longer network news could be seen. Cronkite's broadcast, according to Cronkite, was so important that he felt local stations really should give New York a "100 pound sack." Yet Cronkite said that for the time a "two pound sack," an hour, would do.[81] In the midst of what *Broadcasting* was calling a "local news phenomenon," even CBS affiliates could not believe Cronkite was serious.

The networks had to confront a local broadcast community whose thinking had profoundly changed. This had been easy to see when the first known public discussion of news consultants occurred, in Seattle in January 1973, when KING-TV program director Robert Guy spoke at the University of Washington. Most expected KING's standard line, an enumeration of the two Peabody Awards, the two DuPont Awards, and the six national Emmy Awards KING and Portland sister station KGW recently had won, followed by an affirmation of KING's commitment to great TV.

But on this day, Guy decided to tell the truth. "KING management wishes to be number one; they're not the number one station in town [now]," he revealed. He then put up a chart, on it a diamond-shaped diagram depicting "Social Class in Seattle," and went on to describe how "lower middle" and "upper lower" class viewers, a group he called the "middle majority," comprise 64 percent of the Seattle population and "spend something like 6.8 hours per day watching television." These people, Guy said, were crucial to KING. "It's a programmer's responsibility to try to hook them, because we . . . sell Campbell's Soup, automobiles, and we used to sell cigarettes." Pointing again to the bulging middle section on the chart, Guy asked rhetorically, "So how do you go about buying programming that will make them tune to you? From the social diamond, you can obviously see that it is not the Boston Philharmonic."[82]

If the middle majority was still Greek to big journalism, the problem of bombed out news operations at the networks' flagship TV stations was not difficult to comprehend. With hour-long newscasts on hold, CBS had another plan: recovering, not with researchers and consultants, but with technical might its rivals couldn't match.

LLOYD WARNER

Modern television news consulting grew from the social class research of famed University of Chicago professor Lloyd Warner, who achieved worldwide acclaim for establishing a class hierarchy in the United States. Warner studied differences between the college-educated upper-middle class and the less-educated yet much larger "middle majority." He helped found the first news consultancy, McHugh & Hoffman, in 1962. Photo courtesy of the University of Chicago.

THE BIG NEWS

The first breakthrough in television newscasting came in 1961 when Los Angeles station KNXT introduced "The Big News." A reaction to the indifference of network news divisions in New York, "The Big News" was one hour in length and was seen two years before the networks expanded their newscasts to a half-hour. Pictured from left: Gil Stratton, Ralph Story, Jerry Dunphy, Maury Green, and Bill Keane. Photo courtesy Robert Nelson.

CHICAGO'S "EYEWITNESS NEWS"

Modern local TV news took form with the joining of this news team—Fahey Flynn (left, front), John Coleman, Bill Frink, and Joel Daly—at Chicago's ABC-owned WLS in 1968. The Flynn-Daly broadcast was the forerunner of Chicago's "Eyewitness News." Formerly the anchor of rival WBBM, Flynn was fired by WBBM's owner, CBS, because of his bow-tie. He brought legions of viewers to WLS and helped cement ABC's supremacy in local TV news. Photo courtesy Joel Daly.

BREAKTHROUGH IN NEW YORK

A defining innovation in local TV news was "Eyewitness News" at WABC in New York in 1968. The concept was pioneered by Al Primo (left) and personified by anchor Roger Grimsby (seated). In background: John Schubeck (left), Melba Tolliver, Bob Lape, Milton Lewis, Tex Antoine, and John B. Tucker. Photo courtesy Al Primo.

GERALDO RIVERA

WABC's Geraldo Rivera was synonymous with both the concept of "Eyewitness News" and the criticism it received. While vilified by journalism experts, Rivera connected with the middle majority. His research was "through the roof." Photo courtesy Al Primo.

"EYEWITNESS NEWS" IN PHILADELPHIA

A force in local TV news was Philadelphia's KYW. Its formidable 1975 "Eyewitness News" team included Al Meltzer (left), Mort Crim, Vince Leonard, Jessica Savitch, and Bill Kuster. KYW's owner, Westinghouse, had a grudge against the New York networks, and this brought energy to local TV news. Photo courtesy Neil Benson.

JOHN FACENDA

A principal victim of the people's news movement was "Mr. Philadelphia," John Facenda, the anchor of CBS-owned WCAU. Facenda's stentorian delivery was perfect for his later role as the voice of NFL Films. Yet Facenda's Olympian style fell out of favor in television news. Photo courtesy Philadelphia Magazine.

JEAN ENERSEN

The first woman permanently to anchor a television newscast was Jean Enersen of Seattle's KING. Enersen was singled out in consultants' research in 1971 and became so dominant in Seattle that consultants wrote of her "token male" co-anchors. Photo courtesy KING.

MARVIN ZINDLER

Unsurpassed in reaching the common person was Marvin Zindler of Houston's KTRK. Best known for exposing "The Best Little Whorehouse in Texas," Zindler was an institution in local TV news. Photo courtesy KTRK.

PHILADELPHIA'S "ACTION NEWS"

A newscast called "Action News"on Philaldelphia's WPVI influenced much of the TV news process. Pictured are anchors Gary Papa, Jim Gardner, and Dave Roberts. "Action News" shortened news stories, sped newscast pace, and gave the media the "soundbite." Photo courtesy of WPVI.

JERRY FOSTER

Pilot-reporter Jerry Foster of Phoenix station KPNX helped ENG achieve new heights. Flying the first jet-propelled helicopter with "live" capability, Foster amassed a string of exclusive news stories. Stations all over the country bought helicopters after seeing Foster's numerous feats. Photo courtesy Arizona Republic.

McHUGH & HOFFMAN

Peter Hoffman (left) and Phillip McHugh were the first news consultants. Seen here in their McLean, Virginia, headquarters, McHugh and Hoffman teamed with researchers trained at the University of Chicago in the studies that cleared the way for "Eyewitness News." From a rivalry between McHugh & Hoffman and Magid in the 1970s would come most of the elements of the modern news process. Photo courtesy Cindy Keeler.

FRANK MAGID

Frank Magid was synonymous with news consulting. Magid achieved prominence after steering the success of "Action News" at Philadelphia's WPVI in 1970. Frank N. Magid Associates eventually advised newsrooms in 165 U.S. cities and in countries all over the world. Photo courtesy Frank N. Magid Associates.

FOUNDERS OF AR&D

Another leading news consultant was the Dallas-based Audience Research & Development, founded by Ed Bewley (left), Bill Taylor (center), and Willis Duff. Bewley and Taylor had begun as Magid consultants. AR&D eventually replaced McHugh & Hoffman as Magid's chief opponent. Photo courtesy Audience Research & Development.

CONSULTANTS IN SLOVENIA

Carried abroad by news consultants, the "Eyewitness" concept redefined TV news in countries behind the former Iron Curtain. Here Natasa Pirc and Matjaz Tanko co-anchor the news on Slovenia's Pop TV. Photo courtesy Istok and Yaka Bartolj.

NEW NEWS ON BRITAIN'S ITV

A surprise to some was the entry of American news consultants into newsrooms in Great Britain. One of the first to greet consultants from Magid was Sir Trevor McDonald, the "Walter Cronkite" of Great Britain and long-time anchor of that country's ITV network, seen here on ITV's revamped and American-looking news set. Photo courtesy ITN.

9

ENG and ENP (1971–1979)

Local television gave the world more than people's news. Video cassette recorders and miniature electronic cameras, the forerunners to home video, had spun from a technological breakthrough at TV's local level in the 1970s, something insiders called "electronic newsgathering." Everyone knew ENG would work, and a few prototype portable video cameras had been around since 1956, when the networks used them to cover that year's political conventions. Like nuclear weapons prior to World War II, full-scale ENG had existed only on paper. It was with a glimpse of an atomic bomb, one that could devastate "Eyewitness News," that the video revolution finally was ignited.

Electronic newsgathering would roll out of the laboratories of CBS and would mark CBS's greatest enduring contribution to TV news. ENG was a passion of CBS owner and chair William S. Paley, who had lost a string of technology battles to RCA, the owner of NBC. The immediate issue was the collapse of CBS local news in places like New York, Los Angeles, Chicago and Philadelphia, which fortified the then-paltry ABC. "We weren't going to let ABC get away with it, and we weren't going to cave in to 'Eyewitness News.' . . . There was a CBS tradition to protect," company executive Ray Beindorf would relate. It seemed the flash of new technology could preserve this tradition by getting the vital mass audience back.

After joining with a Tokyo company, in a partnership that heralded Japan's entry into the U.S video market, CBS would throw itself into ENG. It meant more flexible and immediate news coverage and a TV picture vastly clearer than any available on the existing medium, movie film. Yet viewers witnessed not just better pictures; they saw an electronic revamp of the entire TV newscast. Where once were seen fuzzy titles, hand-painted weather maps, and cumbersome microphones on the studio desk, miniaturization, computerization and more gadgetry gave the newscast its modern electronic look. All of the new inventions were tested and unveiled at the local level, mainly at CBS-owned stations. Not until 1979, when 86 percent of local newsrooms had some ENG, would the network news divisions convert.

Interesting twists would abound. To use the speed-of-light technology the way CBS intended, to knock out competitors, TV newsworkers had to work faster and faster. And because ENG absolutely had to be used, it determined the content of newscasts. Also unexpected was a spin-off of ENG—"ENP," electronic news promotion. As ENG grew from a plaything into a multi-million-dollar investment, managers could not sit back and wait for the payoff. Promotion increased ratings and expedited the return. The many antics of ENP dramatized how far the people's news movement had reached.

In the end, ENG did not destroy people's news. To the contrary, in trying to counter "Eyewitness News" CBS actually wound up strengthening the concept. Predicated on visuals, personalities and action, ENG fit with "Eyewitness News" like a video cassette inside one of the machines. CBS's technical magic would only succeed in making its veterans look older and put them in a fighting mood.

Sick and tired of what he called "these newer, warm-and-fuzzy newscasts," Beindorf, a 20-year CBS executive, had been the first to paint a picture of ENG's potential effect. It was an image that had stuck in Beindorf's mind since 1952, when he'd watched scenes of maelstrom and gigantic mushroom clouds beamed live to Los Angeles by station KTLA from the Yucca Flats nuclear weapons site in Nevada, 300 miles away.[1] The atomic bomb coverage on KTLA had been one of the first major feats of early TV news and an event that had left KTLA the trend-setter in electronic production. In 1955, KTLA began carrying live reports in its nightly newscasts. Then in 1958, its engineers figured a way to televise a live picture from a hovering helicopter.[2] KTLA went on to claim a Peabody Award for its aerial coverage of the Watts riots in 1965. Although Beindorf's station, CBS-owned KNXT, had the largest news operation and the biggest ratings in Los Angeles, he nevertheless had been awestruck by KTLA's breakthroughs.

After becoming KNXT general manager in 1966, Beindorf purchased a prototype video camera and gave it to a news reporter named Clete Roberts, who in his spare time conducted more than 100 tests. Beindorf wanted to know if these video units could completely replace film cameras, which KTLA continued to use on routine stories. Roberts had worked at KTLA. He had been a protégé of the far-sighted Klaus Landsberg, the engineer-producer who had developed the first, albeit cumbersome, live news cameras and whose first live spectacle had been KTLA's coverage of the Kathy Fiscus tragedy in 1949. Roberts had assisted Landsberg with the bomb coverage, which Landsberg had masterminded, and with most of KTLA's other triumphs in the 1950s.

But at KNXT, Roberts concluded that the video camera he was given wouldn't work and that a more durable unit would be required for day-to-day news work. By 1968, Beindorf had put the idea to rest. KNXT's "Big News" was sailing, its profits enhanced because all of the film cameras had been paid for. The film gear was sturdy, too, and rarely broke down. Why replace fully depreciated equipment, Beindorf reasoned, if it might last forever?

Three years later, however, everything changed. In 1971 Beindorf was promoted to CBS headquarters and named executive vice president of the CBS local television stations. Beindorf's job was to straighten out the problems at the CBS stations in New York, Chicago and Philadelphia. "I did not have much regard for that 'Eyewitness' stuff," he would exclaim to associates. And "I just knew right off it was a competitive edge to have this technology. . . . We had it and knew how to work it better than they [ABC] did. Winning was what this thing was all about." He fought what he called "traditionalists within my own company," mainly CBS accountants dumbfounded by the costs. "It was force feeding," he would explain.[3] Beindorf was in luck. He found an ally in Joseph Flaherty, the president of the CBS engineering division and, more importantly, a figure with considerable muscle in the company. Chief engineers kept stations and networks on the air and therefore had a direct pipeline to the highest executive suite. The video revolution began when Flaherty told Beindorf "Let's see the boss."

William Paley was all ears the day the two men came to call. While to Paley "Eyewitness News" was a minor worry, he was intrigued by this "bomb" idea and knew of a place where he wanted it dropped—not in California but three blocks away at Rockefeller Center, where RCA was headquartered. Chaired by David Sarnoff, RCA had taken credit for almost every technical innovation since broad-casting began. A bone in Paley's throat was color TV, which CBS actually had invented. Paley watched in dejection as RCA created a different system and then arm-twisted the FCC into forcing CBS and everyone else to use it. Concerned about costs, Paley finally consented to a crash program if the company could locate another party to shoulder the research and development load, preferably someone well along in the science of miniaturization.

There was but one place to look. Beindorf and Flaherty headed for Tokyo and negotiated an agreement with the Ikegami Tsushinki electronics corporation. Within days CBS was shipping technical expertise and operating specifications to Ikegami in Japan, which began inventing a new camera. Beindorf looked ahead to marketing the devices by trademarking the name "Mini Cam."[4] While not trademarked, the label "electronic newsgathering" also was coined at this stage. Beindorf credited the term "ENG" to Flaherty, who in turn credited Beindorf. In any case, the two men envisioned an entirely new system for news coverage.

The devices Ikegami would perfect were identical in principle to big studio cameras. They converted light into electronic signals that could be recorded on videotape and enhanced with computers. The picture was crystal clear, and ENG had a potential cost advantage over film because videotapes could be reused. Flaherty was projecting industry-wide savings of $40 million because of the elimination of 250 million feet of expendable news film.[5] That much film, enough to stretch from New York to Los Angeles and halfway back, was being shot and discarded by TV newsrooms each year. As a bonus, the same electronic signals could be fed into microwave transmitters, sent back to studios and broadcast live into viewers' living rooms.[6]

But by mid-1972 it was apparent the new cameras would not be available for at least another year. As it turned out, they wouldn't be ready for another two years, not until mid-1974. Beindorf decided he could wait no longer. Grudgingly, he diverted around $240,000 from the development budget for the purchase of four cameras manufactured by the Phillips company, at $45,000 each. With the $60,000 that was left, Beindorf bought three lesser-quality units manufactured by Akai.

Beindorf shook his head because it had been flaws in the almost-viable Phillips camera that had caused CBS to turn to Ikegami in the first place. The Phillips system did produce a good picture. However, the unit was so heavy, around 65 pounds, that a photographer needed a metal harness to use it. Worse, it was a glutton for electrical power; large batteries accounted for much of the weight. The cheaper Akai cameras had different problems. While this camera could be operated with one hand, its picture looked little better than the first images transmitted from the moon. To get a usable picture from the Akai units, tremendous lighting was needed. When they finally arrived, the Ikegami devices would produce a clearer picture than some of the best studio cameras and the whole unit weighed only 22 pounds.[7]

Realizing the cameras he had just bought were obsolete, Beindorf nevertheless sent the first Phillips system to Philadelphia, where WCAU had been preparing to fire John Facenda and nearing disaster. ENG began in Philadelphia in 1972. Beindorf also decided that all three of the Akai cameras—enough for a complete film-to-ENG conversion—would go to KMOX in St. Louis. Of the five CBS stations, KMOX, which had the highest ratings, was located in the smallest market. Thus, it was least at risk if breakdowns proved catastrophic. KMOX was also not a union shop. It would be free from challenges CBS was expecting from the International Brotherhood of Electrical Workers, whose contracts specified that only technicians could operate electronic hardware.

KMOX became the CBS Los Alamos. By September 1974 KMOX had the first fully outfitted ENG newsroom.[8] The crux of the activity in St. Louis was live telecasting, accomplished by connecting one of the Akai cameras to a microwave transmitter in a Chevrolet Econoline truck.[9] During the experimental phase, several breaking events, including a plane crash at Lambert Airport and a series of weather emergencies, had upheld the reliability of KMOX's live system.[10] According to KMOX general manager Tom Battista, every newscast had an "election night kind of excitement."[11]

With the first Phillips camera in service in Philadelphia and the three Akai units in St. Louis, Beindorf then had to decide where to send the three remaining Phillips cameras. His temptation was to ship all three to Chicago, where ratings problems were acute and where WBBM general manager Robert Wussler was campaigning for the gear.[12] Wussler shortly was promoted to the network level and later became CBS president. His successor at WBBM, Neil Derrough, wanted the equipment more than Wussler had.[13]

The issue was settled when Beindorf announced that WBBM would get the first Ikegami cameras, and that for now the three Phillips cameras, one each, would go to WBBM, WCBS in New York and KNXT, the Los Angeles station.[14] This guaranteed that Beindorf's former station, KNXT, would be served.

By making this decision, Beindorf enabled CBS to again assume undisputed leadership in local TV news, if only for one memorable day. It began about an hour before KNXT's "The Big News" was scheduled to begin on May 17, 1974, when the newsroom received a tip that police had stumbled onto a hideout believed to be the base of a terrorist group known as the Symbionese Liberation Army. Three months before, the SLA had kidnapped heiress Patricia Hearst, who, rather than remaining a kidnap victim, joined her captors in their terrorist activities. In April, Hearst, with a machine gun, had helped the SLA rob a San Francisco bank. That spring, the Hearst kidnapping vied with Richard Nixon's impending impeachment hearings as the most-widely reported news story in the country. Everyone assumed that once police had tracked down the SLA, they also would find Hearst.

Reporters Bill Deiz and Bob Simmons boarded the live truck and sped to the hideout, a house in south Los Angeles. The live signal kept fading in and out, each time with the scene shifting back to anchor Jerry Dunphy in the studio. "It's getting hot down there," Dunphy said.

Finally, the link was established and Deiz was seen in an alley that pointed across a boulevard to the house, where SLA members had ignored orders to surrender. Behind Deiz could be seen armed police staking positions behind telephone poles, cars and buildings. Popping noises could be heard. The pops, gunshots as reproduced by live television, gave way to a crescendo of gunfire so loud that Deiz couldn't be heard. Then, suddenly, Deiz dived out of the picture as a bullet came whizzing at the KNXT camera. A few minutes later a bomb squad arrived and police could be seen telling each other to evacuate. Deiz was not sure why, but it didn't take him long to find out. Authorities fire-bombed the house, screams could be heard, and flames could be seen leaping so high that trees were engulfed. The inferno continued for 45 minutes. "I don't know how anybody could still be alive," Deiz said. The implication, that Hearst was one of the dead, was stirred by Simmons. "Witnesses saw Patty Hearst in that house last night," Simmons exclaimed.[15]

Six SLA members were killed, although by happenstance Hearst had not been among them. Like millions of others, she witnessed the spectacle on "The Big News." This was in a second hideout, a motel, where she and two others had been holed up. "There in living color," Hearst related, "we could see what seemed like a regular cops-and-robbers show; an army of policemen, wearing gas masks and battle fatigues. . . . Hand-held cameras jerked every which way while the news reporters described in simplistic detail what we could see on the screen." Disturbed by "the fate I had so narrowly escaped," Hearst said that "[to] me, it all looked surreal."[16]

Patty Hearst was part of an audience estimated at around 20 million viewers. KNXT offered its live coverage to all of the other Los Angeles television stations, as well as to 50 others on the West Coast.[17] Not since the shooting of Lee Harvey Oswald in 1963 had anything like it been seen on live television.

That summer, the CBS Chicago station, WBBM, received the first Ikegami cameras. On-the-spot telecasts of a hazardous chemical spill and a collision between two commuter trains were WBBM's first ENG exclusives.[18] Later WBBM pushed the limits of ENG by showing such things as police patrols and actual negotiations during threatened strikes. WBBM routinely originated live coverage of pre-planned events such as news conferences, which alert newsmakers took to scheduling at 6 and 10 p.m., when WBBM's news was on the air.[19]

Patty Hearst gave CBS other opportunities as her arrest in September 1975 and subsequent trial marked the first application of satellite newsgathering, later known as "SNG." By connecting a portable camera to a satellite uplink, geographical barriers were removed. WBBM sent a crew to San Francisco for the "trial of the decade," an important showcase for young anchor Bill Kurtis, the person who had had the dubious distinction of replacing Fahey Flynn on WBBM after the bow-tie dustup in 1968. Unable to avert WBBM's plunge in the ratings, Kurtis was fired. Rehired by Wussler, Kurtis came back to WBBM and with his co-anchor Walter Jacobson excelled in every ENG outing.[20] WBBM's feat of bringing local coverage to a far-off event hinted at an important strength looming in the local news system. Networks weren't needed anymore in the origination of distant news.

While "Eyewitness News" on rival ABC held ground in the ratings, what mattered at the moment were several sets of CBS local ratings that had in fact shot up. In Chicago, for example, WBBM had rocketed out of last place. Having nearly doubled its audience share to "30," it was challenging the Flynn-Daly combination on ABC's WLS. "I think what really made the difference," WBBM news director Van Gordon Sauter maintained, "is when we came to recognize that this TV camera gives us the speed and mobility of radio."[21]

Yet Derrough, the general manager, would explain the difference more the way Beindorf would, as a definitive weapon in a news war. "I'll never forget at WBBM where we would have a live picture of a reporter talking to somebody on a remote [and] WLS and WMAQ would be talking to same the person on the phone. We forced the other stations into ENG. There was no doubt about it."[22] After a late start, the NBC stations finally staked a major position after their parent company, RCA, unveiled what it called the TK-76 camera.[23] But in the latest go-around with new technology it was CBS, not RCA, that had won the prize.

With proven technology, CBS and Ikegami began a new crash program—to sell the camera to other local TV stations, ostensibly CBS affiliates. The campaign began with massive publicity. The spin was "big breakthrough in journalism," and even elite outlets like the *New York Times* and the *Wall Street Journal* got behind it. An article in *Time* magazine entitled "The Handy Looky" heralded an electronic phenomenon in local TV news and noted that the new cameras had brought a new dimension of immediacy to local newscasts. This article was dressed by a two-column picture taken by a CBS publicist, that *Time* had obtained, of the first Ikegami camera. It contained a flattering pose of its user, Bill Kurtis.[24]

Even so, "journalism breakthrough" was not the clarion call to those on the front lines of the video revolution. Buyers were hearing "big ratings" instead. For months, Ikegami ads proclaiming "the first piece of hardware to have a substantive effect on [your] news ratings" would blanket trade publications. Displays all over the magazine *Broadcasting* found new ways to entice owners and managers into being "the first 'instant news' station in your market."[25] Station managers attending the annual convention of the National Association of Broadcasters were able not just to observe but to roll up their sleeves and actually tinker with the hardware at a booth CBS had set up.[26]

Then in June 1974, in the first extensive trade analysis, *Variety* reporter Morry Roth spelled it all out. Not swayed by ENG's journalistic potentials, Roth wrote an article headlined "Minicam As WBBM-TV Weapon That Leapfrogs Chi News Field."[27] Roth's "Minicam as Weapon" article had struck the golden chord with local broadcasters weighing the cost benefits of adopting the new gear. *Broadcasting* added to the interest with another analysis, part of it titled: "WBBM-TV finds portable cameras have helped boost its ratings."[28] Adjacent to *Broadcasting's* report was a story about one of the first non-CBS ENG purchasers, WTOG in Tampa-St. Petersburg. "The new equipment," readers learned, "has given [WTOG its] only leverage" in the ratings.[29]

The buying spree then began, and within six months both Ikegami and RCA had backlogs of orders. The fever was so intense that 58 stations did not wait for the advanced cameras. They went ahead and launched ENG operations the same way CBS had: with obsolete Phillips and Akai hardware. "That's what they wanted us to use," Ridge Shannon, the news director of Detroit's WJBK, recalled, "so we used it."[30]

Indeed, despite all the pro-journalism hoopla, news directors were divided. They did not protest ENG the way some had opposed the news consultants. ENG glittered and gleamed, and in many newsrooms a dozen people would crowd around to uncrate the next new camera or tape machine. Still, news directors had to bow to station managers who had no intention of handing news departments hundreds of thousands of dollars of equipment and not seeing it used. Newsworkers began to complain of contrived news stories and "going live for the sake of going live." Meanwhile, an already awkward relationship between news people and technicians was seriously complicated by labor pressures. At KIRO in Seattle, jurisdictional disputes were so confused that a strike broke out, not directly between labor and management, but because management had not resolved a conflict between two unions, the IBEW, whose members included the engineers, and the International Alliance of Theatrical Stage Employees, whose members included anxious news photographers.

The most unsettling ENG issue for news directors was their dealings with station promotion managers. To serious news directors, promotion was a time-consuming diversion of duties and downright disgusting. Promotion managers were just as happy to stay clear of news directors. At most TV stations, news promotion barely existed. In a single ENG blink, though, this would change. Station managers insisted that ENG be promoted. The technology so simplified news advertising that wave after wave of promotion was not just possible, it was inevitable.

ENG was an advertiser's delight. For years, the Broadcast Promotion Association had taught the value of buzz words. Half of the buzz words in one BPA primer could have been lifted straight off the pages of one of Ikegami's sales brochures. These words had included "new," "fast," "quick," "improved," "here," "now," "live" and "first."[31] Beyond this, ENG was a growing, evolving development that boded well for infinite newsgathering possibilities and promotional strategies. Stations that began with ENG cameras could then trumpet live coverage and later interconnected bureaus, helicopters, weather graphics, computerized newsrooms and satellite newsgathering.

Interestingly, the first "promos" were not as TV spots but were embedded in actual newscasts, where ENG could be effectively touted without excessive fanfare. Managers of the ABC-owned stations circulated to news producers the first policies on how an "ENG effect" could be achieved in a newscast. "Whenever a 'live' ENG report is broadcast," the ABC stations were told, "the fact the report is 'live' must be emphasized with supers [words on the screen]. The super 'LIVE' should be seen throughout most of the report." We must "stress the visual and/or [the] exclusive."[32]

Other stations had similar rules. Instructions in Peoria, the 110th market, were common all over the country: "Action Cam will be promoted at least once each newscast, either orally or by means of a . . . super. This identification will be made on stories which are the latest breaking or have the most action."[33] In 1976, *Broadcasting* went so far as to show what this looked like, with photos of actual newscasts. Almost every photo had "Live" somewhere on the screen. Viewers of Denver's KMGH saw "Live Insta-Cam," those of WCAU "Live Mini-cam" and those of Houston's KPRC "Live Big 2 Instant News Camera." In the Houston photo, the word "Live," in slanted italic letters, was larger than the face of reporter Cal Thomas.[34]

But this inside-the-newscast ENP could not reach viewers who tuned to competitors. Persuading viewers to switch channels was the ballgame, and this meant ongoing flights of TV commercials when news was not on the air. Broadcasters had been slow to yield this lucrative commercial airtime. But the airtime was less valuable to a second or third-place outlet than to the already No. 1 station. Those in the basement not only had less to lose in ENP; over the long run they had the most to gain if promotions caused news ratings to increase.

While numerous lagging local stations would back ENG with all-out ENP, two sister stations in the West, both owned by the Gannett company, were in a class by themselves.

In Denver, station KBTV had been fighting not for first place but to stay out of last place. With "24" shares, KBTV and rival KOA had been swamped by a third station, KLZ, which had had "40" shares since the early 1960s.[35] At KBTV, there was a ray of hope when Time Inc. sold KLZ to McGraw-Hill, a book publisher whose TV credentials looked thin. This quiver soon turned to a rumble when KBTV station manager Charles Leasure, managing news director Roger Ogden, executive news producer Tom Kirby and promotion director Harvey Mars noticed something odd. McGraw-Hill renamed the station KMGH and then brought the first ENG cameras to Denver in 1975. However, as Mars recalled, "We waited and waited and they never promoted it." As near as Mars could determine, the technicians at KMGH were running things. He also suspected that, flying high,

KMGH had balked at freeing up commercial airtime to vaunt its ENG breakthrough.[36]

At KBTV news and promotion factions were not fighting each other but were united in wanting a news war. Even though KMGH had it, ENG had not caused a ripple in Denver. Leasure bought a quarter-million-dollars of ENG equipment, and Kirby and Mars guaranteed him the Mile High City would hear about it.

It would become TV's most sophisticated ENG advertising campaign. KBTV backed away from the "Buck Rogers" strategy that many other stations had used. Such promotion was typically a video montage of the equipment's whistles and bells, with an announcer saying "Here it is and here's what it does." Mars felt this made ENG too remote. He wanted the new technology to evoke an emotional response. Part of the plan was to minimize announcers and let music underscore a statement. "We purposely avoided needle-drop music that said 'industry on parade'" in favor of softer numbers "that created a mood" about the ENG experience "and put the benefits of ENG in real-people terms," Mars recalled.

The effects quickly multiplied. KBTV decided to name its device the "Action Cam" and followed with several supplemental steps, including the painting of all its news cars, live trucks, and cameras, in Mars' words, "with red, white, and blue racing stripes." This American flag color scheme was replicated on KBTV's studio set, the "Action Center." The same stripes even appeared on the jackets worn by reporters, photographers and engineers, all of whom would be seen in promos. In a masterstoke, Ogden would have Mars contact a hobby company, which manufactured a model helicopter adorned with the racing stripes. Thousands of Denver children relished these "9 News" helicopters as their favorite toy.

The blitz began, timed with the arrival of KBTV's first Action Cam. Denver viewers saw again and again a music-adorned ad capturing the Action Cam, the live truck and a lone reporter from 20 different angles. "It's called Action Cam," a voice from off-screen chimed in. "Whenever news happens, wherever it happens, live Action Cam is there. . . . Action Cam. From the time it leaves the scene until the time it reaches you: less than one-thousandth of a second. Live!"[37]

After promos on the cameras ran their course, KBTV started on the helicopter. Swirling music showed the craft dramatically emerging from a mountain scene and then flying directly overhead. "Sky 9," the announcer noted. "Whenever you see this, you know news is happening."[38] Next was a campaign about KBTV's four interconnected news bureaus in Colorado Springs, Boulder, Ft. Collins and on Colorado's Western slope. "It's all right here on Channel 9," these latest ads proclaimed.[39]

In lulls between the arrivals of big-ticket gear, lesser ENG strides came to centerstage. One was a new telescoping transmitting dish that enabled more distant coverage. Mars devised a promo with uplifting music that featured scenes of a Colorado sunset. In the foreground a lone engineer polished the dish and watched it ascend 30 feet into the air.[40] After the dish-polishing promo, the station heralded "Snow 9," a snowmobile equipped with ENG equipment that could reach plane crashes and other breaking news in remote mountain terrain. In yet another KBTV promo, an announcer began, "News coverage of a protest in Springfield, Colorado, was limited. . . . But 'Jet 9' changed the way it could be done. Extra crews, extra views. . . . 'Jet 9.' Just another reason that wherever news is, 9 News is there."[41]

Ogden explained, "The real point is to take advantage of the latest technology, to create the perception in the viewer's mind that Channel 9 is the place to turn to see the news."[42] Within three years KBTV had a "54" share, a larger audience in Denver than the three network newscasts put together.[43] It was the last great local news rating sensation, and like those in the past it stirred national media coverage.

Noting that KBTV's newscast had become "the most dominant local-news show in a major American city," Ben Daviss in a *TV Guide* article entitled "Man the Minicams, Rev Up the Choppers," called the "quietly polite, curly-haired Ogden . . . the Genghis Kahn of Denver television." The effect was so sweeping, Daviss said, that "KBTV has run its closing credits against a filmed background of school children, downtown shoppers or any other available group, holding index fingers erect in tribute to the station's top ratings status."[44]

In a different article, "Selling Souls for a Thirty Share," writer Joe Popper observed that "top executives at Gannett . . . didn't plow millions of dollars into technology just to have toys to play with. They did it because they came to understand that it was the route to the top." KBTV, which Gannett renamed KUSA, "promoted the hell out itself," Popper declared, and "drummed home its message: We're Number One!"[45]

Its sister station in Phoenix also promoted itself, only KPNX hit pay dirt with only one innovation, its helicopter. For 20 years, KPNX had trailed station KOOL, one of the last stations in a large market to still use its news director as its main anchor. KPNX hired Magid, whose research revealed that the best-liked personality in Phoenix had not been the KOOL news director but the KOOL helicopter pilot.[46]

Starting with a homemade gyroplane pilot Jerry Foster had been providing aerial coverage for KOOL since 1970.[47]

KPNX general manager Pep Cooney orchestrated a raid, luring Foster from KOOL, not just with an anchor-level salary, but with a pilot's dream: a jet-propelled Hughes helicopter costing a half-million dollars. It was outfitted with a new type of aerial transmitter enabling the helicopter to beam live pictures while actually in flight and from any direction. Until then, helicopters could cover the news only in a hover position. Foster's helicopter could reach speeds of 180 miles per hour forward—75 miles per hour backwards—while beaming a live picture in flight anywhere within a 150-mile radius of Phoenix.[48] KPNX rolled out "Sky 12" at a special public demonstration on September 1, 1978. "It's a super go, fast chopper," a beaming Foster declared after finishing the first official flight.[49]

Foster lived up to both this advanced publicity and to Gannett's insatiable ratings expectations. KPNX had had only 19 percent of the audience when Foster joined.[50] Three years later in 1981, KPNX was No. 1 with shares in the thirties.[51] Foster in turn became the symbol of Phoenix local news. His helicopter was routinely airborne throughout KPNX's "Action News," and from the cockpit Foster was cast just like an anchor who looked down on the city with weather and traffic reports.

But the greatest excitement came during breaking events, such as fires, holdups and major accidents, when Foster was instantly over the scene. One of his hundreds of exclusives was an interview with Arizona Senator Barry Goldwater, himself a pilot, from inside "Sky 12" shortly after a DC-10 airliner crash in Chicago.[52] Foster also regularly joined local authorities in search and rescue missions; innumerable times KPNX viewers watched as Foster plucked stranded hikers from mountaintops and saved people trapped in cars during flash floods.[53]

The promotion of Foster and "Sky 12" covered every angle. "It was Friday, September 14," one of the promos began. "Assignment editor Roger Ball called Jerry Foster at home—a big fire had erupted. . . . At 7:25 viewers of the Today Show watched the first report on a two-million-dollar fire live!"[54] Three-second promos showing Foster, with headset, inside "Sky 12" ran day and night.[55] According to the research, the single most popular promo was one shot with a second helicopter. From an airborne position viewers first saw "Sky 12" in horizontal flight. Then it began ascending ever-higher altitudes as a popular tune called "The Eagle and the Hawk" by singer John Denver played in the background.[56] More publicity was unleashed when Foster received the Harmon Award for outstanding contribution to aviation from President Ronald Reagan.[57] He was the subject of two separate *TV Guide* articles and in 1983 was flown to Burbank to be showcased on NBC's prime-time "Real People" series.[58]

Yet Foster's most important promotional feat came in September 1979, when he took off from Phoenix, flew 300 miles to the north and landed in the parking lot of Caesars Palace in Las Vegas. There, hundreds of station managers and news directors had gathered for the annual RTNDA convention. Spellbound, the attendees had been watching a presentation by KPNX news director Al Buch, who had just shown a videotape of some of Foster's achievements, including two rescues and a three-minute segment that showed a panel truck speeding down Phoenix freeways and side streets with police in hot pursuit. Foster had captured the entire chase while flying overhead.[59]

Just as Buch was wrapping up, Foster made a surprise entrance. Those in the hall jumped to their feet and gave him a standing ovation. Stepping before the microphones, Foster recounted how earlier that day he had covered a school bus accident and had done his noon news weather segment near the Grand Canyon while flying to Las Vegas. Outside, the TV executives waited in line to look at "Sky 12" for themselves. In the article recapping the convention, the *RTNDA Communicator* stated, "Foster and the Hughes 500D helicopter he pilots for KPNX-TV in Phoenix literally stole the show."[60]

Starting with those first five CBS local stations in 1973, the number of local newsrooms with video capability would reach 550—86 percent of the total—in 1979.[61] No technology in the history of television had caught on so suddenly. Home video was just a step away. Altogether, local stations had spent more than $1 billion on ENG and its many add-ons, including helicopters, during the 1970s. Eight months after Foster's exhibition in Las Vegas, securities of Textron, the parent company of Bell Helicopters, surged on the New York Stock Exchange after word seeped out that Bell had just received 100 orders. Asked for a reaction, Bell executive Gordon Moody told the *Wall Street Journal*, "We have a saying around here. If you sell one, you sell three—one to each (network) affiliate. It's usually the No. 2 or No. 3 station that buys the chopper first. Then No. 2 becomes No. 1, and we sell the others."[62]

Although the arrival of electronic news had been inevitable, when it did strike in the 1970s not just breakthroughs but dilemmas ensued. The public would see a new image of TV news in movies showing frantic producers crashing into walls and sprinting down hallways to get the latest material on the air. Hollywood did not exaggerate. These became everyday scenes in real newsrooms as speed-of-light technology kept pushing deadlines to the very last second.

Meanwhile, live news reporting had opened a raft of ethical questions, including the one provoked by coverage of the SLA shootout. Caught up in the moment and now live on TV, reporters had indicated that Patty Hearst was dead. That she was still alive raised concerns about whether facts would or even could be checked when a live camera was in use. Further, newsrooms relearned a fact of newsroom life, that truly big events like the SLA shootout were few. *Newsweek* reported that Detroit's WJBK had "sent its electronic unit to a downtown tree to cover the rescue of a Siamese cat." Not to be outdone, Washington's WRC carried a live interview with a Taiwanese acrobat who, as viewers and a surprised WRC reporter were to discover, could not speak English.[63] The form-over-substance problem, of turning routine stories into live spectacles, would never disappear.

Almost completely overlooked in the rush to ENG was its assessment by those for whom it was intended. Average viewers quite simply could not get their fill of it, and this, more than any other factor, had rallied the technology. According to the research, ENG had suddenly become "a major function of TV for the middle majority." Yet there had been an intriguing additional finding. It was evidence that ENG at the local level was making worse the mass audience's perception of network news. The networks had continued to avoid "eyewitness" coverage. Yet as local TV expanded such coverage with ENG, the networks were perceived as more biased. This was because ENG could not color or interpret accounts but instead showed the actual news.

In almost all research, a certain proportion of respondents regularly cited instances of one-sided reporting. Yet noteworthy were 1977 data from McHugh & Hoffman, in which the number of those complaining of bias in network news had climbed to more than 60 percent. The comparable figure for local news had dropped to around 40 percent. "The bias described [in network news] was not of a particular political orientation (i.e., 'right wing' or 'left wing'). Rather, it was one of 'not showing all the facts,' thus 'distorting the news.'" This stemmed from the networks' practice of having its newsmen merely read stories from scripts. "In contrast, the local reporter [defers] to film and tape [for] visually supporting the reporter's statements. If the viewer finds contradictions between what he sees and what he hears, he is at liberty to ignore [the reporter]—and the issue of bias is not raised." Emphasizing the extent the networks had not adapted to this crucial characteristic of TV viewing—that pictures overpowered the words—McHugh & Hoffman went on to predict "audience interest in network news will inevitably decline."[64]

The following year in Boston, McHugh & Hoffman would probe these perceptions in greater detail. Definitively, assessments of ENG broke on class lines. Upper-middle viewers were not enamored. A Boston doctor who had watched local news criticized coverage of a snow storm and holiday travel. "Everyone knew it was snowing, who needed to look at it? . . . Also, Memorial Day traffic, standing out on the highway and cars whipping by. They could have told you about the traffic in one sentence and dropped it," he protested.

But in the same study middle and lower status viewers were overwhelmed and repeatedly expressed the benefits of "seeing it yourself." "I love to watch live coverage. There's not enough now to suit me," a lower-middle class respondent said. Another described "a truck that was under a bridge and didn't make it. They were cutting the driver out of the truck. You could become part of it." Yet another recounted "[t]he house that blew up in Madden. I liked seeing that they sent a reporter to cover the helpless family." Many cited ongoing local coverage of the 1977 Boston busing crisis. An upper-lower class woman said ENG meant "uncut, fresh, live news so you can see the news for yourself and you know it's the truth."

Just as arresting was evidence in the same study that average viewers reacted as much to the ENP as the ENG. In the Boston study, without any prompting or aids, 34 percent not only volunteered the name "Instant Eye" but correctly identified it with WBZ. Thirty-three percent correctly linked "Action Cam" to WCVB and almost as many volunteered "Electricam" as the device of WNAC. The consultants could not get over the number of times these marketing handles were routinely used in conversations as middle and lower class respondents described the experience of watching local news. As one of them stated, "With the Action Cam, . . . they can film it at the disaster or whatever instead of seeing it later." Recalling one of the racial disturbances, another explained how "the Instant Eye camera took all kinds of camera shots showing the school buses pulling up . . . and showing all the police milling around." Another commented, "I've seen a lot of holdups and fires and the Action Cam has been right there to take pictures. It's very exciting to see these action films."[65] There was no questioning the impact of the video revolution within the middle majority.

To another group of onlookers, it was conclusive testimony of a television journalism gone mad. Happy talk and action visuals had been bad enough. Now there were helicopter spectacles, racing stripes, and people using index fingers to help stations signal "We're No. 1!"

This was the breaking point. Walter Cronkite, at the peak of his popularity as CBS News anchor, joined an army of critics. Speaking before the annual conference of CBS affiliate managers on May 5, 1976, Cronkite condemned "the razzle-dazzle of a promotion campaign" and questioned "whether we are indulging in show business rather than journalism." Cronkite accepted ratings competition, but not "cosmetics," "pretty packaging" and news consultants. He told local station managers they were "suckers for a fad: editing by consultancy." "Yes, suckers," Cronkite continued, "because there is no evidence that this formula news broadcasting—the top 20 hit news items—works to permanent advantage."[66] Coming from the person then known as the "most trusted man in America," Cronkite's judgment seemingly meant a lot.

It didn't. The next big event in local TV news—a critical firestorm—would show why. Critics like Cronkite would exhort the news values of the upper-middle class. They were clueless, though, as to just how imposing people's news and editing-by-consultancy had become.

10

Armageddon
(1973–1977)

In February 1977, the Trendex research corporation conducted a nationwide public opinion survey on TV newscasts. Eighty-one percent of the 1,500 randomly sampled respondents said local television was doing a good or an excellent job of covering the news. Eighty-two percent voiced approval for the men and women who delivered the news; 69 percent felt local newscasts accurately showed the real world, and 54 percent said local news was free of bias. Local news bested network news in every category.[1] With the ratings services linking legions of first-time news viewers to local news, with pollsters charting overwhelming public approval and with the FCC's community ascertainment mandate fulfilled, it surely had seemed that local news was doing what it should.

Not a chance. The most impassioned news war of the 1970s would not be fought in newsrooms or on home TV screens but in an outpouring of articles, books, columns, commentaries, and speeches condemning local TV news as a public disgrace. Ignited in 1973 by the first accounts of the news consultants, a firestorm would burn almost continuously for three years. Never in the annals of American journalism had so many media experts had so many bad things to say.

Some of the criticism was justified. Happy talk had given viewers frisbee exhibitions, dart contests and other stunts. The advent of news promotion, ENG and whiz-bang studio technology had added to the distress.

The opponents of local news had a bigger axe to grind. They demanded that news research end, consultants be put out of business and local newscasts stop dumbing the American public. From Walter Cronkite on down they would storm local news seeking reform, only to finish by giving history another Pickett's Charge.

It was revealing to look at how insulated the New York media establishment really was. It was a very special look, too, for although big journalism had assaulted presidents, military leaders, churches and all parts of corporate America, it had never attempted to smear another component of the news media. To get their point across, leaders of the big media used public channels in a most questionable way. Their accounts of local TV news were scathing. Yet in the name of good journalism, paragons of the field had not checked facts, had not interviewed essential sources and had selectively chosen material. The facts on local news often arrived when experts who had never worked in the field quoted other such experts. The result was a shrieking public display that raised, within the profession, the first serious questions about the credibility of the major media. It was a lesson to future critics that as much as emotion makes good copy, thinking leads to the truth.

The misguided attack on "little journalism" would not be an episode highlighted in the numerous books and articles that bowed to the New York media. Yet it proved one of the major turning points in American TV news. While denigrating and embarrassing local TV stations, the big networks were spurring their campaign for nightly national newscasts of 60 minutes or longer. With 24-hour news channels like CNN on the horizon, the networks knew they were in trouble if they were limited to 30 minutes. They also knew they couldn't expand without the cooperation of local TV stations.

But the local stations didn't cooperate. Instead, local TV rolled up and returned this network news expansion plan, happy to tell those in New York where they could put it.

Years before New York media experts had even heard of news consultants, local news directors had tangled with them. Rare was the news director who had not put up some kind of protest when word was given, usually by owners or top station executives, that consultants were coming. At the outbreak of the long march in 1971, scores of news directors had been visited by these outside advisors. Hundreds of others knew they were next.

Because arrangements to hire news consultants had always been made in the executive suite, not in the newsroom, news directors had been kept in the dark. They had learned what they could from each other. Their favorite meeting place was the annual conventions of the Radio-Television News Directors Association. These were stellar social occasions whose purpose was not controversy. Thus, the very first grumblings about consultants, at the 1971 convention in Boston, were conspicuous. As if playing a game of 20 questions, news directors in corridors and elevators, at receptions and other events, had tried to determine which ones had Magid or McHugh & Hoffman affiliations, and, then, the details. With rumors circulating that these consultants were out to eliminate them, news directors continued to sound off through the RTNDA's Washington office. This continued at the 1972 convention in Nassau where Phil McHugh appeared and stirred more mystery and bad feeling.[2]

When the RTNDA opened its October 1973 convention in Seattle, anxieties were at fever pitch. By then, several members had been demoted or fired allegedly because of consultants, who sensing retaliation stayed clear of Seattle.[3] Hoping, though, to finally air the issues, the RTNDA had two prominent news directors, Lou Prato of Detroit's WWJ and By Williams of Pittsburgh's WIIC, lead a discussion on "The Value of Research Firms for News." The session turned into a free-for-all. One by one a dozen news directors, Prato the loudest, unloaded on the consultants.[4]

The debate resumed at a board meeting the final day and escalated when Miami news director Ralph Renick, waved on by Prato, demanded a resolution condemning consultants. Renick, a former president of the RTNDA, had been priming for this moment. That October he was locked in a dispute with the management of his station, WTVJ, over its contract with Magid. Renick wanted something to bolster his case that Magid should be fired. However, consensus reigned that news directors did not know enough about consultants to render the verdict Renick sought.[5] It ended with RTNDA president Bosworth Johnson accepting a resolution mandating a blue ribbon investigation.[6] "I'm concerned that we look at the matter intelligently and without the hysteria which I feel was operative on the fringes of our Seattle discussions," Johnson told Richard Yoakam.[7]

Yoakam, an Indiana University professor, had supported the fact-finding over Renick's plan for a preemptive censure. Yoakam saw the rhubarb as emblematic of a broader transition within the TV news field. Older news directors who were usually also the anchors were clashing with an influx of younger people rising from positions totally behind the scenes. "The older news directors wanted consultants run off immediately," Yoakam noted, "while the newer members had more of a wait-and-see attitude."[8] In selecting the four-person panel, which would include Yoakam, Johnson wanted news directors who represented these differing points of view.

The panel chair was Ray Miller, whose career at Houston's KPRC had begun 23 years earlier. He'd anchored the news at KPRC since 1952 and had served as news director since 1959. "I did not rejoice over their arrival," Miller said in recalling his first encounter with the Magid consultants in 1970.[9] It was an understatement. Miller had instigated the anti-consultant movement and had fervently backed Renick.

A younger Ed Godfrey, the news director of KGW in Portland, a Magid client, felt Miller and Renick were overreacting but was not pro-consultant either. The fourth member was a still younger figure named Pat Polillo. The news director at WAGA in Atlanta, a McHugh & Hoffman client, Polillo's career had been shaped by the people's news ferment in the big cities of the Northeast. Johnson had wanted a fifth member, an Oklahoma City news director named Richard Townley.[10] But rather than taking part, Townley had other plans. Townley was preparing a series of articles in *TV Guide*.

While not part of the panel, Renick was eager to speed the outcome. In February 1974 he finally succeeded in having WTVJ end its relationship with Magid, a development Renick was convinced would set the agenda for the entire RTNDA probe. Following Magid's recommendation that WTVJ's "Ralph Renick Report" be changed and that Renick be paired with a co-anchor, Renick had paid a surprise visit to Magid headquarters. Three others from WTVJ and David LeRoy of Florida State University went along and Magid's contract was terminated after a confrontation.[11]

Immediately in contact with Johnson, the RTNDA president, Renick again pressed for a condemnation.[12] "We drove the rascals out and celebrated with champagne," Renick told the RTNDA board.[13] But informed that nothing could happen until the Miller panel reported, Renick began circulating his own packet of information. In it were confidential Magid materials, a report by LeRoy questioning some of Magid's research procedures, and quotations from news directors.[14] "Consultants are a little like the Soviet Army in World War II," read one of the quotes, from Renick himself. "They come in to liberate and end up an army of occupation, and, often, to remove the consultant's grip, a news director must wage a counter-attack, with results all too likely to be similar to the Hungarian revolt of 1956."[15]

With Renick's feelings thoroughly known, the RTNDA panel began its work. In March 1974 Miller outlined the probe at what proved an auspicious occasion. In his home city of Houston, Miller appeared before the National Association of Broadcasters, populated by station executives whose cooperation the news directors absolutely needed.[16] The news directors' fears that station executives might resist greatly were eased when attendees watched aghast as CBS's Dan Rather publicly insulted President Richard Nixon during a news conference televised from the NAB. Studying Rather's behavior, appalled station managers were more sensitive to what their news directors meant by "show business" journalism.

The panel eventually conferred with 50 stations known to be clients of consultants. The team visited newsrooms, interviewed newsworkers and monitored newscasts. Magid and McHugh & Hoffman cooperated by allowing examination of research reports. The RTNDA invited its members to submit written comments, anonymously if necessary.[17]

It was clear by no later than June 1974 that Renick's concerns were exaggerated and the controversy was dying out. Notably, Miller's view of news consultants was taking a 180-degree turn. While the panel did observe almost boilerplate proliferation of the "Eyewitness" format, Godfrey pointed out that the three networks also had identical news formats. Godfrey insisted that if "formula news" was not a concern of the networks, it should not be singled out locally. Grudgingly at first, Miller conceded Godfrey was right. The panel saw no case in which consultants were dictating news content. Nor was there evidence consultants fired and demoted station personnel. Only the stations could do that. The research reports were rife with personnel evaluations, but as they almost always involved people in front of the cameras, newscaster removals seemed the desire of the public, not the consultants.[18]

Finally, the panel investigated the research itself—to disagree vehemently with Renick's conclusion that the research was rigged. Data by a few very small consulting firms were questioned. A bigger issue, though, had been similarities in Magid's and McHugh & Hoffman's recommendations, presumably from independent studies in cities at great distances from one another. The consultants addressed this with national reports showing similar news viewing preferences. The panel was impressed that the research was performed by social scientists with Ph.Ds. Short courses on qualitative methods, moreover, mitigated Renick's allegation of bias. According to Godfrey, "You could see that the information was freely volunteered in interviews," as many as 1,000 in some of the studies.[19] A year before, Miller had wanted the consultants wiped out. Incredibly, he would now go before the RTNDA and announce, "Research conducted by news consultants is one of the greatest tools a news director ever had."[20]

The RTNDA board approved the panel's report and presented it to the full membership on September 10, 1974, at a convention in Montreal. The main conclusion, that station managers must confer with news directors prior to hiring consultants, steered the report's acceptance. As it turned out, a lack of involvement was the only matter troubling most news directors.[21] In finalizing the report, Johnson stated, "Legitimate market research, which forms the basis of a consultant's recommendation, is undeniably valuable. . . . [T]he consultant may be what he should be—an advisor."[22] Miller agreed to remain indefinitely as the RTNDA's official liaison to the consultants.[23]

On the eve of the convention, the RTNDA had sent letters to Magid and McHugh & Hoffman, not only informing them of their acquittals but inviting them to attend the Montreal gathering. For both the moment was sweet, like the end of hell week at a college fraternity, with smiles, handshakes and welcomes. The Miller Report defused so much controversy that a resolution was passed allowing news consultants to become RTNDA members.

Knowing what was to come, Renick did not attend. "Ray Miller, [and] I must say RTNDA wasn't too concerned about this," Renick complained 15 years later. "I guess I was emotionally attached to the issue and I thought RTNDA or Miller did not stand foursquare, at least float the flag and say 'danger, storm warnings, look out.' These guys," the consultants, "aren't what they claim to be."[24]

Yet Renick knew there were others who would listen.

They were experts and opinion leaders in the media power centers of New York, who at any other time would have turned deaf ears to the travails of a Florida news director. The guardians of national TV, New York media critics had almost never stooped so low as to comment on local broadcasting. But something new had just emerged—a local New York television venture so disturbing that it needed national attention. It was "Eyewitness News" on WABC.

The first concerted attacks on any TV newscast began in January 1971, when *Newsweek,* referred to "Eyewitness News" as "a journalistic 'Laugh-In'" whose ratings had "cut cruelly into those of NBC and CBS." Alarmed at too many happy anchors and too much visual news, *Newsweek* carried two articles on this New York debacle.[25]

Quickly joining in, *Time* reduced WABC to a "happy-go-lucky bunch of banana men," while John Leonard, writing in *Life*, would declare, "I'm tempted to call it *Eye-witless News*, but I'll settle for *Malapropaganda*, . . . that process by which incompetence is converted into cuteness."[26]

After *New York* magazine accused WABC of "raising holy hell," readers of *TV Guide* got yet another account. "New York's television news, for what it should be, is pretty bad. . . . [T]his Eyewitness (bleep) is a lot of (bleep)."[27] Dan Menaker of the *New Yorker* would upbraid WABC for "happy-news" prepared and delivered by "vaude-villians."[28] According to nationally syndicated columnist John O'Connor, "Nothing, evidently, is beyond the competitive vision of anchors Roger Grimsby and Bill Beutel."[29]

The excoriation of WABC in the national media continued for two years, although by mid-1973 critics had moved to other things. The New York local media had always been home to the unusual, and "Eyewitness News" was not going to disappear. Above all, the writers realized that no one outside New York could view WABC's news anyway. Yet it was out of this tempest that the true firestorm began.

In late 1973, just weeks after the RTNDA had refused to condemn the news consultants, Renick contacted the Columbia University journalism school in New York. He'd just been there himself, WTVJ having received one of Columbia's coveted DuPont broadcast journalism awards. Renick's packet of materials made its way to an alert Edward Barrett, who quickly spotted a vital piece of inside information. It amounted to a list showing which local newsrooms had contracts with consultants, then a closely guarded secret. Looking for "WABC," Barrett found it not once but twice, across from both Magid and McHugh & Hoffman. Struck not just by this, Barrett also could see that these same two consulting firms had strung clients from coast to coast. All of sudden "Eyewitness News" no longer seemed a provincial plague on New York. Barrett conceived a national conspiracy like Watergate, dominating the news at the time.

Writing in the *Columbia Journalism Review*, Barrett exposed a "phenomenon that has now spread across the country: the current breed of consultants moving in to reshape local television in the image they say the public wants." Consultants "begin by selling top station management on doing a survey. . . . Then the news department is converted, often reluctantly, to going along." By using the listing of clients that Renick had supplied, Barrett was able to contact and interview offended news directors. One of them complained that Magid "wanted an actor, and I'm a newsman." Another stated, "They are not concerned about quality but about style and flash." Barrett's startling account was must reading in elite circles. The consultants, he wrote, have no regard for "the conventional wisdom of the news fraternity"; what matters is not "what the public wants," but "what the public should have."[30] Within weeks, other authors were associating the "action-oriented 'happy talk' format," allegedly for "people who can't stand television news," with news consultants.

Using those words, and reviling a newscast designed for what he called "Billy Blue Collar," Richard Townley fired the second big volley by blasting Magid and McHugh & Hoffman in a two-part *TV Guide* series in March 1974. Townley was the same person asked to serve on the RTNDA's panel. Rather than engaging in the fact-finding, he cut loose in the national media. Townley reported that news consultants are a "danger to TV news integrity [and] a hindrance to public understanding of complex issues." His case in point was a new revelation, that a station in Boston, WNAC, had followed WTVJ in eliminating Magid. According to Townley, there was "mounting antagonism" within the RTNDA.[31]

Mounting antagonism? Ray Miller would ask, but barely before the next negative account appeared a month later in *The Quill,* the magazine of the Society of Professional Journalists. Once more, Magid and McHugh & Hoffman were linked to the "happy talk" news format and accused of using research to dictate news content. "It had happened in New York, Chicago, San Francisco, Los Angeles—where strange things are supposed to happen. But now," readers were told, "it was in Middle America City, USA." According to the article's source on consultants, a local reporter in Baton Rouge, "Magid says say it even if you don't have anything to say."[32] It caused Miller and some others to again do a double take.

By the middle of 1974, a critical campaign against local TV news had exploded. In the *New York Times,* O'Connor objected to "the huckstering of independent 'consultants,' [and their] race for show-business and sensationalism."[33] Another columnist, Gary Deeb of the *Buffalo Evening News,* contacted Buffalo's WBEN and WKBW and sure enough found news consultants. Already shocked by the depravity of people's news, Deeb said he "couldn't believe these stations would allow news consultants to come into the newsroom and run it by remote control. . . . We in the print field had a duty to call this to the public's attention."[34]

Deeb moved to Chicago. Largely because of him, Chicago would compete with New York as the mecca for print-directed attacks on local news reporting. While the *Chicago Sun-Times'* Ron Powers would later gain attention for his scathing 1977 book *The Newscasters,* Deeb would stand head-and-shoulders over all newspaper critics as the scourge of local TV news. His column in the *Chicago Tribune* was syndicated nationwide. Each day broadcasters all over the country could expect to find some type of broadside from Deeb. In the process, Deeb would make ABC-owned WLS, the birthplace of "happy talk," as infamous as its New York sister station WABC. "Channel 7's 'Happy-Talk' approach, which has been copied by stations all over the country," Deeb told the nation, "is bent on winning its audience with 'tranquilizers' that sooth the nerves of viewers who have no stomach for the reality of the news."[35] Later detailing Chicago's "hot battle for the powderpuff championship," Deeb hailed WLS as "the Clown Prince of News Fluff."[36]

With fires intensifying, the assault on local news would take on dramatic new meaning the night of April 22, 1974, when famed commentator Eric Sevareid entered the fray. At first, the affair had been limited to writers and critics mostly obscure to the general public. No more. For three ear-piercing minutes on the "CBS Evening News," Sevareid lambasted the pretty faces and trivial content of local newscasts and branded them as "burlesque." Fingering the news consultants, Sevareid exhorted, "The astounding daily story of the astounding human race is apparently now regarded by many local station managers as not compelling enough. Reality itself must be jazzed up . . . [by] actors, very bad actors." According to Sevareid, "any day now, one of them will sing the news while doing a buck-and-wing stark naked."[37]

Sevareid's missal, a rallying point for critics, had followed and drawn from the first major network expose on local news. Before 50 million viewers, this had played out on the CBS "60 Minutes" program the night of March 10, 1974. "In San Francisco," correspondent Mike Wallace began, "the latest wrinkle is 'tabloid' news. And because KGO-TV, Channel 7, there has one of the highest-rated eleven o'clock newscasts in the country, '60 Minutes' went to San Francisco to take a look." For the next 16 minutes, Wallace unmasked a seemingly systematic emphasis on crime, degradation, and sex-driven news stories on ABC-owned KGO and Westinghouse-owned KPIX. As people talked, CBS crawled sideways across the bottom of the screen a list of news stories these local stations had not covered, including British miners, Pentagon spying, and Watergate developments in Washington.

According to Wallace, all of this was an insult to a third station, KRON, which had finished first in a content study CBS had commissioned. KRON opted for a newscast that in Wallace's words "is the most traditional . . . probably the most informative and perhaps the least entertaining." KGO station manager Russ Coughlan, KGO anchor Van Amburg and KPIX news director Jim Van Messel had been grilled by Wallace. In contrast was the cool, no-worry environment Wallace allowed when interviewing KRON president Al Constant. "Sensationalism in the news is not a proper standard," Constant waxed to Wallace. "We're not going to bastardize our news ratings."[38]

Notably, this "60 Minutes" exposé had been the first since Barrett's to not identify Magid. Noticing both this and the exemplary news operations at KRON, Miller and this time several additional news directors were again saying "hum." But there was no time to dwell as more and more bullets from network news came whizzing their way. In a speech that May, CBS News president Richard Salant publicly condemned Magid, McHugh & Hoffman and the TV managers who hired them, demanding that news judgments "can't be shared [and] can't be delegated. . . . [T]he whole business of journalism is a great deal more than [what is] agreeable to a majority of people."[39] After this ABC executive Av Westin declared, "We will never turn to 'happy-talk' or 'tabloid' journalism" at ABC News.[40] Joining the CBS and ABC factions was John Masterman of NBC News. Masterman called news consultants "money-sucking leeches."[41]

Then came CBS correspondent Charles Kuralt. "I hate what those guys are doing. . . . I think [the consultants] are cheapening news," Kuralt vented at the 1975 RTNDA convention. "My overwhelming impression [of local news] . . . is of hair. . . . Hair carefully styled and sprayed, hair neatly parted, hair abundant and every hair in place. . . . But I can't remember much that came out from beneath all that hair." Interesting to the news directors had been Kuralt's further remark, "Now nothing I say here should be construed as relating in any way to Dan Rather," a person with a shock of hair who was an associate of Kuralt's at CBS.[42]

Soon, the nation's elite newspapers were back at it. The lead paragraph to an article in the Pulitzer Prize-winning *Washington Post* would read: "Ralph Renick, the longtime news director and anchorman at WTVJ in Miami, is something of a hero among the nation's 1,200 news directors."[43] The news in this *Post* report was Renick's ouster of Magid and how this was fueling a rebellion against consultants in newsrooms everywhere. The removals of Magid by Renick's station, WTVJ, and by Boston station, WNAC, also were themes in two more articles in the *New York Times*. The first, in October 1975, stretched over three pages. "Broadcast consultants have sent shocks of alarm through the industry they claim to serve because of their make-or-break say over careers, and their influence on news and feature content. . . . The country is dotted with disgruntled TV news personnel who have suffered at the hands of Magid," Johanna Steinmetz reported.[44] In December 1975, a front-page *New York Times* article about the "profusion of 'action news' programs" was pegged to Magid's firing by WNAC, this because of recommendations for fewer political stories.[45] It was now two years since the WTVJ and WNAC firings had occurred.

Also in 1975 came the first bashings of local news in books. Edwin Diamond in *The Tin Kazoo* would write, "Up until a few years ago, television news was in the hands of professional news directors and producers, traditionally trained in newspaper or magazine work or broadcast journalism. It still is, at the networks. But local station management has not had the same professional approach . . . ." Doubting whether research was used, Diamond explained that consultants defer to "self-evident truths." While no one from Magid or McHugh & Hoffman was interviewed to find out if this was true, Diamond did draw from Townley, Salant and Mike Wallace.[46]

In another book, *Moments of Truth?*, Marvin Barrett issued another call for the consultants' removals. Like Edward Barrett, Marvin Barrett was associated with the DuPont-Columbia University journalism awards, whose top honor in 1975 had gone to CBS for that "60 Minutes" report by Wallace on the shame of San Francisco. Barrett elaborated on the hopelessness of news consulting and praised network news for finding at KRON a model of news excellence. Barrett began: "While the networks were nervously backing their news departments in the struggle to meet the momentous events of the day, local broadcasters were electrifying and, in some instances, electrocuting their news departments in the process of making a short circuit through them to the cash. Frank Magid and his associates, among other news consultants, were doing the wiring."[47] Later Barrett stated, "If they are going to feed the American public crap, this is going to have a long-term impact on the moral and intellectual fiber of the nation."[48]

By 1976 it was open season on local news. NBC News vice president Lee Hanna railed against "the evils of consulting."[49] CBS News vice president William Small denounced local TV news as "an abomination."[50] CBS News Washington bureau chief William Leonard told the Nieman Fellows at Harvard, "One of the frightening things that is happening in local TV news is that it's becoming successful."[51] NBC News anchor John Chancellor referred to local news as a "frightening thing."[52] Salant, again, would reiterate local TV's "tendency . . . to go tabloid."[53] Leonard, again, deplored show business news, claiming local TV's best hope was local newspaper critics who can "concentrate on local news efforts" in order to keep them "honest."[54]

With this, the stage was set for the arrival of Walter Cronkite. Until that May 5, 1976 speech before the CBS affiliate managers, Cronkite had kept mum. As a result, his lightning-bolt investment against "editing by consultancy," in which he'd called station managers "suckers for a fad," was a blockbuster. "Let me say right here," Cronkite had warmed up, "I am not one who decries ratings. . . . [But] there is no newsman worth his salt who does not [see through] advisors who dictate that no item should run more than 45 seconds, that there must be a film story within the first 30 seconds of the newscast and that it must have action in it . . . . For one thing, these fly-by-nights," the consultants, "don't know the territory."[55]

But even Cronkite could tell that this speech, the most widely reported and analyzed of any he would deliver, was not having the intended effect. Then came an opening Cronkite felt made-to-order: an invitation to give the keynote address at the next RTNDA convention. Cronkite assured himself that if he couldn't get through to profit-hungry station managers, he surely would reach the news directors. Indeed, from everything he had read in the New York media, they were in a state of nearly armed revolt. Not only this, Cronkite was peaking. He had just been named "the most trusted man in America" by *U.S. News and World Report*.

Thus, that December, Cronkite flew to Miami and reprised the same speech. Abhorring "Derek Drylook," Cronkite asserted that the time had come to start hiring "the best newspaperman in your town as an on-air broadcaster." Although newspapermen "may be bald [and] may wear horn-rimmed glasses," they are vastly superior to a "young fellow from 500 or 1,000 or 2,000 miles away that some consultant tells you got good ratings there." He assailed visualization, action video, on-set conversation and "pretty anchors," saving his sternest words for the news consultants. "Let me play consultant for a moment," he continued. "The reason you are being taken is that the answer to your news problem probably is right under your nose. In the first place, why buy somebody else's idea . . . . Don't you know what sort of person your neighbors like? Don't you know better than any outsider the tastes of your friends and acquaintances?" If not, Cronkite urged, "I suggest that maybe you ought to be the one to move along." You're "suckers for a fad: editing by consultancy," Cronkite told the news directors.[56]

Back in New York the media establishment was cheering him on. Even the news directors in Miami had given him a rousing ovation.

But then came a very unsettling sensation for Cronkite. Much like the station managers, the news directors had left their applause in the convention hall and went home as if nothing at all had been said.

Cronkite's public acclaim, shaped during the momentous events of the 1960s, when he'd tempered seriousness with human displays and won over both elite and working class viewers, was not a product of media hero-worship. In 1968, Cronkite's objections to the Vietnam War forced Lyndon Johnson out of office. Johnson said, "If I've lost Walter Cronkite, I've lost Middle America." In 1972, Cronkite's decision to run the Woodward-Bernstein exposés on CBS drew the first national attention to the Watergate scandal, and the end for Richard Nixon. With the power to influence wars and presidents, Cronkite should have been potent in his own field of TV news.

Yet to the news directors gathered in Miami, it was as if "the most trusted man in America" had just landed from Mars. Part of the breakdown was a generation gap; only when the sky turned pink were these younger news directors going to put "bald newspapermen" on TV. But the biggest problem had been Cronkite's failure to follow his own hard-and-fast lesson: don't talk until you get all the facts. He was painfully unaware that the news directors had already probed and sanctioned the news consultants. Remarkably, just before Cronkite's speech, Ray Miller had reported to the RTNDA that in two years' time there had not been a single additional complaint.[57] Worse, high on the convention's agenda was a new issue Frank Magid had wanted opened, a research procedure called the "skin test." It came up because Cronkite's own company, CBS, had been using this controversial technique. "I don't think you could say Walter Cronkite was serious. Local news was a way for him to say the right things and be quoted by the establishment in New York," Miller concluded.[58]

Respecting Cronkite as an elder statesman, local news directors were not ready to test him. Yet while caring little about the New York reaction, they were considerably attuned to how Cronkite's speech had "played in Peoria," the symbol of home. Ominously for Cronkite, it didn't play well. Writing in the *Peoria Journal Star* on December 17, 1976, editor C. L. Dancey fumed: "Walter is right, of course, when he reports that TV news is 'distorted' [but it] is interesting that it has taken him a lifetime at the camera's tip to discover this. Now he passes the buck to 'local newscasts' where he criticizes local stations for hiring unqualified people because they 'look good' or 'sound good.'"

According to Dancey, "local TV has been more responsible here in Peoria, at least, in the effort to do as clean a job as possible than have the networks. It doesn't enhance Mr. Cronkite's dignity as the dean of network anchor men to try to unfairly put the heat on others in order to escape it at the network level."[59]

Peoria mattered. Exactly three years and two months later, CBS would give the nation the word, that "the most trusted man in America," his ratings going down, was being taken off the air.[60]

If willing to look past Cronkite, thousands in local TV news were enraged at the rest of the big media. *TV Guide* had reported "mounting antagonism" at the very moment just the opposite was true. The Society for Professional Journalists (SPJ) had used reporters as sources on consultants, though reporters had no direct contact with consultants at the time. Elite publications had kept reporting that broadcasters were dropping news consultants even though out of 150 clients only two, WTVJ and WNAC, ever did. Almost everywhere Renick was portrayed as a hero even though he had boycotted the news directors after they'd turned their back on him. Inexplicably, the same Columbia University factions who were excoriating consulted newsrooms were giving their prestigious DuPont award to the very same newsrooms. In 1975, seven of the nine DuPont winners were Magid or McHugh & Hoffman clients. This never was reported.

In the meantime, local broadcasters were astounded by yet another facet of the affair, the assertion that stations hiring news consultants flirted with FCC license revokations. The FCC had given birth to consulting through the community ascertainment policy and had affirmed the use of the consultants' research again and again. This was left out of every known criticism of the consultants. The source Marvin Barrett and others had used in tying the consultants to FCC rules violations was Florida State University's David LeRoy, the person Renick had hired to examine one Magid research report. Years later as a consultant himself, LeRoy would deny he had made such claims. More serious questions were raised when LeRoy revealed that he had never been contacted by any of the writers who quoted him. "I guess they got what they think I said from Ralph and then quoted each other," LeRoy surmised.[61]

But most nagging—largely because Frank Magid made sure numerous local broadcasters never forgot it—had been that "60 Minutes" expose in March 1974. In it, the news coverage of San Francisco station KRON had been hoisted as a model of journalistic excellence. CBS did not inform viewers that KRON was a Magid client and had been for nearly two years. Had CBS reported this fact, the controversy would have ended. It would have clarified either that the consultants did not dictate news content, the most insidious allegation, or that if they did they proceeded in a positive way. At first, it had seemed an innocent oversight, that CBS did not know of the Magid-KRON relationship. As it turned out, not only was CBS aware of Magid's role at KRON; Wallace had interviewed Frank Magid about it at the CBS studios in New York. All of this was left out of the report, as was any mention of news consultants.

The "60 Minutes" episode had come smack at that moment when the RTNDA was investigating the consultants, and when Edward Barrett's article in the *Columbia Journalism Review* had started the firestorm. Already immersed in the wider controversy, Magid's clients were all ears, even though they knew Wallace, like any reporter, was not obliged to broadcast any interview he'd recorded. "The report was about the news in San Francisco, not news consultants," Wallace would recall. When he himself was interviewed in 1996, Wallace could not remember his two-hour encounter with Frank Magid in the CBS studios and, indeed, had thought Magid had gone out of business.[62]

However, Magid had a riveting recollection. Playing it back like a tape recorder to station managers and news directors, Magid assured everyone there was nothing to fear. New York's campaign to reform local TV news had rested on its allegations of low standards and irresponsible journalism. Yet Magid's account was evidence that New York was really the irresponsible party.

This was what he told them: "After working all day, I caught a flight to New York and arrived at the West Fifty-seventh Street studios at 6:30; the first thing I noticed something very peculiar, that they did not offer to let me wear makeup or freshen for the interview," Magid's conclusion the obvious, that CBS had wanted him to look haggard and unprepared. "Then, Mike came in with a folder [containing] . . . our clients' research," private and sensitive company files that CBS somehow had acquired and, which Magid sensed, was willing to broadcast to 50 million viewers without their owners' knowledge. "Going through the folder, Mike kept confronting me with 'Let me read you this.' 'Let me read you this.' One after another." As this went on "I must have been having a good night . . . [because] as he kept asking questions he pounded on the chair, kept saying 'cut,' and then said, 'Damn it, why don't you tell me the truth?'" Magid replied, "Mike, I am telling you the truth and that's why you're so upset. Furthermore, Mike, I will bet you that not one foot of what you've just shot will ever be aired." Magid was right. He recalled, "I just sat there and said to myself, 'So this is the great American news media?'"[63]

Thus, as the offensive had gained momentum, the victims in local news had simply shrugged. Finally, they became convinced that critics who kept demanding local news shouldn't "give the public what it wants" were really only saying, "I'm not getting what I want." According to Lou Prato, after Renick the most outspoken local news director, "I became angered more by the critics of local news than the consultants. . . . The public was sold a bill of goods that local news was bad by people who only wanted to get attention." The critics had been so relentless, Prato added, "that a point was reached where news directors felt the most responsible thing was ignoring them and doing the job our own way."[64]

The result was plain in the next wave of industry statistics. By the end of 1977, 18 months after Cronkite's first attack on "editing by consultancy," station managers and news directors at 100 additional TV stations had gone out and hired news consultants.

The backlash would have another outcome when the same local stations responded to the other issue big journalism had floated: that plan for long-form national news. This move required a vote of the networks' local stations, whose schedules would have had to be altered. This matter was resolved in early 1977, shortly after Cronkite's fusilade at the news directors at the 1976 RTNDA convention. Although last-place ABC had not discussed newscast expansion, both CBS and NBC had been conducting private dress rehearsals on an hour-long newscast. CBS, in fact, succeeded in getting one of them on the air by using the airtime it had been given by affiliates for coverage of the 1976 Republican convention. The CBS and NBC broadcasts had been ready to roll and waiting only for their affiliates to give their okays.

Yet the public was going to see them over the dead body of at least one person, Ancil Payne, the head of KING-TV in Seattle, who said he was tired of New York flaunting its greatness.[65] Payne was chair of the NBC affiliates board. He and other members of this board were so upset at the networks that they tabled NBC's proposal. When it became clear that NBC would not have an hour-long newscast, CBS backed away. Shortly before this, *Broadcasting* had polled NBC and CBS affiliates to determine their position on the issue. Seventy percent of local stations managers, some concerned that they'd just been called suckers by the networks, said they opposed expanded network news.[66]

One local station owner who had not taken part but who nevertheless was elated was Ted Turner, the head of an independent outlet in Atlanta called WTGC, later WTBS. Seeing that the networks had been straight-jacketed by their affiliates, Turner began planning a

24-hour news channel on cable. Turner's Cable News Network was announced only a matter of months later in 1979 and began telecasts the following year. The Atlanta-based CNN would speed the decline of news-from-New York.

Having brushed aside the greatest of the networks greats, those in local TV flowed with the tide of people's news. Yet despite all the bad words, barely a peep had been heard about news' true dilemmas, such as TV journalists with college degrees being forced to communicate to a high school-educated audience. No one had talked about the constant state of news war and the toll this had taken on the profession. Many journalists got out; others were bounced out, as a revolving door became the newest news image. For those who had entered this door as stars, the trip back out often was just a research report away.

11

Anchors

The viewers were happy to leave the arguing to others. Across America TV news had become one of nation's great glamour professions, and most folks wanted to know: What was it like to be a local news anchor? Who were those friendly faces on the news, the ones with celebrity status, prestige, and million-dollar contracts? Above all, now that a person no longer had to be a Cronkite to be on the news, how could one sign up?

While the TV screen did a good job of transmitting the stars, it hid from view the other side of the coin: a star system, the most mysterious manifestation in the new world of people's news. Yes, news anchors did enjoy fame and fortune. And yes, almost anyone could give it a whirl. But the life of the on-air news personality was not for the faint of heart. The day had passed when those in front of the cameras could escape the scrutiny of owners, news directors, and, especially, news consultants, whose research now allowed viewers to decide an anchor's fate. As competition invited newer prospects, the machine moved faster, and the riskier an anchor's job became. Finally achieving flank speed in the late 1970s, the star system would sort the stars with abandon, accepting some but kicking out vastly more.

The stars were not just points of public curiosity. At stake in their affairs was the question of just who could report the news. Besides dramatizing the backstage influence of news consultants and the imperative of being No. 1, the story behind the star system would bring forth, often poignantly, some of the most familiar personalities local

TV news would ever produce. They'd be challenged not just by viewers but by their corporations. Some were star-laden; others, notably CBS, star-crossed. At the local level, the tiffany company would fumble and bumble and indirectly gild the modern star system by giving the TV industry one of its greatest comedies of errors.

Anchoring looked easy. There was so much interest in it that *Forbes,* a business magazine, would report on "moms and dads . . . prodding their attractively coiffured sons and daughters in front of the glaring lights."[1] But each ratings book and research report was an anchor's moment of reckoning with the people. Among them was Mike Landess of Denver's KUSA, the station with the racing stripes that had the nation's highest-rated television newscast. Even so, a "54" share was not enough for job security. "If somehow that starts to slip, even if it has nothing to do with me at all, then I'm just not valuable anymore and I'm gone," Landess explained. "Every day of my life," he added, "I wake up feeling like some stupid duck in a shooting gallery."[2]

Landess had good reason to feel this way. The linchpin of the star system was research, which the anchors rarely saw. Yet people like Landess had become crucial to TV news because of a routine qualitative research question: "Why do you watch Channel X for local news?" Almost always, "personalities" was the leading middle majority response. Remarkably, only slivers of the audience fathomed superior news content and chose newscasts for that reason. Data reported in 1984 by Selection Research, Inc., for example, showed that only 9 percent of the audience chose a local newscast because of "local news coverage." This compared to 40 percent who volunteered "best personalities."[3] In some of the Magid studies, as many as 80 percent said "personalities."[4]

No longer could TV stations pin hopes on a Fahey Flynn, who at WLS had shifted 15 to 20 ratings points—not with hundreds of younger anchors coming up. It was logical to expect a personality to shift one or two points, though. Research could pinpoint this contribution. Because virtually all stations had converted to people's news, denying each other an edge, a small ratings shift was all that was needed to significantly increase profitability.

As the audience for local TV news swelled, so had its advertising base. Ad rates varied by the rating point. In the fiftieth market,

Scranton-Wilkes Barre, Pennsylvania, the approximate cost-per-rating point for local news was $30. A $30 CPR meant that a sponsor placing a 30-second ad on a newscast with a "10" rating would have to pay $300. If a broadcaster in Scranton found a way to add just one rating point, the extra $30 when multiplied by 16 ads per newscast, then by 260 weeknight newscasts per year, would produce $125,000 in additional revenues, a staggering amount if all this required was replacing Anchor A with Anchor B. In New York, Los Angeles, and Chicago, one rating point translated into over a million dollars. The star system was wrapped around these equations. A personality found to be adding even a tiny amount to the ratings was worth millions. Conversely, an anchor who could not do this was in big trouble.

With so much at stake in personalities, the appetite for research grew, and broadcasters wanted it now. A solution to this frenzy was something called "real-time" perception analysis. Requiring no field surveys, real-time analysis took place in auditoriums where 50 to 100 subjects watched test recordings of newscasts and had their reactions elicited on the spot. For decades, real-time methodology had been used in college research, and many were certain it was better than survey research because one technique theoretically ensured 100 percent reliability. This technique was known as the "galvanic skin response."

Its use was spearheaded by Willis P. Duff, who after Phil McHugh and Frank Magid was news consulting's third major pioneer. Beginning as a disc jockey at a 250-watt country music station in Bonham, Texas, Duff had risen as a program executive, and in 1969 ran KSAN-FM in San Francisco, the first "underground" radio station and a trend-setter in fighting the establishment's approach to news. Previously, at KLAC radio in Los Angeles, Duff had introduced the first 24-hour talk radio format. One of Duff's announcers at KLAC was a highly controversial figure named Joe Pyne, who with Duff had helped define the "vox populi" radio genre.[5] In a 61-page handbook on talk radio that was his springboard into consulting, Duff observed, "99 percent of all the books, all the magazines, all the plays, television and movies, all the newspapers, are written by less than 1 percent of the population—the professionally literate 1 percent. The rest of the people, the muscle, sinew, and soul . . . of this country make up the silent 99 percent."[6] Duff was perfect for news consulting.

In 1973, working out of an artist's loft in San Francisco, Duff formed a company called Electronic Response Analysts. His partners were Sebastian Stone, a former disc jockey, and David Crane, a TV journalist at public station KQED, who in the 1960s had helped

KQED create an eclectic newscast called "Newsroom" which was a model for "Eyewitness News." A fourth person, a professor at Texas Woman's University named Thomas Turicchi, would move this group to national prominence.

Turicchi had been putting GSR devices on students to compare their subliminal responses to classical and pop music. Envisioning commercial applications, Chicago radio station WCFL hired Turicchi, who in turn gave Duff and ERA exclusive rights to further market the GSR. Figuring he'd do well to attract more radio stations like WCFL, KSAN, and others on the fringe, Duff was stupefied when the fortress of the broadcast establishment, CBS, came forward, signed a half-million-dollar long-term contract, and guaranteed the fortunes of his firm. It was an event that did not make the "CBS Evening News."

The miscues of the CBS local TV stations, which began with the firing of Flynn by WBBM in Chicago back in 1968, continued after the firing of Flynn's replacements, Bill Kurtis and Peter Hyams. CBS launched a gigantic promotional campaign to regale its next Chicago anchor, Robert McBride. Holding a CBS microphone, Chicago's new "Walter Cronkite" peered out from an animal costume that made him look like a cross between Porky the Pig and the Werewolf of London. Then a distant third in the Chicago ratings and far behind "Eyewitness News," CBS announced, "Our only hope was to . . . hire the world's first ugly news broadcaster." CBS had headlined this ad: "Oh, look at us now."[7] McBride never had a chance. The WBBM ratings fell further. It was at that point in Chicago that Kurtis had returned, but not before CBS had fired its Philadelphia "Walter Cronkite," John Facenda. The Los Angeles "Cronkite," Jerry Dunphy, was moving to the guillotine.

Eight years after CBS told McHugh it would never again use news consultants, it hired the consultants of ERA. The deal was quarter-backed by a young CBS executive named Neil Derrough, who referred Duff to D. Thomas Miller, the president of the CBS television stations. By 1975 ERA had entered the newsrooms of WBBM and WCBS in New York, KNXT In Los Angeles, WCAU in Philadelphia and KMOX in St. Louis. ERA then signed WMAR in Baltimore, KING in Seattle, KOA in Denver, KOVR in Sacramento, WPLG in Miami, WLOS in Asheville and KOLD in Tucson.[8] Another ERA client was WNAC in Boston, the same TV station New York media experts were still hailing for having ousted news consultants in 1973. Nobody reported that the same station applauded for firing consultants had brought consultants back.

What became known in television news as the "skin test" was born. Turicchi's methods were nearly identical to those common in scholarly research.[9] The GSR worked like a lie detector test. Subjects could not exaggerate or manipulate how they felt. They couldn't talk at all. Taking seats in an auditorium, they attached electrodes to each forefinger of one hand. Wires converged at a computerized control panel, which converted accumulated sweat readings into numerical scores which were plotted with needles on a moving chart. The diagnostic report of a GSR session in San Francisco detailed the rest. From a "field survey [of] 1,024 San Francisco persons, . . . a panel of 80 was assembled for viewing the test tapes." According to ERA, to assess "emotional response, the panels are observed by Galvanic skin potential. This procedure measures the physiographic changes of panelists. . . . The result is a stack of computer printouts six inches thick."[10]

Six inches of printouts hardly were needed to give CBS what it wanted. Just glancing at the charts, it was easy to see which personalities hadn't registered. What followed from this, across the five CBS-owned television stations, was TV journalism's equivalent to a Stalinesque purge. Nearly 100 frontline news figures—almost all anchors, reporters, sportscasters, and weathercasters—were let go. CBS maintained that no one had been fired because of skin tests.[11]

The victims, though, found this hard to believe. The Chicago and Philadelphia stations were badly hit, but nothing compared to the spectacle at KNXT in Los Angeles, where CBS gutted its news team on two occasions. In June 1975, CBS fired Dunphy, lead reporter Bill Stout, sportscaster Gil Stratton and weathercaster Bill Keene.[12] The following spring co-anchors Sandy Hill and Patrick Emory led another CBS news staff out the door. With a photograph that would have done justice to Salvador Dali, the *Los Angeles Times* immortalized what CBS had done. On June 28, 1976, the newspaper carried on Page 1 a group portrait of 12 familiar people smiling to the camera as if enjoying the California sunshine. The caption explained they all were CBS news employees who had lost their jobs.[13]

As the media elite kept fawning CBS as "tiffany," those who'd worked for CBS uttered a collective "You've got to be kidding." In July 1976, the talent union AFTRA filed a grievance against CBS, and a closed-door settlement averted what might have been an embarrassing class action lawsuit.[14] In the meantime, CBS lawyers had been kept busy with individual lawsuits. KNXT reporter Bill Applegate alleged in court that CBS accommodated the skin tests by changing his contract so it had to be renewed every four weeks.[15] "Sevareid, Cronkite, the bunch of them, they turned their backs on us. It didn't matter to them that we worked for CBS, too, and we were losing our jobs. . . . My feelings were hurt," Emory would relate.[16] Because he had chosen to go public and lead his campaign for better TV news, one thing Cronkite could have done, they felt, would have been to stop haranguing other local TV stations until he'd confronted the management of CBS. Applegate was livid. "Anyone could see we were upside down," Applegate recalled. "You've got to admire the fortitude of Cronkite for not caring about what was happening [at CBS], then telling everyone in country how they should be doing local TV news."[17]

In response, Cronkite stated, "I didn't follow the local station management too closely. My role was at the network news division in New York."[18] The skin test was used only at local stations. Cronkite was never subjected to it.

Another immense controversy in local news quickly ensued. This time, obviously, CBS could not join in. The rest of the establishment in New York was again content to overlook another CBS escapade. Elsewhere, though, there had been no shroud. "This ERA thing is frightening. I'm sure if they showed Adolf Hitler up there on that screen, the needle would jump right out of the glass," ignited George Putnam, TV's very first superanchor in the 1950s who had just retired in Los Angeles.[19] Chicago critic Gary Deeb did the most to waken the public to this unseemly process after disguising his way into a CBS GSR session. "About 100 specially selected viewers are bused to a screening room where electrodes are attached to their fingertips. . . . [It is] a grotesque sight, to say the least."[20]

Once again it took local news directors to steer the eventual course. At the 1976 RTNDA convention, the one where Cronkite had savaged news directors for using consultants, the headline event was a face-to-face showdown between Magid and Duff. Duff said he felt like "Copernicus defending his theory." But with Duff sitting next to him, Magid pronounced the skin test as "nothing more than a sham."[21] Soon after this, the skin test suffered a quiet death.

Magid, though, would not hear the last from Duff. While disdaining the skin test, local broadcasters liked the idea of a Copernicus. In 1981, Duff's ERA would merge with the venture started by former Magid consultants Bill Taylor and Ed Bewley. The new firm would be based in Dallas and called Audience Research & Development. In the battle for news consulting supremacy, AR&D would replace McHugh & Hoffman as Magid's chief foe. As the owner of Preview House, a well-known Hollywood TV testing facility, AR&D would remain at the forefront of real-time research, although with a less controversial method that allowed subjects to consciously rate news personalities with dials and push buttons. Anchors and reporters could expect to have their work shown in auditoriums like Preview House, where 100 average people would decide if they were very good, good, normal, dull, or very dull.[22]

But a thousand Preview Houses could not answer the question of the day: What did it take to succeed on TV news? Only by going out into the field and surveying the public could anybody know. At least this much was certain: neither a pretty face nor an exceptional command of journalism were enough. The vital element was a bonding effect between news personalities and the audience. The idea that viewers formed friendships with personalities went far back and had been one of the important offshoots of Lloyd Warner's social class research at the University of Chicago. There, in 1956, two of Warner's associates, Donald Horton and Richard Wohl, detailed "the illusion of face-to-face relationship[s] . . . between spectator and performer," those in the lower-middle and upper-lower classes often dependent on this "para-social interaction."[23]

The consultants' job was breaking down this para-social phenomenon into a framework that could be used for testing every person on the news. To do this, the consultants asked viewers to rank leading qualities in the "perfect" news anchor. From this it was an easy matter to rate the actual faces; those with bonding potential were those strongest in the strongest categories. Although bonding criteria varied from study to study, they gave vital insights into what a TV news anchor had to achieve. Understandability, friendliness, enthusiasm, credibility, and personal appearance were unequivocal expectations. One framework consisted of "works to gain your interest and attention," "understands the news," "takes pride in the station," "is naturally confident," "is sincerely interested in the viewer," "is intelligent," "shares information enthusiastically," "has wide interests," "is more interested in the viewer than in him or herself," "is more than just a reader of the news" and "makes you feel good even though the news isn't always pleasant."[24] Another framework included "likes his or her job," "is clear," "is a team player," "has a good voice," "has good looks," "is relaxed," "is believable," "is friendly," "is talking, not reading," "is knowledgeable," "has the right attitude," "is comfortable," "is interesting" and "has energy."[25]

Another way researchers learned about bonding was simply through the qualitative input volunteered on specific personalities. Researchers would not let respondents wiggle away with a few general comments. They probed and probed. The verbatim commentary on anchors eventually filled entire books. A McHugh & Hoffman questionnaire illustrated the approach: "I'd like to ask you about two newscasters on local newscasts. The first is ___, the Channel ___ newscaster. What do you think of him as a newscaster? (PROBE: In what ways does he appeal to viewers interested in the news? Tell me about his manner, his appearance, and how he strikes you as a TV personality. What is most likeable about him? What is not so likeable about him, what do you wish were different about him? Do not accept only 'good' or 'nice' or similar words as description. Get a specific description and write it all down.)."[26]

Careers depended on the results. For example, an important market for McHugh & Hoffman was Indianapolis after the first research was performed on a WISH-TV reporter named Jane Pauley. "She looks good and her voice is good and she represents women well," one respondent commented. She is "very pretty—talks nice—plain. [She] goes to schools and tells things about the Indianapolis area that are interesting to the viewer," said another. Positive sentiment about Pauley was echoed again and again.

But at the other extreme in Indianapolis was a personality given the qualitative kiss of death. He was a WLWI weathercaster named Dave Letterman. "He makes light of it," one respondent complained. Another likewise found irritating Letterman's "way of giving the local and national weather. He does it like a big joke to everybody. Like who really cares—a 'don't give a care' attitude." Yet another Indianapolis viewer observed, "His personality is no good. I can't understand his forecasts. He tries to be funny and doesn't make it doing weather."[27] The research predicted the paths they would take: Pauley to NBC as a news anchor, Letterman to the networks as one of the nation's renowned comedians.

Another personality weeded out by research was a Baltimore news anchor named Oprah Winfrey. Among the comments: "She's like a fish out of water." "She fluffs it a lot and then doesn't know where she's at." "She has a gorgeous voice. . . . I have learned other stations are trying to buy her, but aside from her voice and appearance I don't know why." "She doesn't pronounce street names correctly." "She seems very unsure of herself. They should have trained her more." But these Baltimore respondents loved the way Winfrey interacted with the other personalities and carried herself while on camera.[28] After leaving Baltimore's WJZ, Winfrey went to Chicago's WLS, became television's most successful talk show host and earned a nine-figure income.

A similar example was the fate of the weathercaster on Los Angeles station KNBC, Pat Sajak. KABC's "George Fischbeck," not Sajak, "is about the only weathercaster in Los Angeles," respondents had decided.[29] Sajak likewise became a national celebrity when he began hosting "Wheel of Fortune," TV's most popular game show. Another career move was possible. This was visible in Seattle, where consultants had raised questions about anchor Rod Chandler and editorialist Charles Royer.[30] Both went into politics, Royer as mayor of Seattle, Chandler as a U.S. Congressman.

The incessant probing of anchors produced by far the largest accumulation of data in typical research reports. Even so, a more straight-forward procedure, the Q score, would carry the bonding effect to the bottom line. Many had heard of Q scores but few knew how they actually worked. Respondents were given the names and/or shown pictures of news personalities and asked two things, whether they knew the person to measure "familiarity;" and what they thought of the person to measure "likability." Different consultants measured likability in different ways, although the most common would be having respondents rate each personality as either excellent, good, fair, or poor. The percentage in the "excellent" column became the operative score.

Few managers and news directors could resist the urge to turn to this page first. All of a city's news, weather and sports personalities were ranked; the readout looked just like baseball and football standings in a newspaper. At a glance, anyone could see who was hot and who was not. Of keen interest were the three or four personalities at the top of the news rankings, which frequently listed as many as 50 anchors and reporters. If any of them was employed by a client, the order was "hands off." Tampering with a top personality for whatever reason was done at a manager's peril. Clients next studied the rest of the rankings, paying close attention to how the standings had changed since the last report, and to the rankings of newly hired personalities researched in a city for the first time.

Q scores confirmed that the best way for someone to bond with the audience was to be a weathercaster. Consistently, weathercasters were the most-familiar and best-liked personalities, and thus expectations were very high. In 1978, KABC weathercaster Dr. George Fischbeck, the person who had towered over Sajak, had a likability rating of 61 percent. By contrast, sportscasters had a more difficult time. Los Angeles's highest-rated sports personalities were KNBC's Stu Nahan and KABC's Eddie Alexander, both with only "19s."[31] Newscasters were in between.

Managers expected an anchor's familiarity score to increase with each report. And while managers expected talent to score high in both criteria, there were many exceptions, one being WABC's Howard Cosell. Despite low likability scores, Cosell's combative style had given him almost 100 percent familiarity. A primary function of Q scores was to star search. A new personality with low familiarity but high likability could be golden. A smart manager moved such an individual into a frontline position and that way maximized likability potential. KYW's Jessica Savitch had been a prime example of this strategy.

While Savitch had been a sensation, there actually was a more celebrated case. The venerable Jerry Dunphy, the longtime anchor at KNXT in Los Angeles before being booted by CBS, had been a newscaster identifiable to millions of Americans. Dunphy had inspired the stilted "Ted Baxter" character on "The Mary Tyler Moore Show." Even so, when word spread that Dunphy had been fired, the TV industry did not quake. It was well-known that KNXT's news ratings had been slipping and that his younger Los Angeles rivals, KNBC's Tom Snyder and, earlier, Tom Brokaw, had been on the rise. It looked like the end of a noble career, one that had delivered television from the dark ages of 15-minute newscasts and given the medium "Big News."

Then, the real intrigue began. Dunphy had not been off the air for more than two weeks before Hollywood was buzzing with rumors that Dunphy was about to join KABC, the "Eyewitness News" station. "Ted Baxter" and "Eyewitness News" went together like pancakes and ketchup, and the very notion that ABC, the vanguard of the youth movement, would absorb a silver-haired, 53-year-old news anchor bordered on the absurd. But it happened, and there was more. Further reports spread that KABC had not bowled over an out-of-work newscaster but, in fact, had just signed one of the biggest personal service contacts in TV history. The truth behind these latest rumors came from the streets of Los Angeles, where Dunphy was seen riding around in an $85,000 Rolls Royce.[32]

Years later, KABC general manager John Severino would share the remaining details, that Dunphy had wound up with salaries, benefits, and perks totaling $500,000—at least double the amount being paid to Harry Reasoner, ABC's network anchor. As for the Rolls Royce, Dunphy simply would say, "Why not?"[33] It was obvious ABC knew something that CBS and its Los Angeles management team, headed by Russ Berry, did not. Close friends, Berry had met Severino on a tennis court and had asked, "If I fire Jerry Dunphy, would you hire him?", to which Severino said "no." After the deed was done, Berry met Severino a second time and queried, "I thought you said you wouldn't hire Jerry Dunphy?" Severino answered, "I lied."[34]

By word of mouth, Severino's "I lied" anecdote spread to station managers and news directors all over the country. It was one of the most-repeated anecdotes during this period of local TV news because it once again captured a CBS above the fray and wallowing in its tiffany image. CBS did not understand the new rules of competitive TV news. KABC had jumped at the chance to hire Dunphy because of 12 years of parallel survey research from both Magid and McHugh & Hoffman showing Dunphy No. 1 in every single study. For CBS it was the Fahey Flynn fiasco all over again. In the November 1975 ratings, the first after Dunphy's debut on KABC, that station almost doubled the audience of its 11 p.m. newscast, a "39" share, while KNXT plummeted to a "20."[35]

The huge contract, though, had a single, yet very important, stipulation, that Dunphy's "Ted Baxter" days were over. Dunphy consented to a partner, a younger Christine Lund. He also agreed to work with the consultants and to adhere to some special surveys. Almost overnight, Dunphy relieved himself of his draconian persona. Out of the cocoon at age 53 came a smiling and gentle man of the people.[36] The chemistry between Dunphy and Lund was exceptional, and soon they commanded larger audiences at KABC than Dunphy had ever had at CBS.

For CBS and KNXT, it was again like walking into an express elevator and pushing the down button. KNXT's "Channel 2 News," anchored by Connie Chung and Jess Marlowe, managed an "8" rating in November 1978.[37] It got so bad for CBS in Los Angeles that on an afternoon when the power went out at KNXT's Mt. Wilson transmitter, only 12 people called in to find out why the station was off the air. There were 15 million people in the KNXT viewing area.[38] The tiffany company's next move was to hire behavioral psychologists from the Athyn Group for encounter sessions to find out why KNXT's news staff didn't like each other.[39] During this confusion, somebody had leaked the results of the latest CBS skin tests to the *Hollywood Reporter*. Its front-page article began: "KNXT management embarrassingly learned last Tuesday that the ERA research test on TV anchor persons showed KABC's Jerry Dunphy . . . as the strongest anchorman in the LA market."[40]

At ABC, they were doubling over with laughter. According to KABC's Michael Silverstein, "We've won in ratings, homes, share, total adults, and viewers. This is how we use research. . . . That's why

we have them both [Magid and McHugh & Hoffman]. And
that's why KNXT used research the wrong way and almost got sued
for it."[41]

Not just Dunphy was shown the money. Around 250 local
anchors were earning six-figure salaries as the 1980s began. In 1981,
CBS paid Chung a $600,000 annual salary. That year Chung
was the highest-paid local news anchor. Four other CBS figures,
WBBM's Bill Kurtis; and WCBS's Jim Jensen, Storm Field and Warner
Wolf had earned a half-million dollars each.[42] But ABC was not to
be outdone. In 1983 *Newsday's* Marvin Kitman obtained, through
agents, revised statistics on local TV news salaries. Kitman revealed
local TV's first million-dollar anchor, WABC's Ernie Anastos, and
then reported that WABC's other anchors, Roger Grimsby, Bill Beutel,
and Rose Ann Scamardella, also had salary packages pushing $1,000,000. Kitman pointed to "an ironic footnote, or bank-
note," that "'Eyewitness News' was popular because it appealed
to the blue collar or lower classes . . . . And here it had all these
semi-millionaires."[43]

This, though, wasn't the only irony. Odder still was the certainty
that large numbers of these semi-millionaires were going to have to
pack. Only a handful could be what they all had to be, No. 1. Few
anchors had dwelled on this fact of life. But working in the background, the consultants knew of the talent field's true structure. It was
not a career ladder but rather a pyramid. At its base were all of the
young newcomers, upwards of 5,000 graduating from colleges and
universities every year, who applied for on-air jobs in TV news. Of the
small number able to land first jobs, usually at small TV stations, only
a fraction would be able to rise to the next-highest level, and fewer
still to the level above that. Each upward move required some form
of ratings and research endorsement. The consultants didn't need
to be geniuses to realize they'd attained a position of enormous
strength. Consultants flagged personalities not tracking toward No. 1.
Moreover, in recommending changes, they could proceed with confidence because only they had the book on the multitude of potential
replacements.

The centralized coordination of news personalities through talent
banks was a cinch activity for a nationally based consulting firm. Consultants were constantly on the road and thus were able to birddog
talent from one end of the country to the other. McHugh had initiated

the first talent bank only months after opening his firm in 1962.[44] Starting with written descriptions, McHugh then purchased eight-millimeter film cameras and gave them to his traveling staff. Moving from city to city, each consultant took home movies of news anchors as they appeared on hotel room TV sets.[45] The next advancement came in 1965, when McHugh & Hoffman rented a videotape machine to record the newscasts, still in the hotel rooms. The firm's Garth Hintz complained that the unwieldy device had to be "hauled in a crate [and] takes two people to lift." Also, there were "quizzical looks" by attendants "in the various motels."[46]

Finally in 1971, upon opening One Research Center, Magid created that first national talent bank by using ENG equipment. The Magid talent bank, containing 1,000 videotapes by 1975, was a hit with broadcasters who until then had had to arrange and pay for live auditions.[47] McHugh & Hoffman would counter with a separate division called TalentBank, Inc., which had 2,000 videotapes by 1979.[48] Not long after this, Don Fitzpatrick, a former ERA consultant, founded a talent bank with 9,000 recordings by 1986.[49] AR&D's would reach 20,000 by 1995.[50]

Increasingly, news anchors who did not hire agents or whose resumés were not in one of these talent banks were out of the loop. Rapidly inundated by job applications, news directors put them aside and called a consultant, who in minutes could target a handful of candidates anytime a job opening occurred. Computerization made this possible. After inputing the vacancy (news, weather or sports), and a TV station's salary, gender, age, ethnic, geographic and physical-feature requirements, out popped a short list. "Looking for work in television? We know where the jobs are," a Magid circular would read. "Will you get hired? That depends on your talent and our clients' needs."[51]

The star system was supported by many anchors. Drake University's Mary A. Bock surveyed local news anchors about this seemingly demeaning "cattle call" in 1986. She was astonished when only 31 percent voiced any negative remarks about the system and fully 94 percent were optimistic about their odds for long-term success. A young newscaster at a Midwest station beamed, "I enjoy anchoring. . . . [A]nchors are paid handsomely, and that's something you don't turn away lightly." Another explained his sensation of "Whoa, I'm on T.V. . . . Lookit [sic] my picture." Yet another looked forward to the news promotion process. "The only (promotion) that ever bothered me," she confessed, "was having my face on the back of the bus and getting mud on it." Meanwhile, 26-year-old Denese Boyer, an anchor at WRAL in Raleigh, thoroughly enjoyed anchor work and was planning the rest of her career. "I'd like to feel I could grey in this business," Boyer related.[52]

The anchor pyramid finally broke when a news anchor in Kansas City tumbled down the side. The case of Christine Craft exposed every cog in the star system and ended with the system stronger than ever before. Allegations of sex and age discrimination and two jury verdicts overturned by judges would keep this case in the headlines for almost three years, even though it started as nothing new. The episode sprang from yet another city's conversion to people's news.

In a battle of Kansas City "Walter Cronkites," KMBC and its man-on-camera Scott Feldman had been trailing KCMO, whose newscast was dominated by superanchor Wendall Anschutz. In early 1980, KMBC hired AR&D, which undertook a massive research study and reported that viewers feel "Anschutz is as comfortable as an 'old shoe.' . . . The best way to develop the necessary degree of comfortability is the addition of a co-anchor person . . . We believe a woman could best accomplish the objective."[53] KCMO, just given identical advice by Magid, paired Anschutz with a co-anchor named Anne Peterson, who instantly caught on. KMBC obtained from the AR&D talent bank 50 videotapes of female anchors. A prospect from Springfield, Missouri, another from Des Moines, and Craft, then the anchor at KEYT in Santa Barbara, were the finalists. Craft was hired in December 1980.

She was first seen by Kansas City viewers on January 5, 1981. There were scattered complaints about her performance and dress, but KMBC was not focussed on these. The No. 2 ratings of its broadcast "The News" were blamed on Feldman, whose contract was about to expire. Not Craft's but Feldman's future was the big question to be resolved in the next AR&D formal survey scheduled for June 1981. Following routine, AR&D researchers prepped this study by conducting focus groups on May 19 and 20. Of 41 total participants in the focus groups, 30 were middle-low status viewers and almost half were homemakers.

During these focus groups KMBC's fears shifted from Feldman to Craft. "She won't make it," one of the homemakers volunteered. A feeling that Craft was "boring and spoke too often about her home in California." was recurrent.[54] The same sentiment was expressed in the 400-respondent formal survey a month later. Her familiarity rating of "74" indicated that most in Kansas City knew her. However, she had a likability rating of "9." This meant that only 9 percent of the respondents had rated Craft as "excellent." By contrast, Feldman had scored a "37," and this saved his job. KCMO's Anschutz had a "36." Conspicuously, Peterson, in her first research outing, had scored a whopping "30." Craft's "9" stood out.[55] AR&D's Steve Meacham presented this research on August 13. The following day, Craft was removed as anchor and named a KMBC reporter. A week later, she resigned.

A year-and-a-half later in January 1983, she filed a $1.2 million lawsuit against KMBC charging sex discrimination, unequal pay and hiring fraud. Just days after Craft's resignation, *Kansas City Star* television critic Barry Garron had published a story in which Craft said she had been told by news director Ridge Shannon, "[You're] not pretty enough and not deferential to men."[56] What a judge termed the "ceaseless incantation" of this accusation inspired worldwide media coverage when Craft's first trial opened in Kansas City on July 25, 1983. Over 11 days, witnesses confirmed that Craft had been counseled on her clothing, makeup, and appearance, and a professor testified that AR&D's focus groups were "backyard gossip." These were keys to her fraud claim.[57] Craft was awarded damages of $500,000. *The Nation* observed, "The jury seemed to sense that Craft was removed because she failed to live up to a sexual stereotype—an ideal of feminine appeal based on youth, beauty, [and] 'warmth and comfort' . . . ."[58] In the *New York Times,* Sally Bedell Smith predicted "significant consequences" including "guidelines that could redefine a local station's ability [for] dismissing an anchor."[59]

The real consequences were previewed in October 1983, when U.S. District Court Judge Joseph E. Stevens, acting on KMBC's appeal, threw out the verdict. Craft's claim that she had been told she was unattractive and non-deferential to men was rejected after Scott Feldman, the only witness, recanted testimony and stated under oath that "he did not recall Shannon making such a comment."[60] Judge Stevens rejected the finding that AR&D's research was fraudulent. Pivotal had been that professor who impugned the focus groups but did not criticize AR&D's 400-respondent formal survey, which was the basis of Craft's demotion. Also important was AR&D's Meacham, who testified that Craft's research was "unprecedented in the history of the consultants."[61] In light of Craft's "9" rating, it looked to the judge like Meacham had been telling the truth.

The pivotal event, though, came when KMBC's attorneys had Stevens review the 1980 ruling of the U.S. District Court in Rhode Island in *Haines* v. *Knight Ridder Broadcasting.* Anchor Mark Haines had gone to court claiming that Providence station WPRI had no right to remove him because he had bad research. But the court ruled: "The news business may indeed have its quirks and vagaries, . . . but consultant's reports and ratings routinely serve as the basis for personnel changes. Furthermore, the ratings and the [research] report provided strong evidence in support of the defendant's decision [to take Haines off the air]."[62] The Craft case was retried with Craft the victor. In hearing KMBC's second appeal, Circuit Judge John R. Gibson cited *Haines* and overturned the verdict.[63] In March 1986, the Supreme Court refused to consider the case.

In defeat, Craft remained a symbol for what she called the "fight [against] unfair labor practices in the media" and "the bigoted mindset that would keep me and other female colleagues in a state of perpetual second-class citizenship." After Craft, every future research-crossed news anchor would have a much bigger fight.

Lost in the furor had been the poignancy of Craft's predicament. In her own words, she had taken the job in Kansas City to sharpen her journalistic "overview" and to get "out in the field."[64] Yet given precisely that opportunity when KMBC kept her as a reporter, she was devastated. She pleaded that had she remained as anchor KMBC's ratings would have increased, not something a social crusader would say. None of this was peculiar. Craft was only reacting the way any fallen star would. Indeed, a year after her demotion but still months before the trial, her instinct was not to rally a cause but to tell a reporter back in Kansas City, "I want my job back."[65] Years later Craft was open in relating the scars left from that conversation with Shannon, in which Shannon had delivered a TV anchor's six dreaded words: "We need to make a change." "I don't think Ridge could have done anything differently," she stated. "He was a victim of the system just like I was. In local news, everyone's the victim." Deciding "life is too short" and "there are more important things," Craft had vowed, "There is no way I'd ever [again] want to be a local news anchor. It's an occupation without a soul."[66] Craft went on to become an attorney.

Finally, on the heels of the Craft case, the pent-up power of the star system was unleashed with widespread personnel changes, demotions and firings. So many accounts were headlined "anchors away" that the whole thing had a sail-on-sailor sort of feel. Some of the original big names in local TV news, people like Miami's Ralph Renick and Cincinnati's Al Schottelkotte, were among the first shuffled off the news.

Not far behind were most of the younger anchors who had been the giants of people's news just a few years before. Moving from Philadelphia to New York, Larry Kane was one of the casualties. Also in New York, the once-prized Rose Ann Scamardella likewise disappeared. In Los Angeles, Christine Lund, Sandy Hill, and a third "Eyewitness" veteran, John Schubeck, were lost in a revolving door. At age 67, Fahey Flynn would anchor on Chicago's "Eyewitness News" until days before his death in 1983. But Flynn's partner at WLS, Joel Daly, was taken off the main news, at about the same time longtime rival Walter Jacobson was axed by WBBM. In San Francisco, the once redoubtable Van Amburg vanished. That skin test victim Patrick Emory became a mandarin of TV news, moving from Los Angeles to St. Louis to Philadelphia to CNN in Atlanta, to Sacramento, and then to Tampa. Cleveland anchor Doug Adair, once the hottest prospect in TV news who had had the chance to be the first anchor of "Eyewitness News," finished his career in Columbus. Just as noteworthy had been the fate of Denece Boyer, the 26-year-old Raleigh anchor who wanted to "grey in this business." She made it to age 34.

The list went on and on. Two of the loudest anchor tumbles were taken by Cleveland's Jim Hale and Boston's Tony Pepper. After his firing by WJW, Hale went to court with a new twist, claiming statements in the press about his bad research had made it impossible for him to find a new job.[67] Hale's complaint did not go to trial. Pepper left WBZ kicking and screaming after anchoring there for eight years. According to Pepper, "If a door's open, and there's a Size 9 on your backside, and a little physical effort is exerted on the Size 9, you go through the door."[68]

After Craft, the most widely reported anchor removal was the firing of WABC's Roger Grimsby in 1986. As the lead anchor of the No. 1 newscast in the nation's largest market, Grimsby stood at the tip of the local news pyramid. But when Grimsby's contract was due for renewal, WABC passed. According to general manager Bill Fyffe, "Roger was going down." Out of work at age 57, and well before retirement, Grimsby was bitter. "The research was fixed," he insisted. "They structured the questions so people would say they didn't like me because Fyffe did not want to pay my salary," an allegation leveled by almost every deposed anchor.[69] Fyffe brushed this off. "Money was not a factor. Anchors earn every penny they're worth. . . . We find the value in ratings and research. These were business decisions," Fyffe explained.[70] Grimsby tried to pick up the pieces of his career as a commentator for WNBC and then as an anchor at KUSI in San Diego.

Only in America could one find celebrity semi-millionaires standing in unemployment lines. This became a common occurrence in local TV news, although usually as a first step toward a lawsuit. In some cases, the personal consequences of trying to be a star were far worse. Reports of marital infidelity and substance abuse were rampant. The RTNDA, which usually did not take up such matters, nevertheless acknowledged the problem in a 1986 national survey showing that 41 percent of respondents drank daily and many had serious health problems.[71] Grimsby, for example, had not hidden the fact that he had frequented a bar near the WABC studios. Few, however, knew that Grimsby's main rival in New York and the No. 2 person on the local news pyramid, WCBS superanchor Jim Jensen, had endured near-fatal bouts with drug addiction. Jensen recovered in the late 1980s after several years of psychotherapy.[72]

In Detroit, Bill Bonds, the immensely popular anchor of WXYZ's "Action News," stirred the community the first time he admitted in public to his own drinking problems.[73] In the Bay Area, longtime anchor George Watson made a similar admission, that he had "worked at KTVU for 18 years [and] drank every day." After winning four Emmy Awards, Watson wound up a tugboat deckhand still hoping to get back on TV. "My strongest emotion right now is fear. . . . People I've known for 20 years are not returning my calls," Watson stated.[74] Then there was the case of Mary Jo West, who was diagnosed with clinical depression, an affliction complicated by her firing after several years as a news anchor in Phoenix. "You find yourself saying, 'What's wrong with me? I haven't done anything wrong,'" related West, who recovered by seeking psychiatric treatment.[75]

While bringing perspective to the star system, cases such as these were rare. Actually, the majority of former news anchors left their jobs voluntarily. A transient lifestyle rendered family life next to impossible, especially for the scores of men and women who lived in one city and appeared on the news in another. Many simply reduced anchor work to a zero-sum ratings-and-research rat race, and one not really very exciting on most days. It was hard to walk away from those lottery-like salaries, though. In 1993, the average salary of anchors in the top-25 markets was $265,000.[76] Still, a 1992 Freedom Forum survey dramatized escalating turnover. The typical local news anchor was only 32 years old, had held three jobs in three cities, and had not worked in any city for more than four years. Every 12 months, 25 percent of the nation's 4,000 news, weather and sports anchor positions changed hands.[77]

A serious challenge to the star system began to materialize in the mid-1990s, when consultants started researching 100-channel cable

TV systems and living room remote controls. Many viewers were by-passing a bonding effect in favor of switching between different local newscasts. In AR&D studies, 20 percent "often switched," and 40 percent "sometimes switched" if a newscast's first story was unap-pealing. Between 1985 and 1995, the number of viewers who watched from beginning to end had declined from 70 to less than 50 percent. Nevertheless, sixty percent of viewers who flipped out of a favored local newscast at the beginning eventually flipped back and stayed because they wanted to see their favorite news, weather and sports personalities mixing it up later in the show.[78] "You couldn't get away from the idea that people just liked watching people," AR&D's Jim Willi observed.[79]

Of the roughly 2,000 principal local newscasters in place at the peak of the anchor explosion in 1975, only 200 were still working in the same cities and fewer than 100 for the same TV station 25 years later. Dominating the survivors was Bill Beutel, who anchored the very first WABC local newscast in October 1962 and was still in the same seat four decades later. Into his seventies Jerry Dunphy contin-ued to anchor local news in Los Angeles. At Chicago's WLS, Floyd Kalber and Joel Daly, both having been bumped and bruised, had re-mained on the air for more than 30 years. Some of the others who made it through were Los Angeles's Paul Moyer, Kelly Lange, and Hal Fishman; Philadelphia's Jim Gardner; Boston's Natalie Jacobson and Chet Curtis; Houston's Dave Ward; Cleveland's Ted Henry; Atlanta's Monica Kaufman and Jim Axel; Seattle's Jean Enersen; Phoenix's Kent Dana; Denver's Ed Sardella; Buffalo's Irv Weinstein; Salt Lake City's Dick Nourse; Norfolk's Jim Kincaid; Tulsa's Clayton Vaughn; Green Bay's Chuck Ramsey; Evansville's David James; Tucson's Patty Weiss; Charleston's Bill Sharp; Topeka's Jim Hollis; Yakima's T. J. Close; and Lafayette's Marie Placer. The odds greatly increased if one could make it into a top-20 market. Trying to survive in any of the 180 markets smaller than about Sacramento seemed to require divine intervention.

The star system remained the greatest anomaly in television news. Even the chosen could not impart a secret of success. "I guess it was a combination of the market and me," Seattle's Enersen related.[80] Beutel believed working class TV viewers "will adopt you and make you feel part of them."[81]

Still, tens of thousands would seek this embrace, have it for awhile and would mysteriously be cut loose. Many blamed a public that kept wanting younger and younger faces. Yet the overwhelming majority who came and went were in their twenties and thirties, and there'd been too many people like Beutel, Dunphy, Kalber and Flynn to validate the age hypothesis.

The problem for anchors was the people, whose attention spans were far shorter than career lifespans. As much as the people adopted newscasters, another instinct, impulsiveness, compelled them to wander in search of new kin. This effect was not limited to news stars. TV's greatest stars, such as Bob Hope, Dinah Shore, Mary Tyler Moore and Bill Cosby, were all canceled in the end. Another, Red Skelton, had parted with a sage insight. Informed of his declining ratings, Skelton was convinced the public had an incurable illness. "They got sick of me," he said. The same malady became a factor in the process of TV news.

12

News Content

No less compelling than the backstage business of the stars was another riddle: What determines the news? For the longest time, it had seemed obvious that news lay at the intersection of great people and big events. Yet in local TV news something was different. The more local newscasts expanded, the more their content puzzled media experts, among them Phyllis Kaniss of the Ivy League University of Pennsylvania, who in a 1991 book called *Making Local News* threw up her hands. Oddly enough a local TV reporter told her "The operative principle we think about all the time is people, people, people." But utterly mysterious was the end result. "No matter how important local government and policy issues may be . . . the coverage of government and policy is always balanced with time for what are typically isolated crimes, accidents, and fires, all of which have relatively limited effects." Why, she asked, "does a typical program begin with a tease about bones in a city park . . . before turning to the coverage of major state legislation?"[1]

It was because the choosing of news had become a thoroughly organized process in which computers at Magid and other research firms had juggled and rerouted the journalists' news values and waved those of the people straight on through. Gone were the days romanticized in movies like *Front Page*, in which a captain of a newsroom could stand up and holler "Stop the press!" When the people said weather was big news, weather was going to appear. When the people said politicians cared only about getting reelected, and that the government they ran was a playground of the elite, these feelings too would steer the news. If there was confusion, it was only because the news bewildering to experts was the news that really mattered to the masses.

There was no better example of this confusion than two of the defining features of the new local TV news: an abundance of crime-related stories and a shortage of government and political news. Like a broken record, the nation's media critics told Americans that crime coverage was ratings bait and ignoring local government was proof of local news irresponsibility. Although each new attack had made it seem like those in local news had given no thought to either topic, in reality they had. The backdrop for this had been the first 20 years of local TV news, when nearly 100 percent of its content had consisted of just these two subjects, crime and government.

This had been easy to see in the very first textbook on TV news in 1968, in which Dr. Irving Fang had taught journalists a two-part program. There was "spot" news, with crime and police, and "institutional" news, with city councils, state legislators and politicians. In 1968, television had recently surpassed newspapers as America's "main source" of news. Because of the switch, sentiment had reigned that TV news must replace the newspaper as the public's "medium of record."

For television to fill the shoes of newspapers, Fang had elaborated, proximity to politicians was a must. The closer a journalist clung to officials the more record-like his or her reporting would be. As Fang explained, top newsrooms should keep "regular staffers in legislative halls and devote most . . . coverage to committee hearings and to interpretive, condensed sound interviewing of key legislators." As for spot news, also part of the record, "[a]ccidents, fires and crime figure significantly in most local newscasts. The fledgling television newsman learns early to cover fires, accidents and police business. But he may not learn to cover them well . . . . He should study techniques used beyond the confines of his own station." In 1968, Fang's examples of quality news coverage had been the "lumber yard fire at night," the "man trapped in head-on collision," the "murder," the "riot," the "demonstration," and the "lost child at police station."[2]

At the time, such logic was based strictly on tradition. The rationale was keyed neither to ratings nor responsibility. Crime and government had dominated newscasts because they were the easiest stories to cover. But there was no indication whether either was fulfilling public interests and needs. Through its community ascertainment policy, the FCC had told broadcasters to find out. Interviewers took to the field, results came back, and almost instantly one of two big areas—government—fell off the charts. According to the vast majority of lower-middle and upper-lower status television viewers, government had cut them adrift.

A center of Magid's earliest research had been Seattle, a locale with a reputation for grassroots politics and citizen interest in them. Thus, much was learned when a 1968 study showed that only 53 percent of Seattle-Tacoma respondents favored routine city-county political coverage on TV, and that only 52 percent favored coverage from the state capitol in nearby Olympia. This compared to more than 80 percent who favored coverage of non-institutional news, including protests over the Vietnam War. Notably, those who did want more government were in the socio-economic strata Magid had designated as "high." While high status viewers wanted news from city hall, the statehouse, Congress, the White House and the United Nations, and were satisfied, lower and middle status viewers—76 percent of the total—were not satisfied and told Magid they needed stepped-up treatment of protest demonstrations, strikes, open-housing controversies, charity ventures and community service activities. Only 29 percent of high status viewers were keen on the protest coverage, while 40 percent of low status viewers wanted protests seen from every angle. This indicated to Magid that something was amiss in journalism's cover-the-officials-until-you-drop priorities.[3]

The same was discovered at McHugh & Hoffman. While more extreme than most, one lower status TV viewer summed up numerous remarks in complaining about the politician's first concern, reelection, and their "gassy platitudes and damned lies when it doesn't mean a thing either way."[4] As the 1960s careened forward, even learned observers aimed suspicions at government because of Vietnam, the urban unrest and what seemed to be a breakdown of law and order. Thus, pivotal at McHugh & Hoffman were findings in its most influential research projects, its first examinations of "Eyewitness News" at WABC in 1969. Politics and government had ranked twelfth out of 15 news content preferences.

This alone was a ground-shaker because it confirmed what Al Primo and others at "Eyewitness News" had suspected, that middle and lower status viewers were estranged from government. Average viewers were interested in the governing process. However, in the words of one respondent, "There is nothing in it for me." They felt politicians were ineffective at solving real-life problems like decaying neighborhoods, crime, drugs, domestic discord and inflation. Over and over they complained of bias when reporters merely put politicians on the air without placing their actions in a real-life context. Many had come right out and volunteered that they did not need a video record of meetings and proclamations. "Eyewitness News" was succeeding in New York precisely because it had abandoned the record and treated the people as the authorities.[5]

The 1970 "Eyewitness" study was more illuminating. Not only had government again ranked near the bottom; remarkably, "Eyewitness News" was perceived as doing what government should have done. An upper-lower status woman wanted more people like "the man on the eyewitness news that goes right to the scene and talks to the people on the streets . . . . It seems like they try to help solve a certain problem that comes up." Another upper-lower woman who had never met a politician became loyal to WABC because "they tell the news about the city [and] they don't push their views on you." Similar was a lower class male who stated, "They wake me up about issues and make me think about them." According to this respondent, "Eyewitness News," not city hall, was "the most socially concerned . . . about local and city problems."[6]

The average person's view of government as a domain of elites would not shift in years of succeeding research. Consultants were not surprised at statistics showing that half of Americans didn't vote in major elections. Also immutable was the view that television news was biased when it merely showed politicians in their natural habitat of meetings, speeches and news conferences. This feeling would resound in a 550-page McHugh & Hoffman national survey in 1983, a year that saw the nation under the grip of its worst recession since the end of World War II. Millions of working class individuals were unemployed. Respondents did not hide their image of government as next-to-useless nor their contempt of TV journalists who just let politicians "run at the mouth." Concerns were mostly directed at network news, although local news did get its share.

It did not make any difference whether a reporter appeared to have a liberal or a conservative bias. Most reporters were perceived as having no political bias but cynical of all politicians. This, too, was irrelevant. To average people, the mere fixation with talking-head politics was running the gamut from A to B. "They repeat and rehash after a presidential newscast. Every time he talks, three or four times a year," a lower-middle female grumbled. A lower-middle male demanded, "[W]hen it comes to political candidates, tell both sides just as they are. The news should let it be known what the meaning of news is." When an upper-lower female was asked how governmental coverage could be improved, she answered, "As far as I'm concerned, just read it and stop editorializing and giving their opinions. Maybe talking to the people involved [would help]." In the view of a lower-middle male, "News in general that is reported is not relatable to the guy watching TV. (Why?) They don't report things that affect me in my everyday life, normally."[7] In a follow-up study, only 17 percent said "always" and 26 percent "usually" when asked whether they were interested in political coverage.[8]

Tens of thousands of identical responses left little doubt that the traditional, give-the-mayor-the-microphone concept of news had to go. "[I]nterest in [raw] government is surprising as this does not surface in too many markets," one Magid report had emphasized.[9] Frank Magid would state, "We never told our clients they should not cover politics and government, but we were specific in telling them they must treat these topics from the perspective of the viewer."[10]

Statehouse bureaus were closed; city council reporters were reassigned, and speeches and news conferences became eight-second soundbites. "The story wasn't there," AR&D's Bill Taylor explained. "If anything government did was important, the real story was out where the people lived."[11] As it moved from consulting reports to a new generation of standard textbooks on TV news, this people-first logic became legitimized. "Try to tell your stories through strong central characters engaged in compelling action," professor Frederick Shook taught students in a textbook published in 1989. "So often reporters try to tell the story . . . using authority figures . . . to explain what ordinary people enact. . . . [Report the news] in ways more compelling than through the world's voices of authority."[12]

The reduction of governmental coverage and the next effect—continuation of crime coverage—had a significant relationship. Clear were the data affirming the need for crime-related news. Average TV viewers were repulsed by crime and had little interest in seeing its spectacle on newscasts. Nevertheless, they insisted crime news appear. The reason had been an exponential increase in crime coinciding with a perception that government was unable or unwilling to act. Crime was the average person's main measure of just how ineffective government had become. Importantly, this had not always been the case.

When consultants first started research in the early 1960s, they had chastised their clients because scenes of stretchers and police barricades, then rife in local news, were "distant [and] not presented . . . in a context of created realism." In other words, viewers didn't relate to crime. The first ascertainment studies in 1961 and 1962 had not shown crime as a community concern that local news needed to address. Respondents volunteered straying reactions to crime, and many said they were weary of seeing it on TV. The coverage of spot news had remained on newscasts only because professionals believed it signaled to viewers "We know how to cover the news."[13]

But by the late 1960s, perceptions had changed. Vandalisms, burglaries, assaults, rapes, murders and arsons tripled and quadrupled in most large cities. Spreading from ghettos onto main streets and then into urban neighborhoods, accelerating crime had been the legacy left from the riots and social unrest. What was documented in FBI crime statistics came to life in the accounts of everyday TV news viewers as elite neighborhoods largely went untouched. Crime almost always struck middle and especially lower class families in crowded working class neighborhoods where TV viewing was extreme.

The difference showed up in the research, in some of the most class-polarized findings consultants ever would produce. While the minority of high status respondents still felt crime was distant and exaggerated, the middle and lower classes gave direct testimony that crime was real. Many volunteered that either they, their families or friends had been victims of crime. More often, middle majority respondents had said they'd seen gang graffiti, smashed windows on parked cars, street corner drug dealings and their own children with drug paraphernalia. Also mentioned was the nightly sounds of sirens. That sirens could be heard, even if in the distance, had been proof that crime was near. McHugh & Hoffman urged clients that viewers "were becoming frustrated that the needed solutions to problems were not forthcoming. As an indication of their reaction, 20 percent of the viewers spontaneously mention violence . . . when asked what the important community problems were. . . . The upper-lower class and the lower-middle class expressed the most critical comments."[14]

Station managers and news directors would question and sometimes scoff at critics who scorned local news for its treatment of crime. Critics appeared to have the same upper-middle class bias that came through in the research. They seemed oblivious to what the majority of people actually felt. The view that crime coverage was an example of local TV news giving the public only "what it wants" was countered by findings clearly showing that members of the mass audience did not prefer to see this subject presented. The larger allegation, that crime coverage was an avenue to big ratings, did not square with evidence showing that average Americans were normal people, not fiends and perverts who tuned in night after night to watch death and destruction on television news. There did remain a core of mostly male viewers between the ages of 18 and 35 who relished the action and excitement of homicides and police raids. But comprising only about 20 percent of regular news viewers, and few women, this group was very small.[15]

In fact, 54 percent of viewers in a 1994 AR&D national study had expressed a wish for totally non-violent newscasts. This finding had been a stepping stone for an experiment advanced at AR&D clients called "family sensitive news," in which coverage of shootings, arsons, hostage situations and such events were eliminated. This idea had mixed results, however, for a reason indicated in the same 1994 study. Fifty-two percent had insisted on coverage of crime because "it accurately portrayed reality and thus was news that was needed." Viewers wanted to know exactly where crime had occurred, exactly what had happened and whether the incident might be repeated. Viewers were interested in whether security measures could have stopped the crime. Above all, they wanted to know exactly what the police were doing about it.[16]

Beginning in the late 1960s and for the next 30 years, the proportion of total respondents who believed crime coverage to be real, not exaggerated and sensationalized, consistently ranged between 45 and 60 percent of the total. In the lower class, this figure often was as high as 90 percent. Usually, only about 25 percent of all respondents felt crime coverage was unreal; others gave don't know or no comment answers. Only in a handful of studies after 1968 was crime not a top-ten item in researched content rankings. AR&D told clients, "Crime: people want to see it, they want to know where it happened, [and] they want balanced coverage between good and bad. . . . The viewer says, 'Tell me how to protect myself, but don't get carried away with blood in the streets.'"[17] Notably, some viewers wanted crime news expressly to discomfort the comfortable. McHugh & Hoffman reported that viewers "do not want it covered up or glossed over. . . . For example, blacks most often want TV exposure to urban crises so whites will have some understanding of the problems with which blacks are faced."[18]

It would not be easy implementing a balance, for although upwards of 60 percent of viewers did insist on crime, the same proportion consistently felt TV stations placed too much emphasis on bad news, namely crime.[19] Moreover, viewers clearly wanted tasteful coverage, what Magid termed "surveillance rather than indulgence." It was nearly impossible to impart this to TV reporters, who instinctively believed that being first with gunshots and screams signified journalistic excellence. The public so adamantly said otherwise that consultants feared for the ratings when "blood and guts" started tracking in a client's research, as a McHugh & Hoffman directive had spelled out: "McHugh and Hoffman, Inc.'s primary recommendation pertains to the training and development of a new type of news editor. It is clearly evident that the day has passed when a news editor can simply focus . . . on the violence itself for attention value, or making the event seem bigger than it is."[20] AR&D continued to ply a semblance of "family sensitive news" by urging that graphic coverage be confined to late night newscasts presumably unseen by children.[21] Part of the problem had been the consultants themselves, who had created an environment for spot news by pressing for new news in each succeeding newscast. Thus, the continuing debate about crime coverage had merit, and those in local news did listen to the critics.

Still, chronic complaints about excessive crime in local news often were insensitive to the real problem, crime itself, and it was meaningful that those most likely to sound off were in the upper-middle class. In McHugh & Hoffman's 1983 survey, 51 percent of upper-middle class respondents said crime coverage on TV had created a false sense of reality. "The news media sensationalize or exaggerate some violence. I suppose [this is] to entice more viewers, to increase ratings," had been a typical upper-middle class remark.

Yet only 38 percent of lower-middle and 32 percent of upper-lower respondents agreed. "[T]here is violence all over in this area [and] there will be violence if it is and if it is not shown on TV," an upper-lower respondent stated. "It's educational and tells how things happen," another noted. Another said, "I think it should be shown because that's what's happening in the world today. You can't bring up a child in complete fantasy." Yet another offered, "It's part of life. . . . It should be handled just the way they are doing it now. Just as it happens." Another emphasized, "It's realistic. We lived in the ghetto at 32rd Street (Chicago) and many children learned what it was all about there. It helps them to fantasize. They need to blow off steam." Still another said, "Show it. Some people grew up with it and others never saw any violence anywhere. We've seen people shot and muggings. I'm just used to it. It's a way of life around here."[22]

That more-privileged Americans did not want this seen was no surprise. Indeed, as Marshall McLuhan had stated, with "audience participation [in TV news], you cannot have a slum that is not also your own home."[23] Thus, for some it was best to keep crime off TV.

If McLuhan had an answer to the controversy over crime coverage, a grassroots vocalist named Ronnie Van Sant may have captured the reason why upper status Americans never got the government news they wanted. "Watergate does not bother me" was Van Sant's message to the elite in the 1974 hit tune "Sweet Home Alabama." It was not just a line from a song but a perception about government deeply embedded in average Americans, and which had resonated in the consultants' research, from Birmingham to Bellingham to Bangor and all points in between.

Still, crime and government were only two of many subjects heavily researched by news consultants. As they numbered news personalities, consultants also ranked news content. This was another extension of the FCC's community ascertainment requirement. Content research was ongoing, and at certain times the public's preferences for news drew special attention when hundreds of local rankings entered into gigantic databases were compiled into one national list.

From top to bottom, AR&D's 1989 rankings read: emergency weather, crime prevention, crime coverage, weather, children's issues, environment, national/international news, education, spot news, investigative reports/corruption, live reports, health, business/economics, housing and minority affairs, military affairs, financial, agriculture, sports, high school sports and entertainment.[24]

The same year McHugh & Hoffman's list would read: weather, local events, crime and corruption, national/international news, business/economics, medicine, crime prevention, people, home protection, children, amusing people, health care, education, technology, personal fitness, travel, sports, consumer news, environment, personal money matters, career opportunities, entertainment, parenting, government and politics, military affairs, women and minorities and boating news.[25]

The two 1989 rankings had 14 subjects in common, which, when compared with an arithmetic calculation, had a similarity factor of 61 percent. This was a high correlation and suggested in these two separate surveys a convergence of the public's news content preferences.

Other features suggested this. Weather finished No. 1 in both surveys. Consistently and sometimes by staggering proportions, weather was a dominant middle majority news viewing expectation. Millions watched local news only to get the weather. At the opposite extreme was sports, mid-range in the McHugh & Hoffman rankings and close to last at AR&D. Indeed, sports segments on local newscasts rarely enticed more than one-third of the audience. A fundamental content objective was broadening the appeal of sports, especially to female viewers. Also consistent with other research were the strong votes of confidence for "news you can use," namely crime prevention, child raising, managing money, personal health and consumer news. That government and politics ranked twenty-fourth out of 27 items in the McHugh & Hoffman survey, and did not even make AR&D's 20-item list, further illustrated how the American public felt about those topics.

Yet no two sets of rankings were exactly alike. Preferences could differ markedly by locale. In 1977, the 10 most frequently named subjects in Detroit, in order, were crime, drugs, the cost of living, unemployment, gun control, school problems, problems of the aged, health care, welfare and the environment. The rankings in Seattle were different. The most frequently named subjects, in order, were special reports, the environment, health, food costs, crime, politics and consumer information. Research in Atlanta created a list topped by "cost of living" and included, in order, inflation, crime, crime and safety in the streets, drug abuse and employment. Different still were the preferences in Indianapolis, where respondents named school busing, street repair, taxes and inflation, crime, drug use among teenagers, incompetent government and traffic.[26]

By far, the greatest variations were brought by the passage of time, with major shifts at about five-year intervals.[27] One occurred around 1980, when, because of double-digit inflation, viewers had strongly preferred news about the cost of living. But then as inflation eased, living costs fell away in the content rankings.

It was one thing to assess the public's news content preferences. A longstanding question was whether content rankings generated by consultants translated into what viewers saw on the news. They did, and sometimes this could be seen by comparing what consultants had privately told clients to findings made public by experts who studied local TV news. An example had been the content observed by Phyllis Kaniss in her 1991 book *Making Local News,* this not long after AR&D and McHugh & Hoffman had circulated their 1989 rankings. A list published by Kaniss of news covered in Philadelphia correlated with the AR&D and McHugh & Hoffman rankings at almost 50 percent.[28] At the time, AR&D consulted Philadelphia station WCAU, while McHugh & Hoffman consulted KYW.

This was of interest because consultants had persistently claimed they did not dictate news content. In truth, consultants had not had to dictate material. Local newsrooms had become so conditioned to what was in the research that they responded by rote. By the 1990s all the consultants would be allowed working contacts with reporters, producers and assignment editors, and, thus, they had occasions directly to impart research-guided news values. In 1986, Magid founded the Frank Magid Institute, the first multi-function people's news journalism school.[29] Yet long before this, real journalism schools had begun training reporters the same way. In a textbook sanctioned by the RTNDA, writers Charles Cremer, Phillip Keirstead, and Richard Yoakam instructed newcomers on "Showing and Telling," "The Anchor Ingredient," "Telling the Story Visually," "Reporting Live, Being Live," and "What Researchers Say."[30] "These things indicated how far we had come with our research," Frank Magid confirmed.[31]

If the journalists hadn't been listening in school, there was a more potent means for getting the research to move: written instructions by the boss. Rules on news had been among the seeds planted during the consultants' long march in the 1970s. The moment management consented to an action plan, provisions had had to be communicated through the newsroom chain of command. A journalist's "freedom of the press" was narrowed by these often exacting materials, and as rules of employment, they had to be followed.

A model was the *Group W Policy Manual* which helped order news selection in the Westinghouse group, a company that had fought the domination of the big networks. This company's zeal for news content that flew in the face of network news was ever-present, as was the impact of its consultant, McHugh & Hoffman. The key guideline read: "We are in the craft of telling people what is happening—when it happens. But we must recognize the very concept of what is 'hard news' has expanded greatly in the past few years. Today, a medical discovery or a scientific advance qualifies as 'hard news' as much as a diplomatic move or a governmental pronouncement; a religious conclave is as 'hard' as a Congressional committee meeting." Further, "It is Group W's goal to present . . . the heavier news of the world's officialdom <u>and</u> those activities that generally run to a lighter vein . . . . [I]n gathering news we will ask ourselves the constant question: Are we deploying ourselves in such a way to accurately reflect the total milieu in which we live? Or are we . . . flocking to the staged happening and simply duplicating what the wire services are offering . . . ?" Thus, "we encourage, indeed insist upon, experimentation."[32]

Another model rulebook was the *Action3News Production Manual,* which administered operations at Cleveland's WKYC in 1980. It began: "Research indicates that most viewers don't completely concentrate when they are watching a news program. When they are forced to concentrate . . . they usually tune out." At WKYC, news stories "that deserve air time" fell into three categories, each defined by "people." They were "stories that directly affect people," including money, health, crime, schools, and safety; "stories that indirectly affect people"; and "unusual or memorable stories," such as people events that "evoke an emotional response." Content rankings inspired more instruction. "Weather," the book noted, "is one of the most popular elements in any news show," while sports needed help. "There has been a lot of research in the area of sports. Most indicates that 25 percent of the audience is comprised of hard-core sports fans. The other 75 percent is comprised of people who range from the 'take it or leave it range' to the 'hate it range.'" As much as "people," WKYC expected "local." "Research," the book went on, "says that most viewers don't have an overwhelming passion for national and international news [but] want to go to bed thinking that they have heard of the important news from around the world." Thus, world news was to be included but limited.[33]

Similar was *The Total News Handbook,* which went into effect at Kansas City's KMBC the same year. "Late, live, and local" were the coordinating themes. "The Ten O'Clock Update will not look like the Six O'Clock Report," was one guideline. "We will update stories while on the air," was another. Reporters were told to challenge print traditions and stop being a "medium of record." "Weather will be the lead when developments demand it," KMBC ordained, and if "our Editor/Specialists have top stories that we know the competition does not have, put them on television news's Front Page, the first section. But their reports better be attention grabbing and holding." After enumerating numerous other content priorities, KMBC laid down a single overriding rule: "We will offer what our audience can't get anywhere else."[34]

As it turned out, KMBC's last provision was not easily fulfilled. This was because its main competitor, Kansas City's KCTV, had also published a newsroom rulebook. Replete with drawings and an appendix, and running 50 pages, the *KCTV 5 News Stylebook and Operations Manual* mandated the same news content as at KMBC. Reporters and producers at Kansas City's "5 News" adhered to checklists. "Are stories included which will also appeal to persons who aren't traditional sports fans?" and "Are there [reports] about activities in which our viewers participate?" In setting up additional lists, the imperative of late, live, and local was augmented by an additional "3-prong test": "heart," "head," and "pocketbook." "Heart stories trigger the empathy one feels for a worker who had lost his job . . . ." Differently, "Head stories make you think: 'Could this be me or my family?'" Finally, "Pocketbook stories: here's where we *bottom line* every story." KCTV went on to alert reporters to five topics, investigative, consumer, medical, science, and economic news, which had topped the research. "Consider this handbook your bible," the KCTV manual had begun."[35]

A TV reporter could not view these instructions as anything less. By bringing teeth to the research process, these rules forced news professionals to think like Joe Six Pack. Rule after rule boiled down to a question Joe Six Pack was asking and which each journalist now had to address. As framed by KCTV, this question was: "What's in it for me?"

It was a task that called many but chose few. What Joe Six Pack really wanted was something the system was not set up to provide: not reporters with college degrees but commoners-turned-reporters who by nature and instinct knew what average people needed to see. The proof was a feisty investigative reporter in Texas who each night went on TV and literally shouted his name, "Marvin Zindler, Eyewitness News." For 30 years the everyday people of Houston couldn't get enough of him.

Raised in a destitute section of Houston, Zindler had had an inborn grudge against the establishment and entered television in a most unusual way—through a Magid research report for Houston's KTRK showing Zindler not only with a very high Q score but as one of Houston's most-trusted personalities. He had not been working in TV at the time. He got those high marks from TV coverage of lawsuits he had brought as a consumer frauds investigator for the Houston D.A. Houstonites were crying for someone who could get the bad guy and stick it to the comfortable. "I told Capital Cities," the owner of KTRK, "that I'm an ugly son of a bitch . . . [and that because] I grew up in Houston, I couldn't speak English. . . . They took me anyway," Zindler recalled.

Zindler needed a special staff to handle the hundreds of letters and calls that came in from Houston's working class. Millions of others knew him too, as the TV reporter played by actor Dom DeLuise in "The Best Little Whorehouse in Texas," a Broadway play and later motion picture headlined by Burt Reynolds and Dolly Parton. The plot had revolved around a house of prostitution known as the "Chicken Ranch" in the small Texas town of La Grange. It was a true story, and Zindler with fellow KTRK reporter Larry Conners had exposed the whole affair on "Eyewitness News." They succeeded in getting the "Chicken Ranch" closed down. "Texas has got a whorehouse in it," Zindler had reported on KTRK.[36]

It was one of the few Zindler exposés with humorous overtones. Later to lose track of the number of people he had sent to prison, Zindler went after banks, car dealers, lawyers, nursing homes, landlords, restaurants, real estate firms and termite control companies. He rode herd on government. One of his persistent targets was the medical field, including a local hospital whose officials, Zindler had shown, had lavishly embezzled funds from an estate dedicated to the indigent and then were accused of selling the organs of deceased poor people who couldn't pay their bills.[37] "I don't consider myself a journalist. I'm a street person. The people are the ones you do the story on, not the politicians and the others who talk in high bullshit. . . . Consultants? You betcha," Zindler would relate. "We were together on many things."[38] Capital Cities agreed and honored Zindler with the only known lifetime contract in the history of local TV news.

But other local newsrooms faced the problem that Zindler could not be cloned and that colleges and universities were turning out "mass" communicators inclined to speak the "high" language Zindler had described. As a result, many additional measures were needed to make sure the news came out right. Not even Zindler's exploits had operated in a vacuum. Indeed, the "Best Little Whorehouse" series and all of Zindler's other reports had been inspired by a need to beat competitors. It was under the pressure of competition that research into news content left its most visible marks.

The sculpting of TV news was never what most people thought, a comprehensive summary of the day's events. The "summary" was there, as burned into the research was the public's need for the day's basic news stories. Yet even at the networks, this blotter of information was not enough. As NBC's David Brinkley admitted, "People usually have the idea that all over the world all of the time all kinds of sensational things are happening. The fact is that in most of the world most of the time nothing is happening."[39] He was right. Ninety-nine percent of the time, the day's basic news was mundane. Worse, newsrooms using only the blotter flirted with competitive disaster. Everybody had access to it. No viewer was going to pick one newscast over another if they all covered the same thing. As soon as this was realized, local newsrooms placed their highest priority on content that was unique. They still carried the day's news, but to attract the middle majority, newscasts increasingly favored pre-built exclusives. Research by consultants made the "scoop" part of the formula for local TV news.

The consultants learned quickly that the real scoop, the hard-hitting undercover investigative report, was the grand slam of all news possibilities. From where the average viewer sat, journalism's detective story was unequalled as a newscast attraction, particularly if such reports unfolded the way Zindler's had—as a white hat-black hat drama that hit at the gut level and unearthed happenings no one thought possible. While Zindler later honed this technique, the "Eyewitness" concept had been legitimized as serious news in 1971 after an investigative series by Geraldo Rivera exposed abuses at the Willowbrook school for the mentally retarded in New York. Rivera's reports led to reform and sealed WABC as New York's leading source of local news. It also had brought WABC both a Peabody and national Emmy award. A year before Woodward and Bernstein and also before CBS's "60 Minutes," Rivera had dramatized the spell that investigative reporting had on the masses.[40]

The popularity of these early investigative ventures had had an additional result: unlocking the door to new thinking on how newscast content could be grooved. The basic idea, promising viewers specific types of news, became entrenched following the success of a new concept that gave viewers a semblance of investigative reporting night after night.

It was a viewer-response segment placed into newscasts somewhat like sports and weather. The beginning of what became an institution in local TV news was a feature called "Action Reporter" on WCCO in Minneapolis, in which Skip Loescher solicited complaints from the little guy and then followed up on TV. The research was so favorable that all the consultants would urge this "ombudsman" idea.[41] McHugh & Hoffman told clients, "[It] encourages viewers to write the station for assistance with problems which require cutting through the red tape of business or government in order to get things done."[42] Eventually, the archetype of viewer-response segments was first called "Help Center 7," then "Seven on Your Side," on WABC's "Eyewitness News." Teams of volunteers headed by Rivera fielded complaints and then confronted governmental agencies, landlords and businesses.[43] Few local stations would not have their own version, known either by these names or as "Action Line," "Call for Action," "Trouble Shooter" and even for a time "The Consumer Cop."

Viewer-response segments cut an enormous swath as for two minutes every night they delivered unadulterated people's news. Even with a Harvard degree, there was no way a TV journalist could controvert the objective. Without delay more specialty segments were established in newscasts, and the groundswell for "news you can use" encouraged numerous ideas. Because health, children, money management, the environment, crime protection and consumer affairs consistently scored high in content rankings, Magid established a half-dozen content designs that stations could select. "Economy and personal health are almost always very popular features across all markets," the firm advised newsrooms.[44] The first viewers to see a complete set were those in Salt Lake City, where Magid client KSL subtitled its "Eyewitness News" as "The News Specialists." KSL reduced its routine news and then divided up the rest of the newscast into five fixed and eventually award-winning specialty segments.[45]

As specialty segments caught on, yet another development would make the news exclusive even easier to pull off. Syndicators, the same ones who distributed game shows and movies, began buying the most popular local news productions. These then were sold to newsrooms all over the country. The largest syndicators, Lorimar and King World, each had contracts with McHugh & Hoffman and AR&D, while a third company, Gilbride, became one of Magid's key non-station clients. Tapping into the consultants' databases, these syndicators easily could spot where, locally, Stories A, B, or C were likely to excel.

Syndicated news had started in 1974 with a special segment on KRON's "News Center 4" called "The Greengrocer." After helping develop it, Magid, KRON's consultant, had proposed similar "Greengrocers" to other clients. Rather than copying the segment, station managers looked at the demonstration tapes and said they wanted the real thing. Hosted by an affable yet knowledgeable grocer-looking figure named Joe Carcione, "The Greengrocer" was shot at supermarkets and advised on such matters as when produce was in season. It was a people's news sensation. For 15 years Carcione's segment was seen nightly on newscasts in 160 of the 200 markets.[46]

Other "news you can use" productions with almost as much visibility had included Dr. Lendon Smith's "The Children's Doctor" from KGW in Portland, Dr. Timothy Johnson's "House Call" from WCVB in Boston, Paul Strassel's tax segment from WJLA in Washington, Art Ginsburg's "Mr. Food" from WRGB in Albany, Steve Crowley's "Money Pro" from Miami's WPLG, Dr. Red Duke's medical update from KTRK, and Dr. Dean Edell's health and fitness report from San Francisco's KGO. These segments were edited so they looked locally produced. Research affirmed that few viewers ever knew they weren't.[47]

Of all these content tacks, none whipped up more attention—by researchers and reporters alike—than the one-time-only showcase report. Sometimes a single report, other times a series stretching over several days in what were called "mini-documentaries," these reports had special importance. They were scheduled during the four monthly rating periods. Daily newsgathering often ground to a halt so these exclusives could be completed on schedule. Then, each February, May, July and November, the public was bombarded by their promotion.

In his attacks on local news, Walter Cronkite had felt news consultants were responsible for the demise of long-form documentaries in local television. Cronkite had upheld critically acclaimed documentary productions, such as those pioneered by Edward R. Murrow, by characterizing local TV's "mini-doc" as "balderdash." While the people hardly perceived them that way, the mini-doc had emerged in local TV pretty much the way Cronkite had surmised. McHugh & Hoffman had not been in business more than two years before its research sounded the death knell for the real documentary. "[T]he problem in such programs is that they are not 'hot news,' as the average person defines 'hot news,'" research in 1964 had shown.[48] But by chopping them to three minutes and packing them with non-traditional content, the mini-doc couldn't miss.

The path-breaker had been that investigative series on the Willowbrook hospital by Geraldo Rivera in 1971. Research performed three years later showed that New Yorkers still recalled Rivera's Willowbrook series.[49] On the heels of Rivera's series were a half-dozen breakthrough documentaries by KYW's Jessica Savitch. One timed for the November 1973 ratings showed a natural childbirth, the first time this had ever been seen on television.[50] In another on rape, timed for the February 1974 ratings, Savitch had taken to the streets and invited what seemed a certain assault.[51] None of Savitch's many mini-docs, though, had a longer afterglow than her five-part series in 1975 on Philadelphia natives who had struck it rich in Hollywood.[52] This series was recalled in research 20 years later. Through the 1970s, ideas had sprung from many other locales, notably Chicago. During the February 1976 ratings, WBBM's Bill Kurtis and WLS's John Coleman both prepared five-part series on UFOs. WBBM's Walter Jacobson and WMAQ's Jim Cummins introduced another mainstay, the runaway-husbands-and-wives special report. A mini-doc on truckers and truckstops by WLS's Joel Daly was copied in local newsrooms from coast to coast.[53]

Although the content system had many hidden spokes, almost all connected to news consultants, who from one city to the next could harvest the nation's crop of story ideas and then recommend them in other cities. Investigative reports always did the best. Usually next were stories that dealt with family matters, from husband-wife issues and sleeping disorders to animal care and the fear of flying. Everyday viewers likewise had a taste for "breakthrough news," such as medical stories, new treatments, discoveries, success stories and "cured folks." The "bizarre," such as UFOs and the paranormal, formed an additional category.[54] Lower in the hierarchy but not to be discounted were stories relating to sex. Overall, stories "most memorable need to hit 'gut issues' [and] evoke real and often complex emotions. . . . The worst try for humor."[55]

Stations had an insatiable appetite for new topics, which the consultants met. One research-devised inventory circulated by McHugh & Hoffman in 1980 included animal diseases and funerals, runaway children, drug use, impact of divorce, loneliness of the single's life, rape, abortion, marijuana, cocaine use, high medical costs, working mothers, school lunches, a day in the life of police, alcoholism, managing money, pill addiction, teenage jobs, family roots, water supply, car purchasing, Born Again religion, remarriage, the control of boxing and fatherhood.[56]

From lists like these would roll stories visible to millions. A special reports list syndicated in 1984, by a distributor called NIWS, included "Trapped in Flight" from KAKE in Wichita, "Psychology of Eating" from KPNX in Phoenix, "Forgotten Babies" from KUTV in Salt Lake City, "Pets: Living the Good Life" from WHO in Des Moines, "Car Wars" from WNEM in Bay City, Michigan, and "Sweet Dreams" from KWTV in Oklahoma City.[57]

The effect was seamless. It took a discerning eye to tell the difference between routine blotter news and that which newsrooms had designed in advance—with the help of data from a consultant's computer. As more and more outside media experts examined local newscasts, though, questions did multiply. Evidence that as much as 70 percent of local newscast content was not really the "day's news" had led Texas Tech researcher Mark Harmon to conclude that the journalism's once-powerful newsroom "gatekeeper" was fading away. Because so many specialists had their hands in it, Harmon speculated, news selection had turned into a science, one organized by forces far from the news desk.[58]

This science, though, undercut the value of those on the news desk. Investigative reports, special segments and mini-docs reduced the amount of airtime producers and assignment editors could control. Veteran producers anguished when they kept seeing the same special reports every couple of years. Of 17 special reports promoted by stations in Phoenix during the November 1995 ratings, among them "Child's Play," "Men and Women" and "UFO Cover-up," all but two had been on that list circulated by McHugh & Hoffman 15 years before.[59] "It's the closest thing to assembly line work I've ever done in my life to be perfectly honest about it," remarked Denver's Roy Weissinger in a 1982 interview on PBS.[60] Later, another Denver figure, Lee Hood, would recall that even though she had a 35-minute newscast to produce, she "got about two minutes" whenever a ratings period came around. "The rest was decided by someone else," she said, and this was one of the reasons she joined tens of thousands of other producers and editors in starting new careers.[61]

Nothing better revealed the shrinking fortunes of the gatekeepers than their low pay. In the first NAB and RTNDA salary reports in the 1970s, producers had been among the highest-paid newsroom employees. By the 1990s top producers even in the largest cities often were young recruits earning $25,000, well below the average income for people with college degrees.[62] In 1992 the on-the-job lifespan of producers had declined to two years.

But local TV news fitted the middle majority like hand in glove. For this reason, news consultants had wanted something they had not yet achieved: professional approval. Trench-level newsworkers, who needed more knowledge, were still off limits. Hundreds of smaller local newsrooms, which could become clients, remained out of reach.

The seal of approval did arrive, but to get it the consultants had needed help. It came from a likely source: the only broadcast institution with "little news" spirit and "big TV" clout.

13

ABC to Z
(1977–1990)

Lively anchor teams and sprightly news content had altered the public's perception of TV news, and yet the rush toward people's news had not seemed entirely real. Local news had "little news" stigma, and news-from-New York had stood fast. The 1980s had begun with network giants still making a sport of scorning local newscasts, while giving every indication New York was America's true source of news. The networks had thousands of reporters and producers and a news-gathering capability that spanned the globe. That the networks' evening newscasts had a combined "50" Nielsen rating, meaning they were seen in one-half of all American homes, had been the rock upon which this confidence was based.

Yet even in the rarified atmosphere of network row, tensions were in the air. That "50" looked good, but the network news divisions were still losing money. CBS's 1980 decision to retire Walter Cronkite had been an ominous sign.

It was inevitable that at least one of the networks would waken to the power of people's news, and, just as certain was that this was going to be ABC, whose local stations were swimming in ratings points and profits because of the success of "Eyewitness News." No longer could this be denied, for despite its starched and above-the-fray image, network news indeed was out on a limb. At ABC, news ratings had remained far below expectations, this as all three networks faced a greater threat: new national networks like CNN planned for cable TV. ABC's immediate solution was notable because it put in motion the capstone episode of the people's news movement. In the first glimmer of what came to be known as the "localization" of network news, and in the calm before a very big storm, ABC became a news consultant not unlike Magid and the other firms.

Few ever knew of this ABC initiative. Nor had ABC anything to gain by telling the world. At a time when local news and news consultants were condemned, it had been unthinkable that one of the big media would stoop so low.

Nevertheless, for nine years a team of ABC executives, most drafted out of "Eyewitness" newsrooms, roamed the country and spread the gospel of people's news. Trading on a welcome they received from almost every ABC affiliate, they seeded the research-consulting process in scores of U.S. cities where some felt it never would appear. The same local news concepts that had enabled ABC to excel in the largest urban markets would work their way to the smallest and most distant locales. Not only had the plan been written in stealth. It had an odd logic typical of ABC. The company had wagered that if its own network newscast could not get off Mt. Olympus, then its 200 affiliates, each with versions of "Eyewitness News," would turn the network around. It was another maverick ABC idea that worked. By spreading incalculable goodwill and healing network-local wounds, ABC in 1980 secured a newscast called "Nightline," the first time affiliates had approved a network news expansion since 1963. Even more of a feat had been a network newscast on the Almost Broadcasting Company that finally became No. 1.

Yet in the end, for network news at large, the screws had turned too far. Network news in its original form did not stay intact. As people's news spread into every city and the networks faced competition for the first time, news-from-New York in the image of Cronkite, Murrow, and other greats was headed for collapse. Ratings tumbled and layoffs multiplied. Inexplicably, the networks became the new target for critics who assailed "local" techniques. ABC's network news felt not just the effects but the irony. This was because another part of ABC, the people's news component, had shown the field the way.

This ABC venture might have been called the people's news Mod Squad. Actually, it was known as the ABC News Advisory Service, and from the beginning it was cumbersome, expensive, ridiculously unmanageable, but destined to succeed. With a budget of around a half-million dollars annually, ABC's plan was giving all 200 affiliates free news consulting. This was new. Because the service was free, ABC realized that the large number of local stations still skeptical of Magid and McHugh & Hoffman would give consulting a try. Further, because these stations would be the first in their markets to attempt people's news, they were certain to gain viewers. The News Advisory Service officially began in 1977 and grew steadily through the 1980s until finally being eliminated as a cost-cutting measure by Capital Cities, ABC's new owner, in 1986.

Throughout these nine years, ABC's dilemma had been the last place ratings of its network newscast. Of that 50 percent of Americans who had regularly watched network news in 1980, 40 percent had been loyal to CBS and NBC. That ABC usually managed a "10" was a problem Roone Arledge, the wizard of the "ABC Wide World of Sports," would be brought in to solve. Yet while Arledge was given much attention for revisions that led to the broadcast "ABC World News Tonight," the News Advisory Service was a bolder solution as for the first time a network would challenge the basic premise of network TV. This premise stated that the main attraction of a network show was the network and the show.

In a corporate culture trained on alternative thinking, factions at ABC had begun to question big television's hypodermic effect. This effect had been taken for granted because Nielsen's national TV ratings, the basis of network decision-making, had ranked programs solely on the basis of national scores. Yet programmers at ABC had taken a closer look at the Nielsen ratings and found something intriguing. Each program's ratings not only differed from city to city but almost always correlated with the known strengths and weaknesses of local affiliates. This indicated that local stations levered the network ratings. While a determinate in prime-time programming, the affiliate factor was absolute in the case of network news. In every city network newscasts were adjacent to or sandwiched between periods of local news. Of particular interest were the numerous cities where local news came first. As the "lead-in" program, the local newscast gathered the audience that fed into network news.

At ABC the spearhead behind this thinking was its research director Marvin Mord, whose data had revealed that 80 percent of the people who watched CBS, NBC and ABC news did so because they'd already selected an affiliate's local newscast.[1] According to Mord, even though CBS's Walter Cronkite was America's "most trusted man," hardly anyone who viewed local news on NBC or ABC affiliates switched stations to watch him. The affiliate factor had been suggested in something most at ABC already knew. While ABC's network news was dead last nationally, it was first in New York,

Chicago, Philadelphia, Detroit and other big cities. This was because in major markets local news on ABC stations was far and away No. 1. Across the U.S., Mord said, Cronkite was No. 1 because CBS affiliates had the strongest local newscasts. Conversely, ABC was No. 3 because its affiliates weren't doing the job.[2]

An internal ABC study went on to confirm this. One-half of ABC affiliates were rated in the lowest category: non-competitive.[3] Dozens of ABC affiliates were new and had been on the air for only a few years. In contrast, almost all CBS and NBC affiliates were pioneer stations that had gone on the air in the 1940s and 1950s. Well into the 1970s, ABC still lacked affiliates in some cities.

Weak affiliates left little doubt as to the merit of an affiliate-wide advising program. Yet given what Mord had said about the levering power of local stations, the company had had an additional reason for welcoming the idea. ABC management had created a monster in its news division and, short of turning to its affiliates, hadn't known what to do.

The ears of ABC chair Leonard Goldenson and company president Elton Rule had been tuned to the voice of owned stations president Richard O'Leary, whose "Eyewitness News" on WABC and elsewhere was lavishing the network with hundreds of millions of dollars in profits each year. The local "Eyewitness News" not only had tremendous ratings; brimming with energy and new ideas, it had been conceived as the counterpoint to those CBS and NBC network newscasts that ABC, at the network level, also needed to counter. It was not clear whether Goldenson and Rule had favored an "Eyewitness" conversion at the network level. Nevertheless, on repeated occasions they had conveyed a wish for more people-oriented news material, up-to-date aesthetic elements, female and minority anchors and other "Eyewitness" effects.[4]

Each overture was rejected. ABC's network news division had become a fortress. Like other bastions of the national news media it was accustomed to directing its own affairs. Ideas from outside the news division were ignored on the grounds they impeded good journalism. Goldenson and Rule backed away out of fears of a flap about corporate level interference. Yet most vexing was an additional realization: The ABC news division was a virtual colony of CBS. In addition to the two top ABC News executives, Elmer Lower and Av Westin, David Schoumacher, ABC's lead correspondent, had just come from CBS. Preceding him had been Howard K. Smith, one of the famed CBS-Edward Murrow protégés. CBS veteran Harry Reasoner had recently been installed as ABC's lead anchor.

With this contingent mired in last place and losing record sums of money, some new blood was injected. Transferred from a local to a network assignment Al Primo walked out and castigated ABC's CBS approach to news.[5] Geraldo Rivera stayed, but his spirit had remained with Primo and WABC. "At Channel 7, we were happening, the news team was the most creative thing in television," Rivera related. But "[a]t the network, they were trying to look like the other guys, at CBS and NBC, and they were failing at it. They were small and shriveled, and we [had been] sexy and thriving."[6] One foresighted move came in 1976 when ABC's Barbara Walters became the first woman to anchor a network newscast. Yet she lasted only a year. The CBS man, Reasoner, had made Walters look like an intruder on the news set.

The official unveiling of the News Advisory Service, at an affiliates confab in New Orleans on January 11, 1977, was memorable. Because ABC had just passed CBS and NBC in the prime-time entertainment ratings, attendees expected a victory celebration. But when the affiliate managers arrived, they found local news the main item on the agenda. Bearing a plea from Goldenson that "ABC will not be the No. 1 network until we are No. 1 in news," ABC network president James Duffy pledged "a new spirit" of news cooperation. John Conomikes, chair of the affiliate Board of Governors, detailed ABC's hope for interdependent local and network news, while vice president Richard Savage reiterated that this goal "can be achieved by raising the level of local news operations." Finally, a figure named Al Ittleson was brought to the microphones and introduced as the vice president of the new ABC undertaking. "There is no magic to this," Ittleson stated, "and no formula."[7]

Yet magic was the intent. Without enlisting a single figure from its network newsroom, ABC brought to headquarters its local "Eyewitness" vanguard. The goal was to replicate the success of "Eyewitness News" at all 200 affiliates. In addition to Ittleson, who'd been the right-arm to Primo in the "Eyewitness" triumph at WABC, ABC hired a management-research specialist named Bryce Rathbone, who as a coordinator of the Arbitron local ratings service, had tracked every phase of the "Eyewitness" phenomenon. Other new ABC executives included Peter Jacobus, who in the 1960s had helped Primo launch "Eyewitness News" at both KYW and WABC, and Don Dunphy, Jr., the son of a famous boxing announcer and also one of the original "Eyewitness News" insurgents at WABC. Joining later was Larry Rickel, who had helped direct "Eyewitness News" in Boston before moving to WABC and to the News Advisory Service.

Although this core was small, it was ringed by very important ABC personnel. The heads of ABC promotion, engineering and research were bound to the News Advisory Service and regularly funneled advice. While not officially linked to the News Advisory Service, members of ABC's network news division also gave guidance.

Very much in this mix were the news consultants Magid and McHugh & Hoffman, still working in tandem for the ABC-owned stations. Irked that Magid and McHugh & Hoffman had stolen the "Eyewitness" concept from ABC, Ittleson at first saw an opportunity to strike back. As it turned out, the News Advisory Service boosted the "real" consultants, who jumped at the chance to participate. This was because the News Advisory Service was not set up to perform research, even though the need for research would emerge as its unifying theme. Thus, a cozy relationship formed. The consultants supplied ABC with needed information, while ABC returned this favor by referring affiliates to the real consultants for research.

Within six weeks, 60 requests for visits were received at the service's small office on the thirty-third floor of "1330," ABC's headquarters on Sixth Avenue in New York. They came from stations as large as WJLA in Washington, D. C., the eighth market, and as diminutive as KOTI in Klamath Falls, Oregon, a locale so small it did not even have a market-size designation. By the time the service hit its stride in the mid-1980s, ABC was trooping into the newsrooms of 120 local affiliates—most in medium and small cities where ABC was weak. This was a big switch for ABC, which had long been identified with the nation's very largest markets. ABC's big-city affiliates were doing well, and most already were partnered with Magid or another consultant. Exceptions were St. Louis, where affiliate KTVI didn't even have a dinner-hour local newscast, and Phoenix, where affiliate KTVK seemed forever consigned to last place.

Still, big gains lurked in small places, where the territory was virgin for people's news. Ittleson and his associates criss-crossed the country to stations they knew nothing about, such outposts as WOWK in Huntington, West Virginia; WSVJ in South Bend, Indiana; WKOW in Madison, Wisconsin; KXLY in Spokane, Washington; and KGUN in Tucson, Arizona.

Descending in these outposts was like touching down on the dark side of the moon. Even at this late date, 1977, smaller TV stations often had skeleton news staffs and covered events with silent film. A winning strategy often was placing most of the news budget on a dominating male anchor who could double as the news director and attempt to become the local Walter Cronkite. "It was another case of us trying to be like CBS," observed Ittleson, who nevertheless was struck by growing numbers of young, energetic newcomers as contemptuous of the "older generation" as he had once been at WABC. "We told them TV news was hidebound by tradition" and that in New York "we at ABC were guerilla fighters who fought from the trees. . . . We impressed upon these young people [that] they could make a difference for themselves and their stations. This caught on everywhere we went," Ittleson explained.[8]

As the program expanded, few details were overlooked. ABC advised on news color schemes, theme music and even where paper should be purchased. A talent service was created so local stations had access to some of the thousands of applications that flooded network headquarters.[9] Adding to this was a stream of newsletters, brochures, tips, guidelines and procedures manuals, each dispatched under a special ABC letterhead highlighted by the slogan "News Is People" embossed on an artistic mosaic depicting different working class walks of life. One of the hundreds of circulars sent to promotion managers read, "Let your news director know what he can expect to promote in his department. . . . Suggest that together you explain to anchors, producers, reporters and photographers how you're going to skyrocket them to stardom."[10]

Not a consulting network like Magid, but a real television network, ABC had yet another way to get through. Every two or three weeks, a News Advisory Service figure or someone the service had appointed appeared from New York in a nationally televised closed-circuit program. The "News Is People" show was sent out on the network line at time periods when ABC was not showing regular programming; only those at ABC affiliates could tune in.[11] Sometimes the advisors answered mail sent in by affiliates. The most talked-about program came the day ABC screened a compilation of promotional ads from WXYZ in Detroit, which had lampooned confusion at its CBS and NBC competitors. One of the promos featured rival anchors playing musical chairs on the anchor desk, while another began "Now its time for disco news!" In a take-off on the movie **Saturday Night Fever,** competing anchors were seen gyrating their way to podiums on a dance floor and then conducting the news, with hand-held microphones, to the pounding beat of disco music.[12] On the many occasions when the advisors had nothing new to say, they had a ready backup: popping in a tape from the previous night's "Eyewitness News" from WABC in New York. There was no better instruction.

The favorite point of contact, though, was regional workshop affairs. Twenty-five at a time, local news directors were flown to a large city such as Chicago, Denver or San Francisco for two days of prepping on research, ratings, promotion and alternative news content.[13] A session entitled "What Is A Leader?" sharpened news directors' interpersonal skills by having them role play with actors who pretended to be prima donna anchors and reporters demanding more pay, more airtime and less work.[14] At a Los Angeles conclave in 1980, ABC greeted news directors from places like Redding, California; Pensacola, Florida; Nampa and Pocatello, Idaho; Lafayette, Louisiana; Ada, Oklahoma; Lufkin, Texas; and Yakima, Washington.[15] After treating them to evenings at expensive restaurants, ABC concluded each event with personalized gifts. "We had one of the largest entertainment budgets ABC had ever seen," Ittleson would relate.[16]

Another token had been a pictorial handbook. So highly polished that it would have looked good on someone's coffee table, **NAS Presents** used visual displays to illustrate the increasing stakes in local TV news. "The rationale for the News Advisory Service is to help affiliates whenever possible in improving and building their local product." A clear understanding that news was people was the place to begin. "Any story, crime, politics, fire, accident, discovery, invention, feature, sports, weather—any story works if it affects, touches, changes, interests or services the People. People are News. Who they are, what they do, why they do it, what's done to them and why. Things are meaningless. Events are empty. News is dumb. Our jobs are self-indulgent—unless we touch the folks. The key is people. NEWS IS PEOPLE—PEOPLE ARE NEWS," ABC had said.[17]

ABC carried this bent to the furthest extreme in the newsrooms, in the first concerted program for reaching TV's thousands of young newsworkers. It was ABC's ultimate task and a major revision in news consulting. Until then, consultants from Magid, McHugh & Hoffman and other firms had had little contact with newsworkers. Almost all their activities had occurred in the offices of top managers. While some anchors had met consultants at the talent schools, most on the front lines had had only a vague idea of who the consultants were.

But at ABC "we did not believe in closed doors," Rathbone related. Although no statistics were kept, Rathbone estimated that at least 5,000 TV reporters, editors and producers heard ABC's discussions on people's news.[18] As these newsworkers spread to different newsrooms, ABC's ideas spread with them. Moreover, in persuading newsworkers away from the traditions and philosophies of CBS and

NBC, ABC capitalized on a powerful effect: Local news people, especially those in smaller markets, were awestruck to be in the presence of those from the network. Indelible impressions were left.

The advisors spent countless hours critiquing the newsworkers' performances, and each session was anticipated with high anxiety. One difficult moment occurred when ABC broke the news to a reporter that he must use a stage name, this because every time he said "This is" and then his real name his credibility was shot. Even though this reporter's actual name was Joe Zass, the recommendation was tough. Yet "the worst part was when you'd make a comment about how they looked on TV, and they burst into tears," Ittleson recalled. "The people we saw were so young—22 and 23 years old. Their lives were totally wrapped up in television, and they were devastated. But you had to be honest about it." The vast majority of these fresh faces, though, accepted the advisors with a loving embrace, this Ittleson recalled after being named by Arledge as executive producer of the ABC newsmagazine "20/20." His only regret was that he was never able to command from "20/20" hosts Barbara Walters and Hugh Downs anything like the adulation he'd received in Ft. Wayne, Fargo and elsewhere.

The focal point of ABC's thousands of seminars were the essentials of people's news. Year by year ABC reiterated the dominance of weather in the research and insisted its stations hire meteorologists.[19] Because of tepid viewer preferences for sports, ABC urged coverage of participation sports like bowling, game highlights, and even bloopers in order to broaden the appeal of sports, especially to women.[20] Toward beating CBS and NBC, personality projection was crucial. Through pie-chart displays, budding on-camera reporters finally found out why six-figure salaries might be in their future. One such chart clearly showed that 53 percent of viewers chose newscasts based on personalties, about 25 percent based on news.[21]

ABC had an innovative strategy for galvanizing the many young minds. Rather than stirring disdain for the network concept of TV news, a tack that would have sent mixed messages, ABC achieved the same result by making the demon the newspaper field. Peter Jacobus, himself only 30 years old, became the most popular of the ABC educators because of his relentless portrayal of people's news as a generational fight for liberation against the greying forces of CBS and NBC—and print. After leaving WABC, Jacobus had become news director at KGO, the station made famous as "kickers, guts, and orgasms" in the Mike Wallace "60 Minutes" exposé back in 1974.

Now to the attentive ears of the young news reporters, Jacobus's theme of a hypocritical establishment struck a chord. As if coming back from a war, Jacobus would recount the many attacks on "Eyewitness News," in which newspaper reporters had torn into ABC for trying to grab the public's attention. "Have you ever seen a newspaper without headlines?" Jacobus would ask. He cut further by pressing an observation few had heard in journalism school. "Look at the newspapers," he would urge, "they're going out of business!" Hundreds of newspapers had, in fact, recently folded. People-to-people TV news, Jacobus insisted, was the highest calling in the electronic age.

ABC advisors taught journalists to replace the newspaper's who, what, when, where and why with simple story-telling techniques. They showed writers how to transform newspaperese into conversational language. Against the prevailing wisdom that national and international news be left for the networks, ABC told local stations, in Jacobus's words, to "go for it." Above all, each newscast had to have human interest at every phase.[22] "Write simple spoken English. Our [stories] should reflect real people talking about real things to other real people. Above all, we must avoid the print form. . . . Writing 'people' talk may be one of the most difficult things we have to do," ABC implored.[23] "They never got this in school. Their eyes really opened," Jacobus recalled.[24]

Testimonials poured in from ABC newsrooms all over the country. Eager to help ABC, for example, had been Jim Riordan of KOAT, whose newscast after using some of the new techniques had leapfrogged from last place to first place in the Albuquerque ratings. "If it worked here, why not at your shop?" Riordan told other ABC news directors.[25] Bill Tell Zortman of KVII in Amarillo then informed the network that after following ABC's advice his station had increased its rating from an "8" to "a 50 to 65 percent share."[26] Rich Gimmel of WTVQ in Lexington detailed a similar success, which validated ABC's "big point," that one must "treat the people as people, not machines."[27]

These testimonials continued. Dick Williams of WXIA in Atlanta reported a doubling of his news ratings after his station adopted the entire "news is people" regimen. "We've been criticized heavily for the sound of our drums and an occasional trip over the line of taste and Southern courtesy. [But] the only Establishment we want to join is the biggest Nielsen family. They're starting to listen," Williams told ABC.[28] From KTVI in St. Louis, Paul Wischmeyer and Rabin Matthews praised ABC for helping "rocket Channel 2 News to the top in less than one year."[29] From KOBI in tiny Medford, Oregon, which had quadrupled its ratings, Ed Zander wrote, "Why are more people watching KOBI Eyewitness News? We stand out. We go to extra lengths to make ourselves visible."[30]

The News Advisory Service accomplished its main goal in May 1983, when Arbitron ratings from the 150 three-station markets showed ABC with more first-place newsrooms, 53, than CBS or NBC. ABC affiliates had increased their share of the local news audience by almost 25 percent.[31] Even though there was no victory celebration, because ABC's own newscast "The World News Tonight" was still in last place, signs were very auspicious. Sure enough, on the heels of the 1983 local results, ABC's newscast finished the 1983-1984 season a hair ahead of NBC. It was the first time since the dawn of TV news that ABC was not in the cellar. Many factors besides the News Advisory Service had contributed, notably Arledge's modernization and peopleization of ABC's newscast, which became a clear alternative to the Olympian standards still set by NBC and CBS. And although no network news division, including ABC, permitted news consultants, the consultants had continued to perform research on network news. The rising Q scores of ABC anchor Peter Jennings against the polarized perceptions of CBS's Dan Rather and the generally neutral perceptions of NBC's Tom Brokaw spelled trouble for ABC's competitors.[32] The News Advisory Service was credited for the sizable local lead-in audiences Jennings's newscast had begun to receive. Rathbone, who by then had succeeded Ittleson as head of the unit, vowed that bigger things were on the way.

It was at that moment that the bottom fell out of all things network. The News Advisory Service was one of the casualties.

The big media had just been broadsided by the sudden popularity of home video and cable TV. Dozens of new national cable channels, including one ABC had started, ESPN, had exploded onto home screens. Yet even ABC, which had anticipated the dilemma and had formed the News Advisory Service as a safeguard, was reeling because of the cable TV phenomenon. Commanding 93 percent of all TV viewers at peak hours in 1980, CBS, NBC and ABC were reaching only 70 percent in 1986. Then in one of the biggest upheavals in TV history, the ownership of all three networks bit the dust. William Paley lost control of CBS to an entertainment tycoon named Lawrence Tisch. General Electric gobbled up RCA, the parent of sagging NBC.

But most unfathomable, at least to New York media experts, was ABC's sale to Capital Cities, of all things a local broadcast group. Anomalous was how some local broadcasters from up the river in Albany had come down and taken over part of network row.

There was, of course, no mystery. For 15 years under Chair Thomas Murphy and President Daniel Burke, Capital Cities had been bank-rolling the hundreds of millions of dollars generated by its "Action News" on WPVI in Philadelphia and by top-rated newscasts everywhere else it owned local stations. Those stations had thrived because of consulting by Magid, not the News Advisory Service. Aware of the project's Achilles heel, that it lacked research, Capital Cities decided that ABC affiliates were best off paying for both research and consulting on their own. The new owners' first priority had been cutting ABC's bloated network budget. The service had ended, though, not with a whimper but with the promotions of Rathbone, Dunphy and others to higher positions in the ABC hierarchy, Capital Cities' way of telling them "job well done."[33]

Although ABC was left the strongest of the original networks, all of network TV looked like a sinking ship. Like the Titanic, the biggest sank the fastest. At CBS, Walter Cronkite had signed off in March 1981 to make way for Dan Rather. When Cronkite departed, the "CBS Evening News" was seen in 20 percent of all American homes and in 30 percent of the homes tuned in at the dinner hour. Over the next nine years CBS news ratings would be cut almost in half. In the first of wave upon wave of network news layoffs and cutbacks, CBS fired 230 of its 1,430 news employees and shut down bureaus in Europe and Asia.[34] A disturbed Rather used his national newscast to express his dismay. After ending a newscast with a plea for "courage," viewers who tuned in late wondered whether the U.S. had just declared war. Nevertheless, Rather went on a week later and said it again in Spanish, "caraje."[35]

After that Rather vented in press interviews. He told **The New Republic** that the budget cuts were causing "a tragic transformation from Murrow to mediocrity" and that it was "something between difficult and impossible" to maintain the Edward Murrow tradition.[36] Even so, with his colleagues losing their jobs, Rather reupped his CBS salary to an estimated $3 million per year. This preceded a network news spectacle in September 1987, when an infuriated Rather walked off the news set because a tennis tournament had run long. Instead of getting the news, CBS viewers got black on their TV screens.

Then the following January, Rather, the man broadcasters still remembered for insulting President Nixon at that NAB convention in 1974, finished the trick by shouting at a Vice President. After deflecting accusations leveled at him by Rather on the "CBS Evening News," George Bush, then running for president, had calm words for CBS's nearly apoplectic news anchor. "How would you like it if I judged your career by those seven minutes when you walked off the set? Would you like that?" Bush asked."[37] Bush went on to win the presidency by a landslide, while Rather lost two more ratings points, about five million more viewers, for CBS. The 1980s had ended with CBS holding on to an "11" rating.

The other pillar of network row, NBC, was having difficulties of its own. Just ahead in the 1990s were a series of ethical transgressions that not only would tar NBC News but raise the first serious questions about the paragon-of-virtue image the networks had shined on themselves. After faking an explosion in a Chevy pickup to make General Motors look bad, NBC then pulled off a network news first: the televising of a domestic disturbance in Florida that ended with a point-blank homicide, gunshots, screams, blood and all.[38] Later, anchor Tom Brokaw would go on national TV and falsely accuse an innocent man of a fatal bombing at the Atlanta Olympics—and then blame the FBI for his mistake.[39] By 1990 NBC had fired almost 300 news personnel. Brokaw, though, kept his $2 million paycheck. Down and down the NBC ratings went. In 1989 NBC's nightly news rating had reached single digits for the first time.

With the total audience for network news continuing the shrink, ABC's newscast held on to a "13" rating achieved at the time of the News Advisory Service. It was because CBS and NBC had lost so many viewers that ABC finally became No. 1. It was a proud moment for ABC insiders, though insignificant to almost everyone else. Who led network news mattered to few. Even in New York media experts were rushing to a new hero, Ted Turner, whose Cable News Network from Atlanta provided news around the clock. At the outbreak of the Persian Gulf War, viewers of ABC, CBS and NBC had seen panel discussions in a studio. On CNN they saw live reporting from where the bombs had actually fallen.[40]

Then came the development that had been most dreaded by those on network row. As the ratings for network newscasts continued to crash, local affiliates began moving them to earlier and earlier time periods. Once near-prime-time fixtures at 7 p.m., network newscasts were now seen in the 5:30 p.m. time slot when most people were still at work. In some locales, affiliates had relegated network newscasts to 4:30 p.m. Viewers who might have continued to watch network news no longer could do so because of the daytime scheduling. It was a nightmare for those who were left in network newsrooms. Having already been devastated in the 1980s, the network news divisions braced for still lower ratings and more layoffs as the 1990s began.

ABC, CBS and NBC did continue nightly newscasts, although by 1990, with the trend going down, there had been talk that one of the network newscasts would be canceled. Actually, cancellation had been unlikely. The broadcasts remained attractive to certain advertisers who saw prestige in sponsoring network news. Meanwhile, the networks' financial turbulence eventually assisted the news divisions. Unable to keep up with the soaring cost of entertainment fare, the networks opened their prime-time periods to less expensive "magazine" shows that the news divisions produced. These prime-time magazines drew large audiences and, coupled with the layoffs, finally enabled the news divisions to achieve profitability. Yet while magazines such as NBC's "Dateline" were popular, they were not newscasts, and they were frequently confused with tabloid shows such as "Entertainment Tonight" and "Current Affair." The more they proliferated, the more they became targets for critics who cited, as did columnist Hal Boedeker, more celebrity "junk."[41]

Network news heaved one last gasp with the first newscast expansions since the debut of "Nightline" in 1980. Few noticed, though. This was because these new network newscasts were televised at two o'clock in the morning when most people were asleep.

The fall of news-from-New York was signalled in additional ways. Brokaw and Rather had become regular guests on the David Letterman late-night comedy show. Later in 1994, network news would broadcast more stories on Tonya Harding, a scandal-ridden celebrity ice skater, than on all events relating to the environment. The following year the networks ran 875 stories on the O. J. Simpson celebrity murder case and only 590 stories on the battle in Congress that led to the first balanced budget in almost 30 years.[42]

No one had been quicker to flag the fall than the people who had first brought network news to prominence. After a dispute with CBS in 1988, Walter Cronkite turned on his former colleagues by telling them they had "gone local" and "thrown in the towel." Elite commentator Bill Moyers walked out of CBS News saying he was disillusioned by the downmarket direction network news had taken.[43] As this had occurred, the often-vocal Reuven Frank, the former president of NBC News, launched the most stinging attacks of his career, his subject the "localization of network news." On the networks Frank saw "news you can use" and "people's health or money" segments. Sensationalism was common, said Frank, and "[c]rime stories abound." Whether the newscast was network or local, he complained, "scandal-tinged celebrities get almost as much attention as they do at the supermarket checkout." All of this, Frank noted, was positive proof that the heart and soul of network news was gone.[44]

Local news had won the local-network news war. More long-time skeptics of local news finally conceded that only local newscasts were making a difference on TV in informing large numbers of Americans. In a 1991 **New York** article entitled "Shrinking The News," Edwin Diamond, one of the most vehement local news critics, nevertheless revealed that ABC, CBS, NBC and CNN had become dependent on local TV stations for much of their daily news coverage.[45] The following year, a study by Nielsen Media Research showed that the daily local news audience of around 150 million viewers was almost five times greater than the audience of all the national broadcast and cable news services, which put together drew around 35 million viewers. Roughly 35 percent of all Americans continued to view 10 and 11 p.m. local newscasts, while another 25 percent watched local news at the dinner hour and yet another 20 percent in the morning.[46] As AR&D's Jim Willi summed up, "Local TV news was destined to be the paradigm. It was the only thing that could cover both your home and the rest of the world. It came out in all of our research: If you couldn't deliver local news you were leaving something out. That was the main thing that killed network news."[47]

Another contributing if unseen factor had been that ABC News Advisory Service. It had begun as a means for helping a national newscast achieve a No. 1 rating, and yet had finished by making the world safe for news consulting. By weaning newsrooms on free consulting and reaching newsworkers who had resisted people's news, those ABC advisors had done much to change the thinking of the profession.

As for local TV news, ABC had left its most enduring mark by its incessant demand that local newsrooms defer to research. "Some stations never make the budgetary commitment necessary to contract the research and market surveys they need. If you're working at one of those stations, don't give up. Pitches to your management from professional consultants are free and may create understanding for what you are trying to do," its advice to affiliates had read.[48] In 1981, ABC published the first directory of news consultants so newsrooms had guidance on where research could be obtained.[49] ABC research director David Bender had reiterated: "There is no substitute for . . . research. [It has] become—for all but a few broadcast geniuses, as necessary in the successful operation of a television station as coaxial cable."[50]

During the time the service was in operation, the number of consulted newsrooms almost tripled from 200 to 525. Consultants had thus entered more than 80 percent of the nation's 650 local TV newsrooms.[51] Further, leading news consultants affirmed that the newest consulted newsrooms almost always were affiliates of ABC. "We had a lot of business with ABC affiliates because of the News Advisory Service," Arnold Reymer, the founder of Reymer & Gersin, recalled. "The smaller stations were not accustomed to spending significantly on research. . . . ABC gave them the first taste of what we could do."[52] Reymer's Detroit-based firm would grow to 60 clients, almost all either ABC outlets or stations part of groups with many ABC affiliates. Al Primo's Primo Newservice likewise benefited, as did yet another new consultant, Broadcast Image, founded by News Advisory Service veteran Larry Rickel. AR&D, which gained two dozen ABC affiliates, grew the most in the period after the News Advisory Service disbanded. Once a consultant was in place at an ABC affiliate, AR&D's Willi would note, "its competitors automatically signed with another consultant."[53]

The result by 1990 was a news consulting field with no geographical limits. En route to penetration in 165 of the 200 total markets, Magid was welcomed into such locales as Jefferson City, Missouri, and Macon, Georgia. McHugh & Hoffman added Abilene, Texas, and Charleston, South Carolina. AR&D consultants fanned into Bryan, Texas; Kennewick, Washington; Great Falls, Montana; Topeka, Kansas; and Jonesboro, Arkansas. When AR&D completed negotiations with KLST in San Angelo, Texas, in 1992, the signing of the contract was a terminal achievement. As market No. 196, San Angelo was about as small as they came.[54] According to Jacobus, "The News Advisory Service gave the Good Housekeeping Seal of Approval to Frank Magid and the other consultants. After we got done, news consultants were everywhere."[55]

Even so, the "getting there" had been more inspiring than the actual arrival. With everyone doing people's news, TV faced a new set of problems. News continued to break, and local TV stations always were there to cover it. Yet unclear after three decades of people's news was a way to work outside this box. Something had to be done because competitors still had to be beat. A 1984 Magid survey had been chilling. "The majority [of people] do not believe there will be a change in the basic local news format," it had stated. Magid's prediction of "more of the same" translated into a brand new question in TV news: Where do we go from here?[56]

The answer would come suddenly, although not from out of the blue but from across it. Just when it seemed the party was over, satellites went up, a wall came down, and more people had decided they'd seen enough of Olympian TV. The spirits of people's news were rejuvenated. A new revolution was at hand.

14

Global Village
(1986–2000)

News consultants had tapped into so many people in so many cities and towns that some had turned to comic relief. If an anchor somewhere in America should happen to sneeze, so went an inside joke, the color of the kleenex would show up in somebody's research. It was an exaggeration, of course, but not by much.

Such comments had abounded in television news in 1986, a year marked by the sudden proliferation of cable television, the rise of the Fox network and the sell-off and downsizing of ABC, CBS and NBC. The consultants would flourish in this reordering of American TV. Over the next decade, the competition for viewers would reach unprecedented levels. At each stage the consulting industry would continue to grow. When local TV news marked its fiftieth anniversary in 1998, and a new millennium two years later, the story was complete. Not only was virtually every local TV station consultant-driven and reliant on audience research; radio stations, newspapers, magazines and finally the major TV networks were in line as well. Even the *New York Times* had become a Magid client.[1]

While journalism remained a field with a paragon tradition, changes in the 1980s and 1990s had been impossible to mistake. Competition from cable, satellites and the Internet had shaken the foundation of traditional news reporting. Particularly when the Internet arrived, and users could design their own newspapers and newscasts, it was undeniable what the consultants had always said: The people count. Although critics continued to excoriate the consultants, their words were zapped of passion because of the commercial trend. Even Hollywood had realized something new. With the "fighting journalist" honored in a string of films from *Front Page* to *All the President's Men,* it was in 1987 that the "system" finally came to center stage. This was in the hit movie *Broadcast News,* about a declining network newsroom, its layoffs and an incapable but handsome anchor who had become Walter Cronkite's heir.

Through more movies, weekly comedy series and even pulp fiction books, popular culture continued to reflect the newsroom's internal intrigue. Yet toward fully revealing "news at work," Hollywood, at least, was still behind the curve. Insiders knew that it was not in the newsroom but in auditoriums like AR&D's Preview House, where average people used dials and push-buttons to judge the news they liked, that the news was actually made. It also was forged in the focus group room, where managers watched through two-way mirrors as more people were heard.[2] No venue, though, was more of a focal point than that facility known as the boiler room, where journalism's most influential input—qualitative surveys by the thousands—poured in.

The modern news system had come to revolve around these gigantic state-of-the-art research factories, the largest occupying the southwest wing of Magid's six-acre complex in Marion.[3] In a room one-third the size of a basketball court, with clocks in front of them set on different time zones, 50 researchers sat in numbered cubicles, each with a computer and a telephone connection. While one researcher probed a television viewer in Philadelphia, the next one over was in contact with a viewer in Fresno. Six supervisors listened for quality control, while a fiber optics switching system enabled station managers and news directors at any Magid station to likewise tap in. An interactive software called "Katy," actually "CATI" for Computer Assisted Telephone Interview system, transcribed every word; entire phrases could be entered with a single keystroke. Beginning at 9 a.m. in the Atlantic time zone and concluding at 9 p.m. in the Pacific zone, a span of 16 hours, three shifts of Magid researchers performed 750 domestic interviews per day.[4]

While these data were raw, their volume was tremendous. On a typical day, Magid could collect as much raw information about the viewing of its clients' newscasts as the written content actually contained in those newscasts.[5] Audience Research & Development could do the same. McHugh & Hoffman, following a 1994 merger with the Detroit-based Market Strategies, had comparable capacity. At AR&D, a new digital research system had gone online in 1995. During one five-day period, between October 9–13, 1995, AR&D

completed 28 500-person surveys, in cities as large as Washington, D.C., and as small as Twin Falls, Idaho.[6] A 1995 year-end report compiled by the AR&D research staff showed that total telephone contacts in just that year had numbered 240,000.[7]

It was with similar superlatives that the total size of the news consulting industry was then spelled out. In the first 50 years of local TV news more than 100,000 station managers, news directors and news practitioners had come and gone. But with one principal function—research—the same news consultants were still around. Frank Magid's Iowa firm and the Dallas-based AR&D had become TV news empires. Magid was partnered with newsrooms in 165 of 200 television markets, with AR&D close to that number and McHugh & Hoffman, Reymer, Primo, Clemensen and Broadcast Image with extensive clientele. What had begun with McHugh & Hoffman's $5,000 research projects back in 1962 had swollen into a $50 million news research industry.[8] News consulting was never big as industries go, but as its commerce was ideas, not toothpaste and shoes, those numbers said a lot.

It was a keen management-age machine, but the machine wasn't perfect. The trouble was that everybody from Philadelphia to Exadelphia was hooked up. And no matter how much the research was made to plumb previously unplumbed areas, there were not many different ways a half-hour television newscast could be conveyed. In focus groups and surveys middle majority viewers had picked over each new set of gimmicks and aesthetic changes, those the consultants had proposed to make their clients No. 1. Yet the research had bottomed out on the same finding that had come through in public opinion polls, that for the most part the people liked local TV news just as it was.

Anxieties about this had started to gather in 1986, a dark year for those in local television. A TV industry that for decades had been rock-solid was starting to come unglued. Not only had cable television and its alphabet soup of new channels—from CNN and ESPN to MTV and TBS—just reduced the network-affiliate audience by 25 percent; a cold wind had blown through the entire U.S. TV industry when in 1986 all of the original networks were sold, ABC to Capital Cities, NBC to General Electric and CBS to Lawrence Tisch. This upheaval continued when an Australian billionaire named Rupert Murdoch was granted American citizenship and, with his citizenship papers, the right to own American television stations. For years broadcasters had dreaded competition from a fourth commercial network. Yet in 1986 Murdoch's Fox network made its debut.

As competition intensified, local news had an ace in the hole. It was local. Broadcasters knew that against the crush of new national cable channels, and Fox, a local program would still stand even if the rest of the network-affiliate system caved in. Yet at an hour of need, when station executives had wanted their local newscasts to step up, the consultants fell mum. There had been that 1984 Magid survey anticipating neither fundamental changes in the basic newscast format nor major openings in a TV field saturated with news.[9] Then in 1985, a McHugh & Hoffman report proclaimed that the big ride was over. "What we are dealing with today are not one or two gigantic trends," this report read, "but an array of individual trends—many of them not large."[10] This meant trouble.

The reason was a factor that those in local TV news knew all too well: While local news had competitive advantages and was still amassing a half-billion dollars in annual profits, what continued to matter was a system that pitted newsroom against newsroom, journalist against journalist, in an environment where they all had to be No. 1. Yet the format was homogenized, news anchors too, and news content had been researched again and again. Weaned on dynamism, the consultants bridled under a 1980s status quo.

Thus, ironically, with their war against their critics over and the consultants finally able to celebrate, the industry sank into malaise. Pioneer figures in news consulting, including Leigh Stowell, Mitch Farris and Harvey Gersin, had left local TV news and started new careers. To these figures and others, the original source of excitement, the people, had become a cause of disillusionment. "Every viewer in America is an executioner. They can turn you on and turn you off," AR&D's Jim Willi would demur.[11] "A new broom comes in and wants to sweep, but that disrupts the image in the mind of the viewer," Peter Hoffman grumbled.[12] Beset by "scarce options" Magid's Craig Marrs concurred, as did Bill Taylor, the head of AR&D. "Television stations aren't as unique as they once were because there's parity in television now. You look around and basically in any market the three local television stations . . . do just about the same thing," Taylor conceded in 1988. Among the most troubled was Al Primo. "[I]nstead of attacking the basics," Primo protested, "[s]omebody says: 'We need a better idea. We need a new twist. We need something brand new and different.'"[13]

But it wasn't there. A private 1986 study of newsroom-consultant relationships had concluded, "It would appear that the ultimate question . . . is 'When will someone come up with another Eyewitness News?'"[14]

If Marshall McLuhan could be believed, no one ever would. The consultants had invoked McLuhan innumerable times. In waging their fight against the establishment, which often had meant looking vogue and futuristic in the eyes of their clients, they had quoted from McLuhan and his praise of "Eyewitness News." McLuhan had called it "teamness news." Yet whatever it was labeled and however it was tweaked, the "Eyewitness" concept was, in McLuhan's view, the nightly newscast's end result. The combination of pictures and people in a live communal setting—what McLuhan had called the million-person "news of the neighborhood"—was as far as TV news could get.[15]

Maybe in the United States. As it turned out, the metaphor most synonymous with McLuhan had also concerned the destiny of television and news, and this was something the consultants had not considered. Yet no sooner had the words "global village" been uttered than the consultants had found a pathway out of the funk.

A Salt Lake City company called Non Stop Productions had down-linked the music, a souped-up 1990s version of Philadelphia's theme for "Action News." A New York production house created the studio set. Strobed to the theme, viewers saw the skyline of downtown Berlin, as the words "Der Tag" ("The Day") swished like a rocket across the screen. Within 20 seconds, all of the day's news had been previewed, in four-second video clips separated by brilliant flashes of white, and then on cue the scene switched to a studio that looked like Houston's Mission Control. There were two young and attractive anchors, a female on the left and a male on the right, their names "Simone Duve" and "Andreas Jüttner" superimposed below them.

After 10 minutes of quick clip reports, then commercials, Simone and Andreas started in on the weather. It was February in Berlin, of interest the arrival of spring. "Why is it that when the seasons change, fashions change, too?" Andreas in German had quipped. "You mean conservative?" Simone responded with a smile while chiding Andreas' straight-laced attire. "Or hip, or feminine," Andreas shot back as he looked suggestively at Simone. The two anchors then addressed a TV monitor that had popped up, in it the word "LIVE" and a laughing Manina Ferreira-Erlenbach, the weathercaster, standing in front of the 400-year-old Berlin Cathedral. "Manina, how is it out there?" Andreas inquired. Amused by what she'd just seen, Manina rocked back and said "Cold! cold!", this her segue to "cool" fashions and her prediction that the color silver would be Berlin's springtime vogue. "From the silver blouse in the office to the silver bikini," she proclaimed, "everything is allowed."[16]

This kind of news in Berlin, the city identified with Khrushchev and Kennedy, the Cold War, and omens of World War III? Yet there it was in the resurrected capital of Germany, a new attraction on German TV. It was a special newscast, too, one that symbolized not only a turning point in world history but a broadcast world and a U.S. news consulting industry about to be turned upside down.

"Der Tag" had precipitated from one of the 20th Century's greatest events, the fall of the Berlin Wall in 1989. When East and West Germany were reunified under a market-based broadcast policy that encouraged the first private ownerships of TV, a Western consortium that included America's Time Warner had rushed to the east side and by 1991 had purchased the former East German TV channel. It became a regional channel that those in the German state of Brandenberg knew as 1A. Commercials were touting Western products seen for the first time. Just two years earlier the studio now home to happy talk and "cool fashions" had been the gun-encircled domain of the German Communist Party. East German dictator Erich Honecker had used the same studio to preach his iron-hand rule. That Honecker had been replaced by Simone, Andreas, and Manina was not the only sign of the times. "Der Tag" was a copy of an American local newscast because consultants from McHugh & Hoffman had been brought over to create it.

It didn't just happen in Germany. In almost the same stroke, McHugh & Hoffman had entered the newsrooms of TV networks in Eastern Europe and Latin America, this while AR&D had pushed into Western Europe and the Pacific Rim. These relationships, though, would be dwarfed in notoriety and significance by a Magid feat in Great Britain, the country whose television was known as the best in the world and where American ventures until now had been greeted with "Yankee Go Home." Nevertheless, in one of the most inexplicable events in the annals of global broadcasting, one of the most maligned names in TV news, Magid, would wind up the partner of the world's most prestigious news organization, Britain's BBC.

Not just years but weeks and days before they began, these moves by American news consultants had seemed unthinkable. Sensing saturation of American local news, the consultants had made their presence known to a large number of non-American television operations. A foray into Canada in the mid 1980s would earn for McHugh & Hoffman one of the plum international consulting assignments.

Yet in every other country, American consultants and non-American broadcasters had had no common ground. While the U.S. had developed a competitive, commercial TV system with three networks and hundreds of local channels, virtually every other country had had one big voice, this owned and operated by the government. "We had just about given up," recalled Jacques De Suze, a former Voice of America correspondent fluent in three languages who became the spearhead of McHugh & Hoffman's overseas push. "Wherever you went, countries had one state-controlled TV channel and one newscast." According to De Suze, "We told prospective clients [that] we had the research and the ideas to bring them closer to the audience. . . . But because there was no competition, they had no need for people like us."17

Then in 1989 came watershed events. Among them were the fall of the Berlin Wall and the impending collapse of Communism. These had dramatized public demands for market systems and private media behind the former Iron Curtain. Yet more consequential had been a simultaneous development in Great Britain, where a state-governed system dominated by the BBC had come under siege. British business interests had demanded that British TV be opened. In a far-reaching decision, one with global repercussions, Prime Minister Margaret Thatcher threw out existing British broadcast regulations and invited commercial competition. Britain's decision to deregulate its media had been a call to other countries to follow. As the 1990s began, most of the world's countries were caught up in this trend toward privatization. Because few countries had had experience with commercial television and market-based competition, a demand for American experts ensued.

A preview of what was to come had occurred across the U.S. border in Canada, where in 1985 De Suze had partnered McHugh & Hoffman with a ramshackle downtown Toronto local TV station that operated on Channel 57. With the call letters CITY, the station had survived in a tiny storefront location with a combination of pornographic movies and offbeat local public affairs shows. To the experts, CITY was an insult to the high standards kept by Canada's elite, government-chartered CBC, a public network like Britain's BBC, which rose from a palatial 10-story courtyard facility just four blocks down the street. Yet the owner of CITY, a former CBC producer named Moses Znaimer, had both a flair for innovation and a vision of bringing the CBC to its knees. Relating their "Eyewitness News" experiences, McHugh & Hoffman consultants encouraged Znaimer to move ahead. Plans took shape when McHugh & Hoffman's research confirmed what Znaimer had felt, that middle majority Canadians, whose taxes paid for the CBC, felt alienated by most of the programs the CBC was carrying.

In the collaboration between Znaimer and McHugh & Hoffman, what became "Citytv" was refitted into that storefront television facility, in a way that in Znaimer's words "reached to the people." Outside it, Znaimer christened a "Speakers' Corner," in which anyone could walk up and be on TV. Inside, they knocked down walls and turned the entire building into one big studio. Headlined each night was the newscast "CityPulse," a shirtsleeve tour of the operation, in which hosts Anne Mroczkowski and Gord Martineau glided about and solicited news not merely from reporters but also from producers, assignment editors and even the photographers. At the assignment desk, live and in full view of the audience, editors manipulated a network of remote cameras in a way that gave viewers a first look at breaking events.[18]

The Toronto studio was a 10-minute drive from where Marshall McLuhan had lived and written about the global village, video involvement and media being the message. Citytv had given these ideas their greatest semblance of physical form. Through McHugh & Hoffman, concept after concept was brought back to the U.S. and employed in American newscasts. Few in the United States knew that the "open studio" and "vox populi" concepts had been developed by Canadians.

Most eye-opening had been the venture's commercial success. True to its name, Citytv eventually linked other Canadian cities and became No. 1 in many of them. In Toronto Citytv consistently beat the CBC in the ratings.[19] Foreshadowing a pattern in numerous other countries, the Canadian government was dumbstruck by the public network's shrinking audiences. Canadian taxpayers had noticed this, too, and they demanded their tax dollars go elsewhere. The CBC went on to lay off so many people that just five years after its opening in 1992 most of its huge headquarters had become empty office space. "Those establishment people sure spend a lot of their time viewing the world with alarm. We think it's okay to be positive," noted Znaimer, who had given U.S. news consultants their first international role.[20]

The pact between Citytv and McHugh & Hoffman had been a meaningful first step. Yet neither that relationship nor two newer international undertakings, by both Magid and AR&D in Australia, had caused the world to take note. The more the consultants moved about, the more they realized that the one country they had written off, Great Britain, was the key to the global aspirations they had. Attempting to drum up business, a Magid salesperson named Joe George had been visiting broadcasters all over Europe and in Asia. As he recalled, "We discovered that it was not the United States but Great

Britain that [broadcasters] in most other countries looked up to. . . . You couldn't get arrested if all you had was an American passport. You had to show experience in Britain."[21]

Even so, the notion of American consultants inside British newsrooms was considered about as likely as the Pope becoming Protestant or the grass turning blue. There had been a long history of British-American program exchange, and the British did have a commercial network that competed against the BBC. Still, Britain had a fully developed broadcast system that although smaller than that of the United States was older and wielded more global prestige. Reaching around the world, BBC radio had been a main source of international news. By 1988 the stature of the BBC was centered in its two domestic television networks, BBC1 and BBC2, which had prided themselves on excellence. Through the 1980s the BBC had supplied considerable programming to the U.S. public network PBS while accepting only a modicum of mainstream American fare—too "downmarket" by British TV standards—in return. "When we did finally get to Britain," George remembered, "the first thing they said was, 'We don't need you. You need us. Your TV is the worst in the world.'"

Just as sociologist Lloyd Warner had indirectly spearheaded domestic news consulting, it was Thatcher, the British prime minister, who would have this distinction at the global level. The turn of events that would finally place Magid in Britain, eventually as the consultant to the BBC, was put in motion when the Thatcher government, in a 1988 White Paper, outlined the process by which British broadcasting was deregulated. While some British factions had insisted that the BBC be privatized, consensus reigned that the BBC must remain under taxpayer-supported public control. Accordingly, Thatcher's plan came to rest on the other provider of British television, that commercial network that had given Britons an alternative to the BBC. Chartered under the name Independent Television, it was known to the British as ITV. It was there that American news consultants would beach on British turf.

Structured somewhat similarly to American TV networks, ITV was a web of 16 regional affiliates each owned and operated by relatively small independent companies. Although privately controlled, ITV had been straight-jacketed by ownership, programming and advertising regulations. By 1988 ITV had become a vortex of corporate sector discontent. Large media corporations had wanted a stake in Britain's one commercial broadcast network. Other corporations were equally irate because they could not advertise on the BBC and thus were limited to the already constrained ITV.

Persuaded by these complaints, Thatcher implemented her privatization plan. The government seized all 16 ITV licenses and then put them up for competitive bid.[22] Companies that bid the most money not only got the licenses but a promise from the government that they could largely do as they pleased. While everyone had understood the cash-on-the-barrel head provision, it was an additional wrinkle, one that swelled as an albatross to the bidders, that finally brought Magid into the UK. To win licenses, companies had to pass a "quality threshold," this to be determined by extensive analysis of the British audience. Few British firms were capable of providing the quantity of research that this task required. But Magid was. In a reversal, some of the same British broadcasters who had snubbed Magid representatives were now pleading with Magid for help.

Magid shined during Britain's famous 1990 "franchise auction." Because this auction gave form to Thatcher's deregulation plan, it was one of the most closely followed episodes in world broadcasting. Nearly $2 billion were paid to the government for the 16 licenses. Later, released from regulation, the 16 ITV companies merged into two big firms. Eleven applicants had hired Magid for the qualitative research needed to complete their bids. When the auction was over, eight Magid companies were winners. Each signed long-term contracts. Four other winning companies that had not relied on Magid during the bidding quickly joined. In one swoop, three-fourths of Great Britain's largest commercial television network was comprised of Magid clients. By 1991, Magid had an entire division based in London for research and consulting at ITV outlets in the UK. And just as the firm had anticipated, the British contract opened doors. By the end of the same year, Magid was consulting new, privately owned news organizations in France, Italy and Norway.[23]

Magid's main role at ITV would end after only three years. In 1994 a controversy about "Americanization" in the London press, one that for a time stigmatized the news-producing unit of the system, would short-circuit the relationship.

Yet in 1991, in the aftermath of the franchise auction, Magid had seemed indispensable. In the deregulated environment of British broadcasting, serious competition was a new concept. Having paid huge sums for the licenses, ITV's new owners had wanted decisive results. This brought an end to a gentleman's rivalry that had existed between ITV and the BBC. Where once the two networks were happy with equal proportions of the audience, ITV now wanted the lion's share. Part of the reason was fears about a new intruder, a direct broadcast satellite service by Murdoch called Sky, which offered a 24-hour news channel comparable to America's CNN.

The Americans' first view of British newscasting had induced culture shock. Not only were these newscasts dominated by government, politics and distant international affairs; they were so much of a "medium of record" that their different segments had concluded with the words "End of Part One," "End of Part Two," etc.

However, because they were getting more American programs from the deregulated ITV and Sky, Britons were becoming uncomfortable with the stodgy style of British TV news. They spoke loudly when Magid's researchers went into their homes and asked how the news could be improved. "The first research in every country was incredibly rich. They had never had qualitative research before," explained George, by then a Magid vice president and the head of the firm's European division based in London. The data showed that newscasts on both the BBC and ITV were "alienating and creating detachment within the mass audience."[24] That Britons were paying taxes for the BBC not only stirred the unrest but was an omen of things to come.

Starting in the city of Leeds at Yorkshire TV and in Belfast at Ulster TV, Magid consultants encouraged what they called the "augmentation" of the staid British approach with many of the same devices that had worked in the United States. In these initial encounters, British viewers for the first time saw 15-second news stories, repeated visualization, reporter involvement and content that stressed "news you can use." In reorganized newsrooms newly anointed teams of reporters instituted high-profile health, money and consumer reports.[25] The Leeds and Belfast ITV local newscasts and others from Norwich, Newcastle, Southampton, Manchester and Plymouth, in the words of Magid's Charles Munro, "went on to just kill the BBC in the regional ratings."[26]

The Cinderella story quickly advanced to a bigger stage. In 1992 Magid was hired by Independent Television News, the unit responsible for national news on both the full ITV network as well as on ITV's startup sister network Channel 4. This was a milepost in the affairs of the news consultants. The opportunity to advise news at a national level was something still denied consultants in the United States. The ITN-Magid relationship, while short-lived, conferred international status on the Americans and provided them a calling card they could use all over the world.

The ITN assignment gave Magid a voice in the British national newscast "News at Ten." Anchored by Trevor McDonald, the Walter Cronkite of Great Britain, "News at Ten" had been the pioneer British newscast and since its inception in 1967 had been seen in prime-time, at 10 p.m. Yet the tide of Americanization had put this British newscast in jeopardy. Keying on American models, the profit-seeking owners of ITV wanted "News at Ten" moved out of prime-time and to a six o'clock dinner hour time period. As was true in the U.S., a prime-time without news gave open field to more profitable entertainment fare. The move seemed logical to ITV, especially when

Murdoch's Sky system provided news around the clock. To those at "News at Ten," the options were clear. They could either improve the ratings of the newscast or see its prime-time status disappear.[27]

Thus began the Americanization of British network news. Reading the research, Magid proposed sweeping changes. Even though ITV was recognized as the working class channel, its news appealed to the upper-middle class. "The old guard of Oxbridge-educated ITV bosses, with their Royal Television Society dinners and endless self-acclamation, could not see . . . their patronising view of 'real life,'" British author Andrew Davidson would observe.[28] Concurring, the Magid consultants had pegged "News at Ten" as grey, lifeless and detached and so devoted to daily activities of Parliament that Munro called it "MPs on parade." The Americans insisted this must change. "We never had a more hostile reaction of news people than at ITN. Their expectations completely differed from the research respondents'," Munro recalled. "Most of the time, the viewers couldn't understand what [the ITN reporters] were talking about. We never said, 'Don't cover Parliament,' but 'Cover it in a way that helps the average person relate.'"[29]

When it finally premiered in November 1992, the peopleized "News at Ten" kicked up a row second only to the firestorm then erupting over the impending separation of Prince Charles and Lady Diana. Sparkling new news music replaced an older ruffles-and-flourishes theme. For 25 years "News at Ten" had begun with a head-on static shot of the clockface of Big Ben ticking toward ten o'clock. Magid's new opening took the viewer in a zoom over the top of Big Ben, still showing the clock, and finally across London to the ITN studios. There McDonald was seen not by himself but alongside several ITN reporters, who in "Eyewitness" style appeared one after another during the broadcast. Much of the program consisted of special segments, including "Focus on Britain" with reporter Julia Somerville and live shots "from hot spots at home and abroad" with Alastair Stewart.[30]

While one contingent of Magid consultants had been at work on "News at Ten," another had been headlong into a revamp of ITV's breakfast newscast. Although a "wakeup" program, ITV's morning news looked like the "MacNeil-Lehrer Newshour," a serious evening report that was a signature of America's PBS. Magid wanted the ITV program fashioned after ABC's "Good Morning America," which had spun from Magid's research in the 1970s and which had just been implemented by Magid clients in Australia and Norway.

In months of research that had involved thousands of British viewers—one of the largest Magid projects ever—the focal point had been a young news presenter named Fiona Armstrong. Her Q scores were low, and she was perceived as icy and aloof. Armstrong would have the distinction of being the first non-American newscaster to be "Magidized." A more colorful and alluring wardrobe was followed by intensive instruction by Magid talent coaches, with program director Elisabeth Howell assisting.[31] Howell finally told the still-resistant Armstrong, "Put a coat hanger in your gob [mouth] and smile."[32]

A host of critics who had witnessed the transformation of "Good Morning," including editors of the newspaper *Scotland on Sunday,* were "appalled" by the "Americanisation" of this long-running British broadcast.[33] As for "News at Ten," Sir William Rees-Mogg of the BBC castigated "wallpaper evenings on the small screen."[34] In the prestigious *Times of London,* Roy Greenslade in telling readers the program was a waste of time said he couldn't believe his eyes. "Mr. McDonald introduced a filmed item by saying: 'Political editor Michael Brunson reports.' Seconds into the film a rather tacky graphic informed [us] that the big man talking was Michael Brunson, the political editor. At the end, Brunson signed off by telling us he was none other than Michael Brunson. . . . Surely with so few words available in a bulletin [newscast], these references are irrelevant," Greenslade demanded.[35]

In another *Times* essay, one that would prove a mixed blessing to Magid, critic Jonathan Miller more clearly saw what was happening: "The critical classes tend to hate every innovation in television," Miller wrote. "Once this might have mattered; today it is largely irrelevant. In the new television environment, the only verdict that matters is the one that will be spewed from the computers of the television audience measurement service."[36] Appearing in November 1993, almost a year after the format revisions, Miller's analysis had been the first to extensively detail the hidden activities of Magid.

Unknown then to Magid, Miller's judgments had been read by a new management team at the BBC. The Americans would be astonished by their discovery, just a few months later, that those at the BBC were impressed.

Yet at ITN, the article in *The Times* had struck a raw nerve. While *The Times* had not condemned the influence of the Americans, the reporting on it had been enough. ITN terminated the Magid contract, and by 1994 the consultants had been shown the door. The news had been received by Brent Magid, the son of the firm's founder and a former Chase Manhattan Bank executive who had succeeded George as head of Magid's London division. "The ITN format change was a watershed mark in British television news," he argued, although "our client did not agree with us about the changes in the way the audience was using TV. They were concerned about bad publicity."[37]

Those at ITN who had made the decision had a different explanation. "The research helped us, but their ideas were American, and they did not appeal to British culture," stated Michael Jermey, ITN's director of development. Magid's recommendation that reporters stand rather than sit during the specialty segments had been one example, according to Jermey, and the effort to make "stars" out of anchors and reporters still another. In the meantime, confrontations had erupted over seemingly minor recommendations, notably Magid's insistence that anchors say "good evening" to viewers with their names superimposed on the screen. While elemental in U.S. TV news, "these things look odd to British viewers," Jermey explained.[38]

It was a sobered and more experienced Magid that finally entered the news division of the BBC, this after a tentative yet auspicious series of steps beginning in late 1994. Out of eyeshot of London, Magid had joined the news unit of the autonomous BBC division in Wales. The relationship tightened in 1995 when a collaboration between Magid and BBC researchers alerted the consultants to concerns within the BBC about declining ratings. Since 1989, the audience share of BBC1, the network that delivered news, had dropped from 40 to 30 percent. In 1996 BBC news executives summoned to their London headquarters a new Magid consultant named Ned Warwick, who in a carefully worded presentation proposed a long-term contract. Although the news directors were convinced, Warwick would deliver the presentation seven more times, to that many additional directors in the BBC hierarchy, before the pact was approved. Magid immediately began consulting the BBC's regional operations, including the one that provided the local news in London. In 1997 Magid officially joined the BBC's world newsroom.

It was another landmark in the legitimization of news consulting. Not only was Magid partnered with the oldest, best-known, and most prestigious name in broadcasting, but no other broadcast news organization exceeded the BBC in size. At a time when the American networks were curtailing international coverage, the BBC, supported by taxes, maintained 50 overseas bureaus and 200 specialty reporters. By 2000 Magid had consulted many of these bureaus and people. Back at Magid headquarters in Iowa, founder Frank Magid felt vindicated as he watched all this take shape. "We had been questioned all those years by the so-called 'greats' of news in the United States, and here we were working with some of the greatest news organizations in the world," Magid said.[39]

Equally true, though, were changes in broadcasting that had played into Magid's hands. Indeed, the BBC Magid had joined in 1997 was not the same as the BBC of 1989, the year Thatcher's White Paper had opened British television to competition. Although the White Paper had protected the BBC's non-commercial "public" status, competition and declining ratings had triggered debates in Parliament about the BBC's $3 billion in annual tax supports. Clearing a path for Magid had been the new chief executive of the BBC, Sir John Birt, who had downsized the system, encouraged the enlistment of outside consultants and made ratings the No. 1 priority. Although the BBC in Warwick's words was a temple of "high-mindedness" and "one of the jewels in the crown of this country," it was in some respects no different than a commercial network that needed to show ratings and share.

Learning from its experience at ITN, Magid placed the entire BBC arrangement under the supervision of one person, Warwick, who had been part of the WPVI "Action News" insurgency in the 1970s but who had then gone on to become the London bureau chief of ABC News. When ABC closed the bureau in 1996, Warwick opted to remain in London and join Magid. With these qualifications Warwick worked from a position of strength. By the time he joined the BBC through Magid, he had lived in Britain for almost 10 years.

Warwick's worst fear had been a media firestorm over "Americanization" like the one that had struck ITN in 1993 and 1994. Happily for Warwick, Magid's role at the BBC received only passing attention in the British press, another sign of how things had changed. In line with the BBC's schoolroom traditions, Warwick's activities largely consisted of classroom sessions and group seminars. Seventeen of these were conducted in just the first two years. There was no discussion about live shots in stories that did not need them, or of anchors and reporters smiling on camera with their names flashed on the screen. "I had been in the UK long enough to know that those things don't work here," Warwick related.[40]

Instead, Warwick concentrated on what the research had indicated was the pressing BBC need, that of making the news more relevant and comprehensible to the British middle class. Because BBC producers and journalists had come to recognize the same need, the American regime of visualization, simple language, reinforcement and reporter involvement hit the mark. According to Warwick, "These were some of the brightest television reporters anywhere, and I knew they were worried about dumbing down the news product." Yet it was because of their extraordinary acuity "that they caught on to seeing news from the perspective of the audience. They'd just never been taught to see it that way before."

In the fall of 1998, BBC1 revised what for decades had been a stately, regal format on its evening newscasts at 6 and 9 p.m. News music fit for the arrival of the Queen was abandoned. In its place was a simple digitized opening showing circular ripples extending from points on the globe, while an unostentatious pulsating theme was heard. In an intimate studio setting, anchors appeared alongside computer-generated pictures and graphics that reinforced the main points. Package stories and live shots by reporters were indistinguishable in form from those in the U.S. News from Parliament was accompanied by reaction from everyday people, and stories about the just-opened London ferris wheel balanced those from 10 Downing Street.

As Richard Sambrook, the chief executive of BBC News, would explain, "We hired Magid for specific purposes [which were] to develop skills to make our presentations more accessible to the public. . . . Ned Warwick was perfect because he knew the cultural thing." At the time Magid was hired, Sambrook would note, the BBC was concerned that "people would think Sky TV is the national broadcaster, not the BBC." Thus, the objective "is not about revenue streams but public perception," that is, "Who do the people perceive as best in news." Building perceptions, said Sambrook, "is the benefit of Magid to us."[41]

A century that had begun with a British Empire and had ended with calls to put the "great" back in Great Britain had finished on a high note for the BBC. Parliament voted to continue the BBC's public charter until 2006. After years of declining ratings, the BBC's "Nine O'Clock News" started inching up. With the "Nine O'Clock News" the most widely viewed news program in Britain, Sky seemed less of a threat, while long-time rival ITV had also been helping. In 1998 ITN's "News at Ten" suffered the same fate that Magid, who had worked there, had been hired to avert. It was replaced by entertainment shows. What was left of the ITV broadcast finally was moved to a six o'clock slot.

While Magid's maneuvers in Great Britain were the breakthrough events in the globalization of American news consulting, they only hinted at just how large this phenomenon would become. By the time Magid had entered the BBC in 1997, its clients included television networks in almost every country in Western Europe. After joining TV2, Norway's second channel and the first there to be privately owned, at its inception in November 1990, Magid then entered Finland's MTV3, Portugal's TVI, Spain's Telecinco and Greece's Antenna. McHugh & Hoffman moved its U.S. base from McLean, Virginia, back to Detroit, its original home, following its 1994 merger with Market Strategies. Yet McHugh & Hoffman had evolved into an almost headquarter-less company, its consultants stretched throughout parts of Latin America and into some of the same Western European

locales where Magid was staked. By the late 1990s, McHugh &
Hoffman had consulted startup newscasts on new networks in France
(FR3), Sweden (TV4), and Portugal (TV Nova). McHugh & Hoffman
was also the advisor to a new European satellite news service called
Euronews.

Reminiscent of their domestic jousts in the 1970s, Magid and
McHugh & Hoffman continued to compete for clients in continental
Europe, even though there it was the other major U.S. firm, AR&D,
that had won the biggest contract. In 1997 AR&D established its first
overseas division in London not far from where Magid's European division was based. AR&D co-founder Ed Bewley left Dallas and settled
in London to head the operation, which assisted in the startup of
Britain's fifth television network that year. Because the news on Channel 5 was provided by the same ITN unit that had booted Magid, the
AR&D partnership was considered somewhat of a coup.

A much larger achievement, though, had been AR&D's 1993
partnership with a television system based in Luxembourg and known
as RTL. It actually stood for Radio Television Luxembourg, and for
decades on radio it had been the only legal commercial broadcaster in
its part of Europe. Luxembourg had been one of the few countries
whose laws had permitted private ownership of broadcast media. At
the outbreak of privatization, investment capital that had poured into
Luxembourg had positioned RTL for massive expansions. The first
had begun in 1984, when what came to be known as RTL1 helped
pioneer private television in Germany. When purchased in 1995 by a
huge German media conglomerate called Bertelsmann, RTL was the
largest private television complex in the world. It operated the dominant private networks in Germany, The Netherlands, Belgium,
Luxembourg and Poland, and it also had channels in Italy, France,
Austria and the Czech Republic. AR&D would advise on news at
most of these RTL properties.

The flagship of RTL were its two networks in Germany, which
had opened news departments and then placed evening newscasts
in competition with those of Germany's long-standing public
channels, ARD and ZDF. "It was not the same situation that Magid
had at ITN," Bewley would note. "RTL was virtually brand new . . .
[and] ARD and ZDF, the public networks, had not developed a tradition for news as [had] the BBC." As Bewley would discover, the
Germans were much more open to Americanization than had been the
British. Both RTL and another new private network, Sat 1, had introduced Germans to an infusion of American programming, from WWF
Wrestling and "Beavis and Butthead" to the talk shows of Oprah
Winfrey, Jerry Springer and Ricki Lake. According to Bewley, the
presence of American programming "affected the research we

conducted on newscasts. Germans did not see news as entertainment, but they wanted a more up-to-date approach."[42]

Using satellite connections and Internet links, AR&D specialists in Dallas studied Germany's signature national newscast, ARD's "Tagesschau," which had featured a silver-haired figure in his sixties reading news stories off pieces of paper on his desk. Nearly identical was the newscast "Heute" on ZDF, likewise dominated by a single male anchor. He spoke into a microphone visible on the news desk and read news stories that went on for two minutes.[43] The consultants noticed that very little of the news on ARD and ZDF was local in orientation and that most pertained to international meetings and other events outside Germany. They also noticed that the news on RTL, their client, looked almost the same.

In 1994 RTL1 revamped its newscast "Aktuell" in order to highlight a youthful news team and a dashing main anchor named Peter Kloeppel. German affairs were emphasized not just in the reporters' live shots and package stories but in an American-style weather segment that contained weather video from scenes around the country. It also gave Germans five-day forecasts. RTL1 then established Germany's first newscast sports segment, a smiling female sportscaster and her on-set interactions with the friendly Kloeppel a trademark of the broadcast. The German soccer team had recently won the prestigious World Cup. Interest in soccer was intense, the research had shown.[44]

Although "Aktuell" did concentrate on indigenous German news, the RTL1 broadcast on October 4, 1995, was a revealing exception. For more than a year ARD and ZDF had been burying brief snippets on the decade's biggest single news story in the United States, the murder trial of football star O.J. Simpson. According to the research, though, Germans were extremely interested in the Simpson trial, which had been treated interminably in the incoming American talk shows as well as in mainstream German newspapers. RTL sent a crew to Los Angeles for the closing arguments. On the morning in Los Angeles when the verdict came in, RTL beamed back to Germany live coverage. Because of the time difference it was seen in Germany in prime-time, and close to one-half of German viewers had tuned in.[45]

By 1995 AR&D's main function at RTL was at RTL2, then languishing in an increasingly crowded German television market. AR&D's assignment at RTL2 was another advance for the Americans as it would mark the first time they would have a voice not just in news but in formulating a network's entire program schedule. Using AR&D's research and acting on the consultants' recommendations, managers of RTL2 canceled the network's general interest fare and introduced programs targeting viewers between the ages of 18 and 34, Germany's "Generation X." A first step in branding the new RTL2 was selecting a logo. AR&D assisted with a videotape compilation of "Channel 2" logos from the United States.[46] The Germans studied about 30 examples, including the "2s" from KHON in Honolulu, WESH in Daytona Beach, and KREM in Spokane, before settling on the one from Atlanta's WSB.

Two hit shows, a weekly sex show called "Peepe" and a home video program called "Bitte Lacheln," helped cement the network's identity, with an AR&D-designed newscast the finishing touch. Female anchors were selected, and they looked like presenters on America's MTV. The American lineage was further hinted in the newscast's title. It was "Action News," with the words "action" and "news" not even translated into German.[47]

In 1996, just 12 years after signing on, RTL1 had overtaken both ARD and ZDF and become No. 1 in Germany. RTL2 was first in Germany's young viewer niche. In The Netherlands RTL4 was No. 1. In Poland, RTL7 was close to the top spot. "The newspapers accused us of putting on hamburger TV," recalled Vic Reuter, the head of RTL news in Luxembourg, "but they couldn't explain why RTL had become so popular." Research, Reuter would stress, "was our basis. For the first time in Europe we were doing inquiries on quality. We said, 'Let the people analyze the program.' They told us the existing news was old-fashioned" and that if RTL adopted American concepts "we would prevail." RTL had not been hesitant about bringing in the Americans. Everyone in Europe, Reuter said, recognized "America [as] the country of TV." After privatization "no TV in Europe could be allowed without consultants. You had to have consultants."[48]

The TV of Eastern Europe had heard Reuter's call. McHugh & Hoffman's Americanized "Der Tag" newscast on the former East German television network had come to fruition in 1994. After that, under Jacques De Suze, McHugh & Hoffman signed an agreement with Central European Media Enterprises, one of the many newly formed consortiums that were generating capital for startup private TV. CME was founded by Ronald Lauder, the heir to the Estee Lauder cosmetics fortune. The McHugh & Hoffman contract was notable because it gave American news consultants their first access to the once forbidden area beyond the former Iron Curtain. Among "everyone there was a sense of the moment—that Communism had just fallen and we were engaged in history-in-the-making," De Suze recalled.[49]

While the Magid-BBC and AR&D-RTL relationships had been eye-opening, no U.S. consulting effort would draw more international attention than that of McHugh & Hoffman in the Czech Republic, where it had entered at CME's Nova TV. Nova had signed on in November 1994. By 1997, on the strength of American entertainment shows such as "Baywatch" and an American-style newscast insiders had called "Eyewitness East," Nova commanded 70 percent of the Czech viewing audience. It had decimated in the ratings the country's two former Communist TV channels. Although the Czech Republic was small, the success of its first private television system was treated as a post-Communist sensation in media sources all over the world. While criticized for rampant Americanization, "TV Nova is a hit. . . . All of Eastern Europe is tuning to the saga of Nova TV," reported the *Wall Street Journal* in a 1997 front-page article.[50]

More than any preceding newscast, the Nova news called "Televizny Noviny" had demonstrated the international appeal of the format for American local news. It became a model for newscasts McHugh & Hoffman subsequently initiated at CME's Pro television in Romania, Pop-TV in Slovenia, and TV3 in Hungary. A riveting experience for those who had grown up with Communist TV were the first sports and weather segments, the first male-female co-anchor team and the introduction of happy talk. At the end of the Nova newscast, the anchors pulled off a feat unimaginable under Communist rule. They smiled.[51] Criticisms of the Nova news were tempered by analyses showing an abundance of investigative reports, many delving into scandals and other affairs the Communists had covered up.[52] Nevertheless, the plan of having the Czech broadcast emulate "Eyewitness News" was so exact that McHugh & Hoffman had members of the Nova news team travel to WABC in New York to see the original version for themselves.[53]

McHugh & Hoffman's eastward move would reach as far as Ukraine, where it briefly consulted at a network called 1+1. It would be another American firm, Story First Communication, that finally would extend the line to Moscow. Founded by American entrepreneur Peter Gewre, who had lived in Russia since 1984, Story First was a Russian-American consortium that in 1996 launched a network called CTC. While small, CTC was the only private network to cover all 11 Russian time zones and thus directly compete with Russia's first channel, the former Communist powerhouse ORT. Like RTL2 in Germany, CTC used American programs such as "Melrose Place" and "Beverly Hills 90210" to target the 18-to-34 demographic group, these viewers significant in Russia because they had few recollections of Communism and unlike middle-age Russians more optimistically reached to the West.

Plans for news had centered on challenging ORT's staid nightly newscast "Vremya," for years a key outlet for Communist propaganda. The venture was consulted not by one of the big firms but by a team of American advisors headed by Tom Battista, a local news veteran who before moving to Moscow had pioneered ENG while running KMOX in St. Louis and then had steered Philadelphia's "Eyewitness News." Although delayed because of a national economic crisis in 1998 and 1999, the first American-style Russian newscast finally took to the air on CTC the following year.

By the late 1990s there was not a continent or region where American news consultants could not be found. As privatization expanded and countries converted to commercial broadcast systems, trade organizations such as the National Association of Broadcasters were kept busy with requests for American experts. More and more independent advisors joined the big firms in moving overseas. In 1998 a cadre of former WABC news managers settled in Bulgaria to begin a new TV newscast there.[54] From Phoenix, a group of advisors headed by broadcast executive Arthur Mobley was shuttling from Arizona to new stations in Africa.[55] Also to surface in Africa was a key figure in Kansas City's Christine Craft affair, news director Ridge Shannon, whose Shannon Communications landed a contract with a new private television channel in Johannesburg called Bophuthatfwana TV.[56] "I had not even considered an international assignment until almost the moment I got on the plane," Shannon would relate.[57] A U.S. company called Atkinson Research had staked a major position in New Zealand.

Magid opened a second international division in Kuala Lumpur, Malaysia. From there Magid serviced a swell of clients in Asia including TV3 in Malaysia, RCTI in Indonesia, RTV in Brunei, BITV in India, SMTV in Singapore and YTN in South Korea. At Magid's expanded research center in Iowa, different languages were heard during telephone surveys which, timed to various parts of the world, now continued around the clock. Looking ahead, a Magid report had indicated that one-half of the firm's total activity would be globally based by 2010.

Then in a surprise 1999 development, the same trend would bring the end to McHugh & Hoffman. After its merger with Market

Strategies, disagreements had emerged over the globalization and far-flung structure of the McHugh & Hoffman complex. De Suze left the company to head a new global consulting unit within Canada's Chum-City corporation. McHugh & Hoffman chair John Bowen then arranged a dissolution of the firm. Headed by Bowen, the former members of McHugh & Hoffman started a new consulting company called Convergent Communications Consultants, or C3. The reconstituted firm continued to consult in Europe, at Euronews and at Britain's Channel 5. Joining Turkey's TRGT in 1998, C3 was the first news consultancy with a major position in the Middle East. In addition, under Bowen, C3 had extensive Latin American ties. Starting with an early relationship with Mexico's Televisa group, McHugh & Hoffman had then entered Brazil's SBT and Banderantes TV, Puerto Rico's TeleOnce and Colombia's Carocol TV.

As the 1990s came to a close, American news consultants were working inside 65 non-U.S. newsrooms in around 25 different countries. At least 50 additional non-U.S. newsrooms had had short-term contracts with one of the three big firms.

The consultants did not completely escape aspersions like those that had greeted them when they first entered the UK. "There was always the danger you'd end up the subject of an article about American bandits imposing their values on the news," Magid's Joe George related.[58] Indeed, after the firestorm in Britain, media critics in Canada and The Netherlands were the next to object.[59] After that came a lambasting of the consultants in New Zealand's national news magazine *Metro,* in which writer Joe Atkinson excoriated that country's first "Barbie and Ken dual-anchor team" and blasted managers for allowing Americans to "potty train" veteran journalists in the TV New Zealand newsroom.[60] "It wasn't as if we hadn't heard that before. For years we had critics in the United States who told us the same thing," Brent Magid observed.

This time, though, there was no Teflon effect. New criticism had formed around an old cachet, "cultural imperialism," a hot button issue in the 1970s and 1980s when a large contingent of mostly Third World countries had gone to the UN and protested American media influence. For the consultants, "cultural imperialism" were two words with bite. As Brent Magid noted, "As time went on we became more and more concerned that we'd be perceived as Ugly Americans. . . . Learning different cultures and blending in became priorities. . . . We sometimes learned the hard way that if you didn't appreciate [other people's] customs and traditions they wouldn't listen to what you were saying."61

Rarely had there been insurmountable language barriers. English was spoken almost everywhere. Daunting, though, was coping with culture and avoiding the Ugly American tag. McHugh & Hoffman consultants would never forget their first encounters in Latin America, where 1 p.m. meetings that had begun an hour late were postponed 30 minutes later because of siesta time. Even in more kindred countries anomalies appeared. One had come in Great Britain, where a misunderstanding of the term "sensationalism" had caused a communication breakdown. When they heard "sensationalism," the Americans had assumed the British were concerned about scurrilous news coverage, which the consultants had not proposed. The British, though, had been referring to items the Americans had indeed recommended, including news teases and superimposing the word "Live," which to the British signified a sensational approach.

Problems had not been limited to people culture. The consultants also had had to learn the political culture of different countries. In less developed countries the fortunes of television clients often had depended on the relationship between the owner and the ruling political regime. While close ties usually expedited the Americans' work, political tensions helped McHugh & Hoffman in Brazil. There McHugh & Hoffman had joined a new network called SBT, the rival to Brazil's powerful TV Globo whose candidate had been elected president of Brazil and then, amid scandal, impeached. Unrest with a government identified with Globo had swayed viewers to the news on SBT. Even so, according to the firm's Robert Morse, "We had never faced a situation [in the U.S.] in which political power and government stability had to be taken into account."62

Sometimes more nagging than factional politics had been politics by red tape. Because of a serpentine bureaucracy, broadcast hardware and material shipped to countries like Russia had stayed with customs authorities for weeks at a stretch. A common experience was that of Story First's Tate Fite, an American whose job required periodic travel between Russia and other CIS countries. Often he would leave for one locale and then discover upon entering the next that visa requirements for American nationals had changed. "When you had the wrong papers," Fite elaborated, "they would put you in 'customs jail' at the airport. To get out you had to write an essay on how you would never do that again."63

Almost every overseas foray had some additional constraint. "When I tell my grandchildren about the first years of international news consulting," Magid's Charles Munro commented, "it won't be the politics or the culture but the weird things we did that stand out."[64] For Munro these experiences had included 10-hour plane flights on back-to-back days and surviving six-hour get-acquainted sessions in which business was not even discussed. On one occasion in the Middle East, American consultants were shot at by an out-of-power political faction eyeing the TV facilities they had to advise.[65] In Greece the consultants had had to wear bulletproof vests and use rear entrances in order to ward off potential sniper attacks.[66]

In the meantime, extraordinary measures often had to be used to fulfill the consultants' basic work. Before Magid opened its London office, its consultants there had had to commute to Iowa every few days. During an 18-month period Magid's Joe George collected 75 British passport stamps. In moving through some countries generators and TV equipment had to be packed. Electricity was not always reliable, and technical standards for television differed from place to place. Although English was common, translation was necessary. Translators not only were hired but sometimes put on retainers and given plane tickets so that reports could be completed in the air prior to a consultant's arrival in the next destination. Research had been the ultimate test. In Malaysia, only one home in 10 had a telephone. Magid consultants acted resourcefully by renting canoes and then paddling up rivers and along shorelines to count television antennas. Samples were then drawn, and using the same canoes the researchers paddled back to conduct the interviews.

Despite obstacles in global consulting, elation set in when one of the ventures succeeded. For Magid this had happened in Greece, where in 1992 the firm had been hired by shipping magnate Minos Kyriakou, who had just licensed and legalized a former pirate television outfit known as Antenna TV. Looking to make money but also dissatisfied with Greece's ruling regime, Kyriakou's hope was to turn Antenna into a news source and thwart the official version of news as seen on the country's 40-year-old government network ERT. Magid's role in the Antenna newsroom, which had launched a newscast called "Ta Nea Toy," culminated in July 1995.

That summer the worldwide "big journalism" agenda had been topped by warfare in Bosnia, a four-hour car ride from Greece. While coverage of Bosnia was included, it was second segment material on Greece's new national news. One edition of "Ta Nea" had opened with team coverage of a Greek basketball star who had signed a new contract. A cocaine bust with all the visual trimmings was the lead story in another. From all over Greece, field reporters contributed live reports, while in the studio a young female sportscaster was brought on with 30 seconds of happy talk. Anchor Terrence Quick was the star of the show. Originally a radio disc jockey, the new Walter Cronkite of Greece had been singled out by Magid, coached by Magid in the Antenna studios and coached again half way around the world at Magid headquarters in Marion. According to magazine polls Quick had risen as the most popular person in Greece. After just two years "Ta Nea" commanded 60 percent of the Greek audience. With a "90" when "Ta Nea" began, ERT had a "9" when the July 1995 ratings came in.[67]

For Magid consultants, the exhilaration of "Eyewitness News" came rushing back. Yet in one respect "Ta Nea Toy" was a bigger triumph. Not figuratively but literally delivered from the bottom of Mt. Olympus, it was the news consultants' coup de grace.

Back in the United States, the consultants never did find the "next Eyewitness News." Yet as local television news entered the new millennium, it no longer mattered. The field had been re-energized by the new competitive environment of American TV. While the news looked the same, there was a lot more of it—and more chances to be No. 1.

The malaise had begun to lift in the early 1990s when broadcasters, consumed by fears of cable TV, turned a minus into a plus by introducing their own cable news channels. Midway through the 1990s more than 50 U.S. cities and regions had 24-hour local news channels on cable, most operated by existing local TV stations. Several of these "local CNNs" were multiplexed so that different segments targeted different suburbs and neighborhoods.

Then in 1997 the industry received more promising news when the FCC gave local broadcasters new channels for their 10-year conversion to digital TV. Jumping on the digital bandwagon, hundreds of local stations unveiled websites that increased their regular output of news. Through direct broadcast satellites and streaming on the Internet, local newscasts from numerous U.S. cities were available all over the world. Only years earlier local news directors were speculating on what jobs and even what newscasts might disappear. Yet in each year of the 1990s, the local news workforce had increased by between 5 and 10 percent.[68]

As the field ventured in new directions, familiar local newscasts on home TV stations continued to center the TV news system. The explosion of new channels and services had fragmented the audience.

The ratings of individual newscasts had gone down. Yet during the 1990s there had been an offsetting effect: a surge of new local newscasts that had added to the total audience. All over the country stations had added local news in morning time periods. In major and large markets, where new stations had opened news departments, local news expanded into the night. The introduction of local news on Hispanic stations affiliated with Univision and Telemundo had greatly extended the field's reach. Thus, despite fragmentation, the aggregate news audience had grown, according to Nielsen, to more than 150 million people each day.[69]

The stakes had been dramatized by Rupert Murdoch in local television's definitive 1990s event. To bolster his young Fox network, Murdoch in 1994 had ponied up more than $1 billion in purchasing 10 major stations formerly part of the Storer and New World broadcast groups. As these stations and dozens of others converted to Fox, ABC, CBS and NBC were forced to realign their affiliate systems. Making deals with new super-groups like Scripps-Howard and Gannett, the networks grabbed the best affiliates they could; the result was a chain reaction of affiliation switches that not only reshaped the television industry but confused viewers in the 75 cities where they had occurred. Led by Murdoch's Fox outlets, local stations stemmed the confusion by doubling and tripling their amount of local news.[70] New jobs abounded, and according to one study morale had soared.[71]

Murdoch had been in step with the times in yet another way. He had focussed his Fox stations on local reporting and not forced them to carry a Fox network news. Fox had not developed a network newscast. During the 1990s the original network newscasts on ABC, CBS and NBC had hung on, but their individual shares of the national audience sank to between 4 and 8 percent. The localization of network news continued when CBS briefly paired Dan Rather with Connie Chung and thus established an "Eyewitness"-style news team. Nevertheless, talk show host Don Imus put the nation in stitches in 1996 by remarking that Rather's CBS newscast still looked like a "hostage tape."[72] Imus had made this remark before President Bill Clinton and a national TV audience while speaking at the news media's annual Gridiron dinner in Washington.

More troubling to the networks had been a 1996 Pew Research Center study. Only 40 percent of those surveyed said they approved network news. Fewer than one-third believed what they saw on networks, and only 35 percent said they had recently watched. Among those under 30, only 22 percent had recently viewed either an ABC, CBS or NBC nightly news.

The same Pew study, though, was another vote of confidence in local TV news. Sixty-five percent had voiced approval, while nearly the same proportion said they watched local news each day. Close to 50 percent of younger viewers had claimed to be part of the audience.[73]

How long this enthusiasm could last was anybody's guess. The local news of 2000 had featured a new news-active TV station, cable service or website in virtually every city. There were thousands of new jobs and, as always, much news to report.

But ratings and research continued to roll, and the revolving door kept spinning. According to a 1999 RTNDA survey, entry-level salaries in local news, at around $15,000 per year, were the lowest among 22 leading professions.[74] Competition had hardly been alleviated. And because the composition of society remained one part upper, four parts middle and lower, Joe Six Pack still had to be served. Thus, while much had changed, the system remained the same.

This system was synonymous with news consultants, who by 2000 had broadened the parameters and amplified the questions by taking people's news worldwide. The American news media had witnessed no more important event than the proliferation of news consultants into almost every newsroom in the United States. Yet even that feat was overshadowed the moment the consultants had entered newsrooms overseas.

The consultants had had little time to ponder the implications. AR&D consultants in Dallas were learning to speak other languages. Without fanfare, Frank Magid had gotten himself elected transportation commissioner so he could arrange international air service at the Cedar Rapids airport.

For Magid, the global village had been one more step. "Our foreign clients recognized that there was no television system more competitive than in the United States. We had been at the center of that competition for 35 years, so it was quite apparent that those in foreign countries would come to the United States, and to us, because we had the research expertise they had to have. . . . Our main function was and always will be research," Magid would state. "We simply told our [foreign] clients that if they wanted to survive they had to listen to the people and not to their peers. This was nothing different from anything we had ever said in the United States."[75]

In September 1993 the experts were at it again. At newsstands around the country, the monthly edition of the *American Journalism Review,* published in Washington, D.C., was devoted to a question bannered in two-inch-high letters on the cover: "Why Is Local TV News So Bad?" A bevy of national pundits, media critics, and college professors gave answers. Todd Gitlin of the University of California wrote of a "scandal"; *Los Angeles Times* critic Howard Rosenberg, of a "big, wheezing laugh." This magazine symposium set the stage for a live version the following January in New York, where Columbia University assembled a 15-person panel of more pundits, critics and college professors. Among them was Columbia's Joan Konner, who scolded the field for "using and abusing the news." "It's another miracle that the electronic media now have in their power the most far-reaching and effective instrument of public education in the world. Maybe there can be another miracle," she said, "journalists [who] show as much interest in ideas, culture and creativity . . . as they do in killer Dillers."[1]

Yet as always happened, the elite lacked the last word. A year later another panel of 15 media experts was convened. Only this time they included a cross-section of the American public, randomly sampled and brought together in New Orleans by AR&D for the first-ever public focus group. It highlighted the RTNDA's fiftieth anniversary convention. Six blue collar workers, two professionals, five homemakers, and two retired people could not figure out why Washington

273

and New York were so upset. Their comments gushed when asked about local TV news. No one talked about abusing the news or lusting for ratings. They considered local news a utility because it was down to earth and close to home. Their contempt centered on a single thing, arrogance, which they identified with the national news media. "Just use non-opinioned people. Just get people that's gonna give you the news, strictly the news, nothing but the news," one stated. And try as they might they could not fathom TV news as an educational experience. "Don't teach me," another insisted, "just give me the news."[2]

Today, the learned sector is right in focussing on local TV news. No longer a domestic phenomenon, it is now determining the flow of news all over the world. But superficial indeed is the question "Why Is Local TV News So Bad?" Local news is a morning, noon and evening companion to 150 million Americans. Just before the 1996 Pew Research Center study, the one giving local news 65 percent public approval, a Bullet Poll national opinion survey had had Americans express their feelings with letter grades. Sixty-eight percent of all respondents and 76 percent of minorities gave local TV news an "A" or a "B." Only 6 percent gave it an "F."[3] Thus, the field's real question is just the opposite: Why is local news so good?

The people are the answer, and as Ma Joad in John Steinbeck's *The Grapes of Wrath* pointed out, they "keep a comin'." Yet they keep getting missed by those in high places where knowledge is shaped. The inevitable result is not insight but frustration when knowledge comes forth. This knowledge gap can be overcome by shifting energies from controversies to several real problems rooted in a daily information system dominated by people's news.

First is the failure of the system to provide a daily TV news service for the upper-middle class. The reason college-educated viewers are angry is that the only TV news they see is designed for someone else. Advertisers demand not only a No. 1 rating but an appeal to younger viewers whose elite sensitivities are rarely pronounced. This furthers a middle majority bias. Historically, the industry has rationalized this matter by arguing that the upper-middle class has greater access to magazines, journals, and the Internet and thus doesn't need TV news. Yet even in the Internet age, TV news still has utility for college-educated users as a service one can sit down and watch. In their rush to castigate all local TV news as "bad," critics rarely ply the more constructive tack of pressing for an upscale newscast, which today may fill a potentially lucrative market niche.

A second and much different issue is the extraordinary turnover among TV news personnel. According to a Freedom Forum study conducted in the 1990s, the typical TV journalist had only eight years of experience and had held three jobs in two different cities; 57 percent of the nearly 2,000 local TV journalists questioned by the Freedom Forum said they wanted out.[4] Americans who might see this as an internal matter and worthy of a So What? have important reasons to care. Not only is good journalism the unlikely domain of unhappy journalists, but the public is spending tens of millions of dollars in tax money on a higher education system which is partly if not largely responsible. Colleges and universities stoke low pay and high turnover by churning out a supply of journalists that by an order of magnitude outstrips the demand. Moreover, taught in journalism schools to scorn people as the "lowest common denominator," those who do get jobs are soon disillusioned by the "real" world. Since only with job security and a passion for the people is today's journalist assured a productive career, a question is whether journalism schools help journalists fail.

Then there is the issue from which local TV news began: social class in America. For too long Americans have falsely believed that class differences are something out of the Great Depression. Today's bounding prosperity has made these divisions difficult to see. Yet according to census data in 2000, only 23 percent of Americans had college degrees. Fifty-five percent have high school educations or less; one-third had household incomes slightly above the government's official poverty line, and more than half worked in unskilled occupations or were part of a semi-skilled white collar rank-and-file. Sixty percent of black children and 25 percent of all children were growing up in single-parent families.[5] Concurrently, AR&D research has located no upward mobility, no increased free time and no greater disposable income, but rather that more and more Americans are pressed for time while trying to make ends meet. That diamond-shaped topology of class stratification still exists. AR&D lists only 19 percent of Americans in its "high" status group. Forty-eight percent are in the middle; 33 percent, at the bottom. As always, those in the middle and bottom are the most avid users of TV.[6]

The problem of inequality is the problem of America itself, and part of the problem may be the expectation that television, specifically television news, is the solution. Lloyd Warner disagreed, and so did his Harvard associate John Kenneth Galbraith, who noted, "People are the common denominator of progress. So . . . no improvement is possible without improved people, and advance is certain when people are educated."[7] By education, Galbraith did not mean television, the "most effective instrument of public education in the world" to those whose thoughts are limited to television. TV can educate a little. Yet no teacher would allow students to come to class with remote controls, eat dinner and play with the kids during the lectures and then call someone educated without earning a grade. To uplift the masses, not television but real education is the challenge and the key. Improvement can come when those who blazon television as the cure-all of society begin to understand the confusion they create.

As for local TV news, improvement is possible when the field is accepted for what it is, not what experts think it should be. It is a news for the masses that the masses embrace.

Every so often, someone comes along who has seen this light and who pictures the mass media as "mass" media. Writing in 1983 in the *Detroit News,* in the city were news consulting was born, critic Mike Bass observed: "Detroiters have this unique fascination with their television news. In this town, a Bill Bonds would get stopped on the street by a passer-by. A Stu Klintenic would be recognized chomping away on some potato skins at a suburban eatery. A Sonny Eliot would be asked to speak before the local PTA banquet." Detroit, Bass said, "is not a martini-extra-dry-and-stir-it-slowly area; this is a beer-and-keep-them-coming kind of town. The aristocrats can jet to New York if they want." Detroiters "would rather see Willie Nelson than the Detroit Symphony. They don't care about Chopin, Mozart. . . . But they do care about their television [news]." The people of Detroit "aren't into impulsive changes. It takes a lot for Detroiters to trust you." Yet "once Detroiters accept a personality, they consider that celebrity as one of them [and] a seemingly unbreakable trust is built." Bass added, "To understand this phenomenon is to understand Detroit."[8]

To understand what Bass was talking about is to understand TV news.

Abbreviations

ABCNAS—ABC News Advisory Service
ARB—Arbitron Archive
ARD—Audience Research &
Development, Inc.
ANM—Action News Materials
ASU—Arizona State University Local TV
News Collection
ASUV—Arizona State University
Television Archive
BOHP—Bonneville Oral History
Project
BTM—Bill Tucker Materials
CBS—CBS Archive
CHSV—Colorado State Historical
Society Video Archive
FCCOS—FCC Office of the Secretary
FCCCC—FCC Correspondence of the
Chairman
FCCD—FCC Dockets
FMA—Frank N. Magid Associates
ICV—Ithaca College Roy H. Park School
of Communication Archive
JFM—Jerry Foster Materials
KGWV—KGW Video Archive
KTRKV—KTRK Video Archive
KYWV—KYW Video Archive
LPM—Lou Prato Materials
MCTV—Marist College-John Tillman
Film Archive

MHI—McHugh & Hoffman, Inc.
PMP—Phil McHugh Papers
PROM—Promax, Inc.
PROMV—PROMAX Audio-Visual
Archive
RBM—Ray Beindorf Materials
RTNDA—RTNDA Archive
RTNDAOH—RTNDA Oral History
Project
SFSV—San Francisco State University
Television News Archives
UCLAV—UCLA Film Archive
VAV—Vanderbilt Archive
VLM—Vince Leonard Materials
WBC—Westinghouse Broadcasting
Company
WCAUV—WCAU Video Archive
WCPOV—WCPO Video Archive
WLSV—WLS Video Archive

Chapter 1

1. F. M. Flynn, "Programming
   Opportunities of the Indie TV
   Station," *Variety,* July 28, 1948,
   p. 36.
2. Pope interview with author.
3. Chapman, *Tell It To Sweeney,*
   pp. 135–145.

4. "Who's TV Now?", WPIX ad, *Broadcasting,* May 31, 1948, p. 19.
5. "TV Costs," *Broadcasting,* May 3, 1948, p. 40.
6. "WPIX Announces Airwave Veterans," June 14, 1948, p. 10; and "Scores WPIX Beat," June 14, 1948, p. 8, both in *New York Daily News.*
7. "Complete Mobile Studios To Screen Spot News," *New York Daily News,* June 14, 1948, p. 8.
8. Pope interview with author.
9. "Lucky 'Levin," WPIX ad, *New York Daily News,* January 2, 1951.
10 "Thousands Here Pick Up Test Pattern of WPIX," *New York Daily News,* June 1, 1948, p. 10.
11. "WPIX Starts June 15," WPIX ad, *New York Daily News,* June 14, 1948, p. 38.
12. "1st on Scene, Screen," *New York Daily News,* June 14, 1948, p. 8.
13. "Leaders, Stars Telecast Hello As Station WPIX Goes on Air," *New York Daily News,* June 16, 1948, p. 3.
14. "WPIX, WFIL-TV's Quickie Crash Reels," *Variety,* June 23, 1948, p. 24.
15. Ben Gross, "The News Ticker," *New York Daily News,* June 19, 1948, p. 10.
16. "Televiewing: The Convention," *New York Daily News,* June 27, 1948, p. 14; and Chapman, *Tell It To Sweeney,* pp. 263–264.
17. Consumer Stories, November 28–December 5, 1956, Reel 107; and "Baby Platypus" and "Bronx Children," June 5–6, 1958, Reel 108, both in "Telepix Newsreel," WPIX-TV, MCTV.
18. "GOP-TV, WPIX," *Broadcasting,* July 5, 1948, pp. 60–61.
19. "Tabloid Technique Gets WPIX Initiation," *Variety,* July 7, 1948, p. 38.
20. "WGN-TV Chicago," *Broadcasting,* March 27, 1950, pp. 60–61.
21. "The Tragedy of Little Kathy," KTTV-TV, April 8–9, 1949, UCLAV.
22. "Television Has 27-Hour Fire Trial," *Los Angeles Times,* April 11, 1949, p. 2.
23. Williams, "Remote Possibilities," p. 7.
24. "In Review," *Broadcasting,* April 28, 1952, p. 52.
25. Mazingo, "Home of programming firsts," p. A30.
26. "KTLA At Forty," KTLA-TV, January 22, 1987, UCLAV.
27. "George Putnam's Fiftieth Anniversary," KTTV-TV, July 13, 1984, UCLAV.
28. B. Allison to B. Tucker, October 1953, BTM, ASU.
29. "KTTV: a Success Story," *Los Angeles Times Seventy-fifth Anniversary,* January 3, 1956, pp. 33, 133; Claudia Puig, "I Broadcast in My Spare Time," *Los Angeles Times,* July 21, 1994, pp. F-1, F-6; and Kitman, "Another Day, Another Million," p. 41.
30. Putnam interview with author.
31. Smethers, "Unplugged," pp. 44–60.
32. Tucker interview with author.
33. W. Engels to W. Tucker, October 1953, BTM, ASU.
34. WMAR to W. Tucker, October 1953, BTM, ASU.
35. J. Byron to W. Tucker, October 1953, BTM, ASU.
36. Walter Cronkite interview, "Later With Bob Costas," NBC-TV, November 1989.
37. P. White to B. Tucker, October 1953, BTM, ASU.
38. R. Renick to B. Tucker, October 1953, BTM, ASU.
39. "A TV Station Tailored for Growth," *Broadcasting,* April 13, 1953, p. 84.
40. "TV Personnel," *Broadcasting,* April 19, 1948, pp. 40, 91.
41. "News Training," *Broadcasting,* November 14, 1949, p. 29.
42. Tucker interview with author.
43. "Tricky Weather," *Newsweek,* April 22, 1957, p. 72.
44. "Fair-Weather Friends," *Time,* April 1, 1968, p. 83.
45. Millstein, "The Weather Girls," p. 64.
46. Francis Davis, "Weather is No Laughing Matter," *TV Guide,* July 23, 1955, p. 10.
47. Smart, *The Outlook Story,* p. 112.
48. "John Facenda: A Man of The People," WCAU-TV, September 14, 1984, WCAUV.
49. Capell interview with author.

50. Weaver interview with author.
51. Daly interview with author.
52. Adair interview with author.
53. Miami report, August 12, 1964, p. 17, MHI.
54. Weaver interview with author.
55. Robert Kelly interview with author.
56. "Nightbeat," KGW-TV, June 15, 1959, KGWV.
57. Capell interview with author.
58. Ross, Schultz, Barker, Schottelkotte, Beutel, Corporon, and Grimsby interviews with author; "Eyewitness News," WBZ-TV, September 16–17, 1983, ASUV.

Chapter 2

1. Nelson interview with author.
2. Beindorf interview with author.
3. "Channel 3 Reports," KCRA-TV ad, February 20, 1961, *Sacramento Union,* p. 3.
4. Robert Kelly interview with author.
5. Sales brochure, "The Big News," KNXT-TV, August 1, 1961, p. 23, RBM, ASU.
6. "Variety Syndication Chart," *Variety,* October 18, 1961, p. 38.
7. Beindorf interview with author.
8. Zelman interview with author.
9. News release, "Ralph Story: The Human Predicament," KNXT-TV, August 1961, RBM, ASU.
10. "The Big News," KNXT-TV, August 1, 1961, UCLAV.
11. Advertising displays, "A Full Hour of Local News Only on Television Two," KNXT-TV, November 1961, RBC; "KNXT Innovation: Stripped News Hour," *Variety,* August 23, 1961, p. 36.
12. *Eye on L.A.,* KNXT-TV, 1966; "Radio-tv covered L.A. fire all the way," *Broadcasting,* November 13, 1961, p. 62; Allen Rich, "The Big News Sets Fast Pace," *Valley Times Today,* June 22, 1962, p. 10; "Vietnam Village War," KNXT-TV, 1966, UCLAV.
13. Sales brochure, "Cost and Commercial Summary," KNXT-TV, 1961, RBM, ASU; and "Chasing the News Dollar," *Los Angeles Magazine,* April 1, 1964, pp. 1–3.

14. Beindorf interview with author.
15. Nelson interview with author.
16. "King Cronkite," *More,* September 1976, p. 10.
17. R. Wood to J. Schneider, 1965, RBM, ASU.
18. "The Hour Versus Half Hour Local TV Newscasts," McHugh & Hoffman, Inc., July 21, 1967, pp. 7–9, MHI.
19. Steiner, *The People Look at Television,* pp. 304–305.
20. See In re Great Lakes Broadcasting Company, Docket 4900, (1928), RG 173, FCCOS.
21. *Public Service Responsibility of Broadcast Licensees,* Pt. 5, Sec. A, FCC, March 7, 1946, RG 173, FCCD.
22. FCC Report and Order, 19 RR 1569, 601–1141, September 21, 1960.
23. U.S. v. RCA, 17 RR 764 (1959).
24. FCC Annual Report, 1958, p. 17, RG 173, Box 1, FCCED.
25. Frederick Ford testimony before Subcommittee on Appropriations, U.S. Senate, 86th Congress, 2nd Session, HR 11776:11775.
26. Programming Policy Statement, July 29, 1960, FCC 60–970, R.G. 173, Entry 35, Box 11, FCCOS.
27. "FCC Still Sitting On 500 License Renewals in Wake of Scandal," *Variety,* January 18, 1961, p. 51.
28. Transcript, Newton Minow speech, Washington, D.C., May 9, 1961, R.G. 173, Box 1, Records Relating to Chairman Minow's Speech, FCCED.
29. Programming Policy Statement, July 29, 1960, FCC 60–970, R.G. 173, Entry 35, Box 11, FCCOS.
30. "A sharper FCC eye on programs," *Broadcasting,* August 1, 1960, pp. 35, 38.
31. Analysis of Letters Received, June 1, 1961, RG 173, Box 1, Records Relating to Chairman Minow's Speech, FCCED.
32. Henry v. FCC, 302 F.2d 191; 371 U.S. 821 (1962).
33. FCC Rules and Regulations, 47 CFR 73.191 (1961).
34. Bagwell interview with author.
35. "How Doerfer's hopes died," pp. 32–33; and "Ford: Soft-spoken

but firm," pp. 34–36, both in *Broadcasting,* March 14, 1960.

36. "FCC Okays Storer Purchases," *Broadcasting,* April 1, 1957, pp. 54, 58.
37. "Storer first quarter double that of '61," *Broadcasting,* April 16, 1962, p. 74.
38. P. McHugh to S. P. Kettler, April 14, 1965, MHI.
39. "Storer Has Option On Toolco's 55% of Northeast Air," *Wall Street Journal,* June 3, 1965, p. 1.
40. *Storer Annual Report 1968,* Storer Broadcasting Company, July 1, 1969, pp. 2–3.
41. Kahn interview with author.
42. W. Michaels to G. Storer, Jr., P. McHugh, and P. Hoffman, May 16, 1962, MHI.
43. Warren Zwicky file, undated, MHI.
44. *Primer on Ascertainment of Community Problems by Broadcast Applicants,* 57 FCC 2d 418, 441 (1976), Pt. C, Question 24.
45. Bagwell interview with author.
46. Kahn interview with author.
47. P. Hoffman to W. Michaels, May 9, 1963, MHI.
48. Contact report, P. McHugh and T. Lee, March 9, 1962, MHI.
49. Hoffman interview with author.
50. "McHugh, Hoffman Form TV Consultancy," *Broadcasting,* March 5, 1962, p. 58.
51. Contact report, T. Lee and P. McHugh, March 3, 1962, MHI.
52. A Report to Storer Broadcasting Company, May 1964, p. 30, MHI.
53. P. McHugh to W. Michaels, August 13, 1962, MHI.
54. Memorandum, W. Michaels to Storer general managers, May 9, 1962, MHI.
55. Ellmore, *Broadcasting Law and Regulation,* pp. 116–117; also see Abel, et al., "Station License Revocations," pp. 411–421.
56. "Renewal forms ready," *Broadcasting,* June 4, 1962, p. 5.
57. *Primer on Ascertainment of Community Problems by Broadcast Applicants,* 27 FCC 2d 650, 682 (1971).
58. *Primer on Ascertainment of Community Problems by Broadcast Applicants,* 57 FCC 2d 418, 441 (1976).
59. *Deregulation of Commercial Television,* 56 RR 2nd 1005 (1984).

Chapter 3

1. Roethlisberger-Dickson, *Management and the Worker.*
2. See Warner, *The Social Life of a Modern Community; The Status System of a Modern Community; The Social Systems of American Ethnic Groups; The Social System of the Modern Factory; The Living and the Dead,* and *Social Class in America.*
3. Warner, *Yankee City,* p. 36.
4. Davis-Gardner, *Deep South;* Warner, *Democracy in Jonesville;* Coleman, *Social Status in the City,* "American Social Classes in the Middle Nineties," pp. 1–2.
5. Warner, *The Social Life of the Modern Community,* pp. 88–91.
6. Warner, *Yankee City,* pp. 36–37.
7. Chase, *The Proper Study,* pp. 23–24; Tumin, *Social Stratification,* pp. 4–9.
8. Standard critiques of Warner's social class thesis include Llewellyn Gross, "The Use of Class Concepts in Sociological Research," *American Journal of Sociology* 54 (1949): 409–421; Harold W. Pfautz and Otis D. Duncan, "A Critical Evaluation of Warner's Work in Community Stratification," *American Sociological Review* 15 (1950): 205–215; Gregory P. Stone and William H. Form, "Instabilities in Status," *American Sociological Review* 18 (1953): 149–169; and R. W. Hodge and D. J. Treiman, "Class Identification in the United States," *American Journal of Sociology* 73 (1968): 535–547. Also see Reinhard Bendix and Seymour M. Lipset, eds., *Class, Status and Power: Social Stratification in Comparative Perspective* (New York: Free Press, 1966).
9. Thernstrom, "Yankee City Revisited," pp. 234–242.

10. "Environment and Education," symposium of Committee on Human Development, University of Chicago, Vol. 1, March 1942.
11. Gardner, *Conceptual Framework*, pp. 20–21.
12. Martineau, *Motivation in Advertising*, pp. 163–172.
13. B. B. Gardner to P. McHugh, "Summary of Credentials of Social Research, Inc.," October 14, 1963, MHI.
14. Coleman interview with author.
15. Warner-Henry, *The Radio Day Time Serial*, pp. 3–71.
16. Horton-Wohl, "Mass Communication and Para-Social Interaction," pp. 215–230.
17. Packard, *Hidden Persuaders*, pp. 23, 98–99, 229.
18. "Riding the TV range," *Television Age*, April 1954, pp. 30–37; "On All Accounts," *Broadcasting*, November 24, 1952, p. 19; "Our Respects," *Broadcasting*, August 23, 1954, p. 20; "Guests in the House," *Fortune*, December 1954, p. 4.
19. Hoffman interview with author.
20. Keeler interview with author.
21. "Panorama," December 27, 1979, WTTG-TV, ASUV.
22. *TV Guide: A Study in Depth*, Social Research, Inc., 1960, pp. 11–16.
23. Glick-Levy, *Living with Television*, pp. 25–39.
24. "McHugh, Hoffman Form TV Consultancy," *Broadcasting*, March 5, 1962, p. 58.
25. Contact report, H. Beville, T. Coffin, and P. McHugh, March 9, 1962, MHI.
26. T. Coffin to H. Beville, April 3, 1963, MHI.
27. Coleman, "Consumers and Television," p. 1.
28. Znaniecki, *The Method of Sociology;* and Bogdan-Taylor, *Introduction to Qualitative Research Methods.*
29. Cleveland questionnaire, October 1962, Social Research, Inc., MHI.
30. Kahn interview with author.
31. Coleman, "American Social Classes in the Middle Nineties."
32. "Continuing Trends in Television," Social Research, Inc., and McHugh

& Hoffman, Inc., February 26, 1962, pp. 27–30, 49–50, MHI.
33. Coleman, "The Continuing Significance of Social Class to Marketing," p. 270.
34. Coleman interview with author. Also Itzkoff, *The Decline of Intelligence in America*, pp. 103–114; Eysenck, *The IQ Argument*, pp. 44–78; Vernon, *Intelligence: Heredity and Environment*, pp. 115–128.
35. Coleman interview with author.
36. Coleman, *Social Status in the City*, pp. 175–176, 186–187, 196.

Chapter 4

1. "Now: X-Ray of the TV Audience," *Broadcasting*, May 1, 1961, pp. 31–41.
2. Glick-Levy, *Living With Television*, pp. 112, 135.
3. Seattle report, August 1968, pp. 71–80, FMA.
4. Glick interview with author.
5. Glick-Levy, *Living With Television*, p. 135.
6. "The Business of TV News," McHugh & Hoffman, Inc., March 11, 1985, p. 4, MHI.
7. "Continuing Trends in Television," Social Research, Inc., and McHugh & Hoffman, Inc., February 26, 1963, pp. 91, 106–110, MHI.
8. "Continuing Trends in Television," Social Research, Inc., and McHugh & Hoffman, Inc., March 1964, pp. 87–88, MHI.
9. Glick interview with author.
10. "Continuing Trends in Television," Social Research, Inc., and McHugh & Hoffman, Inc., February 26, 1963, pp. 83–84, MHI.
11. "Continuing Trends in Television," Social Research, Inc., and McHugh & Hoffman, Inc., March 1964, pp. 73–79, MHI.
12. "Huntley-Brinkley Report," NBC-TV, January 2, 1969, VAV.
13. "CBS Evening News," CBS-TV, January 2, 1969, VAV.
14. "CBS Evening News," CBS-TV, August 16, 1977, VAV.

15. Hoffman interview with author.
16. Manchester, *Death of a President,* p. 512.
17. Kennedy assassination coverage, CBS-TV, November 22, 1963.
18. "Continuing Trends in Television," Social Research, Inc., and McHugh & Hoffman, Inc., March 1964, pp. 74–87, MHI.
19. Hoffman interview with author.
20. Ed Bark, "Survey says 'Uncle Walter' still gets nod as TV's favorite news personality," *Dallas Morning News,* February 1, 1995, pp. 1C–2C.
21. Apollo 4 coverage, CBS-TV, November 9, 1967.
22. Apollo 11 coverage, CBS-TV, July 20, 1969.
23. New York report, February 1965, pp. 198–199, MHI.
24. Boston report, August 1977, pp. 306–308, MHI.
25. Coleman interview with author.
26. "Network Newscasts," in *The Challenge of Change,* McHugh & Hoffman, Inc., April 1983, pp. 243–252, MHI.

Chapter 5

1. "Continuing Trends in Television," Social Research, Inc., and McHugh & Hoffman, Inc., February 26, 1963, p. 14, MHI.
2. Kahn interview with author.
3. Meeting minutes, McHugh & Hoffman and Storer general managers, September 8, 1962, Box 17; and W. Michaels to Storer general managers, September 13, 1962, both MHI.
4. Milwaukee report, July 11, 1969, p. 18, MHI.
5. P. Hoffman presentation to WJBK, July 1962, MHI.
6. Detroit report, July 1962, pp. 134, 166, MHI.
7. *Standing Recommendations,* ERA Research, Inc., 1980, p. 31, ARD.
8. "Continuing Trends in Television," Social Research, Inc., and McHugh & Hoffman, Inc., February 26, 1963, pp. 108–109, MHI.

9. *The Elements of a Television Newscast,* McHugh & Hoffman, Inc., September 1971, pp. 22–23, MHI.
10. WJBK ad, *Detroit News,* July 18, 1965, p. C-17.
11. W. Michaels to Storer general managers, December 14, 1962; and Detroit report, July 20, 1964, p. 4; both MHI.
12. Contact report, P. McHugh and Storer management, New York, June 3, 1964, MHI.
13. W. Michaels to P. McHugh, November 28, 1962, MHI.
14. Arbitron ratings, Cleveland, November 1962, ARB.
15. W. Michaels to P. McHugh, February 26, 1963, MHI.
16. Adair interview with author.
17. "What Catches the Teenage Mind," *Time,* September 27, 1963, p. 55.
18. "Continuing Trends in Television," July 21, 1967, McHugh & Hoffman, Inc., pp. 1–4, MHI.
19. "Radio-tv pinch hits for newspapers," *Broadcasting,* April 30, 1962, p. 54.
20. Cleveland report, July 1962, p. 2, MHI.
21. Bagwell interview with author.
22. Cleveland tracking report, July 1963, pp. 63–72, MHI.
23. Cleveland report, July 10, 1964, p. 3, MHI.
24. Monitoring report, Cleveland market, September 23, 1963, MHI.
25. Daly interview with author.
26. "Joel Daly Years to Remember," WLS-TV, August 15, 1987, WLSV.
27. Hoffman interview with author.
28. Cleveland report, July 20, 1963, p. 3, MHI.
29. "Central Bank, Guthrie Bargain," *Cleveland Plain Dealer,* September 6, 1963, p. 10.
30. "Daly Aids New Channel 8 Look," *Cleveland Plain Dealer,* September 15, 1963, p. 14.
31. "Thirty Years of Memories," WJW-TV, December 17, 1979, ASUV; and "Joel Daly Years to Remember," WLS-TV, August 15, 1987, WLSV.
32. Adair interview with author.
33. Cleveland report, July 1964, p. 36, MHI.

34. Arbitron ratings, Cleveland, May 1964, ARB.
35. Monitoring report, Cleveland market, September 23, 1963, MHI.
36. Cleveland report, July 1964, p. 61, MHI.
37. Primo interview with author.
38. Cleveland report, July 1964, pp. 61–62, MHI.
39. Cleveland report, July 1964, pp. 61–62, MHI.
40. "Thirty Years of Memories," WJW-TV, December 17, 1979, ASUV.
41. Cleveland supplemental report, July 10, 1964, p. 13, MHI.
42. James B. Flanagan, "NBC Returns to Cleveland," June 20, 1965, *Cleveland Plain Dealer*, p. 32.
43. Wagy interview with author.
44. Bagwell interview with author; Marcia Lamier, "Cleveland's City Camera News," *Storer Story*, March–April 1972, pp. 8–9.
45. Primo interview with author.
46. "Reporter Involvement," McHugh & Hoffman, Inc., 1967, pp. 4–5, MHI.
47. Adair interview with author.
48. Daly interview with author.
49. "NBC Comes Back Tomorrow," *Cleveland Plain Dealer*, June 18, 1965, p. 16.
50. Cleveland supplemental report, July 10, 1964, p. 6, MHI.
51. Arbitron ratings, Cleveland, November 1966, ARB.
52. Telephone memorandum, T. Lee and P. McHugh, June 2, 1966, MHI.
53. Detroit report, April 1968, p. 134, MHI.
54. Detroit tracking study, May 24, 1968, p. 17, MHI.
55. P. Hoffman to P. Kettler, March 18, 1965; and P. McHugh to P. Kettler, October 21, 1996, both MHI.
56. "Channel 2 Joins in Sending Riot Special to BBC," *Detroit News*, July 28, 1967, p. 4-B.
57. Bennett interview with author.
58. Detroit report, April 1968, pp. 133–135, MHI.
59. John Kelly interview with author.
60. *Storer Broadcasting Annual Report*, Storer Broadcasting, July 1, 1969, pp. 1–3.
61. Bettelou Peterson, "WXYZ Best on Riot News," *Detroit Free Press*, July

27, 1967, p. 6-D; Frank Judge, "TV, Radio Praised for Riot Coverage," *Detroit News*, July 25, 1967, p. 18-A.
62. Detroit report, April 1968, p. 113, MHI.
63. Berkery interview with author.
64. "CBS Evening News," CBS-TV, July 28, 1967, transcript in Fang, *Television News*, pp. 259–264.
65. "Continuing Trends in Television," July 21, 1967, McHugh & Hoffman, Inc., pp. 33–37, 46, MHI.
66. *Storer Broadcasting Annual Report*, Storer Broadcasting, July 1, 1969, p. 10.
67. T. Lee to P. McHugh, September 12, 1967, MHI.
68. P. McHugh to W. Michaels, September 30, 1966, MHI; "Two Analysts Weigh the Anchors," *People Weekly*, December 24, 1979, p. 139; and transcript, Phil McHugh speech, New York City, November 12, 1975, PMP, ASU.

Chapter 6

1. Cronkite interview with author.
2. O'Leary interview with author.
3. Arbitron ratings, Chicago, November 1967, ARB.
4. "O'Leary Unveils Extensive Plans For WBKB's Chicago Image Quest," *Variety*, March 15, 1967, pp. 39, 48.
5. O'Leary interview with author.
6. "Fyffe New Maestro of WBKB News," *Variety*, May 1, 1968, pp. 37, 42.
7. Daly interview with author.
8. Adair interview with author.
9. Daly interview with author.
10. "WBBM Denies Fahey Flynn on Way Out," *Chicago Tribune*, July 11, 1967, p. II-3; Herb Lyon, "Tower Ticker," *Chicago Tribune*, January 29, 1968, p. 19; and "Fahey Flynn Says Good-Bye to Channel 2," *Chicago Sun-Times*, January 30, 1968, p. 1.
11. Flynn interview with author.
12. Clay Gowran, "Fahey Flynn to Quit CBS After 27 Years," *Chicago Tribune*, January 26, 1968, p. 16;

Herb Lyon, "Tower Ticker,"
Chicago Tribune, February 1, 1968,
p. 23; and O'Leary interview with
author.
13. Bill Granger, "The Great Bow Tie
Controversy," *Chicago Sun-Times
Midwest,* November 14, 1976,
pp. 4–7.
14. P. McHugh to R. O'Leary, 1968,
MHI.
15. "May the Wind Be at Your Back,"
August 11, 1983, WLS-TV, WLSV.
16. Clay Gowran, "Many Laud That
Fahey," *Chicago Tribune,* February
26, 1968, p. 23.
17. O'Leary interview with author.
18. "Flynn-Daly News," WBKB-TV,
February 12, 1968, in "May the
Wind Be at Your Back," August 11,
1983, WLS-TV, WLSV.
19. "Eyewitness News," WLS-TV,
February 12, 1979, WLSV.
20. "WLS-TV's Daly Names a Tipster,"
Variety, May 5, 1971, p. 34.
21. Daly interview with author.
22. Bridges, "Smile When You Say
That," p. 29.
23. Chicago report, June 30, 1970, p. 4,
MHI.
24. Chicago reports, November 1967;
November 1968; November 1969;
February 1970; November 1971;
ARB.
25. Norman Mark, "Fahey Flynn
returns to top of ratings," *Chicago
Daily News,* March 11, 1972,
p. 19; Bruce Vilanch, "TV War at
10 O'Clock," *Chicago Today
Magazine,* September 20, 1970,
pp. 3–4.
26. Jon Anderson and Robert Enstad,
"Fahey Flynn, Chicago TV news
legend," *Chicago Tribune,* August 9,
1983, p. 14.
27. Roth, "O'Leary's (Sacred) Cow,"
pp. 37–38.
28. Primo interview with author.
29. B. Lemon to V. Leonard, January 5,
1960; and WRCV Ratings Analyses,
January 1963 and January 1964,
VLM, ASU; Rex Polier, "What
Makes Fans Choose One Newsman
to Another?, *Philadelphia Bulletin,*
June 19, 1965, p. 17.
30. Arbitron ratings, Philadelphia,
November 1967, ARB.
31. Beesemyer interview with author.

32. Primo interview with author.
33. Skinner interview with author.
34. Tolliver interview with author.
35. Ittleson interview with author.
36. Primo interview with author.
37. Tindiglia interview with author.
38. "Eyewitness News," WABC-TV,
May 9, 1972, in "TV News: Behind
the Scenes," Encyclopedia
Britannica, 1973; and "Eyewitness
News," WABC-TV, May 19, 1977,
in "Six O'Clock and All is Well,"
1977, both ASUV.
39. Ken McQueen, "If We Have To Go
Out and Find a Witness," *Variety,*
September 3, 1969, p. 39.
40. Jack Gould, "TV: 6-Part Prostitution
Report Begins," *New York Times,*
February 25, 1969, p. 87.
41. Paul Klein, "Happy Talk, Happy
Profits," *New York,* June 28, 1971,
pp. 60–61.
42. Rivera-Paisner, *Exposing Myself,*
p. 77.
43. Scamardella interview with
author.
44. Arbitron ratings, New York,
November 1969, ARB.
45. Beesemyer interview with author.
46. New York report, March 6, 1969,
pp. 41–45, MHI.
47. Goldenson, *Beating the Odds,*
p. 374.
48. Chicago report, April 10, 1969,
pp. 7–8, MHI.
49. New York report, March 6, 1969,
p. 46, MHI.
50. Grimsby interview with author.
51. Beutel interview with author.
52. Tindiglia interview with author.
53. Joseph Morgenstern, "Cheer
Leaders," *Newsweek,* January 4,
1971, p. 9.
54. Bill Greeley, "Pursuit of Happiness
News," *Variety,* June 9, 1971,
pp. 31, 43.
55. "Eyewitness News," WABC-TV,
February 15, 1975, ASUV.
56. Arbitron ratings, New York,
November 1971, ARB.
57. Duffy interview with author.
58. Rodman interview with author.
59. "Will Success Spoil Fahey Flynn and
Joel Daly?" promotion, WLS-TV,
1968, WLSV.
60. "Chicago—A New Concept in News
Reporting Flashes Across the Night

Sky," promotion, WLS-TV, 1969, WLSV.

61. "How Did Channel 7's Great News Team Get Together?" promotion, WLS-TV, 1971, WLSV.
62. "Klopfmann Institute Encounter Therapy," promotion, WLS-TV, 1971, WLSV.
63. "Good Evening Americans, This is H. P. Vandakott Taking the Pulse of the World," promotion, WLS-TV, 1970, WLSV.
64. "How Did John Drury Get To Be the Newest Member of Chicago's Hottest News Team?", promotion, WLS-TV, 1972, WLSV.
65. Duffy interview with author.
66. "What Did Seven Say?" promotion, WABC-TV, 1969, ASUV.
67. Paul Klein, "Happy Talk, Happy Profits," *New York*, June 28, 1971, p. 60.
68. "Peacock Feathers," promotion, WABC-TV, 1970, ASUV.
69. "The Eyewitness News Family," promotion, WABC-TV, 1972, ASUV.
70. "We Let the Sun Shine In," promotion, WABC-TV, *Television/Radio Age*, June 29, 1970, p. 74.
71. Joseph Morgenstern, "Cheer Leaders," *Newsweek*, January 4, 1971, p. 9.
72. Jack Gould, "TV: 6-Part Prostitution Report Begins," *New York Times*, February 25, 1969, p. 87.
73. Dominick, et al., "Television Journalism vs. Show Business," p. 214.
74. Primo interview with author.
75. Chicago report, June 30, 1970, pp. 28, 32, MHI.
76. New York report, February 1970, pp. 99–109, MHI.
77. New York report, July 14, 1971, pp. 86–88, MHI.
78. New York report, August 11, 1977, pp. 8, 31–40, MHI.
79. Daly interview with author.
80. O'Leary interview with author.
81. Bill Greeley, "WNBC-TV News Skid," *Variety*, September 15, 1971, pp. 27, 64.
82. Robert Daley, "We Deal With Emotional Facts," *New York Times Magazine*, December 15, 1974, p. 62.

83. McLuhan, *Sharing the News,* pp. 4–6, 26, 30.

Chapter 7

1. Schottelkotte interview with author.
2. Leo Willette, "Clear Channels," *RTNDA Communicator,* March 1971, p. 6.
3. Schottelkotte interview with author.
4. "The Al Schottelkotte News," WCPO-TV, January 1960, WCPOV.
5. Schottelkotte interview with author; "Al Schottelkotte Twenty-fifth Anniversary," WCPO-TV, June 1, 1984, WCPOV.
6. Arbitron ratings, Cincinnati, November 1971, ARB.
7. "Schottelkotte," WCPO-TV ad, *Television/Radio Age,* July 12, 1971, pp. 4–5.
8. Haralson interview with author.
9. Frank Magid interview with author.
10. "TV News Skin Test Consulting," December 14, 1976, Box 78, RTNDA.
11. Quarton interview with author.
12. Cronkite interview with author.
13. "Quarton to Be New Chairman," *Broadcasting,* April 8, 1957, p. 38.
14. "KIRO-TV Eyewitness News Team," Bonneville, Inc., ad, *Television/Radio Age,* October 1, 1973, p. 144.
15. Seattle report, August 1968, p. 21, FMA.
16. Hoffman interview with author.
17. Frank Magid interview with author.
18. Madsen, BOHP, pp. 33–37.
19. "KSL-TV Takes the Big One," *RTNDA Communicator,* September 1982, p. 8.
20. Early interview with author.
21. Frank Magid interview with author.
22. McCurdy interview with author.
23. Primo interview with author.
24. Koehler interview with author.
25. Philadelphia report, June 1969, pp. 35–36, FMA.
26. Kampmann interview with author.
27. "John Facenda: A Man of The People," WCAU-TV, September 24, 1984, WCAUV.

28. Philadelphia report, June 1969, pp. 52, 65, 318, FMA.
29. Thomas, *Winchell,* pp. 123–128.
30. Philadelphia report, June 1969, p. 330, FMA.
31. Koehler interview with author.
32. Philadelphia report, June 1969, pp. 196, 291, FMA.
33. McCurdy interview with author.
34. Mandel, "Manufacturing the News at Channel 6," p. 67.
35. Platt, "Larry Kane Nobody Knows," pp. 65, 69.
36. "News Time," August 1969, WFIL-TV, ASUV.
37. Prospectus, The Lilyan Wilder Group, 1970, p. 1, ANM, ASU.
38. Philadelphia report, October 1970, FMA.
39. Philadelphia report, June 1969, pp. 52, 65, FMA.
40. Philadelphia report, June 1969, pp. 74–78, FMA.
41. *Channel 6's New News,* WFIL-TV, 1970, p. 2, ANM, ASU; "Action News," WFIL-TV ad, *Philadelphia Daily News,* April 20, 1970, p. 18.
42. Mandel, "Manufacturing the News at Channel 6," p. 66.
43. Arbitron ratings, Philadelphia, November 1973, ARB.
44. Cooney, *The Annenbergs,* pp. 369–370.
45. Dolan interview with author.
46. Philadelphia report, September 1977, p. 101, MHI.
47. Koehler and Mike Davis interviews with author.
48. McCurdy interview with author.
49. "People are Moving to Channel 6's News," WFIL-TV ad, *Philadelphia Inquirer,* November 3, 1970, p. 25.
50. Philadelphia report, June 1969, p. 244, FMA.
51. Mike Davis interview with author.
52. "Film Truck," promotion, WPVI-TV, 1971, NYCV.
53. "Sometimes It's Tough to Find Room in the Show For Larry," promotion, WPVI-TV, 1971, NYCV.
54. "Elevator," promotion, WPVI-TV, 1971, NYCV.
55. "Action News Is the Show For the People," promotion, WPVI-TV, 1994, NYCV.
56. Ham interview with author.
57. "Move Closer to Your World," Mayoham Music Publishing Company, Inc., 1971, ASUV.
58. Client lists, "Move Closer to Your World" and "Part of Your Life," The Music of Your Life, Inc., 1971, ANM, ASU.
59. Stephen Seplow, "You like to watch," *Philadelphia Inquirer,* August 4, 1996, pp. 8–21.
60. "Trends in local news," *Broadcasting,* September 20, 1971, p. 32.
61. Koehler interview with author.
62. Kampmann interview with author.
63. WPVI ad, *Broadcasting,* January 24, 1972, front cover.

Chapter 8

1. Stone, "News Operations Surveyed on Use of Consultants," p. 4.
2. "TelCom Wing To Consult On News," *Variety,* March 21, 1973, p. 57.
3. "Keeping TV journalism close to the wind," *Broadcasting,* December 18, 1978, p. 105.
4. Primer on Ascertainment of Community Problems by Broadcast Applicants, FCC Docket 18774:4098, March 3, 1971, FCCD.
5. "How We Came To Be," Frank N. Magid Associates, Inc., 1994, p. I–9, FMA.
6. Helm interview with author.
7. Steinmetz, "'Mr. Magic—The TV Newscast Doctor,'" pp. 2–25.
8. Kristine Hofacker, "Coaching Your People," Newsletter, January 1983, p. 4, ABCNAS, ASU.
9. Stowell interview with author.
10. "Ex-Magid employees form firm," *Television/Radio Age,* November 6, 1978, p. 49; and Bill Greeley, "Gift of The Magid," *Variety,* April 28, 1976, pp. 44, 60.
11. Client lists, Frank N. Magid Associates, 1976, FMA.
12. Stowell interview with author.
13. "The New Breed," *Newsweek,* August 30, 1971, pp. 62–63.

14. "The non-retiring ways of a nonagenarian newswoman," *Broadcasting,* July 4, 1983, p. 103.
15. Louisville report, August 26, 1969, pp. 14, 18, MHI.
16. Philadelphia report, May 1969, p. 327, FMA.
17. Indianapolis report, June 3, 1966, p. 6, MHI.
18. Cleveland report, June 30, 1967, p. 6, MHI.
19. Hoffman interview with author.
20. Bill Greeley, "Pursuit of Happiness-News: Pros & Cons Re McHugh-Hoffman," *Variety,* June 9, 1971, p. 43.
21. Seattle report, August 1969, p. 130, FMA.
22. Bremner interview with author.
23. Seattle report, March 16, 1971, pp. 7–8, MHI.
24. Enersen interview with author.
25. Seattle report, May 24, 1977, p. 24, MHI.
26. Walker, "Newswomen and Television," pp. 4–8.
27. "KIRO-TV Eyewitness News Team," Bonneville, Inc., ad, *Television/Radio Age,* October 1, 1973, p. 144.
28. Linn interview with author.
29. Louisville report, May 31, 1974, p. 37, MHI.
30. Atlanta report, January 24, 1975, p. 18, MHI; "David Susskind Show," February 11, 1980, WETA-TV, ASUV.
31. Davis interview with author.
32. Indianapolis report, September 1974, p. 48, MHI.
33. Tucker interview with author; "News Shakeup Again at KSTP," *Variety,* January 23, 1974, p. 34.
34. Minneapolis-St. Paul report, July 29, 1977, p. 26, MHI.
35. Chagall, "Only As Good As His Skin Tests," pp. 6–10.
36. Joan Lunden study, August 31, 1976, p. 6, MHI.
37. New York report, February 28, 1975, p. 32, MHI.
38. Mary Nachman, "How To Find Your Most Magnetic Self," *More,* June 1975, p. 22.
39. Washington report, March 21, 1979, pp. 17, 47, MHI.
40. Denver report, June 4, 1976, p. 19, MHI.
41. Bowen interview with author.
42. American University, *Broadcast News Doctors,* p. 34.
43. Yu interview with author.
44. West interview with author.
45. Yu interview with author.
46. "Action News," WTLV ad, *Broadcasting,* May 20, 1974, p. 41.
47. Boston report, July 11, 1974, p. 14.
48. Atlanta report, January 24, 1975, p. 10.
49. Baltimore report, July 6, 1977, pp. 18–21.
50. Tucker interview with author.
51. "We've got what you wanted," promotion, WXYZ-TV, 1975, PRMOV.
52. Arbitron ratings, Detroit, May 1975, ARB.
53. Nye interview with author.
54. "John Facenda: A Man of the People," September 24, 1984, WCAU-TV, WCAUV.
55. Morse interview with author.
56. Louisville report, January 28, 1971, p. 6, MHI.
57. Philadelphia report, September 17, 1974, p. 192, MHI.
58. Bowen interview with author.
59. Philadelphia report, September 17, 1974, p. 107, MHI.
60. Bowen interview with author.
61. Philadelphia report, September 17, 1974, p. 43, MHI.
62. Levy, "We Interrupt This Issue," pp. 155–156.
63. Arbitron ratings, Philadelphia, November 1974, ARB.
64. Savitch, *Anchorwoman,* pp. 109–110.
65. Philadelphia report, September 19, 1975, pp. 61–62, MHI.
66. Topping interview with author.
67. Meeting notes, P. McHugh and client news directors, New York City, March 11, 1974, MHI.
68. Arbitron ratings, Philadelphia, November 1975, ARB.
69. Tindiglia interview with author.
70. Kenneth D. Tiven, "ENG At KYW-TV Broadens News Opportunities," *RTNDA Communicator,* November 1977, p. 3.
71. Frank Magid interview with author.
72. Kampmann interview with author.

73. Savitch, *Anchorwoman*, p. 169.
74. See Blair, *Almost Golden* and Nash, *Golden Girl.*
75. "Larry Kane Farewell," WPVI-TV, 1977, ASUV.
76. "Action News," WPVI-TV, October 27, 1976, ASUV.
77. "Newswatch 5:30," and "Eyewitness News," KYW-TV, February 11, 1977, KYWV.
78. Jefferson Davis interview with author.
79. "Trends in local news," *Television/Radio Age,* September 20, 1971, p. 62.
80. "Appeal of local news," *Broadcasting,* December 2, 1974, p. 3.
81. Transcript, Walter Cronkite speech, Bal Harbour, Fla., December 13, 1976, CBS.
82. Transcript, Robert Guy speech, Seattle, January 24, 1973, Box 2, PMP, ASU.

Chapter 9

1. "KTLA At Forty," KTLA-TV, January 22, 1987, UCLAV.
2. "KTLA (TV) 'Up in Air' With Telecopter Unit," *Broadcasting,* July 28, 1958, p. 76.
3. Beindorf interview with author.
4. Greg Holzhauer, "ENG: The New Way to News Gather," *CBS Columbine,* April 1975, pp. 4–5.
5. Flaherty, "Television News Gathering," p. 645.
6. Memorandum, R. Beindorf to CBS staff, "Why Minicam?," March 3, 1973, RBM, ASU
7. "New(s) Deal For CBS O & O," *Variety,* January 31, 1973, p. 39; "Film Still Dominates in News," *Broadcast Management/Engineering,* January 1973, pp. 30–31; and "TV Journalism," *Broadcasting,* August 20, 1973, pp. 17–23.
8. Flaherty, "The All-Electronic Newsgathering Station," p. 961.
9. Beindorf interview with author.
10. Flaherty, "The All-Electronic Newsgathering Station," pp. 658–661.
11. "KMOX-TV: out with the old (newsfilm) and in with the new," *Broadcasting,* August 19, 1974, p. 46.
12. Wussler interview with author.
13. "WBBM changes tune," *Chicago Tribune,* July 31, 1974, p. 8.
14. News release, "CBS Television Stations Add Minicam to News Departments," CBS, February 26, 1973, RBM, ASU.
15. "The Big News," KNXT-TV, May 17, 1974, UCLAV.
16. Hearst, *Every Secret Thing,* pp. 222–223.
17. Dick Adler, "SLA Coverage: KNXT Shines in the Line of Fire," *Los Angeles Times,* May 21, 1974, p. 14.
18. Gary Deeb, "Top Executive Axed," *Chicago Tribune,* May 15, 1974, p. 17.
19. Gary Deeb, "A New Look," *Chicago Tribune,* July 22, 1974, p. 20.
20. Kurtis interview with author.
21. Roth, "Minicam As WBBM-TV Weapon," p. 42.
22. Derrough interview with author.
23. "KCMO-TV Designs Two Unique Mobile TV Systems," December 1976, pp. 4–11; "TK-76 Performs Like a Real Champ," January 1977, p. 20; and "Taking the TK-76 Down Under, April 1979, pp. 27–30, all in *RCA Broadcast News.*
24. "The Handy Looky," *Time,* September 9, 1975, p. 51.
25. "This Is News: See It Now On the Five CBS Stations," Ikegami ad display, 1974, RBM, ASU; "Ikegami: The Micro-Mini Electronic News Gathering System," Ikegami ad, *Broadcasting,* July 22, 1974, p. 68.
26. "Little Cameras Make Big Splash at Convention," *Broadcasting,* March 25, 1974, pp. 63–64.
27. Roth, "Minicam As WBBM-TV Weapon," p. 42.
28. "WBBM-TV finds portable cameras have helped boost its ratings," *Broadcasting,* August 19, 1974, p. 48.
29. "Portability gives Florida UHF an advantage," *Broadcasting,* August 19, 1974, p. 48.
30. Shannon interview with author.

31. "Promoting News," Broadcast Promotion Association, 1979, pp. 1–7, PROM; and Bergendorff, *Broadcast Advertising and Promotion,* p. 164.
32. "News Writing Guidelines," ABC Owned Stations, 1977, ABCNAS.
33. "Guidelines for Reporters," Peoria TV, June 1977, p. 3.
34. "Moving into high gear with ENG," *Broadcasting,* August 23, 1976, p. 26.
35. Arbitron ratings, Denver, November 1973, ARB.
36. Mars interview with author.
37. "Action Cam," promotion, KBTV, 1976, CHSV.
38. "Sky 9," promotion, KBTV, 1978, CHSV.
39. "It's All Right Here on Channel 9," promotion, KBTV, 1980, in "That's Thirty," KRMA-TV, July 22, 1983, CHSV.
40. "ENG Engineer," promotion, KBTV, 1977, CHSV.
41. "Jet 9," promotion, KBTV, 1982, CHSV.
42. Popper, "Selling Souls for a Thirty Share," p. 44.
43. Arbitron ratings, Denver, November 1979, ARB.
44. Daviss, "Man the Minicams," p. 35.
45. Popper, "Selling Souls for a Thirty Share," p. 44.
46. Ken Hoffman, "Researching the News," *Phoenix Gazette,* November 26, 1982, p. E-10.
47. Brochure, "KOOL Skywatch," KOOL Radio, 1970, p. 1, JFM, ASU.
48. Deborah Laake, "It's Gall Right Here," *New Times,* pp. 13–25.
49. Thomas Goldthwaite, "KOOL-TV 'Sky Eye' to join KTAR-TV," *Arizona Republic,* September 2, 1978.
50. Arbitron ratings, Phoenix, February 1978, ARB.
51. Arbitron ratings, Phoenix, July 1981, ARB.
52. "Action News," KPNX-TV, May 26, 1979, ASUV.
53. "Brushfire," 1979; and "Salt River Flood," 1980, in "Action News," KPNX-TV, ASUV; "Flying High A Way of Life," *Gannetteer,* June 1983, pp. 8–9.
54. "It was September 14," KPNX ad, *TV Guide,* October 12, 1979, p. E-17.
55. "Jerry Foster and Sky 12," promotion, KPNX-TV, 1979, ASUV.
56. "The Eagle and the Hawk," promotion, KTAR-TV, 1979, ASUV.
57. "Reagan honors pilot Jerry Foster," *Mesa Tribune,* December 8, 1982, p. B5.
58. Sam Lowe, "Flying His Beat—From Canyons to Floods," *TV Guide,* December 1, 1979, pp. 45–47; Michael Levin, "Rising Above the News," *TV Guide,* September 6, 1980, pp. 6–8; "Real People," NBC, December 9, 1983, ASUV.
59. "Action News," KPNX-TV, 1979, ASUV.
60. "Workshops and Panel Discussions Range Widely, Emphasize Futurism," *RTNDA Communicator,* October 1979, pp. 14–15.
61. Stone, "Radio-Television News Directors and Operations," pp. 5–12, and "ENG Growth Documented," p. 5.
62. Jonathan Kaufman, "TV Stations Raise Coverage of News To a Higher Level," *Wall Street Journal,* April 11, 1980, pp. 1, 37.
63. Betsey Carter, "Minicam Revolution," *Newsweek,* July 19, 1976, p. 57.
64. "Television Trends," May 1977, McHugh & Hoffman, Inc., pp. 18–28, MHI.
65. Boston report, August 24, 1977, pp. 388–390, MHI.
66. Transcript, Walter Cronkite speech, Los Angeles, May 5, 1976, CBS.

Chapter 10

1. "Major Study of Viewer Attitudes," *Television/Radio Age,* June 20, 1977, pp. 30–31, 56–58; and "Coming Age of the TV Viewer," *Broadcasting,* June 6, 1977, p. 35. Additional components of the Trendex study appear in "Television Trends," McHugh & Hoffman, Inc., May 1977, pp. 16, 19–20, 26, MHI.

2. "'Happy Talk' or 'Humanizing' News Is Question," RTNDA Newsletter, December 1, 1972, p. 2.

3. T. Linn to RTNDA board, August 1, 1973, Box 71, RTNDA.

4. "Williams, Prato Argue Value of Research Firms For News," RTNDA Newsletter, October 12, 1973, p. 2.

5. Prato interview with author.

6. Minutes, Board of Directors meeting, October 13, 1973, Box 71, RTNDA.

7. B. Johnson to R. Yoakam, November 21, 1973, Box 71, RTNDA.

8. Yoakam interview with author.

9. Miller interview with author.

10. B. Johnson to R. Townley, November 12, 1973, Box 72, RTNDA.

11. Jack Anderson, "Channel 4, Renick Flee Era of Franchise News," *Miami Herald*, October 14, 1974, p. 17.

12. Johnson interview with author.

13. Meeting notes, RTNDA Board of Directors meeting, June 1, 1974, LPM, ASU.

14. LeRoy interview with author.

15. Leslie Fuller, "News doctors: taking over TV journalism?" *Broadcasting*, September 9, 1974, p. 22.

16. "NAB Panel Weighs News Consultants," *Variety*, March 20, 1974, pp. 34, 54.

17. Minutes, Board of Directors Meeting, June 8, 1974, Box 72, RTNDA.

18. Miller interview with author.

19. Godfrey interview with author.

20. "Consultant Debate Continues," RTNDA Newsletter, September 14, 1974, p. 2.

21. Report of the Consultants Committee, September 10, 1974, Box 72, RTNDA.

22. Message of the President, *RTNDA Communicator*, July 1974, p. 8.

23. Minutes, Board of Directors Meetings, September 10, 14, 1974, Box 72, RTNDA.

24. Renick, RTNDOH, pp. 9–10.

25. Joseph Morgenstern, "Cheer Leaders," *Newsweek*, January 4, 1971, p. 9; "Happy Talk," *Newsweek*, February 28, 1972, pp. 46, 51.

26. "Happy News," *Time*, February 8, 1971, p. 65; John Leonard, "There's bad news tonight," *Life*, February 5, 1971, pp. 12–13.

27. Paul Klein, "Happy Talk, Happy Profits," *New York*, June 28, 1971, pp. 60–61; Townley, "Put the Newsman Back in News," pp. 30–35.

28. Dan Menaker, "Unfortunately, Rain Drops Keep Falling on Their Heads," *New York Times*, August 19, 1973, pp. 15, 20.

29. John J. O'Connor, "TV: Frequently It's Those Little Things," *New York Times*, June 18, 1972, p. 91.

30. Barrett, "Folksy TV News," pp. 17–20.

31. Townley, "The News Merchants," pp. 6, 11.

32. Czerniejewski-Long, "Local Television News in 31 Flavors," pp. 10, 21, 26–28.

33. John J. O'Connor, "Battle Behind News," *New York Times*, March 8, 1974, p. 67.

34. Deeb interview with author.

35. Gary Deeb, "Ch. 7 news act is a soft shoe," *Chicago Tribune*, March 26, 1974, p. 10.

36. Gary Deeb, "TV news brings out the fluff," *Chicago Tribune*, February 18, 1976, p. 12.

37. Eric Sevareid commentary, "CBS Evening News," CBS-TV, April 22, 1974, VAV.

38. "Local News: The Rating War," CBS-TV, March 10, 1974, ASUV.

39. "Salant meets critics head-on," *Broadcasting*, May 20, 1974, p. 53.

40. Gary Deeb, "At ABC, net's set for happy-talk," *Chicago Tribune*, February 4, 1976, p. 10.

41. "Local television's best foot forward," *Broadcasting*, January 5, 1976, p. 85.

42. Transcript, Charles Kuralt speech, Dallas, September 18, 1975, Box 75, RTNDA.

43. John Carmody, "In a High-Risk Profession: The Image Shapers of TV Journalism," *Washington Post*, February 10, 1977, pp. D1, D10.

44. Steinmetz, "Mr. Magic," p. 25.

45. Joseph Lelyveld, "Consultant Helps TV Decide What's News," *New York Times,* December 25, 1975, p. 1.
46. Diamond, *The Tin Kazoo,* pp. 91, 94.
47. Barrett, *Moments of Truth?,* pp. 89–90.
48. Daniel Henninger, "Doctoring the Evening News," *National Observer,* February 17, 1976.
49. "University of Colorado, KWGN Host Successful Regional," *RTNDA Communicator,* August 1975, p. 4.
50. Robert Scheer, "The Selling of TV Local News Shows," *Los Angeles Times,* June 6, 1977, p. I–3.
51. Thomas Griffith, "Happy Is Bad, Heavy Isn't Good," *Time,* May 17, 1976, p. 79.
52. Karen Garloch, "John Chancellor Says News Doctors Missing the Point," *Cincinnati Enquirer,* June 3, 1978, p. D-3.
53. Len Butcher, "Interview With Richard Salant," *Las Vegas Sun,* September 7, 1979, p. 3.
54. "Keep Show Biz Out of News, Leonard Warns," *Variety,* April 30, 1975, p. 41.
55. Transcript, Walter Cronkite speech, Los Angeles, May 5, 1976, CBS.
56. Walter Cronkite speech, Bal Harbour, Fla., December 13, 1976, Box 89, RTNDAV.
57. Report of the Consultants Committee, December 12, 1976, Box 77, RTNDA.
58. Miller interview with author.
59. C. L. Dancey, "Walter Changes His Tune," *Peoria Journal Star,* December 17, 1976, p. 6.
60. Harry F. Waters, "Dan Rather, Anchor Man," *Newsweek,* February 25, 1980, pp. 71–72.
61. LeRoy interview with author.
62. Wallace interview with author.
63. Frank Magid interview with author.
64. Prato interview with author.
65. Corr, *KING,* p. 198.
66. Edmund Rosenthal, "Two thirds of stations oppose longer web news," *Television/Radio Age,* October 25, 1976, pp. 29–31, 60.

Chapter 11

1. Byrne, "If you're so good," p. 134.
2. Popper, "Selling Souls," p. 42; Landess interview with author.
3. "Reasons for Watching the Early and Late News," Selection Research, Inc., October 1984, pp. 6–7, ASU.
4. George interview with author.
5. "Changing with change," *Broadcasting,* December 4, 1972, p. 69.
6. Willis P. Duff, *Talk Radio Handbook,* 1969, p. 9, ARD.
7. "Oh, look at us now," WBBM-TV ad, *Chicago Tribune,* November 14, 1971, p. 20.
8. Crane interview with author.
9. See Elliot McGinnies, "Emotionality and Perceptual Defense," *Psychological Review* 61 (1954): 194–204; Lester Luborsky, Burton Blinder, and Jean Schimek, "Looking, Recalling and GSR as a Function of Defense," *Journal of Abnormal Psychology* 70 (1965): 270–289; Lewis Donohew and John R. Baseheart, "Information Selection Processes and Galvanic Skin Response," *Journalism Quarterly* 51 (1974): 33–39; and J. D. Snoek and Marian F. Dobbs, "Galvanic Skin Responses to Agreement and Disagreement in Relation to Dogmatism," *Psychological Reports* 20 (1976): 195–198.
10. San Francisco report, Electronic Response Analysts, March 3, 1976, pp. 2–4, 7–8, ARD.
11. D. Thomas Miller letter, *TV Guide,* April 16, 1977, p. 8.
12. Barbara Zuanich, "New Era of News at KNXT," *Los Angeles Herald-Examiner,* July 20, 1975, p. 20.
13. James Brown, "KNXT Firings: Is Bad News Good News for Viewers?", *Los Angeles Times,* June 28, 1976, pp. 1, 21–22.
14. "AFTRA deplores audience tests," *Broadcasting,* July 19, 1976, p. 41.
15. "Applegate to Sue CBS," *Hollywood Reporter,* June 30, 1976, p. 1.
16. Emory interview with author; Pete Rahn, "Cronkite got 'bum rap' on

radio's Emory yarn," *St. Louis Globe-Democrat,* July 5, 1976, p. 14.

17. Applegate interview with author.
18. Cronkite interview with author.
19. Chagall, "Only As Good As His Skin Tests," p. 8.
20. Deeb, "Skin tests 'make' the news," p. 2 and "It's the press 1, technology 0," p. 16.
21. "TV News Skin Test Consulting," Bal Harbour, Fla., December 14, 1976, Box 89, RTNDAV.
22. *ASI All Media Center,* AR&D, Inc., July 1995, p. 5, ARD.
23. Horton-Wohl, "Mass Communication and Para-Social Interaction," pp. 215, 221–223.
24. Magid report, June 1983, p. 52, FMI.
25. Talent Perception Factors, National Normative Data Base, October 1995, ARD.
26. Questionnaire, KPR Associates for McHugh & Hoffman, 1987, ASU.
27. Indianapolis report, September 1974, pp. 49, 109, MHI.
28. Baltimore report, July 6, 1977, p. 49, MHI.
29. Los Angeles report, March 16, 1978, p. 122, MHI.
30. Seattle report, February 6, 1973, p. 6; and Seattle report, May 24, 1977, p. 36, both MHI.
31. Los Angeles report, March 16, 1978, pp. 32–34, MHI.
32. Dick Adler, "Dunphy: 'Not Coming Back,'" *Los Angeles Times,* July 2, 1975, p. 17; "Dunphy's KNXT-it to KABC," *Variety,* July 9, 1975, p. 49, 56; John Carnay, "KABC Declares All-Out War on TV News," *Hollywood Reporter,* p. 1.
33. Dunphy interview with author.
34. O'Leary and Fyffe interviews with author.
35. Arbitron ratings, Los Angeles, November 1975, ARB.
36. "Eyewitness News," KABC-TV, November 1, 1975, UCLAV.
37. Arbitron ratings, Los Angeles, November 1978, ARB.
38. Sauter interview with author.
39. Hillman interview with author.
40. "Survey Shows Dunphy Best-Liked Anchor," *Hollywood Reporter,* June 30, 1976, pp. 1, 10.

41. Chagall, "Only As Good As His Skin Tests," p. 10.
42. Byrne, "If you're so good," p. 134.
43. Kitman, "Another Day, Another Million," pp. 39–42, 58.
44. P. McHugh to R. Guy, November 6, 1963, MHI.
45. Contact report, P. McHugh and Storer managers, March 22, 1965, MHI.
46. G. Hintz to W. Michaels, May 7, 1965, MHI.
47. Steinmetz, "Mr. Magic," p. 2–25.
48. J. Bowen to P. Boyer and J. Topping, November 20, 1979, MHI.
49. Don Fitzpatrick Associates ad, *RTNDA Communicator,* February 1987, p. 22.
50. "AR&D 1995 Research and Consulting Proposal," July 1995, p. 16, ARD.
51. "Looking for work in television," Frank N. Magid Associates, Inc., undated, FMA.
52. Bock, "Smile More," pp. 107, 141–143.
53. Kansas City report, August 1980, pp. 20–21, ARD.
54. Notes on Model Audience Probe Session, May 19, 1981, ASU.
55. Kansas City report, June 26, 1981, p. 4, ARD.
56. Barry Garron, "KMBC's co-anchor a casualty of public whim," *Kansas City Star,* August 17, 1981, p. 2B.
57. Craft v. Metromedia, Inc., 572 F. Supp. 868 (W.D. Mo. 1983).
58. "Cosmetic News," *The Nation,* August 20–27, 1983, pp. 132–133.
59. Sally Bedell Smith, "TV Newswoman's Suit Stirs A Debate on Values in Hiring," *New York Times,* August 6, 1983, pp. 1, 44.
60. Christine Craft v. Metromedia, Inc., No. 83-0007-CV-W-8, W. D. Mo., October 31, 1983, p. 18; and No. 84-1336, 1380, 8th Cir., June 28, 1985, p. 11.
61. Craft v. Metromedia, Inc., 572 F. Supp. 868, at 874 (W.D. Mo. 1983).
62. Haines v. Knight-Ridder Broadcasting, Inc., 32 FEP Cases 1116, D. R. I., July 3, 1980.
63. Christine Craft v. Metromedia, Inc., No. 84-1336, 1380, 8th Cir., June 28, 1985.

64. Craft, *An Anchorwoman's Story,* pp. 10, 38, 219.
65. Popper, "Inside TV News," p. 66.
66. Craft interview with author.
67. "Jim Hale Charges TV8 With Libel," *Cleveland Plain-Dealer,* June 23, 1978, p. 5.
68. "Eyewitness News," WBZ-TV, September 16–17, 1983, ASUV.
69. Grimsby interview with author.
70. Fyffe interview with author.
71. Stone, "Personal Problems," pp. 66–68, 100, 102.
72. "Jim Jensen: A Profile in Survival," WCBS-TV, February 13–16, 1990.
73. See Tim Kiska, "Fired Anchor Bonds Vows to Return to TV—Absolutely," *Detroit News,* January 12, 1995, p. 1; and "Bonds Gets the Boot," *Detroit Free Press,* January 12, 1995, p. 1.
74. Mike Antonucci, "Anchored in Despair," *San Jose Mercury News,* December 6, 1995.
75. "Anchorwoman overcomes darkness of depression," *Tempe Daily News Tribune,* October 7, 1993, pp. 1, 4.
76. Stone, "TV News Pay," pp. 12–13.
77. Stone, "TV Journalists."
78. "Viewing Habits," National Normative Data Base, July 1994; "AR&D 1995 Research and Consulting Proposal," July 1995, ARD, p. 27, both ARD.
79. Willi interview with author.
80. Enersen interview with author.
81. Beutel interview with author.

Chapter 12

1. Kaniss, *Making Local News,* pp. 101, 111–123.
2. Fang, *Television News,* pp. 147–160.
3. Seattle report, August 1968, pp. 71–80, FMA.
4. "Continuing Trends in Television," Social Research, Inc., and McHugh & Hoffman, Inc., February 26, 1963, pp. 94–95, MHI.
5. New York City report, March 6, 1969, p. 155, MHI.
6. New York City report, February 1970, p. 149, MHI.
7. *The Challenge of Change,* McHugh & Hoffman, Inc., April 1983, pp. 248, 260–261, 271–272, MHI.
8. "Continuing Trends," McHugh & Hoffman, Inc., September 1990, p. 3, MHI.
9. Empire report, August 1979, p. 21, FMA.
10. Frank Magid interview with author.
11. Taylor interview with author.
12. Shook, *Television Field Production and Reporting,* pp. 7–8.
13. "Television Trends," McHugh & Hoffman, Inc., May 1977, p. 39, MHI.
14. "Sex and Violence on Television: Viewer Reaction," McHugh & Hoffman, Inc., September 12, 1969, p. 10, MHI.
15. *The Challenge of Change,* McHugh & Hoffman, Inc., April 1983, pp. 291, 315–316, MHI.
16. "Crime and Violence," National Normative Data Base, July 1994, ARD.
17. Audiotape, Columbus research presentation, Jim Willi file, October 10, 1995, ARD.
18. "Television Trends," McHugh & Hoffman, Inc., May 1977, p. 37, MHI.
19. "News Viewer Topology Based On Early and Late Evening Local Newscast Fans," KPR, Inc., and McHugh & Hoffman, Inc., July 1985, p. 13, MHI.
20. "Sex and Violence on Television: Viewer Reaction," McHugh & Hoffman, Inc., September 12, 1969, p. 17, MHI.
21. J. Willi to clients, "Family Sensitive Newscasts," October, 1994, ARD.
22. *The Challenge of Change,* McHugh & Hoffman, Inc., April 1983, pp. 297–301, MHI.
23. McLuhan, *Sharing the News,* p. 28.
24. "News Content," National Normative Data Base, 1989, ARD.
25. "Continuing Trends," McHugh & Hoffman, Inc., September 1990, pp. 1–3, MHI.
26. Detroit report, April 28, 1977, p. 198; Seattle report, May 24, 1977, p. 38; Atlanta report, January 24,

294   Notes

1975, p. 29; Indianapolis report, September 1974, p. 24, MHI.
27. "Business Concepts," McHugh & Hoffman, Inc., undated, p. 11, MHI.
28. Kaniss, *Making Local News,* p. 123.
29. "Magid Institute," Frank. N. Magid Associates, 1996, p. 1, FMA.
30. Cremer, Phillip O. Keirstead, and Richard D. Yoakam, *ENG Television News.*
31. Frank Magid interview with author.
32. *Group W Policy Manual,* Part 5, pp. 77–78, April 1976, WBC.
33. *Action3News Production Manual,* WKYC-TV, 1980, pp. 1–10.
34. *The Total News Format,* KMBC-TV, December 12, 1979, pp. 3–8.
35. *KCTV5 News Stylebook and Operations Manual,* KCTV, January 1985, pp. 2, 5, 29, 32.
36. "Eyewitness News," KTRK-TV, July 23–27, 1973, KTRKV; King, "The Best Little Whorehouse in Texas," pp. 130–132, 219–226.
37. "Eyewitness News," KTRK-TV, January 4, 7–11, 1985, KTRKV.
38. Zindler interview with author.
39. Neil Hickey, "David Brinkley debunks some of journalism's most sacred dogmas," *TV Guide,* December 8, 1979, pp. 4–8.
40. "Willowbrook: The Last Great Disgrace," WABC-TV, February 2, 1972.
41. Minneapolis-St. Paul report, February 29, 1972, p. 9, MHI.
42. *The Elements of a Television Newscast,* McHugh & Hoffman, Inc., September 1971, p. 27, MHI.
43. Rivera, *Exposing Myself,* pp. 237–239; New York City report, August 25, 1972, pp. 14, 30, MHI.
44. Empire report, August 1979, p. 21, FMA.
45. "KSL-TV Takes The Big One," *RTNDA Communicator,* September 1982, p. 8; Gale interview with author.
46. "Joe Carcione Is Eleven," Mighty Minute Programs ad, *RTNDA Communicator,* September 1985, p. 51.
47. Gilbride interview with author.
48. "Continuing Trends in Television," Social Research, Inc., and McHugh

& Hoffman, Inc., March 1964, pp. 87, 90, MHI.
49. New York City report, February 28, 1975, p. 15, MHI.
50. "Natural Childbirth," November 1973, KYW-TV, ICV.
51. "Rape: The Ultimate Violation," February 1974, KYW-TV, ICV.
52. "Philadelphians in Hollywood," November 1975, KYW-TV, ICV.
53. "Truckers and Truck Stops," in "Joel Daly Years to Remember," August 1987, WLS-TV, WLSV; Gary Deeb, "TV news brings out the fluff," *Chicago Tribune,* February 18, 1976, p. 12.
54. San Francisco report, January 1980, p. 14; Standing Recommendations, February 10, 1981, p. 32, both ARD.
55. Chicago report, February 10, 1978, p. 45, MHI.
56. New York City report, June 6, 1979, p. 40, MHI.
57. "NIWS: The Content Cooperative," Lorimar ad, *RTNDA Communicator,* May 1984, pp. 20–21.
58. Smith, "Mythic Elements in Television News," pp. 75–76; Harmon, "Mr. Gates Goes Electronic," p. 860; and Harmon, "Consultants and Gatekeepers," Broadcast Education Association, 1994.
59. "Phoenix Topical Reports, November 1995," Arizona State University, January 1996.
60. "Smith and Muse," KRMA-TV, 1982, CHS.
61. Hood interview with author.
62. Stone, "Journalists," Freedom Forum, p. 3; Bob Papper, Andrew Sharma, and Michael Gerhard, "Salaries Moving Up," *RTNDA Communicator,* February 1996, pp. 16–23.

Chapter 13

1. *NAS Presents,* ABC News Advisory Service, 1979, p. 2, ABCNAS, ASU.
2. "Local news audience leaders," and "Network news audience leaders

locally," *Television/Radio Age,*
October 1, 1973, pp. 63, 65.
3. "ABC To Offer Affils News
   Advisory Service," Newsletter,
   December 1976, pp. 1–4, ABCNAS,
   ASU.
4. O'Leary interview with author.
5. "Primo Exits ABC News in a Huff,"
   Variety, June 16, 1976, pp. 33, 48.
6. Rivera, *Exposing Myself,* p. 136.
7. "Seminar Talks Cover Writing to
   Ratings" and "Ittleson Heads News
   Advisory Service," Newsletter,
   March 1977, ABCNAS, ASU.
8. Ittleson interview with author.
9. Transcript, Nick Archer speech,
   Chicago, January 9, 1975,
   ABCNAS, ASU.
10. *Hints on News Promotion,* ABC
    Promotion Board, 1980, ABCNAS,
    ASU.
11. *NAS Presents,* p. 10; "News
    Advisory Closed Circuit,"
    Newsletter, April 1982, p. 3,
    ABCNAS, ASU.
12. "ABC News Advisory Service
    Affiliate News Promotions," 1979,
    PROMV.
13. "Regional Workshops," Newsletter,
    April 1981, p. 3, ABCNAS, ASU.
14. "What Is A Leader?", Chicago
    workshops, August 27, 1980,
    ABCNAS, ASU.
15. Memorandum, ABC to Los Angeles
    attendees, August 1, 1980,
    ABCNAS, ASU.
16. Ittleson interview with author.
17. *NAS Presents,* pp. 1–2.
18. Rathbone interview with author.
19. John Coleman, "Everybody Talks
    About the Weather," September
    1978, p. 4; and "Weather and Local
    News," October 1981, p. 2;
    Newsletters, ABCNAS, ASU.
20. Jacques Minnotte, "Sports and
    Local News," Newsletter, January
    1982, p. 4; and *NAS Presents,*
    pp. 8–9, ABCNAS, ASU.
21. Jon Beacher, "Positioning Your
    Newscast, Newsletter, July 1981,
    p. 1, ABCNAS, ASU.
22. *NAS Presents,* pp. 6–9.
23. *News Writing Guidelines,* ABC
    Owned Stations, 1982, pp. 7, 13,
    126, ABCNAS, ASU.
24. Jacobus interview with author.
25. Jim Riordan, "KOAT Wins On
    Conversion," Newsletter, January

1979, pp. 1–2, ABCNAS,
ASU.
26. Bill Tell Zortman, "KVII-TV Uses
    70 Stringers in 4 States," Newsletter,
    January 1979, pp. 1, 4, ABCNAS,
    ASU.
27. Rich Gimmel, "Re Loss of Talent,"
    Newsletter, December 1977, p. 4,
    ABCNAS, ASU.
28. Dick Williams, "Shakeup Ups
    Ratings At WXIA," Newsletter,
    February 1978, p. 3, ABCNAS,
    ASU.
29. Paul Wischmeyer, "KTVI Scores Big
    In News Ratings," Newsletter,
    January 1982, p. 1, ABCNAS, ASU.
30. Ed Zander, "How To Win In a
    Small Market," Newsletter, October
    1981, pp. 3–4, ABCNAS, ASU.
31. "TV Station Shares,"
    Television/Radio Age, August 1,
    1983, pp. 24, 55–63.
32. "Networks and Affiliates: The
    Relationship," AR&D, Inc.,
    pp. 14–15, ARD.
33. Rathbone interview with author.
34. David Lieberman, "Rhetoric Vs.
    Real Issues in Network News
    Cutbacks," *Business Week,* March
    30, 1987, p. 33.
35. Mark Harrison, "Save CBS,"
    Entertainment Weekly, March 9,
    1990, pp. 32–39.
36. "Welcome to the Rustbelt," *The
    New Republic,* March 30, 1987,
    pp. 4, 41–42.
37. "CBS Evening News," CBS-TV,
    January 25, 1988, VAV.
38. "NBC Nightly News," NBC-TV,
    January 19, 1993, VAV.
39. Lawrie Mifflin, "NBC Pays to Avert
    a Suit," *New York Times,* December
    10, 1996, p. 16.
40. Patrick Mott, "New king of the
    hill," *The Quill,* pp. 14–16.
41. Hal Boedeker, "Dateline Diluted by
    Gimmicks," *Orlando Sentinel,*
    August 10, 1997.
42. Howard Kurtz, "Does the
    Evening News Still Matter?" *TV
    Guide,* October 12, 1996, pp.
    20–23.
43. Dan Rottenberg, "And That's the
    Way It Is," *American Journalism
    Review,* May 1994, pp. 34–37;
    "Taking CBS to Task," *Newsweek,*
    September 15, 1986, p. 53.

44. Reuven Frank, "Localizing Network News," *The New Leader,* September 20, 1993, pp. 20–21.
45. Edwin Diamond, "Shrinking the News," *New York,* May 27, 1991, pp. 20–22.
46. "Local TV News Census," Nielsen Media Research, Inc., November 1992. See Geoffrey Folsie, "Ratings Up in Top 25 Markets," November 2, 1992, pp. 30–32; and Folsie, "Top Markets See Ratings Rise," November 9, 1992, pp. 34–35, both in *Broadcasting.*
47. Willi interview with author.
48. *Hints on News Promotion,* ABC Promotion Board, 1980, ABCNAS, ASU.
49. "News Consultants," Newsletter, April 1981, p. 2, ABCNAS, ASU.
50. "Research: The Local And Network Relationship," Newsletter, January 1982, p. 1, ABCNAS, ASU.
51. Butler, "Consulting Firms and Stations," pp. 22–24.
52. Reymer interview with author.
53. Willi interview with author.
54. "Welcome to AR&D," AR&D, Inc., July 1993, ARD.
55. Jacobus interview with author.
56. "Future Trends in Broadcast Journalism," Frank N. Magid Associates, Inc., October 1984, p. 6, Box 129, RTNDA.

Chapter 14

1. "Frank N. Magid Associates, Inc.: Publishing Clients," March 1990, FMA.
2. Willis Duff, "Research for the 100-Plus Station Operator," January 1987, pp. 2–3, ARD; and *Small Market Television Manager's Guide,* National Association of Broadcasters, 1987.
3. "How We Came To Be," Frank N. Magid Associates, Inc., July 1995, p. I-9, FMA.
4. Audrey Howe Report, Frank N. Magid Associates, Inc., September 20, 1995, FMA.
5. Howe interview with author.

6. Weekly In-field Report, AR&D, Inc., October 9, 1995, ARD.
7. 1994 Annual In-Field Summary, AR&D, Inc., January 1995, ARD.
8. *Dun's Directory of Service Companies 1991,* pp. 95, 200; Butler, "Consulting firms and Stations," pp. 22–24.
9. "Future Trends in Broadcast Journalism," Frank N. Magid Associates, Inc., October 1984, pp. 4–6, FMA.
10. "The Forgotten Ten Percent," McHugh & Hoffman, Inc., March 11, 1985, p. 1, MHI.
11. Willi interview with author.
12. Eileen Norris, "Consultants tackle TV stations' main mistakes," *Electronic Media,* June 8, 1987, p. M1.
13. Barry Garron, "TV news consultants decry frills," *Kansas City Star,* January 21, 1988, p. 20.
14. News Consultant Image Study, KPR Research, May 1986, p. 17, ASU.
15. McLuhan, *Sharing the News,* pp. 10–11.
16. "Der Tag," 1A, February 3, 1995, ASUV.
17. De Suze interview with author.
18. "CityPulse," City TV, June 7, 1993, ASUV.
19. Karen Murray, "Budget-wise CITY-TV Tops in Toronto's 6 p.m. News," *Variety,* February 11, 1991, p. 54.
20. "Znaimer on City TV," City TV, 1995, ASUV.
21. George interview with author.
22. Home Office, U.K., *Broadcasting in the '90s: Competition, Choice, and Quality,* (London: Her Majesty's Stationery Office, 1988).
23. "Frank N. Magid Associates, Inc.: International Clients," July 1995, FMA.
24. Brent Magid interview with author.
25. "Calendar," Yorkshire TV, January 1993, FMA.
26. Munro interview with author.
27. "Stars without Stripes," *Scotland on Sunday,* January 17, 1993, p. 2.
28. Davidson, *Under the Hammer,* pp. 111–112.
29. Munro interview with author.
30. "News at Ten," ITN, November 9, 1992, FMA; and "ITN renews the

news," *The Times*, November 10, 1992, p. 2.

31. Munro interview with author.
32. Jonathan Miller, "How the news doctors make breakfast more palatable," *Sunday Times*, October 1, 1993.
33. "Stars Without Stripes," *Scotland on Sunday*, January 17, 1993, p. 2.
34. William Rees-Mogg, "Wallpaper evenings on the small screen," *The Times*, September 20, 1993.
35. Roy Greenslade, "Sorry, I missed the point," *The Times*, November 11, 1992, p. 32.
36. Jonathan Miller, "Anchor aweigh," *The Culture*, in *The Sunday Times*, Nov. 22, 1992, p. 23.
37. Brent Magid interview with author.
38. Jermey interview with author.
39. Frank Magid interview with author.
40. Warwick interview with author.
41. Sambrook interview with author.
42. Bewley interview with author.
43. "Tagesschau," ARD-TV and "Heute," ZDF-TV, 1994 and 1995 newscasts, ASUV.
44. Elizabeth Anderson interview with author.
45. "Aktuell," RTL-TV, October 4, 1995, ASUV.
46. Channel 2 Logo compilation, AR&D, 1995, ASUV.
47. "Action News," RTL2-TV, September 28, 1995, ASUV.
48. Reuter interview with author.
49. De Suze interview with author.
50. Robert Frank, "U.S.-styled TV Station is a Hit Among Czechs," *Wall Street Journal*, April 30, 1997, pp. 1, 8–9.
51. "Televizny Noviny," 1994 broadcasts, Nova TV, ASUV.
52. Allen, "American News Values," pp. 16–18.
53. De Suze interview with author.
54. Mitchell interview with author.
55. Mobley interview with author.
56. "Plan for News Writing-Gathering and Video Script Presentation at BOP-TV, Mmabatho, South Africa," Shannon Communications, Inc., Overland Park, Kansas, June 15, 1990.
57. Shannon interview with author.
58. George interview with author.
59. Jim Bawden, "Morning Glory," *Starweek*, October 5, 1994, pp. 4–5; Chris Fuller, "Public Humiliation," *TV World*, April 1993, p. 23.
60. Joe Atkinson, "Hey Martha! The reconstruction of One Network News," *Metro*, April 1994, pp. 94–101.
61. Brent Magid interview with author.
62. Robert Morse interview with author.
63. Fite interview with author.
64. Munro interview with author.
65. Scott Tallal, "Consulting at Gunpoint," *ShopTalk*, May 2, 1995, p. 8.
66. George interview with author.
67. "Ta Nea Toy," Antenna, September 4, 1995, ASUV.
68. Bob Papper and Michael Gerhard, 1999 Newsroom Workforce Survey, RTNDA, 2000.
69. "Local TV News Census," Nielsen Media Research, Inc., New York, N.Y., 1992. See summary in Geoffrey Folsie, "Ratings Up in Top 25 Markets," November 2, 1992; and "Top Markets See Ratings Rise," November 9, 1992, both in *Broadcasting/Cable*.
70. "New life for local TV news," *Broadcasting & Cable*, October 10, 1994, pp. 68–69.
71. Stacy Lane, "Fox's Entrance Into the Newsroom," Arizona State University masters thesis, May 1999.
72. Transcript, Don Imus speech, Washington, D.C., March 21, 1996, ASUV.
73. "TV News Viewership Declines," Pew Research Center, Washington, D.C., May 13, 1996.
74. Bob Papper and Michael Gerhard, "Starting Salaries: A Crying Shame," *RTNDA Communicator*, May 1999.
75. Frank Magid interview with author.

Conclusion

1. Transcripts, Alfred I. duPont Forum, "Declining Standards in News: Is It All Television's Fault," New York City, January 27, 1994, Columbia

University Graduate School of
Journalism, p. 7.
2. New Orleans focus group,
September 9, 1995, ASUV.
3. In this Bullet Poll survey of 1,500
randomly selected respondents from
around the United States, 64 percent
of respondents had additionally
noted they watched local TV news
daily, and 67 percent had a favorite
newscast. Nearly one-half of
African-American and Hispanic
respondents gave local TV news an
"A" in the quality analysis. See
"Viewers give local news high
marks," *Electronic Media,*
September 4, 1995, pp. 1, 29.

4. Stone, "TV Journalists," pp. 1–2.
5. National Demographics and
Lifestyles and SRDS, *The Lifestyle
Market Analyst,* Des Plaines, Ill.,
1995, pp. A-34, A-35.
6. "SES," and "Income," National
Normative Data Base, October
1995, ARD.
7. Galbraith, *Economic Development,*
p. 21.
8. Mike Bass, "Awareness of media
personalities sets Detroit apart,"
Detroit News, September 2, 1983,
p. 5-C.

Interviews

By Author

Doug Adair, Columbus, Ohio, March 23, May 12, September 14, 1994

Guy Adams, Norwich, UK, January 11, 2000

Elizabeth Anderson, Dallas, Texas, September 1, 1997

Steve Antoniotti, Detroit, Mich., June 13, 1995

Bill Applegate, Calabasas, Calif., February 12, 1996

Ken Bagwell, Paradise Valley, Ariz., May 14, 1994

Eddie Barker, Cooper, Tex., September 22, 1994

Tom Battista, Old Greenwich, Conn., October 27, 1997; July 13, 1998; January 15, 1999

Richard Beesemyer, Tucson, Ariz., June 29, 1995

Ray Beindorf, Los Angeles, Calif., October 10, 17, 1994; January 4, 1995

Bob Bennett, Detroit, Mich., May 13, 1995

Ron Bergamo, Phoenix, Ariz., April 15, 1993

Dan Berkery, Tempe, Ariz., October 4, 1996

Bill Beutel, New York, N.Y., March 21, May 8, October 18, December 19, 1995; June 13, 1996; April 15, 1998

Ed Bewley, Dallas, Tex., October 9–10, 1995

Arta Boley, La Junta, Colo., January 28, 1994

Jack Bowen, McLean, Va., July 6–7, 1993; June 12–13, 1994; Las Vegas, Nev., March 17, 1994; Southfield, Mich., May 15, August 17, 1995; Phoenix, Ariz., February 6, 1998; September 1, 1999

Eric Bremner, Seattle, Wash., September 15, 1994

Jack Capell, Portland, Ore., December 5, 1994

Igor Chernishov, Kiev, Ukraine, April 23, 1999

Doug Clemensen, Fairfield, Conn., October 1–2, 1994

Richard P. Coleman, Manhattan, Kan., April 5, 1996

Sandra Connell, Dallas, Tex., October 10, 1995; July 15, 1996

Pep Cooney, Phoenix, Ariz., October 4, 1997

John Corporon, New York, N.Y., August 18, 1994

David Crane, Orlando, Fla., September 18, 1995

Christine Craft, Sacramento, Calif., September 21, 1995

Dallas Cronk, Wichita, Kan., December 9, 1994

Walter Cronkite, Phoenix, Ariz., November 16, 1994

Joel Daly, Chicago, Ill., August 5, September 17, November 13, December 5, 1994; May 8, July 13, 1995; July 30, 1997; September 1, 1998

Jefferson Davis, Cedar Rapids, Iowa, September 22, 1994; Phoenix, Ariz., March 2, 1995

Mike Davis, Ardmore, Pa., December 20, 1994; February 6, 1995

Gary Deeb, Chicago, Ill., March 1, 20, 1995

Neil Derrough, Tempe, Ariz., April 18, 1994

Jacques De Suze, Washington, D.C., August 9, 1995; March 15, 1997; November 1, 1999

Tom Dolan, Chicago, Ill., August 1, 1997

Willis Duff, Dallas, Tex., July 26, 1993

Chris Duffy, Indianapolis, Ind., September 8, 1994

Jerry Dunphy, Los Angeles, Calif., May 12, July 7, 1994

Mike Early, New Orleans, La., October 1, 1994

Douglas Edwards, Sarasota, Fla., August 29, 1988

Patrick Emory, St. Petersburg, Fla., April 10, 17, 1996; May 1, 1997

Jean Enersen, Seattle, Wash., February 2, 9, 1996

Tate Fite, Moscow, Russia, April 26–27, 1999

Jerry Florence, Dallas, Tex., July 26, 1993

Mary Flynn, Chicago, Ill., September 13, 1995

Jerry Foster, Mesa, Ariz., January 23, 1996

Bill Fyffe, La Quinta, Calif., September 21, 1995

Don Gale, Salt Lake City, Utah, October 8, 1993

Lynn Gartley, Dallas, Tex., October 9, 1995

Joe George, Marion, Iowa, July 10, August 21, 1995; March 25, 1998; October 6, 1999

Walter Gilbride, Boston, Mass., February 20, 1995

Ira Glick, Chicago, Ill., September 1, 1994

Ed Godfrey, Louisville, Ky., September 7, December 13, 1994; February 27, March 14, 1995

Roger Grimsby, New York, N.Y., May 8–9, December 6, 1994; February 6, 1995

Peter Groome, London, UK, January 12, 2000

Marion Gruntman, Berlin, Germany, December 12, 1995

Al Ham, Huntington, Conn., June 17, 1996

Lee Hanna, Sandisfield, Mass., February 10, 1994

John Haralson, Denver, Colo., September 6, 1994

Naida Helm, Marion, Iowa, July 10, 1995

Lorraine Hillman, Los Angeles, Calif., October 7, 1994

Peter Hoffman, McLean, Va., June 7, August 13, 19, 1994

Lee Hood, Washington, D.C., August 11, 1995

Audrey Howe, Marion, Iowa, September 12, 19, 1995

Steve Hurlbut, Toronto, Ont., June 3, 1997

Al Ittleson, San Diego, Calif., January 24, February 7, 1995; February 1, 1997

Peter Jacobus, San Diego, Calif., October 8, 1990

David Jennings, Norwich, UK, January 11, 2000

Michael Jermey, London, UK, January 10, 2000

Bos Johnson, Huntington, W.Va., April 17, 1995

Earl Kahn, Scottsdale, Ariz., March 14, 1994

Karen Kammer, Chicago, Ill., October 4, 1995

Mel Kampmann, Washington, D.C., October 10, November 15, 1994

Larry Kane, Philadelphia, Pa., September 16, October 23, 1994; April 20, 1997

Nigel Kay, London, UK, January 12, 2000

Cindy Keeler, Hume, Va., September 14, 1994

John Kelly, Detroit, Mich., June 19, 1995

Robert Kelly, Tacoma, Wash., January 9, 1996
Tom Kirby, New York, N.Y., September 7, 1994
Bert Kleinman, Pacific Palisades, Calif., July 11, 1999
George Koehler, Pilesgrove, N.J., January 30, August 10, 1995
Tom Kounelis, Moscow, Russia, April 27–29, 1999
Charles Kuralt, Tempe, Ariz., November 21, 1996
Bill Kurtis, Chicago, Ill., November 10, 1994
Mike Landess, Atlanta, Ga., April 9, 24, 1996
Jeff Lehrer, Moscow, Russia, April 29, 2000
Vince Leonard, Las Vegas, Nev., November 8, 1995
David LeRoy, Tucson, Ariz., March 27, 1995
Ed Lewis, Phoenix, Ariz., July 20, 1995
Walter Liss, Phoenix, Ariz., July 8, 1996
Victor Litenko, Moscow, Russia, April 28–29, 1999
Elmer Lower, Tempe, Ariz., January 26, 1994
Brent Magid, London, UK, September 19, 21, 1995
Frank Magid, Marion, Iowa, June 15–16, 1993; March 30, April 20, 1994; July 10, July 12, 1995; May 1, 3, 1996; Santa Barbara, Calif., March 14, 1994; April 25, 1996
Harvey Mars, Atlanta, Ga., September 7, 1994
Eugene McCurdy, Doylestown, Pa., October 18, 1994
Peter Menkus, New York, N.Y., February 17, 1995
Ray Miller, Houston, Tex., July 18–19, 1994; February 21, 27, 1995
Winstron Mitchell, Las Vegas, Nev., April 7, 1998
Arthur Mobley, Phoenix, Ariz., June 7, 1999
Bob Morse, Washington, D.C., June 15, 1994; Louisville, Ky., September 16, 1994
Charles Munro, Marion, Iowa, July 13, September 5, October 11, 1995
Bob Nelson, Los Angeles, Calif., October 10, 17, 1994; January 4, 1995

Phil Nye, Bakersfield, Calif., June 30, 1995; New Orleans, La., March 1, 1996
Richard O'Leary, Rancho Santa Fe, Calif., August 2, 4, 1994; September 1, 1995
Peter O'Neill, Toronto, Ont., June 5, 1997
Natalia Osychuk, Moscow, Russia, April 29, 1999
David Percelay, Santa Monica, Calif., April 28, 1996
Roman Petrenko, Moscow, Russia, April 27–28, 1999
Diego Planas, Lima, Peru, February 15, 1999
Leavitt Pope, New York, N.Y., September 30, 1994
Ron Powers, Middlebury, Vt., March 2, 1995
Lou Prato, Washington, D.C., March 27, August 11, 1995
Bob Priddy, Jefferson City, Mo., March 17, 1995
Al Primo, Old Greenwich, Conn., June 20, July 21, September 13, 1994; Tempe, Ariz., February 27, 1995; July 20, 1998
George Putnam, Glendale, Calif., December 20, 1994; Burbank, Calif., January 4, 1995
Bill Quarton, Cedar Rapids, Iowa, August 26, 1994
Bryce Rathbone, New York, N.Y., August 14, 1990
John Renelagh, London, January 11, 2000
Arnold Reymer, Detroit, Mich., February 28, 1993; June 2, 1995
Vic Reuter, Luxembourg, Lux, January 31, 1997
Larry Rickel, San Antonio, Tex., September 19, 1990; February 3, 1993
George Rodman, Carmel, Calif., January 17, March 5, 1995
Richard Ross, Portland, Ore., March 3, 1995
Mort Sahl, Burbank, Calif., January 4, 1995
Milana Saigina, Moscow, Russia, April 27, 1999
Joe Saita, Washington, D.C., December 28, 1993
Richard Sambrook, London, UK, January 10, 2000

Van Gordon Sauter, Tempe, Ariz., March 25, 1996
Rose Ann Scamardella, Salisbury, Conn., August 8, 1996
Al Schottelkotte, Cincinnati, Ohio, July 18, 1994
Ernie Schultz, Washington, D.C., July 18, 1994
Ridge Shannon, Shawnee Mission, Kan., September 7, 14, 1994; July 18, 1995
Steve Skinner, Los Angeles, Calif., September 14, 1994
Pat Stockwell, Kansas City, Mo., August 2, 1995
Leigh Stowell, Seattle, Wash., September 9, 1993; September 14, 1994
Harry Sweet, Sacramento, Calif., January 9, 1996
Bill Swing, Portland, Ore., July 20, 1994
Bill Taylor, Dallas, Tex., July 26, 1993
Ron Tindiglia, Harrison, N.Y., August 29, September 3, 1994; February 6, 1997
Melba Tolliver, New York, N.Y., May 1, 1995
Jim Topping, San Francisco, Calif., October 6, 1994
Bill Tucker, Tucson, Ariz., May 15, September 28, 1994
Norm Wagy, Homossasa, Fla., February 16, 1996
Mike Wallace, New York, N.Y., April 24, 1996
Ned Warwick, London, UK, January 10, 11, 2000
Bob Weaver, Miami, Fla., December 13, 1994
Alan Weiss, New York, N.Y., May 1, 1995
Mary Jo West, Tempe, Ariz., October 3, 1995
Jim Willi, Dallas, Tex., October 10, 1995; July 1, 1996; August 15, 1998
Robert Wussler, Potomac, Md., May 17, 1996
Richard Yoakam, Bloomington, Ind., March 1, 1995
Linda Yu, Chicago, Ill., August 1, 1997
Leonid Yurgelas, Moscow, Russia, April 28, 1999
Sam Zelman, Corvallis, Ore., November 9, 1994
Marvin Zindler, Houston, Tex., May 31, 1996

Moses Znaimer, Toronto, Ont., June 3, 1997

By Bonneville Oral History Project (BOHP)

Arch Madsen, September 1, 1986

By RTNDA Oral History Project (RTNDAOH)

Eddie Barker, September 30, 1993
Ralph Renick, March 12, 1989
Ernie Schultz, February 23, 1989

Video Sources

Chicago, Ill.: WLS Video Archive (WLSV).
Cincinnati, Oh.: WCPO Video Archive (WCPOV).
Denver, Colo.: Colorado State Historical Society Video Archive (CSHV).
Houston, Tex.: KTRK Video Archive (KTRKV).
Ithaca, N.Y.: Ithaca College Roy H. Park School of Communication Archive (ICV).
Los Angeles, Calif.: PROMAX Audio–Visual Archive (PROMV).
Los Angeles, Calif.: UCLA Film and Television Archive (UCLAV).
Nashville, Tenn.: Vanderbilt Archive (VAV).
Philadelphia, Pennsylvania: KYW Video Archive (KYWV).
Philadelphia, Pa.: WCAU Video Archive (WCAUV).
Portland, Ore.: KGW Video Archive (KGWV).
Poughkeepsie, N.Y.: Marist College-John Tillman Film Archive (MCTV).
San Francisco, Calif.: San Francisco State University Television News Archives (SFSV).
Tempe, Ariz.: Arizona State University Television Archive (ASUV).
Upper Darby, Pa.: New York Communications Video Archive (NYCV).

Manuscript Sources

Athens, Ga.: Hargrett Library, University
of Georgia.
Arbitron Archive (ARB)
Dallas, Tex.: Audience Research &
Development (ARD).
Iowa City, Iowa: University of Iowa.
RTNDA Archive (RTNDA)
RTNDA Oral History Project
(RTNDAOH)
Los Angeles, Calif.: Promax, Inc.
(PROM).
Marion, Iowa: Frank N. Magid
Associates (FMA).
New York, N.Y.: CBS Archive (CBS).
New York, N.Y.: Westinghouse
Broadcasting Company (WBC).
Salt Lake City, Utah: Bonneville Oral
History Project (BOHP).
Southfield, Mich.: McHugh & Hoffman,
Inc. (MHI).
Tempe, Ariz.: Arizona State University
Local TV News Collection (ASU)
Action News Materials (ANM)
Ray Beindorf Materials (RBM)
Jerry Foster Materials (JFC)
Vince Leonard Materials (VLM)
Phil McHugh Papers (PMP)
Lou Prato Materials (LPM)
Bill Tucker Materials (BTM)
Washington, D.C.: National Archives.
Records of the Federal
Communications Commission
Records of the Executive Director
(FCCED)
Office of the Secretary
(FCCOS)
Dockets (FCCD)

Articles and Books

Abel, John D., Charles Clift, III, and
Frederick A. Weiss, "Station
License Revocations and Denials of
Renewal, 1934–1969." *Journal of
Broadcasting* 14 (1970): 411–421.
Allen, Craig. "Priorities of General
Managers and News Directors in
Anchor Hiring." *Journal of
Media Economics* 8 (1995):
111–124.
___. "American News Values Abroad:
The Spread of U.S. News

Consultants," International
Communication Association, 1998.
American University, Graduate Students
in Broadcast Journalism. *Broadcast
News Doctors: The Patient is
Buying the Cure.* Washington, D.C.:
American University, 1979.
Barrett, Edward W. "Folksy TV News."
Columbia Journalism Review,
November–December 1973, pp.
16–20.
Barrett, Marvin. *Moments of Truth?*
New York: Crowell, 1975.
Bergendorff, Fred L., Charles H. Smith
and Lance Webster, *Broadcast
Advertising and Promotion.* New
York: Hastings House, 1983.
Berkowitz, Dan, Craig Allen, and Diana
Beeson. "Exploring Newsroom
Views About Consultants in Local
TV." *Journal of Broadcasting and
Electronic Media* 40 (1996):
447–459.
Blair, Gwenda. *Almost Golden: Jessica
Savitch and the Selling of Television
News.* New York: Simon and
Schuster, 1988.
Bock, Mary A. "Smile More: A
Subcultural Analysis of the
Anchor/Consultant Relationship in
Local Television News Operations."
Drake University master's thesis,
1986.
Bogdan, Robert, and Steven J. Taylor.
*Introduction to Qualitative
Research Methods.* New York:
Wiley, 1975.
Boulding, Kenneth E. *The
Organizational Revolution.* New
York, Harper, 1953.
Bridges, Les. "Smile When You Say
That, Pardners," *Chicago Tribune
Magazine,* May 9, 1971, pp. 24–29.
Butler, Charles. "Consulting Firms and
Stations," *View,* Apr. 1988,
pp. 22–24.
Byrne, John A. "If you're so good, why
the hell are you in Topeka?"
Forbes, December 7, 1981,
pp. 133–136.
CBS, Inc. *Television News Reporting.*
New York: McGraw-Hill, 1958.
Chagall, David. "Only As Good As His
Skin Tests." *TV Guide,* Mar. 26,
1977, pp. 6–10.
Chapman, John. *Tell It to Sweeny: The
Informal History of the New York*

Daily News. New York: Doubleday, 1961.

Chase, Stuart. *The Proper Study of Mankind.* New York: Harper, 1948.

Coleman, Richard P., and Bernice L. Neugarten. *Social Status in the City.* San Francisco: Jossey-Bass, 1971.

—, Lee P. Rainwater with Kent A. McClelland. *Social Standing in America: New Dimensions of Class.* New York: Basic, 1978.

—. "The Continuing Significance of Social Class to Marketing." *Journal of Consumer Research* 10 (1983): 265–280.

—. "Consumers and Television," Kansas State University, 1995.

—. "American Social Classes in the Middle Nineties," Kansas State University, 1995.

Cooney, John. *The Annenbergs.* New York: Simon and Schuster, 1982.

Corr, O. Casey. KING: *The Bullitts of Seattle and Their Communications Empire.* Seattle: University of Washington, 1996.

Craft, Christine. *An Anchorwoman's Story.* Santa Barbara, Calif.: Rhodora, 1986.

Cremer, Charles F., Phillip O. Keirstead, and Richard D. Yoakam. *ENG Television News.* New York: McGraw-Hill, 1996.

Czerniejewski, Halina J., and Charles Long, "Local Television News in 31 Flavors." *The Quill,* May 1974, pp. 21–28.

Dary, David. *TV News Handbook.* Blue Ridge Summit, Pa.: Tab, 1971.

Davidson, Andrew. *Under the Hammer: The Inside Story of the 1991 ITV Franchise Battle.* London: Heinemann, 1992.

Davis, Allison, Burleigh B. Gardner, and Mary R. Gardner. *Deep South.* Chicago: University of Chicago Press, 1941.

Daviss, Ben. "Man the Minicams, Rev Up the Choppers." *TV Guide,* Nov. 6, 1982, pp. 34–38.

Deeb, Gary. "Skin tests 'make' the news." *Chicago Tribune.* Mar. 7, 1978, pp. II-1, II-2.

—. "It's the press 1, technology 0 as CBS 'skin tests' turn out negative." *Chicago Tribune,* May 18, 1977, p. 16.

Denney, Charles M. "Measuring the Effectiveness of Television News Consultants." University of Tennessee master's thesis, 1992.

Diamond, Edwin. *The Tin Kazoo.* Cambridge, Mass.: MIT Press, 1975.

Diamond, Nina L. "Targeting the Television Set." *Miami.* Mar., 1983, pp. 56–57, 80–83.

Dominick, Joseph R., Alan Wurtzel, and Guy Lometti. "Television Journalism vs. Show Business: A Content Analysis of Eyewitness News." *Journalism Quarterly* 52 (1975): 213–218.

Ellmore, R. Terry. *Broadcasting Law and Regulation.* Blue Ridge Summit, Pa.: Tab, 1982.

Eysenck, Hans J. *The IQ Argument.* La Salle, Ill.: Library Press, 1971.

Fang, Irving E. *Television News.* New York: Hastings House, 1968.

Flaherty, Joseph A. "Television News Gathering." *Journal of the Society of Motion Picture and Television Engineers* 82 (1973): 645–648.

—. "The All-Electronic Newsgathering Station." *Journal of the Society of Motion Picture and Television Engineers* 84 (1975): 958–962.

Galbraith, John Kenneth. Economic Development. Cambridge, Mass.: Harvard University Press, 1964.

Gans, Herbert. *Deciding What's News.* New York: Pantheon, 1979.

Gardner, Burleigh B., and David Moore. *Human Relations in Industry.* Homewood, Ill.: Irwin, 1945.

—, and Sidney J. Levy. "The Product and the Brand." *Harvard Business Review* 33 (1955):33–39.

—. *A Conceptual Framework for Advertising.* Chicago: Crain, 1982.

Glick, Ira O., and Sidney J. Levy. *Living With Television.* Chicago: Aldine, 1962.

Goldenson, Leonard H. *Beating The Odds.* New York: Charles Scribner's Sons, 1991.

Hafer, Mark C. "The Impact of Community Ascertainment: An Analysis of Television Station Ascertainment Reports to the F.C.C., University of Georgia master's thesis, 1980.

Harmon, Mark. "Mr. Gates Goes Electronic: The What And Why Questions in Local TV News." *Journalism Quarterly* 66 (1989): 857–863.

Harr, Candace C. "A Study of Consulting Firms and Television Newsrooms." Iowa State University master's thesis, 1974.

Hartshorn, Gerald Gregory. "The Impact of Consultants on Local Television Stations." University of Maryland master's thesis, 1980.

Hearst, Patricia C. *Every Secret Thing.* Garden City, N.J.: Doubleday, 1982.

Herrnstein, Richard J. *The Bell Curve : Intelligence and Class Structure in American Life.* New York : Free Press, 1994.

Horton, Donald, and R. Richard Wohl. "Mass Communication and Para-Social Interaction." *Psychiatry* 3 (1956): 215–230.

Itzkoff, Seymour W. *The Decline of Intelligence in America.* Westport, Conn.: Praeger, 1994.

Kaniss, Phyllis. *Making Local News.* Chicago: University of Chicago Press, 1991.

King, Larry L. "The Best Little Whorehouse in Texas." *Playboy,* April 1974, pp. 130–132, 219–226.

Kitman, Marvin. "Another Day, Another Million." *Washington Journalism Review,* September 1983, pp. 39–42, 58.

Levy, Maury. "We Interrupt This Issue To Bring You An Eyewitness News Bulletin." *Philadelphia,* March 1975, pp. 82–87, 148–160.

Lower, Elmer W. "Bottom-line value of superanchors." *Television/Radio Age,* July 27, 1981, pp. 34–38, 72–86.

Luttwak, Edward N. *The Endangered American Dream.* New York: Simon and Schuster, 1993.

Maier, Roger David. "News Consultants: Their Use By and Effect Upon Local Television News in Louisiana." University of Southwestern Louisiana master's thesis, 1986.

Manchester, William. *Death of a President.* New York: Harper and Row, 1967.

Martineau, Pierre. *Motivation in Advertising.* New York: McGraw-Hill, 1957.

Mandel, William K. "Manufacturing the News at Channel 6," *Philadelphia,* July 1972, pp. 64–69, 132–139.

Matusow, Barbara. *The Evening Stars.* Boston: Houghton Mifflin, 1983.

Mazingo, Sherrie. "Home of programming firsts." *Television/ Radio Age,* Mar. 1987, pp. A1–A62.

McLuhan, Marshall. *Understanding Media. The Extensions of Man.* New York: McGraw-Hill, 1964.

——. *Sharing the News.* New York: McLuhan and Associates and ABC, 1971.

Millstein, Gilbert. "The Weather Girls Ride Out a Storm." *New York Times Magazine,* October 8, 1961, pp. 62–64, 69.

Murray, Michael D., and Donald G. Godfrey. *Television in America: Local Station History From Across the Nation.* Ames: Iowa State University Press, 1997.

Nash, Alana. *Golden Girl: The Story of Jessica Savitch.* New York: Dutton, 1988.

O'Donnell, Michael Joseph. "Newscast Content of Six Iowa Television Stations." Iowa State University master's thesis, 1978.

Packard, Vance. *The Hidden Persuaders.* New York: McKay, 1957.

Peale, Betsey, and Mark Harmon. "Television News Consultants: Exploration of Their Effect on Content." Association for Education in Journalism and Mass Communication, Aug. 1991.

Platt, Larry. "The Larry Kane Nobody Knows." *Philadelphia,* September 1994, pp. 65–69, 123–129.

Popper, Joe. "Selling Souls for a Thirty Share." *Denver Magazine,* November 1981, pp. 41–44, 114–121.

——. "Inside TV News." *Kansas City,* September 1982, pp. 54–69.

Powers, Ron. *The Newscasters.* New York: St. Martin's, 1977.

Quinlan, Sterling. *Inside ABC.* New York: Hastings House, 1979.

Rauzin, Erica M. "Turning the Channels on the Evening News." *Miami,* Mar., 1983, pp. 61, 84–86.

Rivera, Geraldo, and Daniel Paisner. *Exposing Myself.* New York: Bantam, 1991.

Robinson, John, and Mark Levy. *The Main Source.* Beverly Hills, Calif.: Sage, 1986.

Roethlisberger, F. J., and William J. Dickson. *Management and the Worker.* Cambridge, Mass.: Harvard University Press, 1939.

Roth, Morry. "O'Leary's (Sacred) Cow Updated As Flynn & Daly Duo Start Another Gt. Fire Under Chi News via WLS–TV," *Variety,* February 11, 1970, pp. 37–38.

———. "Minicam As WBBM-TV Weapon That Leapfrogs Chi News Field," *Variety,* June 5, 1974, p. 42.

Rugg, William James. "The Use and Acceptance of Electronic News Gathering Equipment by Local Television News Departments in the United States." University of Mississippi master's thesis, 1980.

Sanders, Keith P., and Michael Pritchett. "Some Influences of Appearance and Television Newscaster Appeal." *Journal of Broadcasting* 15 (1971): 293–300.

Savitch, Jessica. *Anchorwoman.* New York: Putnam's Sons, 1982.

Shook, Frederick. *Television Field Production and Reporting.* New York: Longman, 1989.

Shosteck, Herschel. "Factors Influencing Appeal of TV News Personalities." *Journal of Broadcasting* 18 (1973–74): 63–71.

Smart, Samuel Chipman. *The Outlet Story, 1894–1984.* Providence, R.I.: Outlet Communications, 1984.

Smethers, Steven J. "Unplugged: Developing Rural Midwestern Television Audiences without Live Network Service, 1949–1952." *Southwestern Mass Communication Journal* 12 (1996): 44–60.

Steiner, Gary A. *The People Look at Television.* New York: Knopf, 1963.

Steinmetz, Johanna. "Mr. Magic—The TV Newscast Doctor," *New York Times,* October 12, 1975, pp. 2–1, 2–25.

Smith, Robert R. "Mythic Elements in Television News," *Journal of Communication* 29 (1979): 75–82.

Snyderman, Mark, and Stanley Rothman. *The IQ controversy, the Media, and Public Policy.* New Brunswick, N.J. : Transaction Books, 1988.

Stone, Vernon A. "Radio-Television News Directors and Operations," *RTNDA Communicator,* June 1973, pp. 5–12.

———. "News Operations Surveyed On Use of Consultants." *RTNDA Communicator,* June 1974, pp. 4–5.

———. "ENG Growth Documented." *RTNDA Communicator,* January 1980, p. 5.

———. "Personal Problems of News Directors Surveyed," *RTNDA Communicator,* September 1986, pp. 66–68, 100, 102.

———. "TV News Pay Lags Cost of Living," *RTNDA Communicator,* March 1993, pp. 12–13.

———. "TV Journalists: Careers Survey Report to Respondents," Freedom Forum, February 1992.

Thernstrom, Stephan. *Poverty and Progress: Social Mobility in a Nineteenth-Century City.* Cambridge, Mass.: Harvard University Press, 1964.

———. "Yankee City Revisited: The Perils of Historical Naivete. *American Sociological Review* 30 (1965): 234–242.

Thomas, Bob. *Winchell.* Garden City, N.Y.: Doubleday, 1971.

Townley, Richard. "Put the Newsman Back in News," *TV Guide,* June 5, 1971, pp. 30–35.

———. "The News Merchants." *TV Guide,* March 9, 1974, pp. 6–11.

———. "Who Decides What Is News?" *TV Guide,* March 16, 1974, pp. 13–16.

Tumin, Melvin M. *Social Stratification.* Englewood Cliffs, N.J.: Prentice-Hall, 1967.

Vernon, Philip E. *Intelligence: Heredity and Environment.* San Francisco: W.H. Freeman, 1979.

Vico, Giambattista. *The New Science.* Garden City, N.Y., Doubleday, 1961.

Walker, Connecticut. "Newswomen and Television—Beauty on the Tube." *Parade,* February 16, 1975, pp. 4–5.

Warner, W. Lloyd, and Paul S. Lunt. *The Social Life of the Modern Community.* Vol. 1, Yankee City Series. New Haven: Yale University Press, 1941.

___, and Paul S. Lunt. *The Status System of the Modern Community.* Vol. 2, Yankee City series. New Haven: Yale University Press, 1942.

___, and Leo Srole. *The Social Systems of American Ethnic Groups.* Vol. 3, Yankee City Series. New Haven: Yale University Press, 1945.

___, and J. O. Low. *The Social System of the Modern Factory.* Vol. 4, Yankee City series. New Haven: Yale University Press, 1947.

___, and William E. Henry. *The Radio Day Time Serial: A Symbolic Analysis,* in *Genetic Psychology Monographs* 34 (1948): 3–71.

___, M. Meeker, and K. Eells. *Social Class in America.* Chicago: Science Research Associates, 1949.

___. *Democracy in Jonesville.* New York: Harper, 1949.

___. *Social Class in America: A Manual of Procedure for the Measurement of Social Status.* New York: Harper, 1949.

___. *The Living and the Dead.* Vol. 5, Yankee City series. New Haven: Yale University Press, 1959.

___. *Yankee City.* New Haven: Yale University Press, 1963.

White, Paul W. *News on the Air.* New York: Harcourt, Brace and Company, 1947.

Williams, Mark. "Remote Possibilities: KLTA's Coverage of the Kathy Fiscus Rescue," Dartmouth University, 1994.

Znaniecki, Florian. *The Method of Sociology.* New York: Octagon, 1968.

M. L. started as secretary.

Melodee Beesmyer